Guy F. Owen
4-3-72

THE UNFOLDING DRAMA
OF REDEMPTION

VOLUME II

KNOW YOUR BIBLE

The Unfolding Drama of Redemption

THE BIBLE AS A WHOLE

VOLUME II

THE INTERLUDE AND ACT II OF THE DRAMA

EMBRACING THE INTER-TESTAMENT PERIOD,
THE GOSPELS AND ACTS

W. GRAHAM SCROGGIE, D.D.

FLEMING H. REVELL COMPANY
OLD TAPPAN, NEW JERSEY

This edition is issued by
special arrangement with
PICKERING & INGLIS LTD.
the British publishers.

First Published - 1957
Reprinted - - - 1970

ISBN 0 7208 0193 1

Printed in Great Britain by Lowe & Brydone (Printers) Ltd., London

Other Volumes in the Series

ANALYSIS OF CONTENTS

CONTENTS

CONTENTS

CHARTS

MAPS

THE UNFOLDING DRAMA OF REDEMPTION

THE INTERLUDE

THE TIME BETWEEN THE TESTAMENTS
FROM NEHEMIAH TO THE MESSIAH
JUDAISM AND HEATHENISM
A PREPARATION FOR CHRISTIANITY

IN THE MIDST OF THE NATIONS

IT was not without design that God set the house of Israel 'in the midst of the nations'. A glance or two at the following map will make clear the situation. All the countries here named made contact with the Chosen Race, and for this reason only are they brought to notice in the Bible record. This record is not history for history's sake, but to show where, when, and how the Drama of Redemption was unfolded. In Canaan the Chosen People were first separated to be taught, and then they were scattered to be used. In this plan the surrounding nations had an important part to play.

The Hebrews made contact first of all with EGYPT when Abram went thither about 1921 B.C., and as late as 605 B.C. they were still in contact with that country. This means that for over 1300 years these peoples occasionally touched one another.

The next oldest contact of Israel was with ASSYRIA in the time of Shalmaneser II, who came to power in 860 B.C., in the period of Assyria's Third Dynasty (Vol. I, Chart 73). It was during his reign that contact was made with Israel, in the time of Ahab; and from time to time this happened during a period of more than 250 years until Assyria finally fell in 605 B.C.

The next oldest connection was with BABYLONIA, at the time when PUL, believed to be TIGLATH-PILESER III occupied for a short time the throne of Babylon (Vol. I, Chart 76). In his inscriptions he mentions some kings of Judah and Israel from 806-719 B.C. This Empire was overthrown in 538 B.C. by Cyrus, and during these 268 years Babylon had much to do with the misfortunes of Judah.

Contact with Judah was made by PERSIA also, contact which was wholly to its advantage, because it was Cyrus who allowed a host of Jewish captives to return to Palestine, and later Artaxerxes followed his example in respect of Ezra and Nehemiah; and it was Ahasuerus who saved the Jews from being massacred in the time of Esther. These favours were shown between 536-433 B.C., a century of helpfulness.

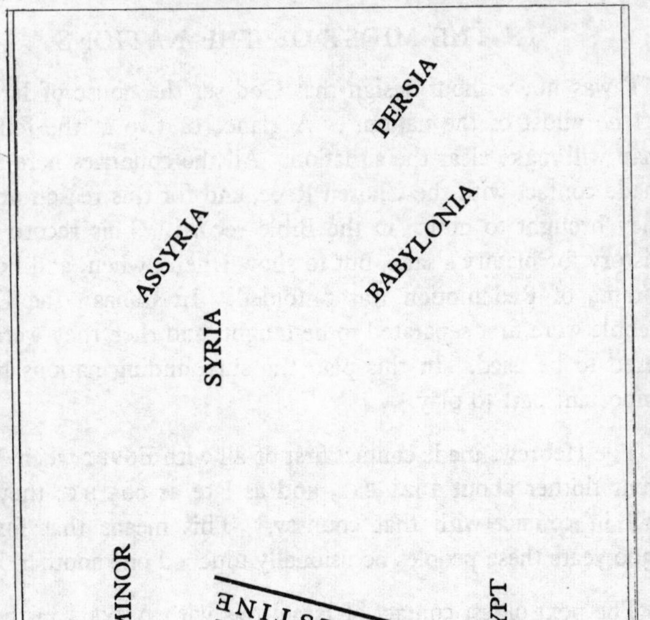

THE INTERLUDE
FROM NEHEMIAH TO THE MESSIAH

MAP 11

PALESTINE IN RELATION TO THE NATIONS

ROME · MACEDONIA · GREECE · ASIA MINOR · SYRIA · ASSYRIA · BABYLONIA · PERSIA · EGYPT · PALESTINE · MEDITERRANEAN SEA

'Thus saith the LORD God: This is Jerusalem; I have set it *in the midst* of the nations and countries that are round about her' (Ezek. v. 5)

In 334 B.C. another power rose to dominion, GREECE, which in ten years under Alexander the Great, the Macedonian, marched victoriously from the Dardanelles to India. He too favoured the Jews directly and indirectly, and by founding Alexandria he furnished them with an Hellenic capital. The contact of the Jews with what was Greek was of inestimable value. 'To them was committed the secular education of the ancient world for Christianity, in the preparation for which their language and philosophy were mighty factors.'

The history of the Greeks goes back to 1100 B.C., but their influence cannot be dated. Some of the most famous battles of the world were fought by them—Marathon, Thermopylae, Salamis—and from 525 B.C. for a hundred years this people was famous for its intellectual brilliance.

After the death of Alexander in 323 B.C. his vast kingdom was divided among four of his generals, as Daniel had predicted it would be (xi. 3, 4). *Cassander* had Macedonia and Greece; *Lysimachus* had Thrace, Bithynia, and some of the adjoining provinces; *Ptolemy Lagus* had Libya, Egypt, Arabia, Petraea, Palestine and Coele-Syria; and *Seleucus* had all that remained, embracing many provinces in Asia Minor, Syria, Mesopotamia, Babylonia, and the East as far as India. Of these generals the last two were to enter deeply into the history of the Jews, because being in conflict with one another, and each being eager to possess Canaan, the Promised Land became the scene of strife, off and on, for two hundred years.

It was during this time that in the Kingdom of the Ptolemies the Hebrew Scriptures were translated into Greek, the Version known as the *Septuagint* (LXX); and in the Kingdom of the Seleucidae arose *Antiochus Epiphanes*, one of the greatest persecutors of the Jews in all time. He too had been predicted by Daniel (xi. 21, 22). This part of Jewish history belongs to the INTERLUDE and is of tragic importance, including, as it does, the Maccabean story.

The final contact of the Jews in this period was with ROME. In 63 B.C. Pompey attacked and captured Jerusalem, and so the scene was laid which, in little more than 60 years, was to witness the advent of the Messiah.

The vital contacts, then, of Israel with foreigners were eight in number.

CHART 113

ISRAEL'S CONTACTS WITH HEATHENISM							
1	2	3	4	5	6	7	8
EGYPT	ASSYRIA	BABYLONIA	PERSIA	GREECE	PTOLEMIES	SELEUCIDAE	ROME
B.C. 1921-	B.C. 860-	B.C. 806-	B.C. 536-	B.C. 334-	B.C. 323-	B.C. 312-	B.C. 63-

FOUR HUNDRED YEARS

The period from Malachi to the Messiah was one of about 425 to 400 years. It has been spoken of as The Period of the Great Silence. That description is correct if what is meant by it is that during that period the voice of prophecy ceased, and that there were no Writings which have been regarded as Holy Scripture; but if anything else is meant the description is most misleading.

There was the less need for prophetic utterance during that period as its course had already been broadly outlined, and in parts detailed, in the Book of Daniel. As this statement will arouse controversy, before proceeding more must be said about it.

THE BOOK OF DANIEL

In this UNFOLDING DRAMA we have made reference scarcely at all to questions raised by Higher Criticism, because scarcely at all is the progressive unfolding of the redemptive purpose affected by matters of authorship, style, and date; but in the case of the Book of Daniel an exception must be made, as the view that is taken of it in these respects must greatly affect one's view alike of prophecy and inspiration.

Of this Book there are two contradictory and irreconcilable views:

(a) That the Book was written by the Daniel of history (Ezek. xiv. 14, 20; xxviii. 3; Matt. xxiv. 15), in the sixth century B.C.; and

(b) that the Book was written by an unknown Jew in the second century B.C., more than 350 years later, and given the name of Daniel.

In the one case it is a genuine work, and in the other, it is a forgery; yet the second is the view of the majority who teach in our Universities and Colleges, and it is supposed to be the voice of scholarship.

Higher Critical Views

The father of this second view, Porphyry, who died in A.D. 304, is one of whom every Christian should be ashamed. He wrote fifteen books against Christianity, and the whole of the twelfth was taken up with an attack on the genuineness of Daniel. Yet in A.D. 1912 Dr. G. Buchanan Gray, writing on Daniel, says:

'The evil genius of this book, though, in accordance with the general rule of apocalyptic literature he is never mentioned by name, is quite clearly Antiochus Epiphanes (175-164 B.C.): and the purpose of the book is to encourage the Jews not to submit to his attempts to seduce or persecute them into the worship of Zeus and disloyalty to their law, but to persist at whatever cost in their fidelity to God'; and he takes the view that Daniel was not yet written in 180 B.C.
('A Critical Introduction to the Old Testament': pp. 233-4)

Dr. H. Wheeler Robinson, in A.D. 1936 says:

'The Book of Daniel—we know to have been written about 165 B.C.'; and, he affirms, 'the evidence for this is overwhelming.'
('The Old Testament, Its Making and Meaning': pp. 200, 127)

And before either of these scholars, in A.D. 1897, Dr. S. R. Driver wrote:

'In face of the facts presented by the Book of Daniel, the opinion that it is the work of Daniel himself cannot be sustained. Internal evidence shows, with a cogency that cannot be resisted, that it must have been written not earlier than c. 300 B.C., and in Palestine; and it is at least *probable* that it was composed under the persecution of Antiochus Epiphanes, B.C. 168 or 176.'
('Introduction to the Literature of the Old Testament': p. 497).

These are fair examples of the views of all Higher Critics, and if the matter were one that can be settled only by scholars, then the unschooled reader could offer little resistance to these verdicts.

The Witness of the Canon
(p. 40)

But this matter is not to be settled by the scholars, but by the common sense of all who have good reason for believing that in the Word of God are miracle and prophecy; that God is His own interpreter, and that He will make it plain.

The above stated view has often been answered by scholars of the class of those quoted, and, to use Dr. Robinson's word, they present 'overwhelming' evidence against his view, and for the former of the two views defined (p. 11*a*).

To go into details here would take us far beyond our purpose and space, but one or two points may be useful as an introduction to a careful study of the whole subject.

1. The crucial point in the controversy is the determination of the date when the Old Testament Canon was finally closed. What evidence is there on this point?

In the Prologue of the apocryphal Ecclesiasticus we have these words:

> 'My grandfather Jesus, when he had much given himself to the reading of *the law*, and *the prophets*, and *the other books* of our fathers'.

The Hebrew original of Ecclesiasticus was written soon after B.C. 200, so that presumably by that date the Canon of the Old Testament Scriptures was closed, for this Prologue refers to the whole collection in the three divisions which were known in our Lord's time as 'the law of Moses, and the prophets, and the psalms' (Luke xxiv. 44). The Jews' Bible, the Old Testament, has always been in these three parts: the *Torah*, or Law; the *Nebiim*, or Prophets; and the *Hagiographa*, or Holy Writings, and these latter included the Book of Daniel.

In Ecclesiasticus is further reference to the Old Testament Scriptures. In chs. xliv-l, which are devoted to the praise of famous men, is a reference to 'the twelve Prophets' (xlix. 10), which shows that in the time of the author of Ecclesiasticus this collection as it appears in the Hebrew Canon had long been in existence. Also in the list of the praised are references to men who appear in each of the three divisions of the Hebrew Bible.

That Daniel's name does not appear is no proof that the author had no knowledge of him, for Ezra's name does not appear, and he certainly would have been known. The argument from silence is very precarious.

It is practically certain that during the two and a half centuries between Ezra and Ben Sirach the Canon of the Old Testament was gradually formed, and though it *may* not have been closed until the second century B.C., the Book of Daniel was included in it as of inspired authority, but none of the apocryphal books were included.

2. All direct citations in the New Testament are made from the O.T. Canon and include from the Hagiographa Collection Job, Psalms, Proverbs, *Daniel*, Ruth, and Chronicles. There are no direct citations from any apocryphal book.

3. In 1 Maccabees, a book of great value, it is recorded what the dying Mattathias said to his sons in B.C. 166; and in this speech he makes reference to the Book of Daniel:

'Ananias, Azarias, and Misael, by believing were saved out of the flame.
Daniel for his innocency was delivered from the mouth of lions'
(ii. 59, 60)

This reference indicates that the Book was well known, and could not, therefore, be a product of the time of Antiochus Epiphanes, or later.

4. It will be well also to mention that Josephus the Jewish historian relates in his *Antiquities* (Bk. xi. ch. viii. p. 5), written about the close of the first century A.D., that Alexander the Great, after his capture of Tyre, marched on Jerusalem. He was met by the High Priest, and later was shown the Book of Daniel wherein it is declared that a Greek should destroy the Empire of the Persians, and he concluded that he was the person referred to, and thereafter he treated the Jews with much consideration. This was in B.C. 330, one hundred and sixty-five years before the Book of Daniel was written according to the Higher Critics.

Whether or not this story is believed, what is impressive is that Josephus believed that the Book of Daniel was in existence in the fourth century B.C.

5. In the Versions Septuagint (Greek), Vulgate (Latin), and Luther's, the Book of Daniel is placed after Ezekiel among the four great prophets. It may safely be said that the Septuagint Version was produced between B.C. 284-200, which was from 119 to 35 years before the time in which the Critics place Daniel.

6. Among the apocryphal books are three additions to Daniel: *The Song of the Three Children*; *Susannah*; and *Bel and the Dragon*. These additions suggest an early date for the Book of Daniel.

7. But for the supernatural in Daniel, the miraculous and the prophetical elements, probably no objection would have been taken to its genuineness; but if this objection be allowed the genuineness of a large part of the Old Testament would be challenged, for much of it is miraculous and prophetical in character.

The Book of Daniel we regard therefore to be trustworthy as a record of fact; genuine, in that it was written by the man whose name it bears, and who in two places claims to be the writer (viii. 1; ix. 2); and integrated in that it is an original whole and not a combination of independent parts. What follows is presented in the belief that the Book was written by Daniel in Babylon in the sixth century B.C.

DANIEL'S PROPHECIES
(cf. Vol. 1, pp. 419-428)

We now go back to the statement in our first paragraph (p. 11a) that the Inter-Testament Period is prophetically outlined in the Book of Daniel. There are five such prophecies: four of them relate to the whole period; and one of them, to a particular part of the whole (Vol. 1, Charts 85-89).

1. *The Great Image* (ch. ii)

In a dream Nebuchadnezzar saw 'a great image', with head of gold; breast and arms of silver; belly and thighs of brass; and legs of iron with feet of iron intermingled with clay. Daniel, in his interpretation, told the king that the four metals represented four kingdoms, beginning with his own, the Babylonian, and followed by the Medo-Persian, the Grecian, and the Roman. These kingdoms are not named in Daniel ii, but his pronouncement of Nebuchadnezzar, 'thou art this head of gold' (38) is the key, and the rest follows inevitably.

2. The Four Beasts (ch. vii)

Daniel himself had a dream in which he saw 'four great beasts' (3). These appeared as a Lion, a Bear, a Leopard, and a fourth not identified. These, we are told, represented four kingdoms, and it is perfectly clear that they correspond to the four metals of Nebuchadnezzar's dream and refer to the Babylonian, Medo-Persian, Grecian and Roman Kingdoms.

3. The Ram and the Goat (ch. viii)

In a vision Daniel saw these two beasts, and it was revealed to him that the Ram represented Medo-Persia, and the Goat, Grecia (20, 21). Details of this vision we need not go into now, but they must be referred to later.

CHART 114

"THE TIMES OF THE GENTILES" Luke xxi. 24			
NEBUCHADNEZZAR'S DREAM: A GREAT IMAGE (ch.ii.)			
Head	Breast and Arms	Belly and Thigh	Legs and Feet
Gold	Silver	Brass	Iron and Clay
DANIEL'S VISIONS: FOUR BEASTS (chs. vii.-viii.)			
Lion	Bear	Leopard	'Dreadful'
	Ram	Goat	
INTERPRETATION			
BABYLONIA	MEDO-PERSIA	GREECE	ROME
B.C. 606-538	B.C. 538-333	B.C. 333-63	B.C. 63-A.D.?
68 Years	205 Years	270 Years	63 Years—

Predictions of over six centuries

4. The Seventy Sevens (ch. ix. 21-27.)

This is a revelation given to Daniel by Gabriel of a period of 490 years relating to the Jews, beginning with a 'commandment to restore and to build Jerusalem', unto a consummation to be determined. This period is divided into three: 'seven weeks', i.e., 49 years; 'threescore and two weeks', i.e., 434 years; and 'one week', i.e., 7 years.

It is beyond the scope of our present study to go into all the details of this amazing prophecy, but what is relevant to our purpose is that the end of the first two periods—49 and 434, i.e., 483 years—brings us to the time of Christ, and apparently, to the event of His death.

> 'Know, therefore, and understand:—
> From the going forth of a commandment to restore and to build Jerusalem *unto an Anointed One, a Prince*, there shall be Seven Sevens and Sixty and Two Sevens. (25)
> And after the Sixty and Two Sevens (the second of the three divisions) *an Anointed One* shall be cut off, and there shall be nothing for Him' (26). CHRIST means Anointed.

We are not here concerned with various chronological calculations which have been made, but it is clear that the 434 years cover the period of the Interlude, the 400 years between the Testaments, and continue in Act II of the Drama up to the death of Christ. Nothing is said in the prophecy of what takes place during the Inter-Testament Period, but provision is made for it, and in the Fifth Prophecy some details are supplied.

CHART 115

THE SEVENTY SEVENS: 490 YEARS			
Seven Sevens	Sixty-two Sevens	One Seven	
49 Years	434 Years	7 Years	
The time of Nehemiah and Malachi	From the cessation of Prophecy to the Death of Christ	3½	3½
		'The time of the end' Dan. xi. 40; xii. 9	
From 445 B.C.	The INTERLUDE or INTER-TESTAMENT PERIOD	Rev. xii. 6, 14; xiii. 5	

5. *'The Scripture of Truth'* (chs. x. 21; xi, 35)

We must accept chs. x-xii to be what they claim to be, a divine revelation vouchsafed to Daniel the prophet, or regard them as a forgery. Porphyry's objection to the Book of Daniel having been written by Daniel in the sixth century B.C. was that it introduced the supernatural, and for that he had no use or place. No objection is taken by Higher Critics to chs. x-xii if it be granted that they were written about 165 B.C., because if written then, they lose their supernatural character. It is the same kind of objection as is taken to the claim that Isaiah the prophet wrote chs. xl-lxvi of the Book which bears his name. However distasteful the conclusion is, we are driven to it, that the objection to the supernatural is the foundation on which modern Higher Criticism builds.

But believing that Daniel wrote these chapters in the 6th cent. B.C., we are confronted with one of the most amazing predictions in all Scripture; predictions which reach from B.C. 530-164, a period of over 360 years, from Cambyses, King of Persia, to the death of Antiochus Epiphanes, King of Syria, in the Grecian period (ch. xi. 2-35); and after that, we believe, the prediction leaps over to a time yet to come, called 'the time of the end'. when Antichrist will appear (xi. 36-xii).

To show how amazing this prophecy is, we place side by side the text and its fulfilment of xi. 2-35. The events recorded in the right-hand column took place, and are matters of historic fact; but that these events were foretold more than 360 years before is more than a dominating School of Criticism can believe, yet the Bible is full of such provisions and predictions.

FROM CAMBYSES TO ANTIOCHUS EPIPHANES

B.C. 530-164 = 366 Years

THE PROPHECY	THE FULFILMENT
2 Behold, there shall stand up yet three kings in Persia;	1 Cambyses, Ahasuerus, B.C. 529-522.
	2 Smerdis, Artaxerxes (not the one mentioned in Nehemiah) B.C. 522-521.
and the fourth shall be far richer than they all;	3 Darius Hystaspes, B.C. 521-485.
and by his strength through his riches he shall stir up all against the realm of Grecia.	4 Xerxes, B.C. 485-465. In 480 at Thermopylae he defeated a small army of Greeks. In 479 his army was defeated by the Greeks. At sea in 480 he was defeated in the battle of Salamis, and in 479 in the battle of Mycale.
3 And a mighty King shall stand up, that shall rule with great dominion, and do according to his will.	Nearly a century and a half later arose Alexander the Great, in B.C. 335. He is the 'notable horn' on the 'he-goat' of Daniel viii. 5-7.
4 And when he shall stand up his kingdom shall be broken, and shall be divided toward the four winds of heaven; and not to his posterity, nor according to his dominion which he ruled: for his kingdom shall be plucked up even for others besides these.	Alexander died in B.C. 323. His kingdom was divided among his four Generals. Cassander had Greece and the adjacent countries. Lysimachus had Thrace, including Asia Minor and the countries lying on the Hellespont and Bosphorus. Seleucus had Syria and Babylon. Ptolemy had Egypt and the neighbouring countries. Fulfilled in the aggressions and conquests of the Romans.
5 And the King of the South shall be strong, and one of his (Alexander's) princes shall be strong above him (LXX), and have dominion; his dominion shall be a great dominion.	Ptolemy Lagi (Soter) of Egypt, B.C. 323-283. Seleucus Nicator, B.C. 312-280. He annexed Macedon and Thrace to Syria.
6 And in the end of years they shall join themselves together; for the King's daughter of the South shall come to the King of the North to make an agreement;	In B.C. 250. Ptolemy Philadelphus, the second King of Egypt, and Antiochus Theos, the third King of Syria, agreed to make peace on condition that Antiochus should put away his former wife, Laodice, and her two sons, and should

THE PROPHECY	THE FULFILMENT
but she shall not retain the power of the arm; neither shall he stand, nor his arm; but she shall be given up, and they that brought her, and he that begat her, and he that strengthened her in these times.	marry Berenice, the daughter of Ptolemy, and that any child of Berenice should be the heir of Antiochus. The marriage took place, but when Ptolemy died Antiochus, in B.C. 247, called back his former wife. Berenice and her young son were poisoned, and Callinicus the son of Laodice was put on the throne as Seleucus II, Callinicus, B.C. 246-226.
7 And out of a branch of her roots shall one stand up in his estate, who shall come with an army, and shall enter into the fortress of the King of the North, and shall deal against them, and shall prevail;	'Her' refers to the murdered Berenice, and 'the one who shall stand up' was her brother, Ptolemy Euergetes, B.C. 247-222, who avenged her death. He invaded the territory of Seleucus Callinicus, slew Laodice the wife of Antiochus Theos, and seized the port of Antioch.
8 And shall also carry captive into Egypt their gods, with their princes, and with their precious vessels of silver and gold; and he shall continue more years than the King of the North.	Ptolemy III carried to Egypt 4,000 talents of gold, 40,000 talents of silver, and 2,500 idols and idolatrous vessels, including those which Cambyses had taken to Persia nearly 300 years before.
9 So the King of the South shall come into his kingdom, and shall return into his own land.	This may mean either that Ptolemy Euergetes successfully returned to Egypt after his invasion of the North, or that Seleucus Callinicus of the North, having unsuccessfully invaded Egypt, returned defeated to Syria.
10 But his sons shall be stirred up, and shall assemble a multitude of great forces; and one shall certainly come and overflow and pass through; then shall he return and be stirred up even to his fortress.	This is a difficult verse. Some think that the reference is to the sons or son of the king of Egypt, Ptolemy Philopater, B.C. 222-205; but the reference is usually taken to be to the sons of Seleucus II, who were Cerannos, Seleucus III, B.C. 222-205, and Antiochus the Great, B.C. 222-186, who was successful in an attack upon the South.
11 And the King of the South shall be moved with choler, and shall come forth and fight with him, even with the King of the North; and he shall set forth a great multitude, but the multitude shall be given into his hand.	In the battle of Raphia in B.C. 217 Ptolemy Philopater of Egypt defeated Antiochus the Great of Syria. 'He' refers to Antiochus, and 'his' to Philopater.

THE PROPHECY	THE FULFILMENT
12 And when he hath taken away the multitude his heart shall be lifted up; and he shall cast down many ten thousands but he shall not be strengthened by it.	Philopater, had he pressed his victory, might have possessed the kingdom of Antiochus, but pride and licentious indulgence prevented him doing this, and so he was not strengthened by his victory at Raphia.
13 For the King of the North shall return, and shall set forth a multitude greater than the former, and shall certainly come after certain years with a great army and with much riches.	In B.C. 203 Ptolemy Philopater having died, and his own son Epiphanes, four or five years of age, having succeeded him, Antiochus entered into an alliance with Philip III of Macedon to partition Egypt between them, the Syrian king attacked Egypt with a larger army than he had had 14 years before, and one result of this was that Antiochus gained possession of all Palestine.
14 And in those times there shall many stand up against the King of the South; also the robbers of thy people shall exalt themselves to establish vision; but they shall fall.	This tells of discontent and sedition in Egypt following the death of Philopater.
	Almost certainly these are rebel Jews who, siding with Antiochus hoped to gain something from him.
	Polybius says that 'Scopas', the general of Ptolemy, 'went in haste to the upper parts of the country, and in the winter-time overthrew the nation of the Jews'. Their apostasy caused them to stumble.
15 So the King of the North shall come and cast up a mount and take the most fenced cities; and the arms of the South shall not withstand, neither his chosen people, neither shall there be any strength to withstand.	In B.C. 198 Antiochus defeated the Egyptians at Paneas, and Scopas the Egyptian general fled to Sidon, one of Egypt's strongest fortified towns. Antiochus laid siege to the town and compelled the Egyptians to surrender.
16 But he that cometh against him shall do according to his own will, and none shall stand before him; and he shall stand in the glorious land, which by his hand shall be consumed.	'Him' refers to Ptolemy, and 'his' to Antiochus whose victory was complete. 'The glorious land' is Palestine. The last clause presents a problem, because Antiochus the Great did not 'consume' the land; but if by 'in his hand shall be destruction' the *ultimate* result of this invasion is referred to, and the imposition of taxes and the ferocity of Antiochus Epiphanes (B.C. 175-164), the difficulty is much reduced.

THE PROPHECY	THE FULFILMENT
17 He shall also set his face to enter with the strength of his whole kingdom, and upright ones with him; thus shall he do (the latter part of this verse has been translated: 'and having an agreement in intention and he shall carry it out'): and he shall give him the daughter of women, corrupting her (Heb. to corrupt her); but she shall not stand on his side, neither be for him.	Antiochus gathered all his forces on land and sea with a view to invading and conquering Egypt, but the Egyptians had sought and obtained the interference of the Romans, which led Antiochus to change his policy. He exchanged force for craftiness, and proposed that his young daughter, Cleopatra, should marry the young Ptolemy Epiphanes (which took place in B.C. 198); his design being that she should work for her father against her husband. But this did not happen. On the contrary, when Scipio defeated Antiochus at Magnesia in B.C. 190, Cleopatra sent congratulations to the Romans.
18 After this shall he turn his face unto the isles, and shall take many; but a prince for his own behalf (Heb. for him) shall cause the reproach (Heb. his reproach) offered by him to cease; without his own reproach he shall cause it to turn upon him.	Antiochus turned his conquests against the isles of the Mediterranean Sea; he took possession of the dominions of Philip of Macedon, crossed into Europe and seized Thrace. The Romans demanded that he should get out of Philip's former dominions. He refused, but a 'prince', Scipio of Rome, resisted him, and turned the reproach back on the Syrian's head.
19 Then he shall turn his face toward the fort of his own land; but he shall stumble and fall, and not be found,	After his defeat at Magnesia Antiochus fled from fort to fort on his way back to Antioch. A heavy tax was imposed upon him by the Romans, and in order to raise the money he assaulted with an armed force by night the temple of Jove (Bel) in Elymais; but the inhabitants slew him and all his forces.
20 Then shall stand up in his estate a raiser of taxes in the glory of the kingdom; but within few days he shall be destroyed, neither in anger, nor in battle.	Antiochus was succeeded by his son Seleucus IV, Philopater, B.C. 187-176. He has somehow to find the taxes imposed upon his father, and it is said that he sent his treasurer Heliodorus to plunder the Temple at Jerusalem, 'the Glory of the Kingdom'. A tradition says that Heliodorus poisoned Seleucus who suddenly disappeared.

THE PROPHECY	THE FULFILMENT
21 And in his estate shall stand up a vile person,	This is the second son of Antiochus the Great, the brother of Seleucus Philopater, Antiochus Epiphanes, B.C. 176-164.
whom they shall not give the honour of the kingdom;	He was not the heir to the throne as his brother, the former king, had a son, Demetrius who was the rightful heir.
but he shall come in peaceably, and obtain the kingdom by flatteries.	He seized the throne at a time when the people were living carelessly, and by intrigue and political favour.
22 And with the arms of a flood shall they be overflown from before him, and shall be broken; yea, also the prince of the covenant.	By an overflowing army he broke all opposition. 'The prince of the covenant' is supposed to be the Jewish high priest Onias III whom Antiochus deposed.
23 And after the league made with him he shall work deceitfully; for he shall come up, and shall become strong with a small people.	The reference here is uncertain. 'Him' may refer to Eumenes, King of Pergamus, B.C. 197-159, with whom, the historian Appian tells us, Antiochus made a league, with no intention of keeping it; or it may refer to feigned friendship on the part of Antiochus with Ptolemy VI of Egypt. To 'come up' means 'to become strong'; and by 'a small people' would seem to mean 'with a small force'.
24 He shall enter peaceably even upon the fattest places of the province; and he shall do that which his fathers have not done, nor his father's fathers; he shall scatter among them the prey and spoil, and riches; yea, and he shall forecast his devices against the strong holds, even for a time.	'Peaceably', as in verse 21, and viii. 25, means, probably, in the midst of security, when men were living carelessly, i.e., unexpectedly. 'The province' may refer either to Coele-Syria and Palestine, or to Egypt. In either case it is known that Antiochus, wherever he went, scattered gifts; the booty he gathered in one place he scattered in another (1 Macc. iii. 30). Meanwhile he was planning the invasion of Egypt; but God had limited his activities; and he was soon to be cut off.
25 And he shall stir up his power and his courage against the King of the South with a great army; and the King of the South shall be stirred up to battle with a very great and mighty army; but he shall not stand; for they shall forecast devices against him.	Antiochus Epiphanes made war with Ptolemy Philometor and speedily defeated his forces. He took Pelusium, advanced to Memphis, and marched toward Alexandria. Ptolemy's defeat was the result of internal intrigue, including that of his brother Physcon who replaced him on the throne.

THE PROPHECY	THE FULFILMENT
26 Yea, they that feed of the portion of his meat shall destroy him, and his army shall overflow; and many shall fall down slain.	This continues the statement of verse 25. Treachery and intrigue caused the overthrow of Ptolemy and the defeat of his army.
27 And both these kings' hearts shall be to do mischief, and they shall speak lies at one table;	The two kings referred to would appear to be Antiochus and Ptolemy Philometor, who consulted together against Physcon the brother of Philometor, how they might dethrone him. The real object of Antiochus was to possess Egypt for himself, not to replace Philometor on the throne; and the real object of Philometor was not with Antiochus to dethrone Physcon, but to unite with Physcon against Antiochus, which he did.
but it shall not prosper; for yet the end shall be at the time appointed.	But these devices did not succeed, for they all reckoned regardless of God's will (cf. 24, 29, 35, 40).
28 Then shall he return into his land with great riches; and his heart shall be against the holy covenant; and he shall do exploits, and return to his own land.	'He' and 'his' refer to Antiochus. The event relates to the Jews. Onias III had been removed from the high priesthood by the treachery of his brother Jason, and three years later Jason was displaced by Menelaus, who had Onias murdered, and plundered the Temple. The Jews rose to defend their Sanctuary, and much confusion resulted. Jason unsuccessfully attempted to recover the high priesthood. Antiochus was in Egypt, and it was rumoured in Judaea that he was dead, which led to much rejoicing among the Jews. Antiochus heard of this and marched against the Jews and Jerusalem. Three days of wholesale massacre followed. Antiochus desecrated and robbed the Temple, and returned to Antioch (1 Macc. i. 20-24; 2 Macc. v. 1-21).
29 At the time appointed he shall return and come toward the South but it shall not be as the former, or as the latter.	Antiochus again attacked Egypt, but not with the success he had the first time (24), or the second (28). The object was to break up the alliance between Philometor and Physcon.

THE PROPHECY	THE FULFILMENT
30 For the ships of Chittim shall come against him; therefore he shall be grieved, and return, and have indignation against the holy covenant; so shall he do; he shall even return, and have intelligence with them that forsake the holy covenant.	It was in B.C. 168 that Antiochus invaded Egypt the third time. The Ptolemies appealed to Rome. When Antiochus was within four miles of Alexandria he learned that a Roman fleet lay at anchor in the bay. He was met by Caius Popilius Laenas who handed him a demand from the Roman Senate to leave Egypt. Antiochus said that, with his advisers, he would consider it; whereupon Laenas drew a circle round him and said, 'Before you step out of that circle give such an answer as I may report to the Senate'. The King replied, 'If it so please the Senate we must depart'; so, grieved, he returned. On his way North he satiated his fury upon the Jews, making use of renegade Jews. It was at this time that he committed those outrages and massacres for which he is so justly infamous, and which have made him the type of the Antichrist (xi. 36-xii).
31 And arms shall stand on his part; and they shall pollute the sanctuary of strength, and shall take away the daily sacrifice,	He shall set physical forces in motion. Antiochus forbade burnt offerings, and sacrifices, and drink offerings in the Temple at Jerusalem.
and they shall place the abomination that maketh desolate.	An idol-altar was built over the altar of Jehovah, upon which swine's flesh was sacrificed. He Hellenized, i.e. made heathen of, renegade Jews.
32 And such as do wickedly against the covenant shall he corrupt by flatteries;	This refers to the uprising and resistance of the Maccabees, who beginning with Mattathias made glorious history, the most heroic in Jewish annals.
but the people that do know their God shall be strong and do exploits.	The period of the Maccabees, beginning in B.C. 165, lasted nearly one hundred years. The story is told in 1 Maccabees.
33 And they that understand among the people shall instruct many;	In the Maccabean crisis arose a class of pious and learned men, called Maskilim—the understanding ones. They did not fight, but taught, throwing light upon the Messianic promises.
yet they shall fall by the sword, and by flame, by captivity, by spoil, many days.	The army of Antiochus attacked a multitude of Jews on the Sabbath day, a day on which the Jews would not fight, and so they fell an easy prey to their enemies (1 Macc. ii. 38).

THE PROPHECY	THE FULFILMENT
34 Now when they shall fall, they shall be holpen with a little help; but many shall cleave to them with flatteries.	When success crowned the arms of Judas some joined the Maccabees who formerly were opposed to them, but their attachment was not genuine.
35 And some of them of understanding shall fall, to try them, and to purge, and to make them white, even to the time of the end; because it is yet for a time appointed.	Judas and his successors were not always faithful, and many fell in battle and persecution, but their trials wrought their purification, and the evil days were not to last for ever; there was a God-appointed 'time of the end'.

Profane history tells us much which Biblical prediction omits, but with it we are not immediately concerned, though, of course, it has its place in the unfolding purpose of God for mankind.

GREAT CHANGES DURING THE INTERLUDE

Not to study the story of the four hundred years between the two Testaments is to be ignorant of the activity of Divine Providence throughout this long period in both Judaism and Heathenism. The New Testament does not begin from where the Old Testament ends. Tremendous changes took place in all directions, and to know what these were, and what was their significance, is of the utmost importance for an understanding of how the story of the first hundred years A.D. was made possible.

All history from the Garden of Eden was a preparation for the Advent of the promised Messiah (Gen. iii. 15), and this is true no less of the Interlude than of every period which preceded it; but with this difference, that the previous method was by separation, and the method during the Interlude was by dispersion; that the scope of operations throughout Old Testament history was national, but during the Interlude it was world-wide.

The importance of the Interlude period can best be understood by contrasting the situation at the close of the Old Testament period with that at the beginning of the New Testament period.

CHART 116

THE TWO TESTAMENTS	
Close of Old Testament	Opening of New Testament
The seat of World Empire was in the East: Asia	The seat of World Empire was in the West: Europe
Medo-Persia was in power	Rome was in power
Artaxerxes was lord over Palestine	Caesar was lord over Palestine
Judaea was under a Jewish Governor	Judaea was under a Roman Deputy
	In Palestine were Greek cities bearing Greek names: e.g., Paneas, Ptolemais, Scythopolis. It was hemmed in by Greek towns on the west, north, and east
The Temple was that built by Zerubbabel	The Temple was being rebuilt by Herod the Great
No mention in the Old Testament or in the Apocrypha of Synagogues	Synagogues everywhere from Jerusalem to Rome
The Scriptures of the Old Testament were in Hebrew	The Scriptures of the Old Testament were in Greek
No Writings by Jews other than the Old Testament Scriptures	There were fifteen Apocryphal Writings (see p. 43) and many Pseudepigrapha.
In the O.T. period there were no Pharisees or Sadducees	These arose in the 2nd cent. B.C.

From this it will be seen that the Messiah came to a very different world from that of the Ezra-Nehemiah period. The time of these men was not ready for the advent of Christ; much had to be done to prepare mankind, in both Judaism and Heathenism, for His appearance and the inauguration of the new age.

JUDAISM AND HEATHENISM PREPARED FOR THE MESSIAH

These two great divisions of mankind, while appearing independently to make each its own history, were in fact both moving toward a predestined goal, Judaism semi-consciously, and

Heathenism unconsciously. Through Judaism God was ap
proaching man from above; and through Heathenism man was
approaching God from below. The guide of the one was revealed
religion, and of the other, natural religion. In Judaism the true
religion was being prepared for man, and in Heathenism man was
being prepared for the true religion. Moving from opposite
directions Judaism and Heathenism met at the Cross.

I. JUDAISM: A PREPARATION FOR THE MESSIAH

The Jews of the   1. Home-land
                  2. Dispersion

In thinking of Judaism in this period we must divide it into
two parts: the Jews of the Home-land, and the Jews of the
Dispersion. The former represented Hebraism, and the latter,
Hellenism.

1. The Jews of the Home-land

(a) HISTORY

Their history during the Interlude age may be divided into
three periods:

(1) *The Pre-Maccabean Period*:

B.C. 400-175

This extends from the end of Old Testament history to the
rise of Antiochus Epiphanes in B.C. 175; a period of 225 years.
Sources of this period are scant, but much information comes to
us through the First and Second Books of the Maccabees, and
from Josephus.

(2) *The Maccabean Period*:

B.C. 175-63

This extends from the rise of Antiochus Epiphanes to the
appearance of Pompey in Palestine; a period of 112 years. This
is one of the saddest and one of the most heroic periods in all
Jewish history. Due to the cruelty and sacrilege of Antiochus

Epiphanes in B.C. 175-164, there was a rising of the Jews under Mattathias and his five sons Johanan, Simon, Judas, Eleazar, and Jonathan.

It was the design of Antiochus IV to Hellenize the Jews, indeed to obliterate the distinctiveness of Judaism, and to merge their religion into the cult of Jupiter, or Zeus, or into the lascivious rites of Syria. And, alas, there was a strong inclination among the Jews to be Hellenized. The high priest Jason was at the head of this faction, and apostasy was widespread. Altars were erected to Zeus throughout the Holy Land. At the little town of Modin there was one of these, and when a Jew at the bidding of an emissary of Antiochus was about to offer a sacrifice to Zeus, Mattathias, an old priest, slew both the Jew and the emissary, and then he and his followers fled to the mountains and caves; but revolt had been raised, and on the death of Mattathias his sons antagonized the spreading paganism, and by valiant victories brought deliverance to Israel.

(3) *The Post-Maccabean Period*:
B.C. 63 A.D.

This period is historically noteworthy for the rise and course of the Herodian Dynasty. After varying fortune Herod the Great was, in B.C. 40, made 'King of the Jews' by Antony and Octavianus. He was notorious for his cruelty, and famous for his rebuilding of the Temple in Jerusalem, the third and last of the Jewish Temples. The outstanding event of his reign was the birth of Jesus the Messiah in B.C. 5-4; and at this point contact is made with the New Testament and the Second Act of the Unfolding Drama of Redemption.

CHART 117

THE CONNECTION BETWEEN MATTATHIAS AND HEROD THE GREAT

B.C. 167-73

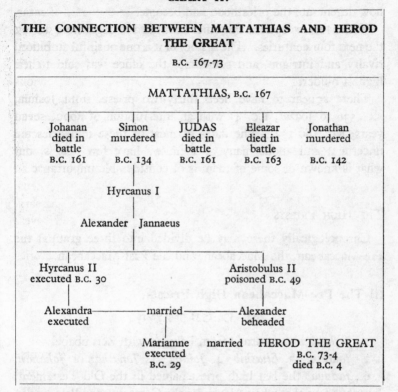

MATTATHIAS, B.C. 167

Johanan	Simon	JUDAS	Eleazar	Jonathan
died in battle	murdered	died in battle	died in battle	murdered
B.C. 161	B.C. 134	B.C. 161	B.C. 163	B.C. 142

Hyrcanus I

Alexander Jannaeus

Hyrcanus II
executed B.C. 30

Aristobulus II
poisoned B.C. 49

Alexandra
executed
————— married —————
Alexander
beheaded

Mariamne   married   HEROD THE GREAT
executed   B.C. 73-4
B.C. 29   died B.C. 4

(b) GOVERNMENT

Zerubbabel was the last of the royal princes, and not again until the Messiah came did there appear a legitimate heir to the throne of David. It was really with Zedekiah in B.C. 586 that rightful kingship ended in Israel.

In the long period of the Interlude the Jewish rulers were priests, not kings, although they combined with their religious functions princely and civil powers. This hierocracy was the governmental feature of this new age. There was a succession of high priests from the time of Joshua, who returned with Zerubbabel from Babylonian captivity, until the birth of the Messiah, a period of over 530 years.

The moral and spiritual condition of the priesthood at the end of the Old Testament period is shown in the prophecy of Malachi.

His indictment of them is stated in chs. i. 6-ii. 9; and in it we see how degenerate the priesthood had become.

With a few exceptions this office continued to degenerate during the next four centuries. The history of it is one of sinful ambition, rivalry and intrigue, and sometimes the office was sold to the highest bidder.

There appear to have been thirty-two priests from Joshua, B.C. 536 to Joazar, B.C. 4; with an interruption of about seven years, B.C. 160-153. The dates of most of these ministries are uncertain, and about many of them we have few details, but what is known of some of them is of considerable importance.

THE HIGH PRIESTS

Chronologically these may be divided into three groups: the Pre-Maccabean, the Maccabean, and the Post-Maccabean.

(i) The Pre-Maccabean High Priests:

B.C. 536-153: 383 years

1. *Joshua*, who returned from Babylon with Zerubbabel
2. *Joiakim* 3. *Eliashib* 4. *Joiada* 5. *Jonathan* or *Johanan*.
6. *Jaddua*: the last high priest named in the Old Testament. Josephus says that when Alexander the Great invaded Palestine in B.C. 333, Jaddua the high priest, then an old man, and a number of Jews went out to meet him. Alexander bowed before them because he had seen this high priest in a vision, and had been assured of victory. It is also said that Jaddua showed to Alexander the prophecies in the Book of Daniel which declared that Greece would conquer Medo-Persia by 'a mighty king' (xi. 3), the 'notable horn' on the head of the goat (viii. 5, 8, 21), which Alexander rightly believed referred to himself. In consequence he treated the Jews with great consideration. The fulfilment of these prophecies was the overthrow of the Medo-Persian Empire and the establishment of the Grecian Empire in B.C. 333-2.

Manasseh, the brother of Jaddua, founded the Samaritan Temple in B.C. 332, from which date the Jews and the Samaritans became totally separated peoples.

7. *Onias I.* He received a letter from Sparta, in which the Lacedemonians claimed kinship with the Jews through Abraham (1 Macc. xii. 5-23).

8. *Simon the Just.* Around this man's tradition and fancy gathered many stories. According to tradition he completed the collection of the books of Scripture begun by Ezra. His praises are sung by Jesus the son of Sirach in Ecclesiasticus l. 1-21; and it may be true that with him ended the purest glory of the priesthood. In his time arose the Chasidim, 'the pious', who were the lineal ancestors of the sect of the Pharisees.

9. *Eleazar*, a brother of Simon the Just. It was in his time, in the reign of Ptolemy Philadelphus of Egypt, that the Hebrew Scriptures, or some of them, were translated into Greek, the Version which is called the Septuagint (LXX).

10. *Manasseh.*

11. *Onias II.* By his refusal to pay the customary tribute to Egypt the virtual independence of Judaea was all but lost. Josephus calls him, 'one of a little soul, and a great lover of money'. By the subtlety of his nephew Joseph, who went to Alexandria as his uncle's representative, he himself became the collector of the royal taxes in Judaea, 'and founded a family which rivalled in influence the high-priestly line, and played an important part in the national history'.

12. *Simon II.* Some think that the passage in Ecclesiasticus l. refers to this high priest, and not to Simon I. When Ptolemy Philopater, a tyrant and voluptuary, attempted to enter the inmost sanctuary of the Temple in Jerusalem, Simon opposed him, and in consequence Philopater persecuted the Jews in Alexandria. The story of this persecution is found in 3 Maccabees (wrongly so called). It was during the ministry of this high priest that a party arose to whom later was given the name of Sadducees.

13. *Onias III.* In 2 Maccabees he is described as 'a virtuous and a good man, reverend in conversation, gentle in behaviour, exercised from a child in all points of virtue' (xv. 12). He was

the head of the Chasidim, the largest and most influential party in Jerusalem. As such he was hated by the Hellenists, who were led by his own brother Jason, to whom later the high priesthood was sold by Antiochus Epiphanes.

It was during the ministry of Onias III that the Syrian king, having heard that there was much money laid up in the Temple at Jerusalem, sent his chief minister Heliodorus to get hold of it. Proceeding to do this he was stricken down by an angelic horseman, and only by the prayers of Onias III was he restored. The story is to be found in 2 Macc. iii.

14. *Jason*, the head of the Hellenizing party in Judaea, secured the high priesthood by bribery. Onias III went to Syria with a view to the restoration of order in Judaea, and during his absence Jason was his deputy; but Onias did not return, and eventually was executed in Syria.

In every way possible Jason promoted the Hellenizing of the people. The money which he had promised to Antiochus he sent to Antioch by Menelaus, who, while there, secured the high priesthood for himself by out-bidding Jason, but his triumph was short-lived. Jason's career ended in disaster, and has been cited as a signal instance of retributive justice for forsaking the laws of the fathers, and throwing open the sacred enclosure of Judaism to the Greek influences. He died a fugitive, and was not 'gathered to his fathers', though he was a high priest of the family of Aaron (2 Macc. v).

15. *Menelaus* was high priest during the tragic period of Antiochus Epiphanes of Syria. He out-bid Jason to get the office, and when he failed to raise the money he had promised to Antiochus he robbed the Temple to secure it. When Antiochus attacked Jerusalem Menelaus guided him to the Holy of Holies, and the Syrian king carried off from the Temple the precious vessels, fittings and furniture.

In B.C. 162 Menelaus was put to death by Antiochus Eupator.

16. *Alcimus*. This man, though not of the high-priestly lineage, was made high priest by Antiochus Eupator. The office should have gone to Onias, son of Onias III, but being deprived

of it he retired to Egypt. Alcimus was a Hellenist and opposed Judas Maccabeus. His story found in 1 Macc. vii, is one of intrigue, and his end corresponded to it, for while removing a wall of the Temple which excluded the laity from the Court of the Priests he was paralysed and died.

(ii) The Maccabean High Priests:

B.C. 153-35: 118 years

17. *Jonathan*: B.C. 153-143.

There appears to have been an interruption of the priesthood for seven years, B.C. 160-153, and then, for about 118 years the office remained in the Maccabean or Asmonaean family.

Mattathias, an aged priest, who in B.C. 167 raised the Maccabean revolt against Hellenism in Judah, died a year later having committed the leadership to his third son Judas.

There is no evidence that Judas held the office of high priest, but in B.C. 153 Balas, who claimed to be the true heir to the Syrian throne, against the claim of Demetrius, appointed Jonathan, the fifth son of Mattathias, to be high priest, and sent him a purple robe and a crown of gold as badges of his sovereign rank. This is important as showing that the sacerdotal and civil offices were combined in Jonathan, who rose to a position of great authority and power.

Tryphon, a Syrian general, fearing Jonathan's power, under a false pretext lured him to Ptolemais and there murdered him.

18. *Simon*: B.C. 143-135.

When Mattathias was dying in B.C. 166, the resistance to paganism and tyranny which he had initiated he committed to his five sons. His third son Judas he made captain of the army, and Simon, his second son, he made the counsellor of his brethren and their followers (1 Macc. ii. 65, 66). Upon the death of Jonathan, Simon entered upon his great ministry as 'the priest and prince of the Jews' (1 Macc. xv. 1), 'the purest height of the whole Maccabean movement'. His period of office was outstanding for several reasons.

His assumption of office and rousing speech to the Maccabean followers recorded in 1 Macc. xiii. 1-9 is a noble example of selflessness and courage. Conscious that he was the last of a family of heroes he built a monument at Modin where were interred the bodies of his father and mother and four brothers, and where his body would lie when the time came. This magnificent monument remained for over five hundred years.

Simon destroyed the strongholds of the Syrians in Palestine, and brought in a period of independence and peace. The record says: 'He made peace in the land, and Israel rejoiced with great joy; for every man sat under his vine and his fig tree, and there was none to fray them' (1 Macc. xiv. 11, 12); words which occur in 1 Kings iv. 25; Mic. iv. 4; Zech. iii. 10.

In his time the Jewish people ceased to pay tribute to the Persian Kings, and contracts were dated 'In the first year of Simon, the great High Priest, and General, and Leader of the Jews'.

In his time also the Jews were allowed to strike coins for themselves which bore the signs of peace and plenty—the cup, the vine the palm-branches, the lily, and the fruit-boughs of Palestine. He made alliances with Sparta and with Rome. In a great assembly held in Jerusalem in B.C. 140 Simon was proclaimed 'governor and high priest for ever, until there should arise a faithful prophet' (1 Macc. xiv. 41).

Simon's daughter was married to a certain Ptolemy, who, being ambitious, and having evil designs, invited Simon and his two sons Judas and Mattathias to a great banquet at Jericho, and at the close of it he murdered the three of them. Thus died the last of the noble sons of the noble Mattathias.

19. *John Hyrcanus*: B.C. 135-106.

The book of 1 Maccabees ends with the high-priesthood of Simon, and there are few reliable sources for the period of John Hyrcanus. But certain things seem to have historical value. Hyrcanus was the first of the Asmonean family. He turned Judaean vassalage into independence, and kept in touch with Rome. At first his sympathies were with the Pharisees, but later he transferred them to the Sadducees.

He absorbed the Edomites into Judaism by circumcision. He destroyed the city of Shechem, and the temple on Mount Gerizim.

Josephus says of him that 'he alone had three of the most desirable things in the world: the government of the nation, the high-priesthood, and the gift of prophecy'.

Probably the apocryphal *Judith* was written in his time; and about the time of his death Pompey and Marcus Tullius Cicero were born.

20. *Aristobulus I*: B.C. 106.

This son of John Hyrcanus was the first of his family to assume the royal title and diadem. He was the first king of the Jews since Jehoiachin in B.C. 562 (2 K. xxv. 27-30). Hyrcanus nominated his wife as his successor, but Aristobulus cast her and all his brothers but one into prison, and there his mother died of starvation. The unimprisoned brother, Antigonus, he murdered in a fit of jealous suspicion, and shortly afterwards died of remorse.

He was known as Phil-Hellen, 'friend of the Greeks'.

21. *Alexander Jannaeus*: B.C. 105-78

The widow of Aristobulus, Salome, liberated the three imprisoned brothers, and Alexander, the eldest of them, succeeded to the priestly and kingly office. Later he married Salome, whose Greek name was Alexandra. This priest-king was aged twenty-two when he came to power, and he died when he was forty-nine years old. He made a hobby of military campaigns, and in them he was frequently successful. He was guilty of the grossest cruelty. As he lay at a feast among his concubines, he ordered 800 Pharisees to be crucified in his presence, after their wives and children had been slain in their sight. His reign was long, adventurous and troubled.

Alexandra: B.C. 78-69.

This once widow of Aristobulus, and now widow of Alexander Jannaeus, whose Jewish name was Salome, now, by the will of her late husband, became the first and only Queen of the Jews during the Interlude period. Josephus says that she was 'a sagacious woman in the management of great affairs, intent always upon gathering soldiers together, so that she increased the army by one half, till her own nation became powerful at home and terrible to foreign potentates' (*Wars*, i. 5. 2).

Her brother, Simon ben Shetach, was the leader of the Pharisees, and Josephus says that 'while she governed the people the Pharisees governed her'. It has been said of her that 'in her devotion to the Pharisees she forgot the duties of a sovereign, and her unwise partiality . . . led quickly to the downfall of her house and to the fresh and permanent subjection of her country'.

22. *Hyrcanus II*: B.C. 69, 63-40.

A woman could not be high priest, so this office was given by Alexandra to her son Hyrcanus, and when she died he was given the crown also. He was a weak and indolent man, and being vigorously opposed by his energetic brother Aristobulus II, he resigned after three months and retired into private life (B.C. 69). At this point nine years of Pharisee tyranny ended.

When Pompey visited Damascus in B.C. 63 he invited all who sought his arbitration to meet him there. Hyrcanus and Aristobulus presented their respective claims, and when later Pompey visited Judaea, he cast Aristobulus into prison, reappointed Hyrcanus to the high priesthood, and entrusted him with the civil administration also of the country, in subordination however to the Roman governor of Syria.

Later the Parthians made Antigonus king, the son of Aristobulus II. Hyrcanus was given up to him, and to disqualify him from again holding office Antigonus cut off both his ears. For a few years he lived among the Jews in Babylonia; and when in B.C. 36 Herod sent for him, he returned to Jerusalem and six years later Herod executed him to get rid of the last male member of the Maccabean family.

23. *Aristobulus II*: B.C. 69-63.

The brother of Hyrcanus II, who deposed him and assumed his office for six years, at the end of which time Pompey reinstated Hyrcanus, and sent Aristobulus as a prisoner to Rome.

24. *Antigonus*: B.C. 40-37.

The rule of this man, whose Jewish name was Mattathias, was undistinguished. At the end of three years he was sent to Antony at Antioch, and after being scourged as a criminal he was beheaded by the axe of the common lictor.

With his death the sovereignty of Judaea passed finally away from the great dynasty of the Maccabees. The dynasty began with Mattathias a hero, and ended with Mattathias a craven.

25. *Ananel*: B.C. 36, 34.

Ananel or Hananeel of Babylon was appointed high priest by Herod, and the choice, involving as it did the passing over of Aristobulus III, the brother of Mariamne Herod's wife, and the son of Alexandra, started domestic troubles which pursued Herod all his life.

Ananel has been identified with the Annas of the Gospels. On account of the storm raised by Alexandra and Mariamne, in B.C. 35 Herod deposed Ananel and appointed in his place, Aristobulus, who was about seventeen years of age, but Herod was jealous of the youth's attractions.

On the appointment of Aristobulus to be high priest his mother Alexandra gave a sumptuous banquet in his honour at Jericho, and Herod attended it. After the feast Herod, Aristobulus and others resorted to the baths and there, without doubt at Herod's instigation, the young high priest was held under the water and drowned. Thereafter Ananel resumed the office of high priest for a short time. So ended in blood and intrigue the succession of Maccabean high priests for nearly 120 years.

(iii) The Post-Maccabean High Priests:
From B.C. 35

Of some of these even the names are not known for certain, and nothing of any consequence can be said of them.

26. *Jesus ben Phabi*. 27. *Simon*, Herod's father in-law. 28. *Matthias*. 29. *Joazar*. 30. *Eleazar*. 31. *Jesus ben Sie*; and 32. *Joazar* a second time.

(c) RELIGIOUS PARTIES

In this Interlude period there must be considered a 'phenomenon', as Dean Stanley says, 'of the most fateful importance for the history of Palestine, and also of the most universal significance for the history of the coming Church. It was the appearance of religious parties and of party-spirit under the name of Pharisee

Sadducee, and Essene, first appearing under Jonathan, developed under John Hyrcanus, leading to fierce civil war under Alexander Jannaeus, and playing the chief part in the tremendous drama which marks the consummation of the period' (*Jewish Church*, vol. III, p. 325).

From our reading of the Gospels we are so familiar with the designations Pharisee and Sadducee that it has not occurred to most people to ask when and how these religious parties arose. For an answer to these inquiries we must go, not to the Old Testament which knows nothing of them, but to the Interlude, the period between the Testaments.

(1) The Pharisees

After the return from Babylonian captivity there arose in Judaism a party who, in view of growing laxity among the Jews, devoted their lives to the upholding of the Law in its integrity. They were known as *Chasidim*—the *Pious*, or as *Asideans*, which is the Graecised form of the Hebrew. They are referred to in 1 Macc. ii. 42; vii. 13; 2 Macc. xiv. 6; and were the lineal ancestors of the *Pharisees*, which means the *Separatists*, a name given to them by their opponents as a nickname. The word *Pharisee* does not occur in the Old Testament or Apocrypha, but Josephus uses it in his annals of Jonathan the high priest (B.C. 153-143), and of John Hyrcanus (B.C. 135-106). They came to prominence and power therefore in the period of the Maccabees.

They were not a political but a religious body, but alas, as Dean Stanley says, their lofty aspirations petrified into hard dogmatic form, their patriotism became partisanship, and their fidelity was corrupted into fanaticism; and these are the Pharisees who appear in the Gospels.

The Pharisees believed in incorporeal beings such as angels; they believed in future reward and retribution, and so in a resurrection, a future life, and immortality. They regarded oral tradition to be of equal authority with the written law; and in the matter of freedom they inclined to fatalism.

(2) The Sadducees

Josephus in his first mention of the Sadducees, in the history of John Hyrcanus (B.C. 135-106) simply says that their 'notions are quite contrary to those of the Pharisees' (Ant. xiii. 10, 6). The power of these opposing parties oscillated in the Maccabean period. The Sadducees were not in the favour of the early Maccabean leaders, but in the time of John Hyrcanus the pendulum swung over, only to swing back in the time of Salome-Alexandra.

It is probable that the name *Sadducee* was derived from *Tsaddiqim*, meaning 'righteous', in opposition to the Pharisees' name *Chasidim*, or 'pious'; but the origin of the designation is not certain.

The Sadducees were never a large party numerically, but they were wealthy and influential. They were the materialists, the secularists, the sceptics, the rationalists of their time. In the Rabbinical writings they are spoken of as heretics. They were opposed to the oral law, on which the Pharisees insisted, and they had no use for the tradition of the elders. On the other hand they interpreted the Law literally and severely, and insisted on the literal interpretations of the *lex talionis* (Deut. xix. 21).

They would believe nothing which the law did not teach, and so they denied the doctrine of immortality, a future life, and so resurrection, retribution, and rewards, the existence of angels, and the dependence of man's free will on the Divine will. Their outlook was limited to this life and world, and their conduct was determined by their outlook. History makes no mention of them after the fall of the Jewish nation in A.D. 70.

The references in the Gospels to this party are noteworthy.

(3) The Essenes

Bishop Lightfoot thinks that this designation comes from a Hebrew word *chasha*, which means 'to be silent'. These strange people arose in the Interlude period, probably about the middle of the second century B.C. The Pharisees were 'separatists', the Sadducees were 'moralists', and the Essenes were 'mystics'. The last may have sprung, as did the Pharisees, from the *Chasidim* of the Maccabean times.

They were a monastic order, and lived generally in little exclusive communities and villages of their own. The community was never large, and membership was conditioned on severe initiation.

D

Their badges were a white dress, in symbol of purity, a leather apron, in symbol of defence from impurity, and a pickaxe or spade with which to dig a hole in the ground to bury impurity out of sight.

An outstanding feature was ablution, and this led them to dwell near water, as, for example, the Dead Sea. They bathed themselves both before and after meals, and after contact with anyone or anything reckoned unclean. All that each of them possessed was the property of the community. They all ate at one table, and began their meals, as well as their daily work, with prayer. Their usual employment was labour in the fields. The keeping of flocks and herds was prohibited, and they did not eat meat. They were forbidden to produce anything harmful, such as weapons of war, swords and spears. They served one another, and accepted statements without oath. Marriage was not prohibited, but few of them married. They offered no animal sacrifices, and in this were distinct from the Pharisees.

They venerated the Law of Moses, and Moses himself. They were severely strict in the observance of the Sabbath. They had a strange regard for the sun as a symbol of the brightness which they imagined invested the Divine majesty. There was a resemblance between their system and the Zoroastrianism of Persia.

De Quincey has argued that the early Christians were Essenes, but while there are some comparisons the contrasts are more and greater. Lightfoot thinks that this Sect is referred to in Colossians ii. 18-23, but they are never named in the New Testament. Nothing is heard of them after the destruction of Jerusalem in A.D. 70. They are referred to by Josephus, Philo, and Pliny.

(*d*) The Canon of the Old Testament Scriptures.

By 'canon' in this connection is meant 'a collection of religious writings Divinely inspired and hence authoritative, normative, sacred and binding'. The word is first used of the Scriptures by the Church Fathers of the 4th cent. A.D.

Our present inquiry is as to when and how the Books of the Old Testament came to be regarded as of Divine authority. A syllogism here will help us: (*a*) in the time of Nehemiah and Malachi the Old Testament as we know it did not exist; (*b*) in the time of our Lord, i.e. in A.D. 1-30, the O.T., as we know it did exist; therefore (c) the O.T., as we know it, must have come into being in the period between Nehemiah and Jesus Christ, that is, in the Interlude period B.C. 400-1. Evidence in support of this fact is ample. What we have said about the Book of Daniel (p. 12) is relevant here, but the larger question may now be summarized.

In the Hebrew Bible the books are in a threefold classification: the *Torah*, the Law, which is what we call the Pentateuch; the *Nebiim*, the Prophets, which consists of Joshua, Judges, 1-2 Samuel, 1-2 Kings, Isaiah, Jeremiah, Ezekiel, and the Twelve Minor Prophets; and the *Kethubim*, Writings, also called the *Hagiographa* or Sacred Writings, which includes the Psalms, Proverbs, Job, Song of Solomon, Ruth, Lamentations, Ecclesiastes, Esther, Daniel, Ezra, Nehemiah, 1-2 Chronicles.

In our O.T. there are 39 Writings, but in the Jews' Bible, by certain combinations of Books, sometimes the number was reckoned as 24 and sometimes as 22.

Now the fact of this threefold division is of great interest and importance, because it suggests, what ultimately is proved, that the Canon was formed gradually across a considerable period of time. It can safely be assumed that the first of these divisions, the *Torah*, was in existence and recognized as of Divine authority in Ezra's time. This is the significance of Neh. viii. 1-6; the date of which would be B.C. 444. Twelve years later, in B.C. 432, the renegade Manasseh founded the community of the Samaritans and built a rival temple on Mt. Gerizim (Neh. xiii. 28. Josephus' *Antiquities* xi. vii. 2—viii. 14), and the Samaritans recognized the Pentateuch and it only, as of inspired authority. That much, therefore, of the O.T. Canon was in recognized existence before the close of the O.T. period.

But it appears that in the Ezra-Nehemiah period and probably long before, public documents and historical records of national interest were being collected. In 2 Macc. ii. 13 we read that Nehemiah founded a library, and 'gathered together the acts of the kings, and the prophets, and of David, and the epistles of the kings concerning the holy gifts'. This would be between B.C. 445-432; and two and a half centuries later, in the time of

Antiochus Epiphanes, an attempt was made to destroy all the sacred books of the Jews. The passage says:

> 'And when they had rent in pieces the books of the law which they found, they burnt them with fire; and wheresoever was found with any the book of the testament, or if any consented to the law, the king's commandment was, that they should put him to death.'
>
> (1 Macc. i. 56, 57).

It was these books which Judas Maccabeus endeavoured to re-collect, books which were the most precious documents which the nation possessed (2 Macc. ii. 14).

We are not told what these books were, but certainly they would include some, if not all, of the O.T. division known as the *Prophets*. From extra-canonical references it seems clear that the second and largest division of the Old Testament Scriptures was in recognized existence in B.C. 200, and probably had been in existence a long time before.

There now remains the third division, called the *Hagiographa*. The contents of this division are strange, and we are led to the conclusion that some considerable time after divisions one and two were completed and regarded as canonical, other Writings were collected which seemed to the Jews to partake of Divine inspiration.

In the Prologue to *Ecclesiasticus* the Hebrew Bible is referred to three times. This Prologue was written by the grandson of Jesus ben Sirach about B.C. 132, and is the oldest witness we have to the threefold division of the O.T. Books. He says:

> 'Whereas many and great things have been delivered unto us by the *Law* and the *prophets*, and by *others* . . .'
> 'My grandfather Jesus . . . had much given himself to the reading of the *law*, and the *prophets*, and *other books* of our fathers . . .'
> 'The *law* itself, and the *prophets*, and the *rest of the books* . . .'

It is eminently probable that at least a century before the advent of the Messiah the Old Testament as we know it was completed in the three divisions of the Hebrew Bible, and by the time the New Testament was written, A.D. 50-100, there was a definite and fixed canon of O.T. Scripture.

In resurrection life our Lord referred to the Old Testament as 'the law of Moses, and the prophets, and the psalms' (Luke

xxiv. 44); and it is noteworthy that citations are made in the N.T., from every book of the O.T., except Esther, Ecclesiastes, Song of Solomon, Ezra, Nehemiah, Obadiah, Nahum, and Zephaniah. This fact is more impressive seeing that no Apocryphal book is quoted in the N.T., though acquaintance with these writings is evident.

What all this serves to show is that whereas no divinely inspired Scripture was written in the Interlude period, what had already been Divinely inspired was collected and canonized.

(e) Non-Canonical Writings

During the Interlude of 400 years in the Unfolding Drama of Redemption no divinely inspired Scriptures were written, but the period did produce many writings of varying character and importance. Of these there are two distinct groups, one *Apocryphal*, and the other *Pseudepigraphical*.

The Old Testament Apocryphal Writings

Of these there are fifteen, written by Jews in Palestine some time between B.C. 200-100, or a little later.

The designation *Apocrypha* means 'concealed', 'obscure', that is, 'things hidden'; but as used to-day of the Writings we are referring to, the word denotes religious books inferior in authority and worth to the Scriptures of the Old Testament.

These books are: 1 Esdras. 2 Esdras. Tobit. Judith. Esther. The Wisdom of Solomon. Ecclesiasticus. Baruch. The Song of the Three Holy Children. The History of Susanna. Bel and the Dragon. The Prayer of Manasses. 1 Maccabees. 2 Maccabees. The Epistle of Jeremy.

The above is the order in the English Versions, but the books may be variously classified.

Historical.	1 Esdras. 1-2 Maccabees. Esther. The Epistle of Jeremy (attached to Baruch). Prayer of Manasses.
Apocalyptic.	2 Esdras. Baruch.
Legendary.	Tobit. Judith. The Song of the Three Holy Children. The History of Susanna. Bel and the Dragon.
Didactic.	The Wisdom of Solomon. Ecclesiasticus.

The history of the O.T. Apocrypha is interesting and important, but it is beyond the scope of this work to review it in detail. Several things, however, should not be overlooked.

1. There is no evidence that the Jews ever regarded these writings as canonical.
2. When the Old Testament Scriptures were translated into Greek in Alexandria, B.C. 250-150—the Version known as the Septuagint —many of the Apocryphal writings were included, and in our present LXX they are intermingled with the Canonical Books.
3. The LXX was the Bible of our Lord and His Apostles, yet they never quote the Apocrypha.
4. When Luther in the 16th century translated the Scriptures into German, he placed the Apocryphal books by themselves between the Old and New Testaments. This means that he, and all early Reformers, did not regard them as of canonical value.
5. Rome, on the other hand, regards these writings as equal in authority and canonical value to the Old Testament Books. The Council of Trent decreed this in April 1546 in the words:

   'If anyone receive not as sacred and canonical the said books entire with all their facts, and as they have been used to be read in the Catholic Church, and as they are contained in the Old Lat. Vulg. let him be anathema.'

6. Contrary to this The Puritan Confession declared that these writings were of a purely secular character.
7. Various Continental and English Versions of the Bible placed the Apocryphal writings by themselves, apart from the acknowledged Books as a kind of Appendix.
8. The first English Version to omit them altogether was an edition of King James' Version published in 1629; but the custom of placing them between the Old Testament and the New Testament continued until 1825.
9. In 1827 the British and Foreign Bible Society decided to exclude them from their publications.
10. Protestants in Great Britain and America have given up the practice of publishing the Apocrypha as part of sacred Scripture.
11. The Church of England, and the American Episcopal Church, do not wholly exclude them, and they read in public selected portions of them.
12. Comprehensively, Roman Catholics accept these writings as Scripture, and Protestants do not.

But from this it must not be supposed that the Apocryphal writings are without significance and value. They reflect the Jewish mind in a very important period of their history, and students of Jewish thought will study them carefully.

The most that here can be attempted is to indicate briefly what each of these writings is about, and to indicate some features of value in them.

(i) Historical Writings
1 Maccabees

This book of sixteen chapters is our chief authority for one of the most stirring periods in Jewish history. It is a sober narration of historical facts, and is of the highest value for the history of the period of which it treats, which is the forty years B.C. 175-135; from the attempt of Antiochus Epiphanes to crush the Jewish religion to the death of Simon the High Priest.

The style is simple and straightforward, and the narrative is in the following sequence:

1. An Introduction covering a period of 155 years, B.C. 331-176, summarizing the events which had placed the Jews under Greek rule (i. 1-9).
2. The attempt of Antiochus Epiphanes and the Hellenizing party in the land to abolish the Jewish religion and to desecrate the Temple (i. 10-64).
3. The revolt of Jews under Mattathias and his sons, and the beginning of the struggle for independence (ii).
4. The struggle under Judas, B.C. 166-161 (iii. 1-ix. 22).
5. The struggle under Jonathan, B.C. 161-143 (ix. 23-xii. 53).
6. The struggle under Simon, B.C. 143-135 (xiii-xvi).

The date of this book cannot be fixed with precision, but probably it should be placed in B.C. 137-105.

It is supposed to have been written by a Sadducee because it contains no miracles, or portents, or supernatural interventions; neither is there any reference to a future life.

Another feature of the book is the absence of references to 'God' or the 'Lord' (a possible exception, iv. 24). It should not be supposed, however, that the writer did not believe in God, but evidently he had lost the sense of His nearness; and for the same reason there is no clear notice of the Messianic hope, though the writer does refer to a coming prophet (iv. 46; xiv. 41).

From these particulars it is evident that the value of the book is not doctrinal but historical.

2 *Maccabees*

There are certain comparisons between 1st and 2nd Maccabees but there are more contrasts. Both books tell of the Maccabean struggle, but the Second begins earlier and closes earlier than the First. The First book deals with the 40 years of B.C. 175-135; but the Second, covers the 15 years of B.C. 176-161, so that the two books are parallel for 14 years. It is most probable that the First book was written by a Sadducee, but it is certain that the Second was written by a Pharisee. The object of the First was historical, but of the Second it is religious. The First as history is more reliable than the Second, but the latter supplies many details which the former omits. The First book is an original work, but the Second is a digest of five volumes by a Jason of Cyrene (ii. 23). The First book was written in Hebrew, but the Second, in Greek; the First, in Palestine, and the Second in Alexandria.

The main narrative is prefaced by two Letters (i. 1-9; and i. 10-ii. 18) which are regarded as of no historical value, and of a Preface which is explanatory (ii. 19-32). The narrative itself is in five parts:

1. The troubles in Judaea from the coming of Heliodorus to the desecration of the Temple (iii-v).

2. The pollution of the Temple and the persecution of the Jews (vi-vii).

3. The revolt under Judas Maccabeus to the death of Antiochus Epiphanes (viii-x. 9).

4. The war of Judas with Antiochus Eupator (x. 10-xiii. 26).

5. The war of Judas with Demetrius I to the death of Nicanor (xiv-xv).

Features of 2 Maccabees are:
The frequent references to God and the Lord. The narration of miraculous occurrences. The hortatory and admonitory character of the record. The extolling of the Temple at Jerusalem, and references to the altar, the priests, the sacrifices, the incense, lights, and shewbread, the Sabbath and the Festivals; also the writer believed in a bodily resurrection and in future rewards; all of which is in striking contrast to 1 Maccabees.

I *Esdras*

This book of nine chapters is not an original work, but a compilation of passages in 2 Chronicles, Ezra and Nehemiah. They are as follows:

i.	2 Chron. xxxv. 1-xxxvi. 21.
ii. 1-15	2 Chron. xxxvi. 22, 23; Ezra i. 1-15.
ii. 16-26	Ezra iv. 7-24.
iii. 1-v. 6	Has no parallels.
v. 7-73	Ezra ii. 1-iv. 5, 24.
vi-vii	Ezra v. 1-vi. 22.
viii-ix	Ezra vii. 1-x. 44; Neh. viii. 1-13.

The only original part of the book is chs. iii. 1-v. 6 that relates a strange story which, however, has a message for us all. Three young men venture to say what in the world is strongest, and their dicta are submitted to the king, Darius, for a verdict. The first said that wine is strongest (iii. 17-24); the second said that the king is strongest (iv. 1-12); and the third said that women are strongest, but Truth above all (iv. 13-40). Then all the people shouted and said 'Great is Truth'. When the king asked Zerubbabel (iv. 13. 42) what he would have as a gift, he requested that the Jews might return to Judaea, which wish was allowed.

The author of the book is unknown. Its chronology is all askew. It was written probably between B.C. 168-A.D. 1.

The motive of the writer seems to have been to stimulate his fellow-countrymen to a more zealous observance of the Law; to win for them the favour of some foreign ruler, and to assure Jewish sufferers that truth was bound to prevail ultimately.

Additions to the Book of Esther

In the Septuagint six passages of added material are inserted in as many places in the canonical Esther. They are placed as follows:

x. 4-xi. 1	at the end of Esther.
xi. 2-xii. 6	at the beginning of Esther.
xiii. 1-7	after iii. 13 of Esther.
xiii. 8-xiv. 19	after iv. 17 of Esther.
xv	an amplification of v. 1-3 of Esther.
xvi.	after viii. 12 of Esther.

It is supposed that these additions were made to supply the alleged lack of the religious element in the canonical Book, where, it is persistently affirmed, the name of God does not occur. In this Apocryphon it occurs forty-five times. But it is not true that the Divine name is not in the Book of Esther. The tetragrammaton Y H V H occurs four times acrostically at critical points in the story. This Apocryphon adds nothing of any consequence to the Book of Esther.

The Epistle of Jeremy

From an early period this Epistle was attached to the Book of Baruch, though for no valid reason. Jeremiah's name is attached to the writing though it was written more than 400 years after Jeremiah's time. The writer may have supposed that as the Prophet had written one letter to the Jews in Babylon (ch. xxix), he may have written others, and this is an imitation of what it was thought he would write.

It is a diffusive and rhetorical exhortation against the Babylonian deities with an ironical description of their nothingness. Two refrains are the only attempt at arrangement in the writing.

'They are known not to be gods, therefore fear them not'
(16, 23, 29, 65, 69)
'How can they be called gods?'
(30, 40, 44, 46, 49, 52, 56)

It has been said of the Epistle: 'From first to last we feel not a breath of the genuine spirit of prophecy; no spark of the fire which burned so fiercely in the words of Jeremiah, and made him so terrible to the sinners of his day: not one sound of the sorrowful sighing of his soul over the sins and calamities of his country' (Dr. E. H. Gifford).

Most of the ideas of the writing are found in Pss. cxv. 4-8; cxxxv. 15-18. Isa. xliv. 9-19. Jer. x. 3-9.

The Prayer of Manasses

Manasseh, surely the worst of all the kings of Judah, was taken captive to Babylon. The Chronicler tells us that there he repented of his sinful past, and prayed for forgiveness and restoration (2 Chron. xxxiii. 11-13, 18, 19), and that his prayer was answered. Further it is said that his prayer was recorded 'in the book of the kings of Israel', and 'among the sayings of the seers'. The writer of this Apocryphon attempts to make good the loss of the original prayer in words simple and dignified. For the most part the prayer is built up of sentences and phrases taken from the Canonical Scriptures. It is a great mercy that forgiveness awaits the penitent. Said R. Johanan: 'Whoso saith, "Manasseh hath no part in the world to come", discourageth the penitent.'

(ii) Apocalyptic Writings

2 Esdras

This book of sixteen chapters is unique among the Apocryphal writings for several reasons: (*a*) chs. iii-xiv were written not in B.C., but almost certainly in the reign of Domitian, A.D. 81-96; and chs. i. ii, xv, xvi, are assigned to A.D. 260-268; (*b*) these four chapters were written probably by a Christian Jew of Alexandria, and the body of the book, by a non-Christian Jew; (*c*) it is the only specimen of apocalyptic literature, as distinct from prophetic; and (*d*) religiously and theologically it is the most important book in the Apocrypha.

The main body of the book is set in a Christian frame, chs. i, ii, xv, xvi.

Ch. i   God's ancient people are reproved for their sins; they are in danger of being cast off, and their privileges given to others.

Ch. ii   The controversy is continued, and if the chosen people will not hear, God will turn to the heathen. There follows the vision of a great multitude on Mount Sion, and in the midst of them is the Son of God wearing a crown.

Ch. xv.   God will take vengeance upon the wicked. A 'horrible vision' from the east is proclaimed against Babylon and Asia.

Ch. xvi.   Plagues are to come and cannot be avoided; the Lord's people can look for troubles; let them not hide their sins but forsake them, and deliverance will come.

The Apocalyptic work consists of seven visions (chs. iii-xiv).

Vision One (iii. 1-v. 20)

Ezra is perplexed at the problem of the sufferings of his own people and the prosperity of their enemies, and asks God for an explanation.

Vision Two (v. 21-vi. 34)

Ezra is dissatisfied with the explanation of the archangel Uriel, and is told that man's judgment is weak, and the Day of the Lord which is approaching will set all things right.

Vision Three (vi. 35-ix. 25)

Ezra and Uriel discuss whether many or few will be saved. There is here a vivid picture of the final Judgment and the future state of the righteous and the wicked.

Vision Four (ix. 26-x. 59)

On the plain of Ardath Ezra meets a mourning woman who has just lost her only son. While he tries to comfort her she vanishes and Jerusalem takes her place.

Vision Five (xi-xii)

Ezra sees in a dream an eagle with three heads and twelve wings, which is destroyed by a lion. The eagle is the fourth kingdom seen by Daniel, and the lion is the Messiah.

Vision Six (xiii)

Another vision of the Messiah who destroys His foes and establishes His Kingdom on earth.

Vision Seven (xiv)

Ezra is warned of his approaching decease, and he dictates ninety-four books, twenty-four of which were to be published (the O.T.), and seventy to be hidden for the use of the wise.

The book deals with an old enigma—the sufferings of God's people—and it should be read with the Book of Job, Psalm lxxiii, Habakkuk i, and Romans ix-xi. The problem is not solved, but the perplexed are reminded of the inscrutable ways of Divine Providence; of God's boundless love; of a future life; and of the Messianic Kingdom. 2 Esdras is a great contribution to the study of this problem.

Its value for religion and theology is found in a number of references: the Messiah (vii. 28, 29; xii. 32; xiii. 32, 37, 52); original sin (iii. 21); a future life (vii: destiny is fixed at death); faith and works are vitally related. The so-called lost Ten Tribes are referred to (xiii. 40).

Baruch

We place this book under apocalyptic only because it is not history, or legend, or wisdom; yet in character it is not apocalyptic as is 2 Esdras.

What is regarded as chapter vi of the book must be completely detached from it, as *The Epistle of Jeremy* has nothing whatever to do with it, though placed here because in history Jeremiah and Baruch were friends.

The five chapters which make up this writing divide into two distinct and unconnected parts: i. 1-iii. 8, and iii. 9-v. 9. So different are these two parts in language and subject-matter that there is little likelihood of their having come from the same hand, and at the same time. Guesses at the dates of these parts cover a period of three centuries, B.C. 200-A.D. 100. Probably the first part was written in Hebrew, and the second part, in Greek. No one knows who wrote this book, but certainly it was not Baruch, Jeremiah's friend of the 6th cent. B.C.

Part 1. Chs. i. 1-iii. 8.

After a historical introduction (i. 1-14) describing the origin of the book, comes the confession (*a*) of the Jews in Palestine (i. 15-ii. 5), and (*b*) of the Jews in exile (ii. 6-iii. 8).

These are worthy utterances and i. 15-ii. 17 follows the prayer of Daniel in his ch. ix. 4-19.

Part 2. Chs. iii. 9-v. 9.

Here the Jews are admonished to return to the wisdom of the Law (iii. 9-iv. 4); and this is followed by words of comfort, encouragement and promise of deliverance (iv. 5-v. 9).

Part 1 is in prose, and this Part is in verse.

The titles of God in this book are noteworthy. In Part 1 'the Lord', and 'the Lord our God' occur frequently. In Part 2 the former titles do not occur, but 'God', and 'the Everlasting' occur frequently; and 'the Holy One' occurs three times.

Both parts of the book deserve careful attention, and may well find a place in our prayers. But there is no reference to the Messiah, the future life, or the resurrection.

(iii) Legendary Writings

Certain of the Apocryphal Writings are best described as legend, romance, or religious fiction, and should not be regarded as anything else. These writings are: the Song of the Three Holy Children; the History of Susanna; Bel and the Dragon; Tobit; and Judith, and each of these has definite moral value.

Three of these are additions to the canonical book of Daniel, and were written probably between B.C. 170—A.D. I.

The Song of the Three Holy Children

In the Septuagint this is placed after Dan. iii. 23. It purports to be a prayer which Azarias uttered while, with his two companions, he was in the fiery furnace for refusing to worship Nebuchadnezzar's Image (3-22); the Song is attributed to the three of them (28-68); and the Prayer and the Song are connected by a description of their preservation, and the destruction of the Chaldean servants (23-27). Only one verse in the Song (66) relates to the circumstances of these Hebrews, and the whole seems to be an expansion of Psalm cxlviii. The Anglican Church has adopted the Song for liturgical use, and it is known in the Prayer Book as the *Benedicite*.

The History of Susanna

Except for the fact that Daniel's name is introduced in this story, it has nothing to do with that man or his Book. The beautiful wife of a wealthy Jew is charged with adultery and is condemned to death. Her accusers were two lustful elders whose designs were frustrated. At the critical moment a young man named Daniel appears and declares that the charge against Susanna is false. By examining the elders separately he proves that this is so, with the result that Susanna is vindicated, and the two elders are condemned. The story is like that of Joseph and Potiphar's wife, only here the accusers are men and the woman is charged.

We may learn from the story that innocence is ultimately proved; that guilt is discovered and punished; and that cross-examination is valuable for both ends.

Shakespeare drew on this story for the words he put into the mouth of Shylock:

> A Daniel come to judgment! yea, a Daniel!
> O wise young judge, how I honour thee!

Bel and the Dragon

There are here two stories which, probably, are quite independent, but they both bring idolatry into ridicule. Both are related to Daniel, and the second connects with the canonical story in the incident of Daniel being put in the den of lions and being preserved from all harm.

In the second part of *Robinson Crusoe*, Defoe makes use of this Apocryphon.

Tobit

This strange story has a definite religious value. It was written probably about the second century B.C., and is a fair example of religious fiction.

Tobit was a God-fearing Jew of the tribe of Naphtali, who, with his wife Anna, lived in Nineveh. They had one son whom they named Tobias. Tobit became blind; and being overtaken by poverty and domestic unhappiness, he prayed that he might die. Far away in the Median city of Ecbatana was another family, also in trouble. Raguel and his wife Edna have a daughter Sara who had married seven husbands, and each of them had died on the wedding day. For this Edna was cruelly reproached and contemplated suicide. The story goes on to tell how these two families met, and the happy result.

Tobit had a kinsman named Gabael who lived in Rages in Media, with whom he had deposited a sum of money. Being now in need of it Tobit decides to send his son to fetch it, and wants him to find a companion for the journey. Tobias finds Raphael, but did not know that he was an angel. The two set out for the home of Raguel; and on the way, when Tobias went down to the Tigris to wash, a fish leaped out of the river. Raphael bade him cut out its heart, liver and gall, and the remainder they roasted and ate.

Raphael told Tobias that the heart and liver would chase away an evil spirit, and the gall would give sight to the blind.

The result of the visit to Ecbatana was that Tobit and Sara married, and the evil spirit Asmodeus which had killed her former husbands fled when he smelled the smoke of the heart and liver of the fish. Raphael went to Rages and got the money from Gabael, and later he, Tobias, and Sara returned to Tobit and Anna in Nineveh. By the use of the fish's gall Tobit was healed of his blindness. Raphael revealed his identity and disappeared. After the death of Tobit and Anna, the young people and their children removed to Ecbatana, and there Tobias died at the age of one hundred and twenty-seven years.

In this story angelology, demonology and magic are introduced, and emphasis is laid on giving alms and tithes, on burying the dead, and on fasting. An outstanding feature of the story is prayer, and besides many references to it, six prayers are reported. It is doubtful if any single aim can be attributed to the writing, but it contains wholesome lessons on family life; parents giving counsel to their children; children obeying their parents; Divine guidance; faithfulness to God in times of personal poverty and national disaster, and in spite of them; and on the truth that at last righteousness triumphs over wickedness. Luther described the book as 'a truly beautiful, wholesome, and profitable fiction'. The Anglican prayer-book makes use of 'Tobit' in its marriage service: 'O God, as Thou didst send Thy Angel Raphael to Tobias and Sara the daughter of Raguel, to their great comfort, so vouchsafe to send Thy blessing upon these Thy servants'.

Judith

In reading this story one is reminded of Delilah, of Jael the wife of Heber, and of Queen Esther, yet it differs widely from all of these. It is fiction with a politico-religious purpose, and was written probably in the Maccabean period of the second century B.C.

The story is that Nebuchadnezzar, King of Assyria, sent an army under Holofernes against the nations between Persia and Memphis which had refused to keep him in his wars. Holofernes approached Palestine and laid siege to Bethulia. He cut off the water supply, and so desperate became the situation in the city that the people besought the rulers to surrender. Judith, a beautiful and wealthy widow, hearing of this counsel obtained permission of the rulers to go to the camp of Holofernes and obtain an audience with him. Having put off her mourning attire, and decking herself in her finest robes, she, with a maid, goes to the camp of the enemy.

She is taken to the tent of Holofernes who, on inquiring why she had come, is told that her intention is to show him how and when he can take Bethulia and subdue Judaea. Holofernes, deeply impressed by her beauty and wisdom, invites her to a feast, and for joy of her company he drinks excessively.

Judith is left alone with him in his tent, and while he lay there 'filled with wine' she took his scimitar which was beside him, and catching hold of his hair 'she smote twice upon his neck with all her might, and she took away his head from him'. This she gave to her maid who put it in a bag, and they both returned to Bethulia.

In the morning when the discovery was made in the camp of the Assyrians, panic seized them and they fled. The children of Israel fell upon them and chased them with a great slaughter.

Thereafter the great event was celebrated with a song of praise, and with burnt offerings.

The object of the book seems to have been to encourage the Jewish people to maintain at any cost their faith and worship. The story faithfully represents the spirit of the Maccabean age. Savage though Judith's patriotism was, it grew out of her faith in God, and it was accompanied by much prayer.

Ruskin in his *Mornings in Florence*, studying that celebrated painting of *Judith and Holofernes*, writes of Judith:

'The conception of facts and the ideas of Jewish womanhood are here, grand and real as a marble statue, a possession for all ages. . . . She is . . . the mightiest, purest, highest type of high passion in severe womanhood offered to our human memory.'

E

(iv) Didactic Writings

'The Wisdom of Solomon', and 'Ecclesiasticus' certainly belong to this class of writing, and Dr. Charles places here 'Tobit', the 'Prayer of Manasses', and the 'Epistle of Jeremy' also.

Among the Hebrews of old there were three great classes of religious teachers—Priests, Prophets, and the Sages. The Priests were occupied with the minutiae of the Levitical Law. The Prophets proclaimed the supreme importance of eternal laws. The Sages taught the lessons of prudential experience, and insisted on the truth that 'the fear of the Lord is the beginning of knowledge', and that 'to fear God and to keep His commandments is the whole duty of man'. To this kind of teaching was given the name of 'Wisdom', and the literature of it was known as '*the chokmah*', or Sapiential literature. In the O.T. canonical Writings are three books of the 'Wisdom' class—'Job', 'Proverbs', and 'Ecclesiastes'; and in the O.T. Apocryphal Writings are 'The Wisdom of Solomon', and 'Ecclesiasticus'. Outside of the canonical and apocryphal Writings in this 'Wisdom' class are the Fourth Book of Maccabees, the Book of Enoch, and Philo's writings.

The Wisdom of Solomon

Farrar says: 'The book marks the highest point of religious knowledge attained by the Jews in the period between the close of the Old Testament canon and the beginning of the Gospel dispensation'. It has also been spoken of as 'one of the most remarkable extant specimens of Jewish Sapiential literature'; as 'the most beautiful of the Apocryphal books'; and as 'a book of great value'.

The *author* must have been an Alexandrian Jew, who was well acquainted with Grecian literature and the philosophy of that time and place. As to *date*, it is not unlikely that the author lived about 120 B.C. The original *language* was Greek, and good Greek. The *style* has been described as 'pompous, sublime, turgid, diffuse, simple, tautological, varying with the subject, and seldom tedious'.

The Writing has been variously divided, but the simplest and most natural analysis is that of three parts: i-v; vi-ix; x-xix.

In Part 1 (i-v) it is shown that Wisdom is the condition of immortality, and here the lot of the righteous and of the wicked is contrasted.

In Part 2 (vi-ix) Wisdom is described and commended. It is the source of all blessing, the secret of power, and the fountain of all that is morally and intellectually to be desired.

In Part 3 (x-xix) by many illustrations Wisdom is shown to be a power in history, and the consequences of pursuing or neglecting it are seen. These illustrations are drawn from (*a*) the primeval and patriarchal periods (Genesis); and (*b*) from the story of the Israelites in their contact with the Egyptians before and after the Exodus (xi, xii, xvi-xix). Between chs. xii and xvi is a long digression on the Folly and End of Idolatry (xiii-xv).

The author personates King Solomon because that monarch was, with the later Jews, the ideal of Wisdom; but, of course, Solomon had nothing to do with the production of this Book.

The *aim* of the book is to commend Wisdom, and to detail the blessings it brings to those who hear and heed it. The writer shows that Wisdom was alike opposed to the perversions of Judaism and the nature of heathenism. His object is to encourage faithful Jews, to warn apostate Jews, and to condemn every form of idolatry.

The book is *an exposition* of Jewish religious philosophy at a certain period. Subjects which enter into this exposition relate to the Being of God, the creation of man, the entrance into the world of sin and death, a future state of rewards and punishments, and the truth of immortality.

In this book, as in Ecclesiasticus, there is no personal and no suffering Messiah; neither is there any reference to a resurrection of the body. But views are present which show Platonic influence such as: the doctrines of the world-soul (i. 7); of the soul existing before the body, and entering into it (viii. 19, 20); and of the body as a poison of the soul (ix. 15); and like the school of Plato the writer reduces all the virtues to four: temperance, prudence, justice and fortitude (viii. 7).

It is claimed that there are traces of this Book in the New Testament, for example:

Rom. i. 20-32: W. xi. 16 xiii. 1-16	Rom. ii. 4: W. xv. 1
Rom. ix. 21-23: W. xii. 20, 21; xv. 7	Rom. xi. 32: W. xi. 23
1 Cor. vi. 2: W. iii. 8	2 Cor. v. 4: W. ix. 15

Eph. vi. 13-17: W. v. 18-20

James i. 5: W. viii. 21	James i. 17: W. i. 14
James i. 19: W. i. 11	James iii. 9: W. ii. 23

James v. 4-6: W. ii. 20

Among many *details* of interest and importance, may be named: that though much of the Old Testament is alluded to in the book, no proper name occurs in it from first to last; that the book was never in the canon of the Jews; that Philo and Josephus do not refer to it; that it is wanting in the catalogues of Origen and Jerome; that many of the Church Fathers made no distinction between it and the canonical writings; that the third Council of Carthage and also the Council of Trent put it among the canonical writings.

Ecclesiasticus
The Wisdom of Jesus the Son of Sirach

This is the longest of the Apocryphal Writings (51 chs.), longer than Genesis, and Ezekiel, and only one chapter shorter than Jeremiah. The *name* 'Ecclesiasticus', which comes from the Vulgate, means 'belonging to the Church', or 'used in the Church', because from an early date it was used in the Western Church as a Lectionary or Reading Book.

It is the only book in the Apocrypha which gives the name of the *author* (l. 27), but beyond this nothing is known of him. He wrote in Hebrew, and his grandson translated his book into Greek (Prologue). The *date* probably is B.C. 250-175. It belongs to the Wisdom literature, but differs from *The Wisdom of Solomon* in that it is a collection of gnomic sayings, maxims, apothegms, proverbs, sonnets, epithets and more elaborate passages, whereas

The Wisdom of Solomon is more or less a treatise on Wisdom. Consequently one will look in vain for divisions in 'Ecclesiasticus', which follows the method of which the Book of Proverbs is the one canonical example.

But though divisions need not be looked for, unity is given to the book by its *subject*, which is Wisdom, and it is insisted on throughout that this virtue is the source of all good and happiness.

By the *themes* which are treated and the manner in which they are treated this book 'affords glimpses of the intellectual history of a period over which otherwise profound darkness would rest' (Edersheim).

Among the scores of themes on which the author writes may be named: old age; behaviour; borrowing; cheerfulness; children; companions; conscience; continuity; conversation; creation; death; enemies; excess; fear of the Lord; the fool; forgiveness; friendship; God; gossip; health; honour; humility; insincerity; instruction; jealousy; judgment; law; lion; loans; love; loyalty; lying; meekness; mercy; miserliness; moderation; mourning; neighbours; outspokenness; parents; patience; the poor; praise; prayer; pride; quarrelling; repentance; reproof; retribution; reward; riches; rudeness; servants; shame; sickness; silence; sin; speech; the tongue; trade; travel; trust in God; truth; understanding; vengeance; the wicked; wife; wine; wisdom; women; and wrath.

There is not a little in this Book which is contrary to true wisdom. A line of conduct is frequently commended which is merely prudential and self-centred. Its general moral tone cannot be said to be lofty. 'The model-man of Ben Sira seems to be always thinking of himself—what men will say of him, or how a thing will affect him either in this life, or when he comes to die.'

There is no reference in the Book to the resurrection of the body, nor to a final judgment, nor to any expectancy of a personal Messiah. The writer's eschatology is dark and forbidding. The spiritual and the eternal are not in his view.

Considerable correspondence exists between Ecclesiasticus and the Book of Proverbs, which leads one to think that the writer was acquainted with the latter. For example:

PROVERBS	ECCLESIASTICUS	PROVERBS	ECCLESIASTICUS
viii. 22	i. 4	xxix. 3	ix. 6
i. 7; ix. 10	i. 14	xvii. 2	x. 25
xxiii. 22	iii. 13	xii. 9	x. 27
xxviii. 14	iii. 26	xviii. 13	xi. 8
xxviii. 27	iv. 5	xix. 4	xii. 9
iv. 7	iv. 12	xxvi. 24	xii. 16
xvii. 5	vii. 11	xv. 13	xiii. 25

In addition to these there are over twenty other close parallels.

The Apostle James seems to have been acquainted with Ecclesiasticus as certain passages selected by Boon would indicate. For example: E. i. 23, ii. 1-5, and J. i. 2-4; E. li. 13, and J. i. 5; E. i. 28, ii. 16, vii. 10, xxxv. 16-21, and J. i. 6-8; E. i. 30, iii. 18, xxxi. 5-9, and J. i. 9-11; E. vi. 2, 3, and J. i. 10, 11; E. vi. 28-31 and J. i. 12; E. xv. 11, and J. i. 13, 14. These, and other references indicate the wide circulation of Ecclesiasticus in the first century A.D.. and also the spiritual difference between the standpoints of the two writers.

Outstanding passages in this Book are *The Song of Praise of the Works of Creation*, xlii. 15-xliii. 33; *The Praise of Famous Men*, xliv. 1-l. 29 (omitting Ezra, Daniel, and Mordecai); *A National Anthem*, xxxvi. 1-17; and *The Praise of God and of Natural Phenomena*, xlii. 15-xliii. 33.

2. The Jews of the Dispersion

THE DIASPORA

One of the most impressive phenomena of history is the ubiquity of the Jews, however the fact may be accounted for. For fact it is that for about 3,000 years voluntarily or involuntarily Jews have been spread abroad. This scattering is called *Diaspora*, an expression which describes Jews living among Gentiles outside of Palestine. Reference to Jewish scattering occurs in the O.T. Apocrypha in 2 Esdras ii. 7, and 2 Macc. i. 27: 'Gather those together that are scattered from us'. In the Old Testament it is frequently spoken of as punishment for their sins (Jer. viii. 3; xvi. 15: Ezek. iv. 13 *et al.*), and from the time of Moses this had been predicted (Deut. xxviii. 25).

But sometimes the *Diaspora* is regarded in quite a different light, as a means of blessing to the Gentiles. Micah (v. 7) says: 'The remnant of Jacob shall be in the midst of many people as a dew from the LORD, as the showers upon the grass, that tarrieth not for man, nor waiteth for the sons of men'; and in the *Apocalypse of Baruch* it is said: 'I will scatter this people among the Gentiles, that they may do good to the Gentiles' (i. 7).

Josephus says, 'there is no people on the earth that has not a portion of us'. Strabo affirms that the Jews had 'entered every city, and no place in the world can be found that has not received this race and been possessed by it;' and the Sibylline Oracles declare that 'every land and every sea is full of them' (2nd cent. B.C.).

This historical phenomenon is referred to several times in the New Testament, and the contexts should be noted (John vii. 34, 35; James i. 1; 1 Peter i. 1).

THE DISPERSION UNIVERSAL

Anyone who would draw a map to show where Jews were located during the Bible period would have to draw a map of the world. In B.C. 722 Sargon removed to Assyria the subjects of the Northern Kingdom of Israelites; and in B.C. 606-586 Nebuchad nezzar removed the subjects of the Southern Kingdom to Babylonia, where for a thousand years a powerful colony was established. It is difficult to say when Jews were first settled in Egypt, but we know that the remnant left in Canaan by Nebuchadnezzar in B.C. 586 went to Egypt, taking Jeremiah and Baruch with them (Jer. xliii, xliv).

From the time of Alexander the Great the Jews flourished in Egypt, and in the time of Philo (B.C. 20-A.D. 40) it was estimated that the colony numbered a million. Of the widespread dispersion of Jews in Asia Minor there is abundant testimony, and they were found in large numbers in Syria and Arabia also. From the Maccabean period began the connection of Jews with Rome, where eventually they were settled in great numbers and exercised great influence.

That they came from far distant places to Jerusalem for their three great feasts Acts ii. 9-11 shows.

A Preparation for Christianity (pp. 76-83)

The fact of the Jewish Dispersion is of interest and importance in itself, but it is much more than this, because in the plan of God it was a preparation for the coming of the Messiah and the establishment of Christianity in the world. Whether this *Diaspora* was promoted by forcible deportation, voluntary emigration, political inducements, or the allurements of trade, the result was the same, it cast up a highway for the spread of the Gospel. It did this in several ways: by the institution of synagogues wherever Jews were located; by the translation of the Hebrew Scriptures into Greek which was universally spoken; by the faith of a strict monotheism; by the maintenance of a religious consciousness; by schools and libraries; by the strict relation to one another of religion and morality; by missionary propaganda, resulting in the adding greatly to their numbers by proselytes and God-fearers, and by the Jewish Canon. In these and in other ways the *Diaspora* was a pathfinder for Christianity. Harnack has said:

> 'To the Jewish mission which preceded it the Christian mission was indebted, in the first place, for a field tilled all over the Empire; in the second place, for religious communities already formed everywhere in the towns; thirdly, for what Axenfeld calls "the help of materials" furnished by the preliminary knowledge of the Old Testament, in addition to catechetical and liturgical materials which could be employed without much alteration; fourthly, for the habit of regular worship and the control of private life; fifthly, for an impressive apologetic on behalf of monotheism, historical theology, and ethics; and finally, for the feeling that self-diffusion was a duty. The amount of this debt is so large that one might venture to claim the Christian mission as a continuation of the Jewish propaganda' (*Mission and Expansion of Christianity*, i. 15).

In different ways, therefore, did Judaism in Palestine, and throughout the world, prepare for the coming of the Messiah and the Christian Dispensation.

II. HEATHENISM: A PREPARATION FOR THE MESSIAH

'When the fulness of the time was come' (Gal. iv, 4). Whatever in its context this phrase meant at the time it was used, it certainly has an application world-wide and age-forming. Christianity had antecedents. 'The same God who planted the Gospel prepared the soil. Men were His servants and instruments then and now, whether conscious of it or not'.

It is not necessary to argue that Judaism prepared for the advent of the Messiah and the spread of Christianity, but it is equally true that, in other ways, Heathenism also was a preparation. The Graeco-Roman world helped to make possible an already revealed Divine purpose. This preparation on the part of Heathenism was both negative and positive: *negative* in what it so desperately needed socially, morally, and spiritually; and *positive* in what it supplied of what Christianity required, in conditions and facilities, for the accomplishment of its great mission. 'To secure the right perspective Christianity must be viewed not only in *contrast* but also in *contact* with its environment'.

NEGATIVE PREPARATION

This consisted in the want of ideals and conditions of life without which peoples can have neither satisfaction nor permanence. Ancient society rested upon the foundation of slavery, an evil which Christianity was to eliminate, not by bloody revolution, but by the establishment of principles which could not but end it. It has been estimated that in the Graeco-Roman world there were 60,000,000 slaves, and their condition was most wretched, for they had neither protection nor rights. Among the Romans gladiatorial displays were immensely popular, men with men and men with beasts. Every excess of cruelty was tried until all sense of disgust was exterminated. In Greece especially the status of woman was one of great degradation. Abortion was widespread, and both Plato and Aristotle recommended it. Vice was rampant, and infidelity in married life was common.

Pagan religions failed to exert any potent influence upon morals. In religion there was no authority for the human spirit, and belief in Fate or Destiny was heavily oppressive. There was widespread disgust with life, and deep-seated pessimism.

The picture which Paul draws of the heathenism of his day is fully sustained by Seneca, Tacitus, Juvenal, and other heathen writers of that age, and shows the absolute need of redemption.

Seneca said: 'The world is full of crimes and vices. More are committed than can be cured by force. Crimes are no longer hidden, but open before the eyes. Innocence is not only rare, but nowhere' (*De Ira*, II. 8). Read Rom. i. 18-32.

This state of things was negatively a preparation for the new age that would dawn, because it revealed how deep was moral depravity, and how urgent was the need of redemption. But the preparation was not negative only.

POSITIVE PREPARATION

The foregoing picture was not unrelieved. Voices were raised against the prevailing conditions, voices crying in the wilderness of Heathenism, preparing the way of the Lord. In quarters the gauntlet was thrown down to a materialised age. There were men who aimed at a moral and religious revival and this was an admission of the need of it. Seneca, Epictetus, Marcus Aurelius, Socrates, Plato, Xenophanes, Virgil, Aristotle, and others reached out to worthy social and moral conditions, and for unity and authority in religion. There was a growing sense of the importance of prayer, and a sense of sin is revealed in the writings of Virgil and Seneca.

(i) *The Greeks*

But in other ways did the Graeco-Roman world prepare for the Christian religion. Notably, Greece gave to early Christianity a world unified in language and culture, and it was the Hellenised world that most eagerly accepted Christianity. Hebrew was dead, and the first Christian missionaries went forth with a language and a Book that could be understood and read by everyone. Alexander the Great, the truest Greek of his age, did an incomparable work for humanity and for Christianity by compelling the old world to think afresh, by extending Greek culture, and by blotting out the distinction between conquerors and conquered. By throwing down national barriers and disregarding racial distinctions he prepared the way for the Gospel message. The Septuagint Version of the Old Testament came within the ambit of Greek thought at a time when it was veering toward the necessity of a Revelation. Hosts of 'God-fearing' heathen heard in Greek a message of salvation; and because the LXX was the first, and for a considerable time the only, Bible of early Christianity it was a potent ally of the Gospel.

(ii) *The Romans*

The contributions of the Romans to preparing the way for Christianity was not cultural, but executive; they were more concerned about politics than about philosophy; their ambition was to unite the world in a colossal Empire which would reach from the Euphrates to the Atlantic, and which would embrace 100,000,000 human beings. The Romans believed that they were called, not to *guess*, but to *govern*. They were builders, and they built for all time; some of their roads and bridges are still standing. Rome unified the world, and laid highways for the feet of the Christian missionaries, and with world-wide commerce went the universal Gospel. By offering their subjects good laws, uniform government and military protection, the Romans gave Christianity the opportunity to promulgate, what they could not provide, a universal religion. They had lost faith in their own gods but they had not found the true God. The Empire which, when Christ came, was free from war, was religiously dissatisfied and disillusioned. Magic, astrology, philosophy and foreign rites had not brought to them what they needed and desired, but Christianity was on the way, and in due course would have its converts in Caesar's household. 'The throne of the human mind' was declared vacant, and Christianity was at hand as the best claimant.

Thus was the way for Christianity prepared on every side. 'Christ', says Schaff, 'entered a dying world as the Author of a new and imperishable life' (*History of the Church*, vol. i, p. 89).

The following chart summarizes the foregoing observations:

CHART 118

PREPARING THE WORLD FOR CHRIST AND CHRISTIANITY		
'When the fulness of the time was come'. Gal. iv. 4		
JUDAISM	HELLENISM	ROMANISM
THE JEWS	THE GREEKS	THE ROMANS
RELIGION	CULTURE	LAW
REVELATION	LANGUAGE	GOVERNMENT
REDEMPTION FOR THE SINFUL	THE GOSPEL IN GREEK	HIGHWAYS FOR THE MISSIONARIES
PROPHECY	PHILOSOPHY	POLITICS
SCRIPTURES	SCHOOLS	SCEPTRES
The title on the Cross was written in		
HEBREW	GREEK	LATIN

THE GOSPEL FOR THE WORLD

The world-preparation and expectation will not surprise any careful reader of the Old Testament for it plainly declares that the promised salvation was not to be the exclusive privilege of Israel, but was to be for all mankind. It is repeatedly affirmed that the blessing was for the Gentiles to the ends of the earth. The Abrahamic Covenant said: 'in thee shall *all the families of the earth* be blessed'; 'in thy seed shall *all the nations of the earth* be blessed'; a promise which is oft repeated. '*All nations* shall call Him blessed'. 'The *Gentiles* shall come to Thy light, and kings to the brightness of thy rising'. 'The *Gentiles* shall see thy righteousness, and all kings thy glory'. 'They shall declare my glory among the *Gentiles*'. '*All nations* shall serve him'. 'The leaves of the tree were for the healing of the *nations*.'

Not only are there these promises but there are not wanting actual illustrations of Gentiles being blessed: Melchisedec, and Jethro, and Rahab, and Ruth, and Naaman, and in all likelihood Job. There was a spiritual Israel scattered throughout the heathen world. It is astonishing, in the light of all this, that even Peter had to receive a revelation before he would go with the Gospel to Gentiles! Nothing less than the whole human race was ever in the redeeming purpose, and in innumerable ways through the ages individuals and peoples were being prepared and were preparing for the coming of the Saviour of souls, and 'when the fulness of the time was come' HE APPEARED.

THE UNFOLDING DRAMA OF REDEMPTION

ACT II

Matthew to Jude

A DIVINE COVENANT OF GRACE EMBODIED IN THE HISTORY AND LITERATURE OF THE CHRISTIAN CHURCH

INTRODUCTION

SCENE I

THE UNFOLDING DRAMA OF REDEMPTION

ACT II

Introduction

THE BACKGROUND OF THE GOSPELS

THE RELATION TO ONE ANOTHER OF THE PARTS OF THE DRAMA

IT is made clear in Volume I of THE DRAMA, Chart 7, page 36, that the unfolding of The Redeeming Purpose is in two related yet quite distinct parts, which we speak of as ACTS I and II. Each of these ACTS is the embodiment of a COVENANT, which, in the first, is one of LAW, and in the second, is one of GRACE. These two words may be regarded as summarizing the entire Biblical revelation, for, as the Apostle John said: 'The Law was given through Moses; Grace and Truth came through Jesus Christ' (i. 17). ACT I has a PROLOGUE; ACT II has an EPILOGUE; and between them is an INTERLUDE representing a period of about four hundred years which forms the transition from the First Covenant to the Second.

THE TWO COVENANTS

ACT I is called The Old Testament or Covenant, and ACT II is called The New Testament or Covenant, and an apprehension of the distinction between these is absolutely vital for an understanding of the Bible.

The Covenant of ACT II is *New* both in time and quality (Heb. xii. 24, and ix. 15), and must never be confused with the other Covenant which is *Old* both in time and quality (Heb. viii. 6-13). See Volume I, p. 25.

73

Failure to distinguish these Covenants is prolific of grave misinterpretation and misapplication of the Scriptures, and must result in obscuring the significance of the course of history.

The distinction between these Covenants is made clear in Galatians. 'Wherefore then serveth the Law? It was added because of transgressions, till the Seed should come to whom the promise was made' (iii. 19). And the 'Law has but been as the guardian-slave that watched over us till we were matured for Messiah, in order that by faith in Him we might be made righteous. Well, faith has now come, and so we are subject to the guardian-slave no more' (iii. 24, 25. WAY'S translation). Also, read carefully Gal. iv. 21-v. 1.

Two things we should be sure not to do, which yet are constantly done, namely, to judge by the New Covenant those who lived under the Old, and to live under the Old Covenant, we whose lot is cast under the New.

The Old Covenant was preparative, but the New is executive. The Old tells us what not to do, but the New tells us what Christ can and will do for us. The Old holds us in bondage, but the New brings us into freedom. The Old involves a curse, but the New imparts a blessing. The Old shows us what we are, but the New shows us what we may become. The emphasis of the Old is on *doing*, but of the New it is on *being*. The Old creates expectation, but the New brings to realization. The Old stirs longing in the human heart, but the New leads to satisfaction. In the Old man seeks God, but in the New God seeks man. By the Old man is condemned as a sinner, but by the New he is delivered from his sin. In the Old God says 'you cannot', but in the New Christ says 'I can'. The Old Covenant is really bad news, but the New Covenant is Good News, that is, Gospel.

The Two Covenants are interdependent; each is incomplete without the other. If revelation had ended with the First Covenant it would have been a lock without a key, a track without a goal, a story without a plot, a promise without a fulfilment, a germ without a development.

If, on the other hand, there had been the revelation of the New Covenant without that of the Old, there would have been an end without a beginning, a fulfilment without a promise, a supply without a need, a superstructure without a foundation, a consummation without a commencement.

It was said long ago, 'The New is in the Old concealed; the Old is in the New revealed'. 'The New is in the Old contained; the Old is in the New explained'. 'The New is in the Old enfolded; the Old is in the New unfolded'. 'The New is in the Old latent; the Old is in the New patent.'

A fundamental distinction between the Two Covenants is in this: that the Old is embodied in a Nation, and the New, in a Church. The Nation was exclusive (Deut. vii. 6-8; Ps. cxxxv. 4; Amos iii. 2); but the Church is inclusive (Gal. iii. 28. Rom. x. 12. Rev. vii. 9). This distinction constitutes two dispensations which together reveal the redeeming purpose and method. If God's dealings with the Jew and with the Christian are not distinguished, great confusion will result in one's attempt to understand the Scriptures.

From all this it will be clear why, in the Drama of Redemption, there are two Acts, and two only. There can be no development in history which will invalidate this revelation, and none which will make any addition to it necessary.

ACT I represents a period of about 2000 years, and ACT II is at present about half a century short of 2000 years.

In ACT I (see Volume I), there are Three Scenes, and in ACT II there are Two Scenes. The First Scene presents *The Introduction of Christianity into the World by Jesus the Messiah*; and the Second Scene shows *The Progress of Christianity in the World to the Close of the First Century A.D.* The first of these covers a period of about 35 years; and the second, a period of about 65 years, and, of course, the Second Scene is still in progress.

This first century of the Christian Era is, beyond all dispute, the greatest in the history of the world. Everything that preceded it led up to it, and everything that has followed has been the consequence of it.

CHART 119

THE UNFOLDING DRAMA OF REDEMPTION	
ACT II	
SCENE 1	SCENE 2
THE INTRODUCTION OF CHRISTIANITY INTO THE WORLD BY JESUS THE MESSIAH	THE PROGRESS OF CHRISTIANITY IN THE WORLD TO THE CLOSE OF THE FIRST CENTURY A.D.
History	*History*
MATTHEW MARK LUKE JOHN	ACTS
	Literature ROMANS TO JUDE
35 Years. B.C.5-4—A.D. 30	65 Years. A.D. 30-95
100 Years	

PREPARING THE WORLD FOR CHRIST AND CHRISTIANITY

(See pp. 62-66)

The followers of Christ were the last of four great peoples which constituted the world of the first century A.D.—Romans, Greeks, Jews, and Christians, which respectively represent Romanism, Hellenism, Judaism, and Christianity. The last of these emerged from the other three, which were at once its challenge and its opportunity. See Chart 118, p. 66.

ROMANISM

The establishment of the Roman Empire and the advent of Christianity were synchronous. This Empire was the final preparation for Christ, and made possible the spread of the universal religion. The whole civilized world was practically at rest when Christianity appeared, and thus the Romans were the harbingers of the 'peace on earth, goodwill to men', of the Evangel.

This, of course, was a condition which gave to Christianity a wide-open door for the promulgation of its message. Universal political order made possible the mission of the Christian Church. If the Empire embraced all men, why should Christianity aim at less. The intermixture of all races and the free exchange of thought which Rome allowed were entirely favourable to Christianity. Also, in material ways, the spread of the Gospel was greatly facilitated by the great highways which Rome built throughout the lands over which it had sway. Its system of roads knit the then civilized world together, and served not only the legions and the imperial escorts, but were of equal service to the missionaries in travelling from one colony to another, and also made possible the communication of churches with one another. These famous roads ran throughout the Empire and formed the main arteries of civilization. They made communication both easy and rapid, and became the guiding lines of the missionary enterprise. Of this facility of intercourse we have ample evidence in the Acts.

The contact of Christianity with Rome during the period covered by the Acts is impressively evident. It appears in such names as Caesar, Augustus, Cornelius, Felix, Festus, Claudius Lysias, Gallio, and Sergius Paulus; and prominently towards the close of Paul's missionary career in Acts xxiii-xxviii.

HELLENISM

Another of the forces with which Christianity was confronted was *Hellenism*, which stood for Greek culture, and did almost as great a work as Rome in preparing the world for Christ. A universal Empire and a universal religion demanded a universal language, and it was Greece that supplied it. Greek was the only linguistic medium which Alexander found available to govern his vast territory, and so from the fourth century B.C. onwards the exclusive Greek dialects gave way to that Greek language known as the *Koine*, that is, 'common language', or Hellenistic Greek, and this is the language in which the New Testament is written, and in which the Gospel was first carried to the nations. The Old Testament in Greek, which had been in existence for over two hundred years, was a potent ally of the Evangel, for it was the Bible of Paul and Luke and the early missionaries who carried the Good News to all the world.

It has been well said that 'it was not by accident that Christianity appeared at the one time in history when Greek was the sole international medium for all the civilised peoples of the Empire. It was the first moment in history when all men could easily exchange thought. The spread of Greek neutralized the confusion of Babel. Greek was the language in which an Aramaic Gospel became a world-evangel. All the missionary activity of early Christianity was practically confined to Greek-speaking people. It was in Greek soil that Christianity took at first its firmest root, and on Greek territory it carried on its most fruitful propaganda, and by means of Greek secured its first footing in the West. Such considerations show us how important and indeed necessary for the success of Christianity was the spread of Greek. That the Gospel was so successful on Greek territory proves that not only the Greek tongue but the indefatigable efforts of the Greek spirit prepared the way for Christ,—if in no other way than by raising problems which only Christianity could solve, and by giving clear expressions to needs that only Christianity could satisfy' (S. Angus. *The Environment of Early Christianity*; pp. 209-212).

It is interesting to find that in early Christianity Hellenists formed an important element among the disciples. In Acts vi. 1, for 'Grecian Jews' read 'Hellenists', who are distinguished from 'the Hebrews', Jews who were born and bred in the Holy Land. When it became necessary to create a new office in the Church to meet a need that had arisen, seven men were chosen 'by the multitude of the disciples', and they all bear Greek names: Stephen, Philip, Prochorus, Nicanor, Timon, Parmenas, and Nicolas 'a proselyte of Antioch' (vi. 5). The synagogue to which Stephen belonged was one belonging to Hellenists; its name was 'of the Libertines, Cyrenians, and Alexandrians' (vi. 9). When the recently converted Saul of Tarsus first went to Jerusalem, 'he preached boldly in the name of the Lord, and disputed against the Hellenists' (ix. 28, 29). The trouble of which we read in ch. viii. 1, began in a Hellenist synagogue, and the chief of those who were scattered were Hellenists (viii. 4; cf. xi. 20). The members of the Church at Antioch were in the main either Hellenists, Jews, or God-fearing Greeks; and as the Hellenist or Greek Church, Antioch was the connecting link between the Hebrew Church at Jerusalem and the churches of the Gentiles (ch. xiii, 1-3). In ch. xi. 19-26, we read that 'certain men of Cyprus and Cyrene' went to the Syrian Antioch and 'spake unto the Hellenists' and 'a great number that believed turned unto the Lord'.

When the result of the Jerusalem Conference (ch. xv) was sent to Antioch, it was entrusted to two delegates, one being a Hebrew, Judas, and the other a Hellenist, Silas (xv. 22-29).

In ch. xvii. 22-31, is Paul's great sermon preached to Greeks in their Capital.

These references will suffice to show, first of all, the opportunity which Hellenism presented to early Christianity, and secondly, to indicate the impact which Christianity made on Hellenism.

JUDAISM

The third power and the most ancient which Christianity had to face was *Judaism*. This differed from both Romanism and Hellenism in that it was divinely originated.

Judaism may be defined summarily as the religion of the Jews, and the Law and Prophecy of the Old Testament are the embodiment of it. Departure from the revealed purpose of God for this people led to the Assyrian and Babylonian captivities, but by the time of the return of large numbers of the Jews from Babylon they had turned from idolatry and reverted again to the Law. However by the time that Christ came they had so overlaid the Law by their traditions as largely to have made it void (Matt. xv. 1-9). 'They analyzed the Mosaic Law to death, and substituted a labyrinth of casuistry for a living code' (Schaff). Yet, notwithstanding the fact that Judaism had to a large extent become petrified, it alone in the world represented true religion. There were elements in their creed which were indestructible, and which Christianity absorbed. The Jews were the only ancient people that firmly grasped the thought of a purpose in history, and while all other peoples saw their Golden Age in the past, the

Jews saw theirs in the future; they were the only optimists of the old world. The dispersion of this race among the nations was to prove one of the largest single factors in the preparation for Christianity. Towards the fulfilment of their divinely-appointed mission there were two distinct stages; one of seclusion, that they might know God, and one of dispersion, that they might make Him known.

'Their first dispersion was Eastward, and was compulsory, and their later dispersions were Westward, and were voluntary. Sennacherib and Nebuchadnezzar did not consult the Jews but commanded them, yet, as we have said, their captivity purged them of idolatry and led them to a devout study of the Law, and these exiles were the founders of a powerful Babylonian colony which was a centre of Jewish life and thought for over 1,000 years' (S. Angus).

Later and voluntarily, allured by trade and other reasons, the Jews spread South and West, as the Sibylline Oracles declare. At Pentecost there were 'Jews from every nation under heaven' (Acts ii. 9-11). Their numbers in the Roman Empire were variously estimated from 8,000,000 and upwards. This dispersion greatly facilitated the spread of Christianity.

But there was a great deal more to it than merely a widespread scattering of Jews. There were certain factors which gave to this scattering its enormous power and influence, chief among which were their system of synagogues, their possession and use of the Septuagint, the Greek Old Testament, and their moral and religious standard and practice.

THE SYNAGOGUE

The Babylonian captivity of the Jews proved to be providential, for, being torn from their ancestral sanctuary, and being no longer able to offer their sacrifices, they were compelled to find a new means of religious worship and fellowship, and this they did in the idea of the *synagogue*, which means a place of assembly, or a company of Jews assembled. But the idea was not confined to captivity conditions. Wherever Jews went the synagogue went. Wherever ten adult males were found in a town a synagogue was formed. In Acts xv. 21, James speaks of synagogues 'in every city'. At one time there were over 400 synagogues in Jerusalem, and the New Testament refers to their existence in Galilee, Judaea, Asia Minor, Macedonia, and Greece; and in the time of Augustus there were many synagogues in Rome.

The services of the synagogue were simple and impressive, and many heathen were attracted to them, of whom some became converts. By their proselytizing activities the Jews became the first great missionary people, and met with much success among Gentiles who were craving for spiritual satisfaction. The synagogue was also the school and the library, and in all these respects it was the precursor of Christian assemblies and Sunday-schools.

We should remember that our Lord began His ministry in a synagogue (Luke iv. 16-30), and that the Apostles frequented and used these meeting-places (Acts xiii. 13-49).

THE GREEK BIBLE

The translation of the Hebrew Scriptures into Greek, which was made more than 200 years B.C., became the Bible of Hellenistic Judaism in Asia and in Europe. It also made available to Hellenistic heathenism the revelation of the Old Testament, and enabled them, in a language they understood, to hear a message of salvation.

This translation became the first, and for a considerable time the only, Bible of early Christianity, and a potent ally of the Gospel. Deissmann has said that 'Greek Judaism with the Septuagint had ploughed the furrows for the Gospel seed in the western world'. Its use in the Greek cities paved the way for the spread of Christianity in the heathen world. Our Lord and His Apostles were familiar with it, and the numerous quotations from the Old Testament in the New are, with few exceptions, taken from this Version. It was the Bible used by the Christian missionaries before Christian writings were made.

JEWISH BELIEFS AND PRACTICE

Christianity was indebted not only to the Jewish Synagogue and the Septuagint Version of the Old Testament, but also to

the morality and beliefs of the Jews. Moral conditions in heathenism in the first century of this era are described in Romans i—
though there was another side to the picture—and the Jews'
enthusiasm for righteousness was a condemnation of every form
of injustice.

Religiously the world was weary, and spiritually it was hungry.
Its look was backward and not forward. The Graeco-Roman
world was heavy-laden. Rationalism and scepticism, stoicism
and fatalism, formalism and religious destitution, pessimism and
exhaustion, were characteristics of that age; and yet, desire,
and hope, and faith of a sort were not dead. 'The pathology of
the soul was studied with a view to know its diseases and so to
discover remedies'. Men were losing faith in the national religion
and were willing to experiment with any substitute. In Greece,
before Christ came, thought moved quite definitely toward
monotheism: Xenophanes said, 'the best can only be One'.
No subject was more discussed in the Graeco-Roman world
than prayer. A growing sense of sin, and a demand for redemption
were becoming more widespread.

These conditions and tendencies in the pagan world of that
time gave the dispersed Jews their supreme opportunity, an
opportunity which they did not fail to embrace. Their synagogue
ministry was the answer to the questions raised by paganism.
Their lofty monotheism, their practice of prayer, their enthusiasm
for righteousness, their faith in the future, their zeal for worship
and the purity of their worship, all made a strong appeal to the
temper of that age, and this accounts for the accessions to their
ranks as proselytes, or God-fearers. These God-fearers appear
in the New Testament as the most susceptible hearers of the
Gospel, and formed the nucleus of many of the first Christian
churches. Of this class were the centurion of Capernaum,
Cornelius of Caesarea, Lydia of Philippi, Timothy, and many
other prominent disciples.

This whole situation was a preparation for Christianity. The
Jewish canon was the forerunner of a Christian canon. The
Christian Church took over the Jewish Bible, and all that was vital
in Judaism Christianity transfigured and adapted to the spirit
and needs of the new dispensation. Of this the Acts gives

evidence. It is the record of the transition from Judaism to Christianity, and this transition was completed in A.D. 70 when Judaism suffered its most staggering calamity.

'Thus', says Schaff, 'was the way for Christianity prepared on every side, positively and negatively, directly and indirectly, in theory and in practice, by truth and error, by false belief and by unbelief—those hostile brothers, which yet cannot live apart—by Jewish religion, by Grecian culture, and by Roman conquest; by the vainly attempted amalgamation of Jewish and heathen thought, by the exposed impotence of natural civilization, philosophy, art, and political power, by the decay of the old religions, by the universal distraction and hopeless misery of the age, and by the yearnings of all earnest and noble souls for the religion of salvation' (*History of the Church*).

THE RISE OF THE NEW TESTAMENT WRITINGS

The first hundred years of this era, A.D., may be divided into three periods: B.C. 5-A.D. 30; A.D. 30-50; and A.D. 50-95.

In the first of these periods the redemptive message was *created*; in the second it was orally *proclaimed*; and in the third it was *recorded* in Writings.

THE PERIOD OF CREATIVE STORY

Christ is the sum and substance of the first period (B.C. 5—A.D. 30), and He wrote nothing. The reason for this is two-fold. First, because the Jews had a Bible, the Old Testament Writings, and Christ pointed to them, and came to fulfil them. He said: 'Think not that I came to destroy the Law or the Prophets; I came not to destroy, but to fulfil' (Matt. v. 17). And secondly, Christ wrote nothing because *He was His message*, a fact which is true of no one else in history. He declared 'I am the truth'; and when He said 'Learn of Me', he did not refer to what He was teaching orally, but to Himself, and so He continued, 'for I am meek and lowly in heart', pointing not to His words but to Himself. Christ's message was not merely or primarily His teaching, but His character, life and work. There was nothing for Him to write, for He was creating the message which afterwards would be written. 'Christianity entered the world not as a written letter, like the Mosaic law, but as a creative fact, as life-giving spirit' (Schaff).

THE PERIOD OF ORAL TRADITION

The second period of this era was one of about twenty years A.D. 30-50, during which the Christian message was being orally proclaimed. This was the period of evangelists, proclaimers of the Evangel. Little need was felt for any written record of the message for it was fresh in the minds of disciples, the Apostles were still alive, and the Old Testament was in the hands of the Christians, mostly converted Jews, and the expectation of Christ's imminent return was widespread. The substance of the oral message is preserved in the address by Peter in the house of Cornelius (Acts x. 34-43). This is a passage of great importance because it is the substance of Mark's Gospel, which is really Peter's, and which was the first of the Gospels to be written.

These and other facts of Christ's public life, and summaries of His discourses were orally circulated by those who had been with Him, and by those whom He had instructed. Light is thrown on this by the qualification necessary for one to become a member of the apostolate. Peter said that it was needful that he should have been in the society of the apostles 'all the time that the Lord Jesus went in and out among us, beginning from the baptism of John until the day when He was taken up from us' (Acts i. 21, 22). The subject of the Evangel, then, embraced the story of Jesus from His baptism to His ascension. This message the Apostles and Evangelists 'ceased not to teach and to preach', the message of 'Jesus the Christ' (Acts v. 42).

But it must not be concluded that no writings appeared in this period because we are not in the possession of any. Indeed, it seems clear that the beginnings of Christian history were recorded in some form. Milligan says: 'It is impossible to doubt that the leading facts of Christ's life and ministry, which had so profoundly stirred the hearts of many, were written down and circulated almost as soon as they took place'; and Ramsay says:

'So far as antecedent probability goes, founded on the general character of preceding and contemporary Greek or Graeco-Asiatic society, the first Christian account of the circumstances connected with the death of Jesus must be presumed to have been written in the year when Jesus died'.

But we are not dependent only on the probabilities of the case, because we know that there were records of Jesus' life and ministry before any of the canonical Gospels appeared. Luke says: 'Many writers have already attempted to draw up a connected account of the events which have taken place among us, as these have been handed down to us by men who were from the earliest days eye-witnesses in the service of the story; therefore, having examined them all carefully from the beginning, I have decided, Theophilus, myself to write a continuous account to your Excellency, in order that you may have trustworthy information about the things that you have been taught' (Luke i. 1-4. Translation by C. K. Williams, 1952).

Also the lost 'Q' document or Sayings of Jesus, used so largely by Matthew and Luke, indicates that there was considerable literary activity in this period, but none of it has survived, except in so far as it has influenced the writers of the canonical Gospels.

THE PERIOD OF THE WRITINGS

By the time the middle of the first century was reached the situation was felt to be changing. The oral tradition had at first a limited field of circulation, but now the field was being enlarged. The Lord had said to His Apostles: 'Ye shall be witnesses unto me both in Jerusalem, and in all Judaea and Samaria, and unto the uttermost part of the earth' (Acts i. 8). This promised enlargement of the field of witness, which had begun, would call for something more than the testimony of individuals.

But further, in the course of years the number of the original witnesses became fewer and fewer. The Apostles and the first disciples would decease, and unless before that time arrived the message was fixed in written form there was every reason to fear that it would become corrupted by omissions, or exaggerations, or interpolations. Dr. Ryle says: 'The lapse of time quickly demonstrated the inefficiency of merely oral teaching.

For while Christian communities everywhere multiplied and the Church spread into far distant regions, the members of the Apostolic circle became fewer. The sacred tradition was committed to those who were not gifted with miraculous powers of memory or inspiration', and so there was the danger that the Apostolic message would suffer in accuracy and proportion.

But before the Apostolic age closed the Christian message was embodied in a permanent form. 'On practical rather than on literary grounds, a number of Christian Writings gradually came into existence, out of which, in time, by a process of selection there came to be formed what we are accustomed to describe as the New Testament Canon, or, more briefly, the New Testament' (Milligan).

It is important to understand that the varying opinions of scholars relative to the date, place of writing, and even the authorship of these Writings in no way affect their value. Here they are; and did we know positively who wrote the Epistle to the Hebrews it would not add to the value of that Writing, though it might add somewhat to its interest; but our not knowing who the author was, in no degree diminishes its value. Critical questions and spiritual values should be considered separately.

THE NEW TESTAMENT LITERATURE

From Chart 120 it will be seen that the Gospels, except Mark, were not written first, but it is practically certain that the Synoptic Records were written before the destruction of Jerusalem in A.D. 70. It is interesting also to notice the order of Paul's Epistles, about which more will be said, and of the place of the Acts in the syllabus.

The rapid spread of the Christian Church, and the multiplication of particular fellowships in different places, afforded abundant cause for correspondence between individual teachers and members; between churches and individual believers who were connected with them, but absent; and between churches in different countries.

CHART 120

THE NEW TESTAMENT LITERATURE

Decade	Writing	Date	Place	Period
A.D. 40-50	JAMES	44-49	Jerusalem	I
50-60	MARK	50-55	Rome (?)	N
	1 THESSALONIANS	52	Corinth	I
	2 THESSALONIANS	53	Corinth	
	1 CORINTHIANS	57	Ephesus	T
	2 CORINTHIANS	57	Macedonia	I
	GALATIANS	58	Corinth	
	ROMANS	58	Corinth	A
	LUKE	58-60	Caesarea	
	MATTHEW	60-66	Judaea	L
60-70	EPHESIANS	62-63	Rome	C
	COLOSSIANS	62-63	Rome	E
	PHILEMON	62-63	Rome	
	PHILIPPIANS	63	Rome	N
	ACTS	63-64	Rome	
	1 PETER	64-65	'Babylon'	T
	JUDE	65-68	Jerusalem (?)	R
	1 TIMOTHY	65-66	Macedonia	
	TITUS	65-66	Ephesus	A
	2 TIMOTHY	67	Rome	
	2 PETER	66	(?)	L
	HEBREWS	67-68 (?)	(?)	
70-80	—	—	—	F
80-90	—	—	—	I
90-100	JOHN	90-95	Ephesus	N
	1 JOHN	90-95	Ephesus	
	2 JOHN	90-95	Ephesus	A
	3 JOHN	90-95	Ephesus	
	REVELATION	68-70(?) 95-98(?)	Patmos	L

In Acts xv. 23-29 a letter is preserved which the mother Church in Jerusalem sent to the churches in Syria and Cilicia with reference to the freedom of Gentile Christians from the observances of the Jewish law; and in Acts xviii. 27, we are told that when Apollos was about to pass into Achaia, the Christians at Ephesus wrote a letter of recommendation for him to the brethren there. All the Epistles of the New Testament are letters of individuals,

G

of Christian teachers, either to particular persons, or to Christian churches in particular places, or scattered over a wide district.

Most of them are written by the Apostle Paul. From him it is that we might expect a widespread correspondence. He who founded many churches naturally kept up a close intimacy with his converts and others, and was ever ready to counsel them relative to matters of belief and conduct. This practice was followed by other Apostles and leading teachers as the Catholic Epistles and the Epistle to the Hebrews show. By the time the first century closed the last of the Apostolic Letters was written, and the last of the Apostles had died.

The complexion of the New Testament Writings and their progressive relation to one another is shown in Chart 121.

CHART 121

THE NEW TESTAMENT WRITINGS CLASSIFIED		
Part 1	**Part 2**	**Part 3**
MATTHEW to JOHN	ACTS to JUDE	REVELATION
Historical	Doctrinal	Prophetical
Evangelic	Exegetic	Apocalyptic
Foundation	Superstructure	Completion
Past	Present	Future
THE CHRIST	THE CHURCH	THE CONSUMMATION

There is a completeness about this collection which cannot be mistaken, and it is all the more remarkable because the writers were aiming at no such result. The plan of the whole was not in their minds but in the Divine Mind. The Great Architect directed His workmen, and the result is this Temple of Truth which we call the New Testament.

BASED ON MARK'S GOSPEL

THE LIFE AND WORK OF JESUS THE CHRIST

	MARK	MATT.	LUKE	JOHN
PART ONE - - B.C. 5—A.D. 26				
The Thirty Years of Preparation				
(i) INTRODUCTORY				
Prologue of John's Gospel	—	—	—	i. 1-18
Preface to Luke's Gospel	—	—	i. 1-4	—
The Genealogies	—	i. 1-17	iii. 23-38	—
(ii) THE ANNUNCIATIONS				
To Zacharias	—	—	i. 5-25	—
To Mary	—	—	i. 26-38	—
To Joseph	—	i. 18-25	—	—
Mary's Visit to Elisabeth	—	—	i. 39-56	—
(iii) THE ADVENTS				
Of John the Baptist	—	—	i. 57-80	—
Of Jesus the Messiah	—	—	ii. 1-7	—
The Angels and the Shepherds	—	—	ii. 8-20	—
(iv) THE INFANCY OF JESUS				
The Circumcision	—	—	ii. 21	—
The Presentation	—	—	ii. 22-38	—
The Wise Men from the East	—	ii. 1-12	—	—
The Flight into Egypt	—	ii. 13-18	—	—
The Return from Egypt to Nazareth	—	ii. 19-23	ii. 39	—

A HARMONISTIC SYLLABUS OF THE GOSPELS (continued)

	MARK	MATT.	LUKE	JOHN
(v) THE YEARS IN NAZARETH				
Jesus' Childhood	—	ii. 23	ii. 39-40	—
The Visit to Jerusalem when Twelve Years Old	—	—	ii. 41-50	—
Eighteen Years More at Nazareth ..	—	—	ii. 51-52	—
PART TWO - A.D. 27. About 3 months				
The Opening Events of Jesus' Ministry				
The Ministry of John the Baptist	i. 1-8	iii. 1-12	iii. 1-20	—
The Baptism of Jesus	i. 9-11	iii. 13-17	iii. 21-23	—
The Temptation of Jesus	i. 12-13	iv. 1-11	iv. 1-13	—
John's Testimony to Members of the Sanhedrin ..			—	i. 19-28
John's Identification of Jesus as the Messiah ..			—	i. 29-34
The First Disciples			—	i. 35-42
Philip, Nathanael, and Jesus ..			—	i. 43-51
The First Miracle—at Cana ..			—	ii. 1-11
Jesus' Sojourn at Capernaum ..			—	ii. 12
PART THREE - A.D. 27. About 8 months				
The Early Judaean Ministry				
(i) IN JERUSALEM				
The First Cleansing of the Temple ..		—	—	ii. 13-22
The First Discourse—with Nicodemus ..		—	—	ii. 23-iii. 21
(ii) IN JUDÆA				
Christ Baptizing		—	—	iii. 22-24
John's Loyalty to Jesus		—	—	iii. 25-36

	St. Matthew	St. Mark	St. Luke	St. John
PART FOUR - A.D. 27. A FEW DAYS				
The Samaritan Ministry				
The Departure from Judæa	iv. 12	i. 14	iv. 14	iv. 1-3
Discourse with the Woman of Samaria	—	—	—	iv. 4-26
Words to the Disciples on Sowing and Reaping	—	—	—	iv. 27-38
The Gospel in Sychar				iv. 39-42
PART FIVE - A.D. 27-29. About 22 months				
The Galilean Ministry				
PERIOD I.—From the Return into Galilee to the Choosing of the Twelve. About 5 months A.D. 27-28.				
(i) THE BEGINNINGS				
The Arrival in Galilee	iv. 12	i. 14	iv. 14	iv. 1-3
Commencement of the Galilean Ministry	iv. 12, 17	i. 14, 15	iv. 14, 15	iv. 43-45
The Healing of a Nobleman's Son at Cana	—	—	—	iv. 46-54
The First Rejection at Nazareth	—	—	iv. 16-30	—
Removal to Capernaum	iv. 13-16	—	iv. 31	
(ii) THE FIRST PREACHING TOUR				
A Miraculous Draught of Fishes, and the Call of Four Disciples to Full-time Service	iv. 18-22	i. 16-20	v. 1-11	
An Unclean Spirit Cast Out	—	i. 21-28	iv. 31-37	
Peter's Mother-in-law Healed	viii. 14-17	i. 29-34	iv. 38-41	
Preaching in Galilee with His Disciples	iv. 23-25	i. 35-39	iv. 42-44	
A Leper Cleansed	viii. 2-4	i. 40-45	v. 12-16	

A HARMONISTIC SYLLABUS OF THE GOSPELS (continued)

	MARK	MATT.	LUKE	JOHN
(iii) GROWING HOSTILITY OF THE SCRIBES AND PHARISEES				
A Paralytic Man Healed	ii. 1-12	ix. 1-8	v. 17-26	—
The Call of Matthew, and the Feast in his House	ii. 13-17	ix. 9-13	v. 27-32	—
The Question about Fasting and three Parables in Answer	ii. 18-22	ix. 14-17	v. 33-39	—
Healing of a Man at Bethesda on the Sabbath, and the Action Defended in a Great Discourse	—	—	—	v. 1-47
The Disciples Pluck Grain on the Sabbath, and the Following Controversy	ii. 23-28	xii. 1-8	vi. 1-5	—
Healing of a Man with a Withered Hand on the Sabbath, and the Following Controversy	iii. 1-6	xii. 9-14	vi. 6-11	—
PERIOD II.—From the Choosing of the Twelve to the Withdrawal into Northern Galilee				
A.D. 28-29. About 12 months				
(i) ORGANIZATION OF THE KINGDOM				
The Widespread Fame of Jesus	iii. 7-12	xii. 15-21	—	—
The Choosing of the Twelve	iii. 13-19	—	vi. 12-16	—
The Sermon on the Mount	—	v. 1-viii. 1	vi. 17-49	—
(ii) THE SECOND PREACHING TOUR				
A Centurion's Servant Healed	—	viii. 5-13	vii. 1-10	—
A Widow's Son Raised from the Dead	—	—	vii. 11-17	—
The Baptist's Inquiry and Jesus' Response	—	xi. 2-19	vii. 18-35	—
Woes upon the Cities of Opportunity	—	xi. 20-24	—	—

Event	Matthew	Mark	Luke	John
Christ's Prayer and Claim for Himself..	xi. 25-30	—	—	—
The Anointing of Jesus' Feet in the House of Simon, and the Parable of the Two Debtors	—	—	vii. 36-50	—
Christ's Companions on His Second Tour of Galilee	—	—	viii. 1-3	—
(iii) A DAY OF TEACHING				
Blasphemous Accusation of League with Beelzebub	xii. 22-37	iii. 19-30	—	—
The Scribes and Pharisees Demand a Sign	xii. 38-45	—	—	—
The True Kindred of Christ	xii. 46-50	iii. 31-35	viii. 19-21	—
The Parables of the Kingdom	xiii. 1-53	iv. 1-34	viii. 4-18	—
(iv) A DAY OF MIRACLES				
Jesus Stills the Tempest..	viii. 18, 23-27	iv. 35-41	viii. 22-25	—
A Gerasene Demoniac Healed	viii. 28-34	v. 1-20	viii. 26-39	—
The Raising of the Daughter of Jairus	ix. 18, 19, 23-26	v. 21-24, 35-43	viii. 40-42, 49-56	—
Healing of a Woman with an Issue of Blood	ix. 20-22	v. 25-34	viii. 43-48	—
Healing of Two Blind Men and a Dumb Demoniac	ix. 27-34	—	—	—
(v) THE THIRD PREACHING TOUR				
The Second Rejection at Nazareth	xiii. 54-58	vi. 1-6	—	—
The Third Tour in Galilee	ix. 35	vi. 6	—	—
The Mission of the Twelve	ix. 36-xi. 1	vi. 7-13	ix. 1-6	—
Death of John the Baptist	xiv. 1-12	vi. 14-29	ix. 7-9	—

A HARMONISTIC SYLLABUS OF THE GOSPELS (continued)

	MARK	MATT.	LUKE	JOHN
(vi) THE CRISIS AT CAPERNAUM				
The Twelve Return and Retire with Jesus for Rest	vi. 30-32	xiv. 13	ix. 10	—
Feeding of the Five Thousand	vi. 33-44	xiv. 13-21	ix. 11-17	vi. 1-13
The Disciples and the Multitude Sent Away, and Jesus Retires for Prayer	vi. 45, 46	xiv. 22, 23	—	vi. 14, 15
Christ Walks on the Sea	vi. 47-52	xiv. 24-33	—	vi. 16-21
The Reception at Gennesaret	vi. 53-56	xiv. 34-36	—	vi. 22-71
Discourse on The Bread of Life	—	—	—	—
Discourse on the Traditions of Men	vii. 1-23	xv. 1-20	—	—
PERIOD III.—From the Withdrawal into Northern Galilee to the Final Departure for Jerusalem. A.D. 29. About 6 months				
(i) IN VARIOUS REGIONS				
Daughter of a Syro-Phoenician Woman Healed	vii. 24-30	xv. 21-28	—	—
Healing of a Deaf Mute in the Region of Decapolis	vii. 31-37	xv. 29-31	—	—
Feeding of the Four Thousand	viii. 1-9	xv. 32-38	—	—
The Pharisees and the Sadducees Seek a Sign	viii. 10-12	xv. 39-xvi. 4	—	—
The Disciples' Perplexity about Leaven, and Jesus' Explanation	viii. 13-21	xvi. 5-12	—	—
A Blind Man Healed near Bethsaida	viii. 22-26	—	—	—
(ii) JESUS AND HIS APOSTLES				
Christ's Inquiry about His Person, and Peter's Confession	viii. 27-30	xvi. 13-20	ix. 18-21	—
Christ Foretells His Death and Resurrection, and Rebukes Peter	viii. 31-27	xvi. 21-26	ix. 22-25	

Passage				
The Coming of the Son of Man	xvi. 27-28	viii. 38-ix. 1	ix. 26, 27	—
The Transfiguration near Cæsarea Philippi	xvii. 1-8	ix. 2-8	ix. 28-36	—
On the Way Down from the Mount	xvii. 9-13	ix. 9-13	—	—
Healing of a Demoniac Boy	xvii. 14-21	ix. 14-29	ix. 37-43	—
Christ Again Foretells His Death and Resurrection	xvii. 22, 23	ix. 30-32	ix. 43-45	—
(iii) IN CAPERNAUM AGAIN				
The Messiah Pays the Half-Shekel for the Temple	xvii. 24-27	—	—	—
Discourse on Humility as a Mark of Greatness	xviii. 1-5	ix. 33-37	ix. 46-48	—
Discourse on Occasions of Stumbling	xviii. 6-14	ix. 38-50	ix. 49, 50	—
Discourse on Forgiveness	xviii. 15-35	—	—	—
Jesus Lingers in Galilee	—	—	—	vii. 1-9

PART SIX   A.D. 29.   About 3 months

The Later Judæan Ministry

Passage				
(i) ON THE WAY TO JERUSALEM				
Jesus' Departure from Galilee	xix. 1, 2	x. 1	—	vii. 10
Rejected by the Samaritans	—	—	ix. 51-56	—
The Cost of Discipleship	viii. 19-22	—	ix. 57-62	—
(ii) IN JERUSALEM				
At the Feast of Tabernacles	—	—	—	vii. 11-52
Story of an Adulteress Brought to Jesus	—	—	—	vii. 53-viii. 11

A HARMONISTIC SYLLABUS OF THE GOSPELS (continued)

	MARK	MATT.	LUKE	JOHN
(ii) In Jerusalem (continued)				
Jesus in Conflict with the Pharisees Exposes them in Discourses on The Light of the World (12-30) and Spiritual Freedom (31-59)	—	—	—	viii. 12-59
Healing of a Man Born Blind	—	—	—	ix. 1-41
Discourse on the Good Shepherd	—	—	—	x. 1-21
(iii) In Judæa				
The Mission of the Seventy and their Return	—	—	x. 1-24	
In Answer to a Lawyer's Question Jesus Speaks the Parable of the Good Samaritan	—	—	x. 25-37	
Jesus the Guest of Martha and Mary	—	—	x. 38-42	
Discourse on Prayer	—	—	xi. 1-13	
Blasphemous Accusation of League with Beelzebub	—	—	xi. 14-28	
Seeking a Sign Rebuked	—	—	xi. 29-36	
Arraignment of the Pharisees in the House of One of Them	—	—	xi. 37-54	
Teaching Concerning Trust in God and Coming Judgment	—	—	xii. 1-59	
All Must Repent or Perish	—	—	xiii. 1-9	
A Cripple Woman Healed on the Sabbath, and Jesus' Defence	—	—	xiii. 10-17	
Parables of the Mustard Seed and the Leaven	—	—	xiii. 18-21	
Jesus at the Feast of Dedication	—	—	—	x. 22-39

PART SEVEN - A.D. 29-30. About 3½ months
The Peraean Ministry

	Matthew	Mark	Luke	John
(i) WITHDRAWAL FROM JERUSALEM				
Jesus Withdraws to Bethany beyond Jordan				x. 40-42
A Question about Salvation			xiii. 22-30	
Reply to the Warning against Herod Antipas			xiii. 31-35	
Discourse at a Pharisee's Table			xiv. 1-24	
Discourse on the Cost of Discipleship			xiv. 25-35	
Discourse on Seeking and Finding the Lost			xv. 1-32	
Two Parables on Stewardship			xvi. 1-31	
Concerning Offences, Forgiveness, and Faith			xvii. 1-10	
Jesus Raises Lazarus from the Dead				xi. 1-44
Jesus Withdraws to Ephraim				xi. 45-54
(ii) THE LAST JOURNEY TO JERUSALEM BY WAY OF SAMARIA AND GALILEE				
The Healing of Ten Lepers			xvii. 11-19	
Discourse on the Coming of the Kingdom			xvii. 20-37	
Two Parables on Prayer			xviii. 1-14	
(iii) IN PERAEA				
Teaching Concerning Divorce	xix. 1-12	x. 1-12		
Christ and Little Children	xix. 13-15	x. 13-16	xviii. 15-17	
The Rich Young Ruler and Teaching on Riches	xix. 16-xx. 16	x. 17-31	xviii. 18-30	
Jesus Foretells His Death and Resurrection	xx. 17-19	x. 32-34	xviii. 31-34	
The Selfish Ambition of James and John Rebuked	xx. 20-28	x. 35-45		
(iv) TOWARDS JERUSALEM				
Blind Men Healed near Jericho	xx. 29-34	x. 46-52	xviii. 35-43	
The Conversion of Zacchaeus			xix. 1-10	
The Parable of the Pounds			xix. 11-28	
Jesus' Arrival at Bethany				xi. 55-xii. 1, 9-11

A HARMONISTIC SYLLABUS OF THE GOSPELS (*continued*)

PART EIGHT - - A.D. 30. One Week

The order of the Passion Week in this Harmony follows the traditional view of the Church, but is not necessarily on that account correct.

The Closing Events of Jesus' Ministry

	MARK	MATT.	LUKE	JOHN
(i) SUNDAY—THE DAY OF DEMONSTRATION				
The Triumphal Entry into Jerusalem	xi. 1-10	xxi. 1-9	xix. 29-40	xii. 12-19
Prediction over Jerusalem	—	—	xix. 41-44	—
Jesus in the City and the Temple, and Retirement to Bethany	xi. 11	xxi. 10, 11	—	—
(ii) MONDAY—THE DAY OF AUTHORITY				
A Fig Tree Cursed	xi. 12-14	xxi. 18. 19	—	—
Second Cleansing of the Temple	xi. 15-19	xxi. 12, 13	xix. 45-48	—
Jesus Works Miracles and Justifies the Praise of Himself	—	xxi. 14-17	—	—
(iii) TUESDAY—THE DAY OF CONFLICT				
The Fig Tree Withered and Jesus' Remarks thereon	xi. 20-26	xxi. 19-22	—	—
Controversy with the Priests, Scribes, and Elders about His Authority	xi. 27-xii. 12	xxi. 23-xxii. 14	xx. 1-19	—

	Matthew	Mark	Luke	John
Controversy with the Pharisees and Herodians about Paying Tribute to Caesar	xxii. 15-22	xii. 13-17	xx. 20-26	—
Controversy with the Sadducees about the Resurrection	xxii. 23-33	xii. 18-27	xx. 27-40	—
Controversy with a Lawyer about the Commandments	xxii. 34-40	xii. 28-34	—	—
Christ's Unanswerable Question	xxii. 41-46	xii. 35-37	xx. 41-44	—
Denunciations of the Scribes and Pharisees	xxiii. 1-39	xii. 38-40	xx. 45-47	—
Jesus Commends the Liberality of a Poor Widow	—	xii. 41-44	xxi. 1-4	—
Greeks Desire to see Jesus, and Jesus' Following Discourse	—	—	—	xii. 20-36
The Jews' Rejection of Christ	—	—	—	xii. 37-50
Discourse concerning the Destruction of Jerusalem and the End of the Age	xxiv. xxv	xiii. 1-37	xxi. 5-38	—
Jesus Predicts His Death as at Hand	xxvi. 1-5	xiv. 1, 2	xxii. 1, 2	—
Anointing of Jesus by Mary of Bethany	xxvi. 6-13	xiv. 3-9	—	xii. 2-8
Judas Arranges to Betray Jesus	xxvi. 14-16	xiv. 10, 11	xxii. 3-6	—

(iv) WEDNESDAY—THE DAY OF SILENCE

(v) THURSDAY—THE DAY OF PREPARATION

	Matthew	Mark	Luke	John
Preparation for the Paschal Meal	xxvi. 17-19	xiv. 12-16	xxii. 7-13	—
Jesus Partakes of the Passover with His Apostles	xxvi. 20	xiv. 17	xxii. 14-16	—
Jesus Washes the Feet of the Apostles	—	—	—	xiii. 1-20
The Betrayer is Pointed Out	xxvi. 21-25	xiv. 18-21	xxii. 21-23	xiii. 21-30
The Apostles Warned Against Desertion	xxvi. 31-35	xiv. 27-31	xxii. 31-38	xiii. 31-38
Institution of the Lord's Supper	xxvi. 26-30	xiv. 22-26	xxii. 17-20	(I Cor. xi. 23-26)

A HARMONISTIC SYLLABUS OF THE GOSPELS (continued)

	MARK	MATT.	LUKE	JOHN
(v) THURSDAY—THE DAY OF PREPARATION (continued)				
Jealousy of the Apostles Rebuked	—		xxii. 24-30	—
Farewell Discourse to the Apostles in the Upper Room	—	—	—	xiv. 1-31
(vi) FRIDAY—THE DAY OF SUFFERING				
Discourse on the Way to Gethsemane	—	—	—	xv., xvi.
Christ's Intercessory Prayer			—	xvii.
Arrival at, and the Agony in Gethsemane	xiv. 26, 32-42	xxvi. 30, 36-46	xxii. 39-46	xviii. 1
The Betrayal and Arrest	xiv. 43-52	xxvi. 47-56	xxii. 47-53	xviii. 2-12
(a) THE JEWISH TRIALS				
First—Before Annas	—	—	—	xviii. 12-14, 19-23
Second—Before Caiaphas and the Sanhedrin	xiv. 53, 55, 65	xxvi. 57, 59-68	xxii. 54, 63-65	xviii. 24
Peter Thrice Denies his Lord and Repents	xiv. 54, 66-72	xxvi. 58, 69-75	xxii. 54-62	xviii. 15-18, 25-27
Third—Before the Sanhedrin, which Passes Sentence	xv. 1	xxvii. 1	xxii. 66-71	—
Remorse and Suicide of Judas	—	xxvii. 3-10	(Acts i. 18, 19)	—
(b) THE ROMAN TRIALS				
First—Before Pilate	xv. 1-5	xxvii. 2, 11-14	xxiii. 1-5	xviii. 28-38
Second—Before Herod Antipas	—	—	xxiii. 6-12	—
Third—Before Pilate Again	xv. 6-15	xxvii. 15-26	xxiii. 13-25	xviii. 39-xix. 16
Jesus Mocked by Roman Soldiers	xv. 16-19	xxvii. 27-30	—	—
On the Way to Calvary	xv. 20-23	xxvii. 31-34	xxiii. 26-33	xix. 16, 17

	Mark	Matthew	Luke	John
(c) CALVARY				
The First Three Hours on the Cross	xv. 24-32	xxvii. 35-44	xxiii. 33-43	xix. 18-27
The Second Three Hours on the Cross	xv. 33-37	xxvii. 45-50	xxiii. 44, 46	xix. 28-30
Phenomena Accompanying Christ's Death	xv. 38-41	xxvii. 51-56	xxiii. 45, 47-49	—
The Burial of Jesus' Body in Joseph's Tomb	xv. 42-46	xxvii. 57-60	xxiii. 50-54	xix. 31-42
(vii) SATURDAY—THE DAY OF ABSENCE				
The Watch of the Women by the Tomb	xv. 47	xxvii. 61-66	xxiii. 55, 56	—

PART NINE - A.D. 30.   About 6 Weeks

The Forty Days of Confirmation

	Mark	Matthew	Luke	John
(i) SUNDAY—THE DAY OF VICTORY AND EVENTS				
The Visit of the Women to the Tomb	xvi. 1	xxviii. 1		
The Earthquake; the Tomb Stone Rolled Away, and the Fright of the Roman Watchers	—	xxviii. 2-4		
The Message of Angels to Women at the Tomb	xvi. 2-8	xxviii. 5-8	xxiv. 1-8	xx. 1
Mary Magdalene and Other Women Report to the Apostles, and Peter and John Visit the Tomb	—	—	xxiv. 9-12	xx. 2-10

A HARMONISTIC SYLLABUS OF THE GOSPELS (continued)

	Mark	Matthew	Luke	John
(ii) APPEARANCES OF JESUS ON THE RESURRECTION DAY				
First—To Mary Magdalene	xvi. 9-11	—	—	xx. 11-18
Second—To Other Women	—	xxviii. 9, 10	—	—
Some of the Guard Report to the Jewish Rulers	—	xxviii. 11-15	—	—
Third—To Two Disciples on the Way to Emmaus	xvi. 12, 13	—	xxiv. 13-32	—
Fourth—The Report of the Emmaus Disciples, and the News of the Appearance to Simon Peter	(1 Cor. xv. 5)	—	xxiv. 33-35	—
Fifth—To Ten Apostles in a House ..	xvi. 14	—	xxiv. 36-43	xx. 19-25
(iii) APPEARANCES OF JESUS AFTER THE RESURRECTION DAY				
Sixth—To the Eleven Apostles in a House	—	—	—	xx. 26-31
Seventh—To Seven Apostles by the Sea of Galilee. A Miraculous Draught of Fishes. Conversation of Jesus and Peter, and an Intimation of Peter's End	—	—	—	xxi. 1-14
Eighth—To Five Hundred Disciples in Galilee	xvi. 15-18	xxviii. 16-20	(1 Cor. xv. 6)	xxi. 15-25
Ninth—To James His Brother ..	(1 Cor. xv. 7)	—	—	—
Tenth—To the Eleven in Jerusalem and on Olivet	—	—	xxiv. 44-49	—
The Last Commission and the Ascension	xvi. 19, 20	—	xxiv. 50-53	(Acts i. 3-12)

THE GOSPELS AND THE MESSIAH

Christ in person dominates the First Scene of Act II, and, all too briefly, we must contemplate His Person and His Work. But as the sources of our knowledge of Christ incarnate are the Four Gospels, a little must first be said about them.

As we study these Records many questions inevitably arise: who wrote them? when were they written, and in what language? what sources had the writers at their disposal? why are there four? how are the differences in them to be accounted for? what are the characteristics of each of them? how is the difference between the first Three and the Fourth to be accounted for? has the credibility of these Records been shaken? These and other such questions are not unimportant (see the writer's *A Guide to the Gospels*, 664 pages), but, perhaps, they have received attention out of all proportion to what is the main value of the Gospels. The object of the writers, as we believe, under the guidance of the Spirit, was to narrate, each from his own standpoint, the story of the Messiah's life and work, with a view to the moral and spiritual benefit of their readers. However the critical questions may eventually be settled the supreme value of the Gospels remains. Intellectual difficulties should not be allowed to rob us of the spiritual values of these priceless Pamphlets.

In these Records Jesus the Messiah is presented in four aspects: as King and Servant, as Man and Son. The first two relate to His Offices, and the next two relate to His Person; and in each pair the aspects are sharply contrasted; Sovereign and Servant; Human and Divine. These are not artificial ideas imposed upon these Gospels, but are found prophetically in the Old Testament.

The Mighty King of Matthew's Gospel is in Jeremiah xxiii. 5:

'Behold, the days come, saith the LORD, that I will raise unto David a righteous Branch, and a *KING* shall reign and prosper, and shall execute judgment in the earth.'

The Lowly Servant of Mark's Gospel is in Zechariah iii. 8:

'Behold I will bring forth My *SERVANT*, the Branch.'

The Ideal Man of Luke's Gospel is in Zechariah vi. 12:

'Behold, the *MAN*, whose name is the Branch.'

H

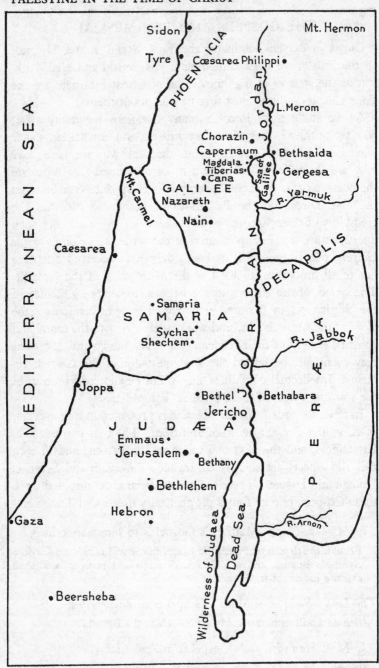

The Divine Son of John's Gospel is in Isaiah iv. 2; ix. 6; xi. 1:

'In that day shall the Branch of the LORD be beautiful and glorious.' 'Unto us a *SON* is given.' 'There shall come forth a Rod out of the stem of Jesse, and a Branch shall grow out of his roots.'

The repeated reference to the Branch in these texts shows in their contexts that it is the Messiah that is spoken of; and the Four Gospels answer, respectively, to these ideas.

Matthew. Unmistakably this Gospel is Royal in complexion. The Messiah is a King, the King of Israel's hopes, though they knew it not. The references in the Record to 'the Holy City', the 'Son of David', the 'Kingdom of heaven', the Mosaic Law; the recurrent phrase 'that it might be fulfilled' and its equivalents, 'which was spoken', and 'it is written', all point in the same direction, to the Messianic King. His genealogy is traced through David back to Abraham the father of the Nation, but not further back as in Luke.

The object of this Gospel is to present the Messiah to men against the sky of the past, against the background of promise, prophecy, type and symbol, that men may recognize in Him the fulfilment of the voice of the past in the actuality of the present. This accounts for the fact that this Gospel is saturated with the Old Testament, there being about fifty-three citations, and about seventy-six allusions, about one hundred and thirty references in all.

Tradition is unanimous that Matthew wrote his Gospel for the Jews, and although it was not the first of the Four to be written, it is placed first because of its relation to the Old Testament.

CHART 122

SUMMARY OUTLINE OF MATTHEW'S GOSPEL			
JESUS THE MESSIANIC KING			
I	II	III	IV
The Coming of the Messiah and His Preparation for Ministry	The Ministry of the Messiah in Word and Deed	The Messiah's Instruction of the Apostles in view of the Cross	The Final Events of the Messiah's Earthly Ministry
i. 1–iv. 11	iv. 12–xvii. 21	xvii. 22–xx. 34	xxi. 1–xxviii. 20

See the author's *A Guide to the Gospels*, pp. 317-324

Mark. This Gospel is characterized by rapidity of action, as is indicated by the occurrence, over forty times, of the word *eutheōs* or *euthus*, translated straightway, immediately, forthwith, and anon. The Record conveys a sense of urgency, immediacy and power. Mark relates incident and action rather than teaching. There is here no genealogy; and the writer has the present rather than the past in mind. He dispenses with introduction and explanation and plunges at once into the narrative. The first chapter tells of the ministry of the Baptist, the Baptism of Jesus, the Temptation, the opening of Messiah's ministry, the calling of disciples, three miracles, the Lord's devotions, and of the many seeking Him.

This Record is the rapid story of a victorious campaign from the Baptism to the Ascension. There is here almost entire absence of discourses, because the writer would present the Messiah as the Worker rather than as the Teacher. The Gospel appears to have the Roman in mind, the typical man of the world, the man of power. The closing word of the Record characterizes the whole, 'the Lord *working* with them' (xvi. 20). Mark's connection with Peter as his *interpreter* is well established, and it was in this relation that he composed his Gospel from the oral teaching of his master who was a man of action rather than of contemplation. This, then, is the Gospel of the Lowly Servant, the Redeeming Worker.

It is impressive that the Messiah is presented first of all as Sovereign and Servant, and that the portrait of the Servant comes first, for as the Incarnate One it is His service that leads to His sovereignty; He stooped to conquer; His deeds are the ground of His demands.

CHART 123

SUMMARY OUTLINE OF MARK'S GOSPEL			
JESUS THE DIVINE SERVANT			
I	II	III	IV
OPENING EVENTS	GALILEAN MINISTRY	PERAEAN MINISTRY	CLOSING EVENTS
i. 1–13	i. 14–ix. 50	x. 1–52	xi. 1–xvi. 20

See the author's *A Guide to the Gospels*, pp. 224-234

Luke. Following the official views of the Messiah in Matthew and Mark come the personal views in Luke and John, and the first of these is of the Ideal Man. This is the Gospel of the Humanity of Jesus. The writer presents the Messiah, not as Sovereign or Servant—though He rules and toils—but as our Fellow and Friend. There is evidence of this at the beginning, where His genealogy is traced back to Adam the father of the race. Luke emphasises the universality of the Gospel, and has much to say about *sinners* and the *Saviour*. The Record overflows with *sympathy*, and is pre-eminently the Gospel of *forgiveness*. Much is said about *prayer* because that is a necessity, and a natural function of man. *Women* and *children* figure largely in this Gospel of Christ's humanity. *Miracles* peculiar to Luke reflect the compassion of Jesus: the widow's son raised; a woman's infirmity cured; ten lepers healed, and other acts of mercy. Also the *parables* peculiar to this Gospel are in keeping with the presentation of Jesus' humanity: for example, the Two Debtors; the Good Samaritan; the Friend at Midnight; the Great Supper; the Prodigal Son, and fourteen other parables.

The author of this Gospel was a Greek, and had the Greeks specially in mind as its dedication to a Greek shows (i. 3). The opening of Christ's ministry at Nazareth strikes the key-note of the Record: 'The Spirit of the Lord is upon Me, because He has anointed Me to preach good tidings to the poor; He hath sent me to proclaim release to the captives, and recovering of sight to the blind, to set at liberty them that are bruised, to proclaim the acceptable year of the Lord' (iv. 18, 19). Renan regarded this Gospel to be 'the most beautiful book in the world'.

CHART 124

SUMMARY OUTLINE OF LUKE'S GOSPEL			
JESUS THE SON OF MAN			
I	II	III	IV
HIS ADVENT	HIS PREPARATION	HIS MINISTRY	HIS TRIUMPH
i. 1–ii. 52	iii. 1–iv. 13	iv. 14–xix. 27	xix. 28–xxiv. 53

See the author's *A Guide to the Gospels*, pp. 382-389

John. This Gospel differs greatly from what are called the Synoptic Records, with a difference which is not contradictory but complementary. The writer has clearly defined his design in these profound words: 'Many other signs therefore did Jesus in the presence of the disciples, which are not written in this book; but these are written that ye may believe that Jesus is the Christ, the Son of God; and that believing ye may have life in His name' (xx. 30, 31). John's selection from the abundant material at his disposal was made with a twofold object in view, namely, to create a particular conviction, and to precipitate a particular experience. The conviction is, 'that ye may believe', and the experience is, 'that ye may have life in His name'. The object of the Gospel is, therefore, to show the Christhood and Godhead of Jesus, by presenting irrefutable evidence, in order to create faith in the hearts of men, with a clear view to their having eternal life.

The thought, though not the basic facts, of the Fourth Gospel is strikingly different from the thought of the Synoptics. They embody the gospel of the infant church, but this one embodies the Gospel of its maturity. 'No writing', says Westcott, 'combines greater simplicity with more profound depths'. Questions of authorship, date, style, language, and so forth, leave the spiritual value of this Writing unaffected. Its teaching could not have been conceived by the mind of man, but bears unmistakable evidence of being a divine revelation. Its vocabulary is limited, but its dominating words emerge from the realm of the unseen and eternal—Father, Word, Life, Light, Truth, Glory, Love, and a score more—and they are not abstractions, but centre in a Person. Much significance attaches alike to words which are peculiar to this Gospel—over eighty—and to those which are not used, such as power, parable, faith, wisdom, gospel, and others.

The presentation of Christ as the *Ego* is noteworthy: I am the Bread of Life; I am the Light of the world; I am the Good Shepherd; I am the Vine; I am the Resurrection; I am the Life; I am the Way; I am the Truth; 'before Abraham was, I AM'. The revelation of the Holy Spirit in this Gospel points on to Pentecost and the future Church, and this, together with striking

omissions—the Birth, Baptism, Temptation, Transfigur:
Institution of the Supper, Agony in the Garden, and the Ascer
—indicate the standpoint and purpose of the writer.

This Gospel will continue to be a subject of controversy, but
it will ever remain the Holy of Holies in the New Testament.
It is 'the golden sunset of the age of inspiration, and sheds its
lustre into the second and all succeeding centuries of the Church'
(Schaff).

The relation to one another of three ideas constitutes the plan
of this Gospel. These ideas may be summarized in the words
revelation, rejection, reception, and all three appear in every part
of the Record.

First, there is a divine *revelation,* and then it is shown that this
revelation must have one or other of two issues in the hearts of
men: either they *reject* it, or they *receive* it; either they disbelieve,
or they believe; unbelief or faith must result from the revelation
made known. John selects no material which does not serve
to exhibit this truth (see the writer's *A Guide to the Gospels*
pp. 407-8, 461-466). The outline of the Gospel is as follows:

CHART 125

SUMMARY OUTLINE OF JOHN'S GOSPEL

JESUS THE SON OF GOD

Prologue	A	B	C	D	E	Epilogue
Revelation of the WORD, and its inevitable consequences of Faith and Unbelief	First Manifestations of the WORD, and the beginnings of Faith and Unbelief	Development of Unbelief in Israel	Development of Faith in the Disciples	Consummation of Unbelief in Israel	Consummation of Faith in the Disciples	Manifestation of the WORD for the Correction of Unbelief and the Confirmation of Faith
i. 1-18	i. 19-iv. 54	v-xii	xiii-xvii	xviii-xix	xx	xxi

See the author's *A Guide to the Gospels*, pp. 461-466

THE WORLD AND THE MESSIAH

In the consideration of this subject there are two matters which claim our attention:

(A) The World into which the Messiah came, and

(B) The Messiah who came into the World.

(A) The World into which the Messiah came

'When the fulness of the time was come'.

While it is true that Christianity originated from above, in the will of God to redeem a fallen race, it is also true that conditions in the world made such a revelation possible. For fructification all seed must have suitable soil, and if two thousand years ago conditions in the world had been inimical to such a revelation as the Christian one, this present dispensation could not have originated at that time. This is what is meant by 'when the fulness of the time was come'. The statement in Galatians iv. 4, 5, certainly refers to a preparation by Judaism for Christianity; it cannot however be limited to this first interpretation but must be understood, as other passages show, to embrace all peoples and circumstances which, either negatively or positively, politically, morally, intellectually, or religiously made possible and necessary the revelation of the New Covenant. (See pp. 74-76).

Failure, in different ways, characterized both Judaism and heathenism at the time that Christ came. The outstanding elements in *Judaism* were formalism, represented by the Pharisees; scepticism, represented by the Sadducees; and mysticism, represented by the Essenes. Yet, in the history of the Hebrew people was alone to be found the true religion, growing through all stages of progress unto its consummation in the Messiah.

In *Heathenism* superstition and infidelity, polytheism and pantheism, stoicism and Platonism had all failed, leaving the world in a state of profound dissatisfaction and of undefined longing.

These features represent the *negative* preparation of Judaism and Heathenism for the advent of the Messiah; but there was a *positive* preparation also.   Augustus Neander has said that the three great historical nations contributed, each in its own peculiar way, to the preparation for the planting of Christianity—the Jews on the side of the religious element; the Greeks on the side of science and art; and the Romans, as masters of the world, on the side of the political element.   Thus it was that both revealed and natural religion cast up a highway for the advent of the Messiah, and the establishment of Christianity.

Before the Bread of Life could be given the world had to become very hungry, and before the Water of Life could be supplied mankind had to become very thirsty; but 'when the fulness of the time was come' there came the Bread and the Water.

The failure of all human resources prepared the world for an entirely new departure in human history.

Schaff has well said that in Judaism the true religion was prepared for man, and in Heathenism man was prepared for the true religion; and that *Jerusalem*, the holy city, *Athens*, the city of culture, and *Rome*, the city of power, stand for the three factors in that preparatory history which ended in the birth of Christianity.

In Judaism, Abraham, Moses, David, Isaiah and Jeremiah anticipated the Messiah; and in Heathenism, Melchisedec, Jethro, Rahab, Ruth and Job did the same.

By the dispersion of the *Jews* the seeds of the knowledge of the true God and the Messianic hope were sown in the field of the idolatrous world.   The *Greeks* furnished the language into which the Hebrew Scriptures were translated two centuries before Christ, thus giving the world access to them.   And the *Romans* by their colossal Empire, stretching from the Atlantic to the Euphrates, and by their vast highways, made possible the work of the Christian missionaries in the new age soon to dawn.   It is not a little significant then that the inscription on the Cross was in Hebrew, and Greek, and Latin. (See pp. 76-81).

This, then, is the world into which the Messiah came; and now attention must be given to:

THE MESSIAH IN THE LAND

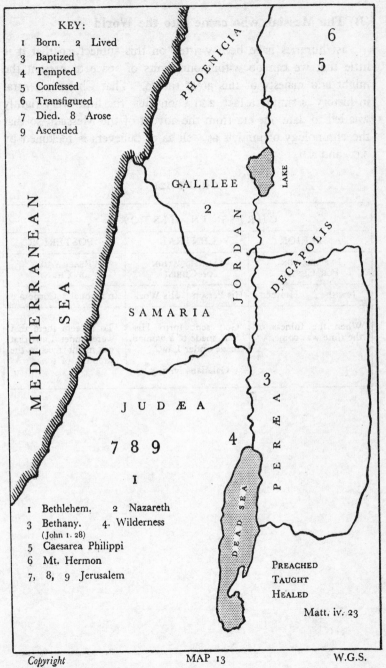

KEY:

1 Born. 2 Lived
3 Baptized
4 Tempted
5 Confessed
6 Transfigured
7 Died. 8 Arose
9 Ascended

PHOENICIA

GALILEE

LAKE

JORDAN

DECAPOLIS

MEDITERRANEAN SEA

SAMARIA

JUDÆA

PERÆA

DEAD SEA

1 Bethlehem. 2 Nazareth
3 Bethany. 4. Wilderness
(John 1. 28)
5 Caesarea Philippi
6 Mt. Hermon
7, 8, 9 Jerusalem

PREACHED
TAUGHT
HEALED

Matt. iv. 23

Copyright　　　　MAP 13　　　　W.G.S.

(B) The Messiah who came into the World

Vast libraries have been written on this subject, so that it is little that we can do within our limits of space to present the might and majesty of this great theme. That Christ is central in history is simply a fact, and Dionysius 'the little' very rightly was led to date our era from the advent of the Messiah, so that the chronology of infidels as well as of believers is reckoned by B.C., and A.D.

CHART 126

CHRIST IN HISTORY					
ANTERIOR		CENTRAL		POSTERIOR	
PREPARATION FOR CHRIST		MANIFESTATION OF CHRIST		REALISATION OF CHRIST	
Jewish	Heathen	His Person	His Work	Individual	Corporate
'When the fulness of the time was come.'		'God sent forth His Son, made of a woman, made under Law.' Galatians iv. 4, 5		'To redeem them that were under Law, that we might receive the adoption of sons.'	

THE UNFOLDING DRAMA OF REDEMPTION

ACT II

SCENE 1

THE INTRODUCTION OF
CHRISTIANITY INTO THE WORLD
BY JESUS THE MESSIAH

THE GOSPELS
THE OLD AND NEW TESTAMENTS

THE FOUNDER AND FOUNDATIONS
OF CHRISTIANITY

THE PERSON OF CHRIST

THE MINISTRY OF CHRIST

THE GOSPELS

The authentic Christian sources for Scene I of Act II—*The Introduction of Christianity into the World by Jesus the Messiah* —are chiefly what we call the Gospels, *Matthew, Mark, Luke* and *John,* but the remainder of the New Testament must also be included, and also the Old Testament Scriptures. This is virtually to say that the whole Bible is about the Redeemer, but the Gospels are distinct in that they are the historical records of the earthly life and ministry of Jesus the Messiah. The most important non-canonical source is Josephus the Jewish historian (A.D. 38-100). References to Christ by heathen writers are very few.

The Old Testament references to Christ, particular and general, issue in His manifestation, and the references to Him from the *Acts* to the *Revelation* emerge from His manifestation; so that what now demand our attention are the *Gospels,* the historical sources. We shall divide the subject into two parts: *The Founder of Christianity,* which will relate to *His Person*; and *The Foundations of Christianity,* which will relate to *His Ministry.* Study carefully the following Chart before continuing to read.

CHART 127

THE UNFOLDING DRAMA OF REDEMPTION			
ACT II		SCENE 1	
THE INTRODUCTION OF CHRISTIANITY INTO THE WORLD BY JESUS THE MESSIAH			
The Founder of Christianity.		The Person of Christ	
HIS REAL HUMANITY	HIS TRUE DIVINITY	HIS PERFECT UNITY	
His Relation to the Human Race	His Relation to the Eternal God	His Relation to the Race and God	

The Foundations of Christianity.		The Ministry of Christ	
HIS TEACHING		HIS WORK	
Features of it	Substance of it	The Attesting Deeds	The Atoning Deed
Manifold	The Great Realities	The Miracles	THE CROSS
Sermon on the Mount	Upper Room Discourse	Wonders. Signs, Powers	**Death** Providing for the Past. Guilt of Sin Removed Romans i-v
The Beginning	The End	In the Cosmic Realm	
Matthew v-vii	John xiii-xvii	In the Human Realm	**Resurrection** Providing for the Future. Power of Sin Broken Romans vi-viii
The Law	The Gospel		
Confirmation of the Past	Intimation of the Future	In the Spirit Realm	

ACT II—SCENE 1

The Introduction of Christianity into the World by Jesus the Messiah

THE OLD AND NEW TESTAMENTS

There are several statements in the New Testament which intimate that there is a connection between ACTS I and II of the Drama and which indicate what that connection is. Examples of these are:

Mark i. 15 - -	'*The time is fulfilled,* and the kingdom of God is at hand.'
I Cor. i. 21 - - -	'After that in the wisdom of God *the world by wisdom knew not God*, it pleased God by the foolishness of preaching to save them that believe.'
Acts xiv. 16 -	'God in times past suffered all nations to walk in their own ways.'
Acts xvii. 26-30 -	'*God hath made of one blood all nations of men* for to dwell on the face of the earth, and *hath determined the times before appointed, and the bounds of their habitation* (Deut. xxxii. 8; Job xii. 23); that they should seek the Lord, if haply they might feel after Him, and find Him, though He be not far from every one of us; for in Him we live, and move, and have our being; *as certain of your own poets have said. "For we are also His offspring"* ... The times of this ignorance God winked at; but now commandeth all men everywhere to repent.'
Gal. iv. 4, 5 -	'*When the fulness of the time was come,* God sent forth His Son, made of a woman, made under Law, to redeem them that were under Law, that we might receive the adoption of sons.'

For an understanding of the world before and after the advent of Christ these passages are momentous and vital.

The Two Testaments, viewed as wholes, are intimately related, and the relation reveals that 'through the ages one increasing purpose runs'. In Genesis to Deuteronomy is the basic *revelation* of the world-religion; in Joshua to Esther is a slow *preparation* for it; in Job to Canticles is a yearning *aspiration* after it; in Isaiah to Malachi is a growing *expectation* of it; in Matthew to John is a Divine *manifestation* of it; in Acts to Jude is a widespread *realization of it*; and in the Book of the Revelation is the perfect *consummation of it*. What are seen as *origins* in Genesis, appear as *processes* in Exodus to Jude, and as *issues* in the Revelation.

The foreshadowing in the Old Testament is fulfilment in the New. The promise of the Old, is performance in the New. The redemption which in the Old is anticipated, is in the New accomplished. All the commencements lead to consummations.

Christ the Redeemer is the sum and substance of both Testaments (Heb. x. 7), and it is He who gives connection and unity to all the Scriptures. In the Old Testament is the preparation for Him; in the Gospels, the manifestation of Him; and in Acts to Revelation, the realization of Him.

I. THE FOUNDER OF CHRISTIANITY

THE PERSON OF CHRIST

Christ was the fulfilment of the past and the promise of the future. In Him one dispensation was consummated and another commenced. In Him Judaism ended and Christianity began. By His advent the Law gave way to the Gospel. One day ended and a new day began.

Christ is the Key to the Scriptures. The Old Covenant Writings reveal Him in prophecy; the Evangelical Records reveal Him in history; and the Apostolical Scriptures reveal Him in experience.

The least that can be said about Christ is that He is the most extraordinary person in all history. This fact has been recognized by men of all creeds and of no creed, by men of every kind of accomplishment, of all nations, and tongues, and climes, and for nearly two thousand years.

How, then, is the uniqueness of Christ to be accounted for? The answer is, by His Person and His Work as these are made known in the authentic Records. It will be well then to have before us a reference outline of the life of the Messiah.

CHART 128

THE LIFE OF THE MESSIAH.

	Preparation			Ministration					Consummation
	I			**II**					**III**
	1	2	3	4 (Galilean)			5	6	7
	The 30 Years	Opening Events	Judaean	First Period	Second Period	Third Period	Later Judaean and Peraean	Closing Events	The 40 Days
		Mark i. 1-13		i. 14-iii. 6	iii. 7-vii. 23	vii. 24-ix. 50	x. 1-52	xi. 1-xv. 47	xvi. 1-20
Matthew i. 1-ii. 23		iii. 1-iv. 11		iv. 12-xii. 14	xii. 15-xv. 20	xv. 21-xviii. 35	xix. 1-xx. 34	xxi. 1-xxvii. 66	xxviii. 1-20
Luke i. 1-ii. 52		iii. 1-iv. 13		iv. 14-vi. 11	vi. 12-ix. 17	ix. 18-50	ix. 51-xix. 28	xix. 29-xxiii. 56	xxiv. 1-53
John i. 1-18		i. 19-ii. 12	ii. 13-iv. 42	iv. 43-v. 47	vi. 1-71	vii. 1-9	vii. 10-xii. 11	xii. 12-xix. 42	xx. 1-xxi. 25

Reference Outline

As this is not an apologetic work we assume the accuracy, reliability and authority of the Gospels. These Pamphlets are of more value than all the Classics which have ever been written, for they are the Sources of our knowledge of the Redeemer of the world.

The three things of vital importance in the Person of Christ are His Humanity, His Divinity, and the Unity of His Person. His Humanity relates Him to the human race; His Divinity relates Him to the Eternal God; and the Unity of His Person relates Him to both God and Man. (Chart 127—p. 118).

1. The Real Humanity of Christ

Though in the Gospels this is obvious, yet it should be considered cautiously and reverently, for in all history we have no standard of comparison. It would be equally easy to affirm either too little, or too much, of the humanity of Jesus; but there are several things which with confidence can be affirmed.[1]

(i) Christ's Humanity was Real and not Feigned

Throughout the Christian era there have been those who have believed that the humanity of Jesus was not real, but was only in semblance; and this view can be traced to one or other of three sources: to the idea that a deeper reverence is paid to His Divinity by denying His humanity; or to the idea that the human body is radically and incurably evil in itself; or to the idea that it is impossible to conceive of humanity and divinity in one personality.

[1] See the author's *The New Testament Unfolded*

But for the truth about Christ's humanity we should not go to human speculation but to the Gospels, in which it is everywhere assumed and declared. In pursuance of this truth let us consider certain facts.

(a) CHRIST'S PHYSICAL LIFE

He was born into the world; he was a helpless babe, dependant on His mother; He was subject to the authority of a home; He grew in stature; He hungered and ate; He thirsted and drank; He worked and wearied; He felt the need of rest and sleep, and His body suffered pain and privation. He learned a trade and worked at it for eighteen years. He made frequent reference to His body and its parts, and His body was endowed with all human instincts. He suffered flogging, and at last He died.

(b) CHRIST'S MORAL LIFE

He had an unswerving sense of duty; a penetrating consciousness of right and wrong which led Him to feel the pressure of temptation, and to resist it. He recognised and accepted opportunity and responsibility. He was loyal to the social and political conditions of His time which it was no part of His mission directly to antagonize—as, for example, the practice of slavery, and Rome's rule of the Jews in Palestine.

Some of the moral ingredients in the character of Jesus were love of God and man, self-control, self-denial, self-respect, transparent sincerity, courage, calmness, patience, prudence, humility, endurance and goodness.

(c) CHRIST'S EMOTIONAL LIFE

He entered fully into experiences of joy and sorrow. He exhibited wonder and surprise. He was no stranger to love and anger, nor to indignation and compassion. He sought sympathy, and felt the pain of disappointment. More than once He wept. His gratitude and zeal were unmistakable, nor must we overlook His sense of humour.

(d) CHRIST'S INTELLECTUAL LIFE

We are told that He grew in wisdom, and what He knew as man He must have learned. He went to school, as did every

Jewish boy, and His mind developed as our minds do. At no time did He know everything. As man He was not omniscient, for omniscience is not a human attribute. He asked questions to elicit information, and acted on information which reached him.

'When Jesus heard of (the death of John the Baptist) He departed thence by ship into a desert place apart.' (Matt. xiv. 13.).

'Jesus heard that they (the Pharisees) had cast out the (man who had been born blind), and when He had found him (apparently after searching for him) He said to him . . .' (Jo. ix. 35).

'When Jesus heard (that Lazarus was dead) He abode two days still in the place where He was.' 'Where have ye laid him (Lazarus)?' (Jo. xi. 6, 34).

'How many loaves have ye?' (Mk. vi. 38).

'Who touched my clothes?' (Mk. v. 30).

He asked the name of the demented Gadarene. He asked a father how long his son had been subject to fits. He went to a fig tree to see if it had any figs on it. He plainly stated that He did not know the hour of an event to come (Mark xiii. 32).

Christ's sense of wonder and surprise indicated that His mental life was conditioned. But it must be affirmed that His mind was not subject to error, for it was unclouded by sin.

The existence of all-knowledge and limited knowledge in one and the same person is part of the mystery of the incarnation, of the Divine and the human in one personality. No theory that we can frame can do justice to all the facts. 'Without His perfect knowledge of Divine things, He could not have been to us the manifestation of God; and without the mental experience involved in those conditions of acquiring knowledge . . . we should not have had among us One who was in all points tried as we are. There would have been something wanting in the perfection of His humanity. But it is for us to see and keep clear and distinct in our minds each fact of His Personality' (Nolloth).

Unless one's judgment is sadly warped he cannot read what Jesus said, as recorded in the Gospels, without being deeply impressed by its simplicity and profoundness, its range and qualities. His thinking was intuitive rather than discursive; concrete rather than abstract; positive rather than negative; and creative rather than critical. No utterances of man have ever been so bracing as those of Jesus, for they are dateless infallible and authoritative.

(e) CHRIST'S SOCIAL LIFE

Jesus was both distant and accessible. He lived a social life. He was a member of a family, having a mother, brothers and sisters. He fitted into the social life of His time. He attended a wedding feast, and accepted invitations to dinner. He had special friends such as Martha, Mary, and Lazarus. He needed and wanted companionship, and found it in the company of His apostles and of those women who ministered to His temporal needs. With His latest breath He made provision for the temporal care of His mother.

(f) CHRIST'S RELIGIOUS LIFE

This is a profound and difficult subject to expound, but the essence of it consists in His relation as man to God. He revealed a deep sense of His dependence on God His Father, and apart from God He had no thoughts, desires, or will. This sense of dependence was repeatedly expressed. 'The Son can do nothing of Himself'. 'The Father abiding in me doeth the works'.

An outstanding expression of Jesus' religious life was *His habit of prayer*, which is prominently recorded in Luke's and John's Gospels. His life was a life of prayer; He taught much on prayer; and we have on record some of His prayers, notably John xvii.

Another evidence of His religious life was His absorbing love for His Father, a love which was the atmosphere in which all His actions were performed, and all His feelings felt.

The Records, then, make it abundantly clear that Christ's humanity was real and not feigned.

But there is a second fact which must be considered, namely that

(ii) Christ's Humanity was Perfect and not Faulty

The first proposition is true of all men—that our humanity is real and not feigned, but this proposition is true only of Jesus. The character portrayed in the Gospels could not have been created by any human mind, and so it must be a photo of facts.

In all the realm of biography the character of Christ stands apart and alone. Study the characters of Shakespeare, Scott,

Dickens, Thackeray, George Eliot, and of all others who have portrayed character, and it is easy to see the presence of qualities which should not be there, and the absence of qualities which should be there, but neither of these characteristics was true of Jesus.

No one can read the story which is recorded in the Gospels without observing that

(a) JESUS HAD NO CONSCIOUSNESS OF SIN

The sinlessness of Jesus relates, not to His Deity—which would be quite impossible—but to His humanity.

It would be nonsense to talk about a sinless God, but it is wonderful to be able to think and speak of a sinless man. Sinlessness does not necessarily carry with it divinity, because some day all believers will be sinless; but in the case of Jesus sinlessness was not something to which He attained—as it will be in our case—but something which was grounded in His Deity. In human nature, as God intended it to be, no provision was made for sin, and it is no proper part of it. What we see in ourselves and all men is not ideal but distorted human nature; but what we see in the sinless Christ is human nature as God intended it to be.

Jesus' sinlessness did not consist merely in the entire absence of evil, but also in the presence of all good; and thus His sinlessness was both negative and positive.

'No miracle of Christ equals the miracle of His sinless life. To be holy in all thought and feeling; never to fail in duty to others, never to transgress the law of perfect love to God or man, never to exceed or to come short—this is a condition outstripping the power of imagination and almost of belief. Here is a casement opening on a Divine world.' (H. R. Mackintosh).

It is simply a fact that Jesus had no consciousness of sin. Sensibilities which characterize the best of men were entirely wanting in Him. He never apologized for anything. He never said He was sorry for anything He had done. He never withdrew anything He had said, nor modified it. He never admitted having made a mistake. He never showed any sign of regret, or of remorse for misused or lost opportunity. He never exhibited any consciousness of guilt. He never acknowledged sin in Himself, and so never asked for pardon. He never felt the pain of an accusing conscience. He never showed any dread of the penal future. He never manifested any trace of healed scars, nor memories of defeat.

In all this, the difference between Him and us is not one of degree, but of type. His was 'the one quite unspotted life that has been lived within our sinful race.' Had He not been sinless, to have made—as He did—such a claim for Himself, would of itself have been sin. This sinless state of His had been foretold by Gabriel to Mary, and was affirmed by those who knew Him most intimately (Luke i. 35. Acts iii. 14. Rom. viii. 3. 2 Cor. v. 21. Heb. iv. 15; vii. 26. 1 Peter i. 19; ii. 23. 1 John iii. 5). It is perfectly clear that the piety of Jesus was impenitent and unrepentant.

(b) JESUS PERFECTLY COMBINED IN HIMSELF QUALITIES WHICH ARE COMMONLY REGARDED AS INCOMPATIBLES.

Solemnity and Joyfulness

On the last journey to Jerusalem He was so solemn that His disciples were afraid (Mk. x. 32), yet, in His last discourse, in the upper room, He repeatedly spoke of His joy.

Aloofness and Sociability

'Rising up a great while before day, He went out and departed into a solitary place' (Mk. i. 35). 'Jesus was called to the marriage' (John ii. 1-10).

Dignity and Humility

Evidence of dignity is illustrated by His composed silence in the presence of Pilate; yet, of Himself He said: 'I am meek and lowly in heart.'

Profoundness and Simplicity

This is abundantly illustrated by the parables which Jesus spoke. These are so simple that any child will be attracted to them, and will understand them; and yet they are so profound that they baffle every attempt to discover their final meaning. As long as language lasts these incomparable parables will draw and hold and thrill the serious mind:

the Sower; the Talents; the Pounds; the Good Samaritan; the Prodigal Son and the Elder Brother; the Publican and the Pharisee; the Good Shepherd; the Friend at Midnight; the Lost Sheep; the Two Builders; the Leaven in the Meal; the Wheat and the Tares; the Unfinished Tower; the Unwaged War; the Rich Fool; the Ten Virgins; and two score more.

Severity and Tenderness

He who lashed the Pharisees with His words (Matt. xxiii) said to the poor adulteress, 'Neither do I condemn thee' (John viii). He who said to Peter, 'Get thee behind me Satan' (Matt. xvi. 23), said from the Cross to the Apostle John, 'Behold thy mother' (John xix. 27), committing to the Apostle His own mother.

Energy and Restfulness

The unceasing activity of Jesus is astonishing. From dawn to night-fall He travelled, and taught, and performed works of mercy, and yet there is no evidence that He was ever flustered or irritated, though, being human, He did tire. His experience was one of unbroken peace within; the peace which at last He bequeathed to all His followers (John xiv. 27).

Haste and Leisureliness

One cannot read the story of Jesus without sensing a certain urgency in His activities, especially towards the close of His life, and yet throughout there is the atmosphere of leisureliness. He was never so busy as not to have time for those who needed Him.

The character of Jesus was held in perfect equilibrium. He had no strong points because He had no weak ones. Everyone else must be conscious of weaknesses and defects, of insufficiencies and excesses, but Jesus had no such consciousness because His character was complete. In the whole range of world-biography, actual and fictitious, no such character has ever been portrayed, and for the simple reason that no such character has ever existed. Christ alone, Who is so like us in some respects, is profoundly unlike us; He is alone and apart in a category of His own.

Not only is it true that 'never man spake like this man', but more, never man was like this man. Prudent in avoiding danger, yet courageous in facing it. Patient under wrong, yet indignant at injustice. Meek and lowly, yet self-assertive. He respected authority, precedent, and the past, yet He was bound by none of these things. A dreamer of dreams, yet He was intensely practical. Tolerant of publicans and sinners, yet He was intolerant of sin. Though He longed for sympathy, yet He took no pains to soften the truth though it cost Him the loss of followers. He who had an eye for details saw the universal reign of God at hand.

These contrasts existed as facts in the character of Jesus, yet they do not impress us as contradictions.

His character was perfect in unity, symmetry, and proportion. Bushnell has well said that it is 'never modified, even by a shade of rectification. It is one and the same throughout. He makes no improvements, prunes no extravagances, returns from no eccentricities. The balance of His character is never disturbed or readjusted, and the astonishing assumption on which it is based is never shaken even by a suspicion that He falters in it.'

His perfect goodness is witnessed to by His Father, His friends, His foes, and by Himself.

When on one occasion He was addressed as 'good Master', and replied 'Why callest thou me good? there is none good but One, that is God', He was not denying that He was good, but, observing that the speaker used this word in an unreal and conventional manner, He expressed His disapproval.

(c) Jesus' self-consciousness was unique

This is true of *the consciousness He had of His relation to God*. How profoundly significant and mysterious are such statements as: 'I and My Father are one'; 'I came forth from the Father'; '*We* will come unto him, and make *our* abode with him'; 'Ye are from beneath, I am from above'; 'No man cometh to the Father but by me.'

It is true also of *the consciousness He had of His distinction from men*.

He never prayed with others, neither did He include Himself in the prayer He taught. 'When ye pray, say—forgive us our debts'. He could not make that request on His own account, for He had no debts, and never did He stand in need of forgiveness.

He distinguished between His own, and His disciples' relation to God. This is emphatic in His words, 'My Father, and your Father; my God and your God' (John xx. 17). Why did He not say, *our* Father, and *our* God? All believers are God's sons, but Jesus Christ is *The Son* uniquely and alone.

Now this fact and truth of Christ's real and perfect humanity is vital for Christian faith. This will become evident as we consider that *he who believes in His humanity believes that God has come right down to us historically.* This means that 'He who was rich became poor'; that in Jesus God took 'the form of a bondslave; was made in the likeness of men, and was found in fashion as a man'. It means that the Incarnation was God's partaking of flesh and blood, and so, that His assumption of human nature, sin apart, was entirely real.

Again, *he who believes in Christ's humanity believes in the possibility and actuality of Atonement.* If Christ was not true and perfect man, reconciliation with God is impossible, and the hope of forgiveness is a delusion. 'Only He can act with God for man who speaks from man's side' (H. R. Mackintosh). Only a man, and such a man as Jesus was, can deliver men from the guilt and power of sin.

And, again, *he who believes in Christ's humanity believes that, apart from sin, Christ is one of us, and one with us*; 'touched with a feeling of our infirmities; in all points tempted like as we are'; and so He is 'able to succour them that are tempted'. For, be it affirmed, when Christ ascended again to heaven, He did not throw off His humanity, but took it with Him, and is to-day a Man at God's right hand.

2. THE TRUE DIVINITY OF CHRIST
(Chart 127)

Christ's humanity reveals His relation to the human race, and His Divinity reveals His relation to the eternal God. Fundamentally the humanity and the Divinity of Christ are inseparable, yet the evidence for each is quite distinct. The evidence for His Divinity may be considered along three lines, the Old Testament anticipation of it; the Apostolic proclamation of it; and Christ's own declaration of it.

(i) THE OLD TESTAMENT ANTICIPATION OF CHRIST'S DIVINITY

This is widespread and manifold, and, indeed, is in the warp and woof of the Old Testament Writings.

There are *hints of a plurality of Persons in the Godhead.* 'God said, "Let *us* make man in *our* image, after *our* likeness".' 'The Lord God said, "Behold, the man is become as one of *us*, to know good and evil".' 'The Lord said, "Go to, let *us* go down and confuse their language".' (Gen. i. 26; iii. 22; xi. 7). The same thing is observable in the threefold priestly blessing in Num. vi. 23-26. 'The LORD bless thee and keep thee. The LORD make His face to shine upon thee, and be gracious unto thee. The LORD lift up His countenance upon thee, and give thee peace'. Also in the Psalter there is frequently a threefold rhythm of praise or prayer, as for example, in Psalm xcvi. 1, 2, 7, 8. 'Sing unto the LORD,' three times, and 'Give unto the LORD', three times.

Again, in Isaiah vi. 3 is the threefold, 'Holy, holy, holy is the LORD of hosts.'

Then there is *the record of Theophanies in the Old Testament.* More than fifty times we read of 'The Angel of the LORD' appearing, speaking and acting; and the contexts indicate that not man, nor mere angel is referred to, but a Divine Person.

Jacob, after he had wrestled with this Angel said, 'I have seen God face to face' (Gen. xxxii. 24-32. Hos. xii. 4). This Angel of the LORD spake to Jacob in a dream and said, 'I am the God of Bethel, where thou anointedst the pillar' (Gen. xxxi. 11, 13).

This Angel appeared to Moses in the burning bush, and said, 'I am the God of Abraham, the God of Isaac, and the God of Jacob' (Exod. iii). The Angel, therefore, was a Divine Person, anticipating the incarnation.

Then there is *the witness of Messianic prophecy.*

There will be a 'seed of the woman' who shall bruise the serpent's head, and that 'seed' will be in the line of Abraham (Gen. iii. 15; xxii. 18).

One called 'Shiloh', 'Star', and 'Sceptre' is to arise and exercise regal and legislative authority (Gen. xlix. 10. Num. xxiv. 17). A Prophet like, but greater than, Moses would come (Deut. xviii. 18, 19). A King will arise Who will establish the throne of David 'for ever', and this King is called the Lord's anointed 'Son' (2 Sam. vii. 16. Psalm ii).

Descriptions of this Royal Messiah and of His Kingdom are given in many Psalms (e.g., xlv; lxxii; cx).

This Messiah will be a Priest as well as a King, and though David's son, He will also be his Lord (Ps. cx. Matt. xxii. 41-45). In the Prophets, especially Isaiah, the coming Messiah will be both a sufferer and a sovereign (Isa. liii. Jer. xxiii. 5, 6). He is called, 'Wonderful, Counsellor, the Mighty God, the Everlasting Father, the Prince of Peace' (Isa. ix. 6).

In Daniel, Micah, Haggai, Zechariah and Malachi, Messiah's Divine Person and everlasting Kingdom are predicted.

Here, then, are numerous converging and consentient lines of prophecy which declare that One would come Who, though human, would be more than human; Who, indeed, would be Divine, God manifest in the flesh.

All this is more than astonishing when we remember that the Jews were strict monotheists, believers in One God only. Their creed was, and is, 'The LORD our God is one LORD' (Deut. vi. 4). This statement says more than appears on the surface. The word 'God' is 'Elohim' (plural), and the word for 'one' does not mean single, or only one, but means a compound unity, one of others. Thus, this ancient formula of the Jewish creed plainly declares that God is One in Essence, but in that Essence there is a plurality of Persons.

The Old Testament, therefore, anticipates the Divinity of Jesus.

(ii) The Apostolic Proclamation of Christ's Divinity

The Old Testament witness to the Divinity of the Messiah is *anticipative*; it looks on to One who will come. But the Apostolic witness to Christ's Person is *affirmative*; it looks back to One who did come.

Nothing is clearer than that the Apostles profoundly believed in the Deity of Christ. Evidence of this is overwhelming and leaves one astonished that this truth could ever have been questioned or doubted.

James represents himself as standing in the same relation to Jesus Christ as to God.

'A servant of God, and of the Lord Jesus Christ'; and he calls Jesus 'the Lord of Glory' (i. 1; ii. 1).

Jude speaks of 'Our only Master and Lord, Jesus Christ'; and he makes distinct reference to the Trinity (4, 20).

Peter, alike in his sermons and Epistles is emphatic about the Divinity of Christ. He says that His name imparts forgiveness of sins to those who believe in Him. 'To Him give all the prophets witness, that through His name whosoever believeth in Him shall receive remission of sins' (Acts x. 43). He calls Jesus 'the Author of Life', and says that 'He is Lord of all', and that there is 'salvation in no one else' (Acts iii. 15; x. 36; iv. 12). He repeatedly affirms that Christ is God. 'In your hearts reverence Christ as Lord'. He calls Him 'the Word of God', and says that 'To Him belong glory and dominion for ever and ever' (1 Ep. iii. 15; i. 23; iv. 11. 2 Ep. iii. 18).

Again, Peter definitely associates Christ with God as the true Objects of knowledge. 'Grace and peace be multiplied unto you through the knowledge of God, and of Jesus our Lord' (2 Ep. i. 2, 8). His power is spoken of as Divine (2 Ep. i. 3); and the Apostle never wearies of uttering the manifold names of Jesus: 'Lord', 'Lord Jesus Christ', 'Lord and Saviour' (2 Ep. i. 1, 2, 14, 16).

These references rise far above any thought that Jesus was only human and plainly affirm His Divine personality.

PAUL. In the Writings of this Apostle is found a great enlargement of the evidence of apostolic belief in the Divinity of Jesus
Christ. He constantly refers to Christ's pre-existent life.

He is 'from heaven' (1 Cor. xv. 47). He who 'was rich became poor'
(2 Cor. viii. 9). He was eternally 'in the form of God' (Phil. ii. 6).
He is called 'God blessed for ever' (Rom. ix. 5); and 'our great God
and Saviour Jesus Christ' (Titus ii. 13).

Perhaps the greatest passage in Paul's Writings on Christ's
Divinity is Col. i. 15-20.

'He is the image of the invisible God, the firstborn of all creation;
for in Him all things were created, in heaven and on earth, visible,
and invisible, whether thrones, or dominions, or principalities, or
authorities; all things were created through Him and for Him; and
He is before all things, and in Him all things consist. And He is the
head of the body the church; Who is the beginning, the firstborn from
the dead, that in all things He might have the pre-eminence. For it
was the good pleasure of the Father that in Him should all the fulness
dwell; and through Him to reconcile all things unto Himself, having
made peace through the blood of His cross; through Him, I say,
whether things upon the earth, or things in the heavens.'

This is a transcendent revelation and affirmation, and it is
marvellous that language can bear the weight of such thought.
Nor must it be overlooked that in the Benediction, perhaps the
most quoted verse in all the Bible, the name of Christ is put,
not only before 'the fellowship of the Holy Spirit', but also before
'the love of God' (2 Cor. xiii. 14).

HEBREWS. Whoever wrote this Epistle, it is true to say that no
book in the New Testament more explicitly asserts the reality of
Christ's Deity. It affirms that He is greater than the great men of
the previous dispensation—Moses, Joshua, Aaron, Melchisedec;
greater also than the God-appointed Institutions of old—the
Law, the Offerings, and the Covenants; and greater than the
unfallen angels (iii-vii; viii-x; i-ii).

He is the Creator of the world, the upholder of the universe,
the radiance of the Father's splendour, the full expression of
God's Being, God's Son. He is worshipped by Angels, is called
God whose Throne is forever, is before and after all things, and
is the origin and crown of all faith. There is no real place for
Christ between humanity and God.

JOHN. Perhaps it is not an exaggeration to say that in the writings of the Apostle John the subject of Christ's Divinity finds its fullest expression.

In the Prologue of His Gospel (i. 1-18) it is emphatically and eloquently declared that Jesus Christ is absolutely God. He is anterior to and independent of all time; uncreated and self-existent. 'In the beginning was the Word'. He is a separate personality in the Godhead, for 'the Word was with God'; and He is Himself God, 'The Word was God'. He is the creator of all things, the Fulness of Life and Light; the Father's Only-begotten Son, and the only true interpreter of God.

The same great affirmations are found in John's Epistles. He speaks of Christ as 'the Word of Life', 'the Eternal Life', and 'the Son of God'. He that has Christ has life, and he that has Him not is dead. He that denies Christ's Deity is a liar; and he that believes that Jesus is the Son of God overcomes the world.

Grace, mercy and peace are jointly from God the Father, and from Jesus Christ the Father's Son.

In the Book of the REVELATION the testimony of the Gospels and the Epistles is continued, and here it shines with dazzling splendour. Christ is the explanation of the past and the significance of the future. He is the Alpha and Omega, the First and the Last, the Beginning and the End. He is 'the Living One', omnipotent and omniscient. He, equally with God, is the Object of worship.

'Every created thing which is in the heaven, and on the earth, and under the earth, and in the sea, and all things that are in them, heard I saying: "Unto Him that sitteth on the throne, and unto the Lamb, be the blessing, and the honour, and the glory, and the dominion for ever and ever".' (v. 13). 'Salvation unto our God who sitteth on the throne, and unto the Lamb' (vii. 10).

'Throughout the Book,' says H. R. Mackintosh, 'the praise of this Divine personality is echoed passionately.' His name is written on the foreheads of the faithful. He is the giver of grace and victory. He is called 'the Word of God'. He is 'King of

kings, and Lord of lords'. (iii. 21; xxii. 21; xix. 13; xix. 16).
Everywhere the transcendence of this Divine Person is declared.

(iii) THE MESSIAH'S OWN DECLARATION OF HIS DIVINITY

The Prophetic anticipation and the Apostolic proclamation of
Christ's Deity meet in His own declaration of it. The Jews
persecuted Jesus, not because He was a good man, but because
He claimed to be Divine. 'He said, "My Father worketh hitherto,
and I work". Therefore the Jews sought the more to kill Him,
because He said that God was His Father, making Himself equal
with God'. (John v. 17, 18; Matt. xxvi. 63 65). The Jews
said to Him: 'For a good work we stone Thee not; but for blasphemy; and because that *Thou, being a man, makest Thyself
God*'. (John x. 33). The Jews said to Pilate: 'We have a law,
and by our law He ought to die, because He made Himself the
Son of God.' (Matt. xxvi. 63-65. John xix. 7).

The consciousness of Christ respecting His rank in the scale
of being is the very heart of Christian truth. Think first of all of

HIS CLAIMS FOR HIMSELF

He claimed to transcend the Mosaic Law.

'Ye have heard that it was said by them of old time . . . but I say
unto you' (Matt. v. 21, 22, 27, 28 *et al*).

He continuously and energetically preached Himself.

'I am the Way, the Truth, and the Life'. 'I am the Light of the
World'. 'I am the Bread of Life.' 'I am the true Vine.' 'I am the
Good Shepherd'. (xiv. 6, viii. 12, vi. 48, xv. 1, x. 11).

He promised that prayer offered in His name will be answered.

'If ye shall ask anything in My name, I will do it'. (xiv. 14).

He declared His pre-existence.

'He that came down from Heaven'. 'The Bread of God is He that
cometh down from heaven'. 'What if ye shall see the Son of Man
ascend up where He was before' (John iii. 14, 13; vi. 33, 42, 50, 51,
62). 'Before Abraham was, I am' (John viii. 58).

He claimed to be the Lord of the realm of death.

'Destroy this temple, and in three days I will raise it up' (John ii. 19). 'The hour is coming, and now is, when the dead shall hear the voice of the Son of God, and they that hear shall live'. 'All that are in the graves shall hear His voice, and shall come forth'. (John v. 25, 28, 29). 'He that believeth in Me, though He were dead, yet shall he live' (John xi. 25).

He invited men to trust in Him as they trusted in God.

'Ye believe in God, believe also in Me' (John xiv. 1).

He said that love of Him was proof that one was a child of God.

'If God were your Father ye would love Me' (John viii. 42).

He affirmed that no one knows the Father but Himself and those to whom He reveals Him (Matt. xi. 27). Of this passage Dr. H. R. Mackintosh says: 'These words (are) the most important for Christology in the New Testament'; and they are 'the climax of Jesus' witness to Himself.'

He accepted the confession of Nathanael and of Peter that He was the Son of God (John i. 49. Matt. xvi. 16).

'Blessed art thou, Simon Bar-Jonah, for flesh and blood hath not revealed it unto thee, but My Father who is in heaven.'

He said that whoever had seen Him had seen the Father.

'He that hath seen Me hath seen the Father. Believest thou not that I am in the Father, and the Father in Me?' (John xiv. 9, 10).

He claimed for Himself the honour which belongs to God.

'All men should honour the Son even as they honour the Father' (John v. 22, 23).

He claimed to have the power to forgive sins, and to give eternal life.

'Son, be of good cheer; thy sins are forgiven' (Matt. ix. 2). 'I give unto (My sheep) eternal life' (John x. 28).

He claimed absolute authority for His teaching (Matt. vii. 24, 26. Luke x. 16).

'I am the Truth' (John xiv. 6).

He declared that He has universal power.

> 'All power is given unto Me in heaven and in earth' (Matt. xxviii. 18)

He united Himself with the Father and the Spirit as together constituting the Godhead.

> 'Teach all nations, baptizing them in the name of the Father, and of the Son, and of the Holy Spirit' (Matt. xxviii. 19).

He affirmed that God and He were One.

> 'I and My Father are one' (John x. 30).

These affirmations attributed to Christ must have been His words, and must be true, because no one could ever have conceived such ideas, or, if that had been possible, no monotheistic Jew would ever have used such language of a man whose home was in Nazareth.

But His claims for Himself are not the only evidence of His consciousness of Divinity. To these must be added

HIS CLAIMS UPON MEN

It may be that our sense of wonder at these has been blunted by our familiarity with them, but, may be, this sense will be sharpened if we think of these claims being made by any one else.

When, as often, Christ says, 'Follow Me', it seems clear that He is not merely inviting but commanding men to be His disciples (Matt. iv. 19; viii. 22; xix. 21; Mark ii. 14); and He affirms that no other claim upon men, however intimate and dear, must interfere with His claim.

> 'He that loveth father or mother more than me is not worthy of me; and he that loveth son or daughter more than me is not worthy of me' (Matt. x. 37).

> 'If any man cometh unto me, and hateth not his father, and mother, and wife, and children, and brethren, and sisters, yea, and his own life also, he cannot be my disciple' (Luke xiv. 26; ix. 59-62).

This is an amazing claim, and can only mean that a man's relation to Christ must take precedence over every other relation; that people must give themselves to Him without reserve; that no rival claims however strong, no natural affection however legitimate and sacred, must stand in the way of His claim upon us.

Christ declares that only by coming to Him can we be delivered from the burden of sin.

'Come unto Me, all ye that labour and are heavy laden, and I will give you rest'.

He also affirms that only as we become like Him in character can we be what we ought to be.

'Learn of Me, for I am meek and lowly in heart, and ye shall find rest unto your souls' (Matt. xi. 28-30).

And, perhaps most astonishing of all, He says that they who obey Him shall never die.

'Verily, verily, I say unto you, If a man keep My word he shall never see death' (John viii. 51).

Truly, 'never man spake like this man.'

To all the wonder of the witness of Prophets, and Apostles, and of Christ Himself to His Divinity, must be added other witnesses manifold (John v. 30-47).

The Father ..	'This is My beloved Son, in whom I am well pleased' (Matt. iii. 17; xvii. 5).
The Holy Spirit	'The Spirit of truth ... shall bear witness of Me' 'He shall glorify Me' (John xv. 26; xvi. 14).
Angels	'There is born to you this day in the city of David a Saviour, who is Christ the Lord' (Luke ii. 11).
Demons	'What have we to do with thee, thou Son of God?' 'Thou art the Son of God' (Matt. viii. 29; Luke iv. 41).
Apostles ..	'Thou art the Christ, the Son of the Living God' (Matt. xvi. 16).
Friends	Martha said, 'Yea, Lord, I have believed that Thou art the Christ, the Son of God' (John xi. 27).
Heathen	A Roman centurion 'feared exceedingly, saying, Truly this was the Son of God' (Matt. xxvii. 54).

The Divinity of Christ is not merely a theological conception, or a matter only of academic interest, but it is a fact and truth of universal, age-long, and vital importance. If Jesus was not God, Christianity is a fraud, and the Christian Church is a farce.

If Jesus was not God, the Bible is a lie, and those who teach it are ignorant and deluded. If Jesus was not God, everything is lost, and nothing but eternal death confronts us. But 'In the beginning was the Word, and the Word was with God, and *the Word was God*' (John i. 1).

3. THE PERFECT UNITY OF CHRIST

His humanity relates Him to the human race; His Divinity relates Him to the Eternal God; and His Unity relates Him to both God and man. Christ is from everlasting the Divine Son, but, in time, He became Man. 'Unto us a child is born; unto us a Son is given' (Isa. ix. 6). The Son was not born, but the child was.

This matter of the Unity of Christ is the profoundest mystery, and the only knowledge we can have of it must be derived from what the Scriptures say, together with reasonable inferences therefrom.

'Great is the Mystery of Godliness: God was manifest in the flesh.' 'This Mystery, which is Christ' (1 Tim. iii. 16; Col. i. 27).

It is perfectly clear that Christ is human, and perfectly clear that He is Divine; but it can never be perfectly clear to our intellects that He is both human and Divine, for the fact is inscrutable. But though the mystery is impenetrable, there are some things which may confidently be affirmed concerning it. The first of these is that *Christ has two natures*, one human, and the other Divine, and that each of these, never mingled nor confounded, retains its own properties and attributes. The human nature remains human, and the Divine nature remains Divine. 'Christ was not a Divine Person who became a human Person. He was a Divine Person who took another nature to His own, maintaining to the full His own original Personality' (Nolloth).

A second, and profoundly important truth is that *Christ is a single Person*. The possession of two natures in Christ does not involve a double personality in the God-Man. The Son of God did not unite Himself with a human person, but with a human nature. There are not two Christs, but only one. There is a duality of natures in the unity of a Person; and these are constant and eternal. This is the marvel and the mystery of the incarnation, and must be apprehended—though it can never be comprehended—if we would understand, in any degree, the work of Christ as Redeemer and Saviour.

> Thou art the Everlasting Word,
>   The Father's only Son;
> God manifestly seen and heard,
>   And heaven's beloved One.
>
> In Thee most perfectly expressed
>   The Father's glories shine;
> Of the full Deity possessed,
>   Eternally Divine.
>
> True image of the Infinite,
>   Whose essence is concealed;
> Brightness of uncreated light;
>   The heart of God revealed.
>
> Throughout the universe of bliss,
>   The centre Thou, and sun;
> The eternal theme of praise is this,
>   To heaven's beloved One.
>
>   (*Josiah Conder*, 1836).

Scene I of Act II of the *Unfolding Drama of Redemption* deals with the *Introduction of Christianity into the World by Jesus the Messiah*, and this we are considering in two parts, The Founder, and the Foundations of Christianity. The first relates to Christ's Person, and the second to His Ministry (Chart 127).

Under the first, we have considered the Humanity, the Divinity, and the Unity of the Messiah, and now we are to consider,

II. THE FOUNDATIONS OF CHRISTIANITY

This relates to the Ministry of Christ, and calls attention to His teaching and His work; to what He taught and what He wrought.

II. THE FOUNDATIONS OF CHRISTIANITY

THE MINISTRY OF CHRIST
(Chart 127)

1. THE TEACHING OF CHRIST

Matthew says, 'Jesus went about teaching' (iv. 23), and this leads us to consider *how* He taught, and *what* He taught; that is, the method and the substance of His teaching.

(i) *How Christ Taught*

As we read the records we must be impressed by the *originality* of our Lord's teaching. In heathendom had been many great teachers, Confucius, Buddha, Plato, Socrates, Aristotle, Caesar, Virgil and others; and in Israel had been Moses, Isaiah, Jeremiah and others, but Christ owed nothing to any of them. 'Ye have heard that it was said by them of old time . . . but I say unto you'. 'When Jesus ended these words, the multitudes were astonished at His teaching' (Matt. v. 21, 27, 33, 38, 43; vii. 28). Christ's was a voice and not an echo.

Another characteristic of His teaching is its *simplicity*. Wendt says that Christ 'aimed at the greatest clearness in the briefest compass'; and of this there are numerous illustrations. No one could fail to know what the Teacher meant when He said; 'No man can serve two masters; for either He will hate the one, and love the other; or else he will hold to the one, and despise the other. Ye cannot serve God and mammon'. Simplicity must not be mistaken for shallowness. The simpleton can never be simple.

The simplicity of Christ's teaching will hide its *profoundness* from the careless reader. Profound means 'from the bottom', that is, deep; and this all Christ's teaching is. Profoundness means knowledge and insight, and is akin to wisdom. 'All that heard Him were amazed at His understanding and His answers', and this was long before He began to teach. He began to teach in the synagogue, and many hearing Him were astonished, saying, 'Whence hath this man these things?' And, 'What is the wisdom that is given unto this man?' 'Whence hath this man this wisdom?' (Luke ii. 47; Mark vi. 2. Matt. xiii. 54). Who has fathomed this exhortation?: 'Love your enemies, and pray for them that persecute you' (Matt. v. 44). 'In the world ye shall have tribulation; but be of good cheer, I have overcome the world' (John xvi. 33).

Another feature of this teaching is its *pregnancy*. Most speakers find it difficult to be compact without being obscure; but Christ taught in crisp pointed sentences which stick like burrs in the mind. Illustrations of this are: 'The Sabbath was made for man, and not man for the Sabbath'. 'Whosoever would save his life shall lose it; and whosoever shall lose his life for my sake and the gospel's shall save it'. 'If any man would be first, he shall be last of all, and minister of all'. 'He that is not against us is for us'. 'Render to Caesar the things that are Caesar's, and to God the things that are God's'. 'God is not the God of the dead, but of the living'. 'Many are called, but few are chosen'. 'It is more blessed to give than to receive'. Such sentences as these are unforgettable.

The *picturesqueness* of Christ's teaching is one of its most striking features. Everywhere are figures, similes, analogies and imagery, relative to natural phenomena, animals, plants, agriculture and commerce; and also to life physical, domestic, social, civil and religious.

He speaks of lightning, earthquakes, fire, storm and light; of oxen, sheep, wolves, swine, dogs, birds and serpents; of olive, fig, and sycamore trees; of lilies, reeds, and thorns; of houses, food, cooking and lamps; of tailors, builders, fishermen, and merchants; of husbandmen, soil, tillage, sowing, growth and harvest; of marriage, hospitality and feasts; of robbery, taxes and punishment; of alms, tithes, fasting and prayer.

Another feature of this incomparable teaching is its *concreteness*. Christ did not speak in the abstract, but concentrated the general in the particular. He embodied principles in examples. When He would urge importunity in prayer, He tells a story about an unjust Judge (Luke xviii. 1-8). When He would contrast pride and humility, He speaks of a Pharisee and a Publican who went to the Temple to pray (Luke xviii. 9-14).

The parables of the Talents and the Pounds teach lessons on opportunity and responsibility. Religious incongruity is set forth by the analogies of the new patch on an old garment, and the new wine in old wine skins. When He would pronounce upon wise and foolish ways of living, He depicts one man building his house on rock, and of another building his on sand, and tells what the results were when a storm struck them.

Further, the *appositeness* of Christ's teaching is impressive. He likens the peevishness of the Jewish people to children playing at marriages and funerals (Matt. xi. 16-19). He ironically compares the carping critic to a man with a 'log' in his eye, squinting round it to see a 'speck' in another man's eye (Matt. vii. 1-5). All His illustrations were adapted to the circumstances before Him.

The *practical* character of Christ's teaching is another of its features. He never sets before us impossible ideals and unattainable heights, but insists on our *doing* what is right. 'This *do* and thou shalt live'. 'If ye know these things happy are ye if ye *do* them'. 'If any man willeth to *do* (God's) will, he shall know . . .'. 'Not every man that saith unto Me, "Lord, Lord", shall enter into the kingdom of heaven, but he that *doeth* the will of My Father who is in heaven'.

Another feature of the teaching is its *brevity*. We shall look in vain for verbosity or prolixity in Christ's illustrations. They are marvels of compression, and yet they are clear and complete. Take, for example, the parable of the leaven in the meal. We do not know how many words there were in the Aramaic in which Jesus spoke, but in the Greek translation there are only nineteen.

'The Kingdom of the heavens is like to leaven which a woman, having taken, hid in three measures of meal until (a double word) all was leavened' (Matt. xiii. 33).

If a hundred words had been used would the picture have been clearer or more complete? Our Lord's longest parables, regarded as stories, are short, and yet, how full they are!

Still another feature of His teaching is its *authoritativeness*. 'He spake as one having authority, and not as the scribes.' They spoke *by* authority, but Christ spoke *with* it. He never made guesses at truth. He never said, 'I submit', or 'I suggest', or 'it is probable', or 'perhaps'. There is nothing tentative about His teaching. His tone is always, 'I say unto you'. 'He that hath ears to hear let him hear'.

Another thing that must impress the careful reader is the *universality* of Christ's teaching. It is true that He said, 'I am not sent but to the lost sheep of the house of Israel', and 'Go not into the way of the Gentiles', but He also said, 'I am the light of the *world*'; 'Go ye into all the *world*'; '*Whosoever* believeth in Me shall never perish'; 'I, if I be lifted up will draw *all men* unto myself'. The most local Man was most universal; the greatest Jew knew no bans or barriers. Luke's Gospel tells on almost every page of the universality of Jesus and His teaching.

'There is that in it which exceeds the bounds of time and space. It passes naturally over the borders of the East, and is recognised by the West as true to the life of the West. Indeed one of the marvels of Christ's teaching is that, though a child of the East it has found in the West its widest and most fruitful acceptance.

'Compare this fact with the fate which has attended the teaching of Buddha or of Mahomet. Each, like Christ, was an Oriental. Each, unlike Christ, has been powerless to influence the West. But the race has yet to be found which cannot find in the teaching of Christ the expression of its best and deepest thought, the answer to its most pressing questions. Authority, sureness, universality of scope and bearing, lift His teaching above that of every other religious Leader'. (Nolloth).

One more feature of this teaching must be noticed, namely, its *finality*. Christ said, 'The word that I have spoken shall judge you in the last day' (John xii. 48). When we have heard Him speak we have put ourselves under an inescapable obligation for He said, 'The words that I speak unto you, they are spirit and they are life'. 'I am the Truth'. The most of what other men have said is out of date, but immortality stamps all that the Messiah said. He is the Omega as well as the Alpha of all utterance. His word is the last word, because He Himself is The Word.

(ii) *What Christ Taught*

Christ's *parables* are incomparable and exhaustless. There are about seventy of them altogether, fifty are parables proper, and twenty are parabolic illustrations, and these treat of a great variety of subjects of supreme importance.

But there are many *discourses* also, about forty-five of them, and all dealing with the great things as God regards them: Blessedness, Confession, Discipleship, Faith, Faithfulness, Forgiveness, the Future, Gaining and Losing Life, the Holy Spirit, Humility, Hypocrisy, the Kingdom of God, Love, Mercy, Offences, Prayer, Regeneration, Repentance, Rewards, Riches, Righteousness, Self-denial, Service, Sin, Stewardship, True Greatness, Unbelief and Watchfulness.

Christ's discourses show that the soul is of more importance than the stomach; eternity, than time; the spiritual, than the material; purity, than pleasure; truth, than expediency; and morality, than money.

Two of Christ's discourses deserve special attention because of their contrasted standpoints—the *Sermon on the Mount*, and the *Upper Room Talk*. The one deals with the Law, and the other with the Gospel. The one looks back, and the other looks on. The one is a confirmation and consummation of the past; and the other is an intimation and anticipation of the future (Matt. v.-vii; John xiii.-xvi).

The *Sermon on the Mount* can never be out of date because it relates to character and conduct, but what it omits to say will become evident as we compare it with the *Upper Room Talk*, the distinctive revelation of which is the Holy Spirit in the Christian Age. (Chart 127).

The Ministry of Christ embraces both His Teaching and His Work, and of these His Work is the more important, because by it, and not by His Teaching, is the power of salvation.

2. THE WORK OF CHRIST

In one sense Christ's whole life was His work, though here we are thinking particularly of His *deeds*. His death must not be regarded as an isolated event, for His whole life was the indispensable foundation of His final sacrifice. The Incarnation made the Sacrifice possible, and the Life made it worthy, and effective when trusted.

The work of Christ is both *evidential* and *atoning*, and though these are intimately related they can be considered separately.

(i) *Christ's Evidential Work*

We are not concerned here with the question of the possibility of miracles, but proceed on the testimony of the Gospels that they did in fact happen. This cannot be regarded as incredible by anyone who believes the witness of the Gospels relative to the Person of the Messiah. If He was sinlessly human and eternally Divine He Himself was the supreme Miracle. His entrance into the world was miraculous; His departure from the world was miraculous; and His life in the world was miraculous. No one who believes in what He *was*, will find it difficult to believe in what He *did*.

Strauss and Hume did not believe in miracles because they did not believe in Christ, for the miracles derive their credibility and their impressiveness for us from their relation to Him. 'We believe in the miracles because we believe in Christ; not in Christ because we believe in the miracles'.

The terms in which the miracles are spoken of in the Gospels are important. Of these there are four. (*a*) Work (*ergon*. John vii. 3, 21), which means a deed designed to arrest attention. (*b*) Wonder (*teras*. John iv. 48), which means a wonderful act; that which creates wonder in those who behold it (Mark ii. 12; iv. 41). (*c*) Power (*dunamis*. Mark. vi. 2, 5, 14). This is translated 'mighty-work' (Acts viii. 10), and indicates the source of the miracle, as *teras* indicates its effect. (*d*) Sign (*sēmeion*. Mark viii. 11, 12), which means a token of the presence and working of God. This is the word which is translated 'miracle' (John iii. 2; vii. 31 *et al*), and more than any of the others it indicates the ethical end and purpose of the act. It declares that the prime object of the miracle is to lead to something out of and beyond itself (Mark xvi. 20)

A miracle, then, is an act of God, which visibly deviates from the ordinary working of His power, designed, while capable of serving other uses, to authenticate a divine message.

A miracle, 'is an occurrence so marked in its departure from the usual order of things as to be to men a sign of God's special power'. It is an interposition of a power above nature and above man.

Miracles are not contrary to nor against nature, but are beyond and above it. They are an invasion of the fixed order, but not a violation of it. When Peter walked on the water the law of gravitation was not violated, but its operation was suspended by the action of a greater law for the time being. The precipitation of natural law is not a violation of it, but is rather an exchange of the instantaneous for the gradual. When Jesus turned water into wine He did instantly what nature does gradually; and this is true also of His feeding the multitudes, of His healing the sick of His withering the fig tree, and of the two draughts of fishes.

The thirty-six miracles particularized in the Gospels were wrought in three realms: the human, the cosmic, and the spiritual, and prove Christ's sovereignty over all realms. In the human realm are all healing miracles; in the cosmic realm are all the miracles involving nature; and in the spiritual realm are the miracles which impinge on other worlds.

The miracles were not designed to create curiosity, but to produce conviction, and in addition to being divine signs they were spiritual symbols.

Fever stayed speaks to us of the stilling of the restless energy of the flesh, of the feverishness of our mortal life. Leprosy healed tells of the removal of sin's loathsome defilement. Paralysis cured points to the removal of sin's helplessness and disability. The withered hand restored proclaims Christ's enablement of men to work for Him. The stilling of the storm shows Christ's power over the upheavals of life. The issue of blood stayed speaks to us of the removal of the weakness and waste caused by sin. Sight given to the blind demonstrates that the Gospel brings illumination to the darkened soul. Deafness healed tells of the divine enabling of men to hear God. Dumbness cured shows that Christ wants men to witness for him. The cursing of the fig tree proclaims the fate of the persistently unfruitful. Feeding the multitudes speaks of the satisfaction which Christ can bring to hungry souls. Raising the dead proves Christ's conquest of death, and of His gift of life to the spiritually dead.

The parables are miracles in words, and the miracles are parables in deeds. Denial of the miracles creates more problems than it pretends to solve. No one can admit, or has ever admitted, the miracle of Christ's Resurrection without granting the other miracles recorded in the Gospels, and the Resurrection of Christ is one of the best authenticated events in all history.

(ii) *Christ's Atoning Work*

What is commonly understood by this is not the redemptive virtue of Christ's whole life and ministry, though there is truth in this view, but His final work in death and resurrection. That everything else in the story of Christ is subordinate to His death and resurrection cannot surely be denied. In prophecy and history, as in exposition and experience, the Cross is central.

(1) *Christ's death is plainly anticipated in the Old Testament.* The keynote is: 'According to the law all things are cleansed with blood, and apart from shedding of blood there is no remission' (Hebrews ix. 22).

The Old Testament anticipation of Christ's death is found not only in statements of principle, such as this, but also in types and prophecies. Illustration of it in *types* are Abel's offering in Gen. iv., and Abraham's in Gen. xxii; in the Passover Lamb, also, and in the Levitical and other blood offerings.

And illustration of it in *prophecy* is found in many passages: notably Gen. iii. 15; Psalm xxii. 1-21; and Isaiah liii. These and many other lines of type and prophecy converge towards Calvary, and find their fulfilment in the death of Christ for the redemption of the world.

(2) *Christ's death is central in the earliest Christian preaching.* In the Acts much is said about the resurrection of Christ, and that, of course, presupposes His death; and about Christ's

dying two things are repeatedly emphasised, namely, (a) that it was foredetermined by God; and (b) that it was the act of wicked men. 'Him being delivered up by the determinate counsel and foreknowledge of God, ye, by the hand of lawless men did crucify and slay' (Acts ii. 23).

In the New Testament Christ's death is never spoken of as God's act; yet the earliest preachers proclaimed it as Good News, the hope and power of salvation.

> 'I delivered unto you first of all that which I also received, how that Christ died for our sins according to the Scriptures; and that He was buried; and that He rose again the third day according to the Scriptures' (1 Cor. xv. 3, 4).

The death and resurrection of Christ cannot be separated, for they are the two parts of one redeeming act. 'I have power to lay down My life, and I have power to take it again' (John x. 18). If Jesus had not died He could not have risen, and if, having died He had not risen there would have been no salvation for us. The death and resurrection of Christ are, therefore, the dominating notes in the music of apostolic preaching.

(3) *The place and significance of Christ's death in the teaching of the Apostles is unmistakable.* Though they wrote independently, at different times, in different places, for different people, from different standpoints, and for different objects, yet their teaching on the subject of Christ's death is in perfect harmony. They all regard it to be a revelation of God's love, to be occasioned by man's sin, and to be redemptive in its purpose and effect.

PETER writes his First Epistle to exhort to patience and constancy Christians who are suffering persecution, but beneath and behind his exhortations lies the dynamic of Christ's Cross and example.

> 'His own self bare our sins in His own body on the tree . . . by whose stripes ye were healed' (ii. 24).

> 'Christ suffered for sins once, the Righteous for the unrighteous, that He might bring us to God, being put to death in the flesh, but quickened in the spirit' (iii. 18).

> 'Ye were redeemed . . . with precious blood, as of a lamb without blemish and without spot, even the blood of Christ' (i. 18, 19).

L

A Christian life is made possible only by Christ's death and resurrection. This is of the essence of primitive Christian teaching.

PAUL leaves one in no doubt about where in his creed and experience he puts the Cross of Christ. The Death occupies the central and fundamental place in the Apostle's Gospel. All else that he believed and taught rested on and radiated from Calvary. He had been preaching for fifteen years before He began to write his Epistles, and then he wrote for fifteen years, but from start to finish he had but one message—Christ's Death. In it, for him, everything was involved, and from it the whole of Christianity was deduced.

In *1 Thessalonians*: Jesus died and rose again, and in consequence all who believe in Him will be raised from the dead, and will live with Him (iv. 14; v. 10)

In *1 Corinthians*: 'We preach Christ crucified'. 'Christ our Passover is sacrificed for us' (i. 23; v. 7)

In *2 Corinthians*: 'He died for all, that they which live should no longer live unto themselves, but unto Him who died for their sakes and rose again' (v. 14, 15)

In Galatians: 'Far be it from me to glory save in the cross of our Lord Jesus Christ' (vi. 14)

In *Romans*: 'God commendeth His own love toward us, in that, while we were yet sinners, Christ died for us' (v. 8)

In *Ephesians*: 'Christ hath loved us, and hath given Himself for us, an offering and a sacrifice to God, for a sweet-smelling savour' (v. 2)

In *Colossians*: Christ has 'made peace through the blood of His Cross' (i. 20).

In *Philippians*: 'He humbled Himself, becoming obedient unto death, yea, the death of the cross' (ii. 8)

In 1 *Timothy*: 'There is one God, one mediator also between God and men, Himself man, Christ Jesus, who gave Himself a ransom for all' (ii. 5, 6)

In *Titus*: 'Christ gave Himself for us, that He might redeem us from all iniquity' (ii. 14)

In 2 *Timothy*: 'Remember Jesus Christ, risen from the dead according to my gospel' (ii. 8)

What Paul calls his gospel is the Christian gospel and the only gospel, the central fact of which is that Jesus Christ died an atoning death to deliver us from sin and our sins, to give to us eternal life, and to bring us to everlasting glory.

Hebrews. Whoever wrote this Epistle had the same creed and experience as Peter and Paul, though he expresses himself differently from them. 'The real content of the Epistle, religious and theological, is in what it has to say of the historical Christ; and that, beyond a doubt, is concentrated in what it has to say of His death'. (Denney). 'Christ has been manifested to put away sin by the sacrifice of Himself' (ix. 26). 'By His own blood Christ entered in once into the holy place, having obtained eternal redemption' (ix. 12; ii. 9, 14; ix. 14, 28; x. 14; xiii. 12, 20).

The Writings of the Apostle JOHN throb with this central truth of the Gospel, that the death of Jesus is redemptive; that His sacrifice was atoning, and that thereby sinners can be reconciled to God.

'The blood of Jesus, God's Son, cleanseth us from all sin.' Christ 'laid down His life for us' (1 Ep. i. 7; iii. 16 *et al*).

Revelation. This Book is full of Christ's redeeming work by the sacrifice of Himself. 'Unto Him that loveth us, and loosed us from our sins by His blood, to Him be the glory and the dominion for ever and ever.' 'The Lamb that hath been slain from the foundation of the world' (i. 5; xiii. 8).

The harmony of all this testimony is profoundly significant, and so long as language has any meaning it cannot be invalidated by sceptical criticism. Men may reject the teaching of the New

Testament on the subject of Christ's death, but they cannot make what it does say to bear any other than its obvious meaning.

(4) To the fact and significance of Christ's death as witnessed to in the Old Testament, in the primitive preaching, and in the Apostolic Writings, must be added *the witness supplied by the Gospel Records*. The importance of the death of Christ in His earthly story is indicated by the proportion of space given to it there. If we remember that the Passion Week is a period of seven or eight days in the thirty-five years of our Lord's life on earth, we shall be able better to appreciate the emphasis in the Gospels on His death and resurrection. This week occupies eight of Matthew's twenty-eight chapters, nearly one-third of the whole. It occupies three of Mark's sixteen chapters, about one-fifth of the whole. It occupies five-and-a-half of Luke's twenty-four chapters, nearly one-fifth of the whole. And it occupies nine of John's twenty-one chapters nearly one-half of the whole. That is, of the eighty-nine chapters in the Gospels, twenty-five and a half are about the last week of Jesus' life; more than one-third of the entire record is given to one week in a life of nearly thirty-five years! The significance of this is that the dominating factor and feature of Christ's earthly life was not His entrance into the world; not His sinless character; not His wonderful teaching; not His miraculous works, and not His peerless example, but *His death and resurrection*. The incarnation and the perfect life without the death and the resurrection would be our greatest condemnation; because 'without shedding of blood there is no remission'.

Christ's death provided for the need of men relative to the past, and His resurrection, for our need relative to the future. By His death the guilt of sin is removed, and by His resurrection the power of sin is broken.

(5) *Christ's own interpretation of His death* seals all other witness to it. The naturalistic view that He never expected to die as He did, and only at the end was disillusioned, flatly denies all reliable testimony. From the outset of His public ministry Christ knew and declared that He would die a violent death (Mark. ix. 31). He taught that He came to die (Mark x. 45); that His death was

one of inward constraint (Luke ix. 22); that it was voluntary (John x. 17, 18); that it was a fulfilment of prophecy (Luke xxii. 37); that He would be 'lifted up', as was the serpent in the wilderness (John iii. 14, 15); that His death would be a 'ransom' (Mark x. 45); that it was a 'baptism' which He must experience, a 'cup' which He must drink, and a 'covenant' which He must fulfil (Mark x. 38, 39; xiv. 24).

Jesus' death was an incident in His life. We cannot tell when the clear consciousness of it came to Him, but we do know that during the period of His ministry that consciousness was clear. The Cross came to Him as the consummation of His life's work; and being fully aware of who He was, He knew that His death would be vicarious and atoning.

This, then, is the Messiah, who consummated the Mosaic Age and inaugurated the Christian Age. It cannot be said with certainty when He became conscious of His Messiahship, but certainly it was not later than His Baptism. That He did believe that He was the Messiah of prophecy, the Christ of God, the Anointed King of His people, the Son of David, cannot reasonably be called into question. Bousset says that it is 'a point which resists the sharpest criticism'. At the time of the incarnation the Jews were expecting the promised Messiah (Matt. xi. 3. Luke iii. 15), but their conception of what He would come to do was very different from His own conception. They envisaged one who would deliver them from foreign domination, and re-establish the Davidic Kingdom with Jerusalem as its metropolis. In their expectation of a King and a Kingdom they were right, but not in their idea of the nature of the Kingdom as national and temporal. The Apostles acknowledged Jesus to be the Messiah (Matt. xvi. 16), but they thought of Him in terms of glory and not of suffering, as the scene at Caesarea Philippi shows (Matt. xvi. 21-23).

It is clear that Jesus accepted acknowledgments of His Messiahship, and claimed to be the Messiah, yet we find Him again and again urging upon people not to make Himself or His doings known (Matt. ix. 30, Mark v. 43; vii. 24; ix. 30). The reason for this must be looked for in the attitude of the people towards the Messiahship and Himself. It was not until He stood before Pilate, and, earlier in the same week, entered regally into Jerusalem, that He made it perfectly clear to all that He was the Messianic King (Matt. xxi. 1-9. Matt. xxvi. 63, 64; xxvii. 11. Mark xi. 1-10. Mark xiv. 61, 62; xv. 2. Luke xix. 29-40. Luke xxii. 70; xxiii. 2, 3. John xii. 12-19). The Jews never associated the Messiah with suffering, and never interpreted Isaiah liii of Him, yet He came to fulfil Isaiah liii, and did so (Acts ii. 36; iii. 13, 18-21, 26).

Because of its vast significance it is difficult for us to apprehend what was taking place in the world by the advent and ministry of the Messiah, for in Him two ages met. But two things should be clearly understood, namely, (a) that Christianity is not a reformed Judaism; and (b) that all that is morally and spiritually vital in Judaism has passed over into Christianity. The natural and local are dropped, but all essentials are perpetuated. The Messiah said: 'Think not that I came to destroy the law or the prophets; I came not to destroy, but to fulfil' (Matt. v. 17); and He fulfilled the law and the prophets by giving to them a new spiritual content. All the Apostles were Jews, and during their association with Jesus, and also after Pentecost, there was no violent break or formal renunciation of Judaism. The Old Testament was their Bible, and the Temple at Jerusalem was their centre of worship, yet, all unconsciously, they were passing from the Old Covenant to the New, and from the Temple and Synagogue to the Church.

Christ never used the word *Church* (Ecclesia) in His public addresses, and only twice latterly in speaking to His disciples (Matt. xvi. 18; xviii. 17), for it would have been difficult for them to understand what He meant by the word; but they and all Jews were familiar with the idea of the *Kingdom*, and so Jesus continued to speak of the Kingdom of God, or the Kingdom of Heaven, thus confining Himself to the expression used previously by the Prophets, and adopted by the Baptist (Dan. iv. 3. Matt. iii. 2. Luke iv. 43). But He did not mean by *Kingdom* what the Jews meant, a kingdom of earthly power and worldly greatness, but that Divine order of things which He had come to establish. His Kingdom, though in this world, is not of it, and by employing the term in its contexts, Christ half-revealed and half-concealed the truth that it was passing from an elect nation to an elect people of all nations, and kindreds, and tongues, a body of Jews and Gentiles who are God's children by faith in the sacrificed Lamb. In this way *Christianity was Introduced into the World by Jesus the Messiah*, and so Scene 1 of Act II of the Unfolding Drama of Redemption prepared for Scene 2, *the Progress of Christianity in the World to the Close of the First Century A.D.*

(For full treatment of the Gospels see the writer's *A Guide to the Gospels*, 664 pages.)

Jesus, Thou Joy of loving hearts,
  Thou Fount of life, Thou Light of men,
From the best bliss that earth imparts
  We turn unfilled to Thee again.

Thy truth unchanged hath ever stood;
  Thou savest those that on Thee call;
To them that seek Thee, Thou art good,
  To them that find Thee, all in all.

We taste Thee, O Thou living Bread,
  And long to feast upon Thee still;
We drink of Thee, the Fountain-head,
  And thirst our souls from Thee to fill.

Our restless spirits yearn for Thee,
  Where'er our changeful lot is cast;
Glad when Thy gracious smile we see, .
  Blest when our faith can hold Thee fast.

O Jesus, ever with us stay;
  Make all our moments calm and bright;
Chase the dark night of sin away;
  Shed o'er the world Thy holy Light.

BERNARD OF CLAIRVAUX

THE UNFOLDING DRAMA OF REDEMPTION

ACT II.

SCENE 2

THE HISTORICAL EXPANSION OF CHRISTIANITY

THE BOOK OF THE ACTS

THE BOOK OF THE ACTS

THE book is beautifully stamped with the individuality of the writer in its amiable catholicity, its "sweet reasonableness", its abounding geniality, its zeal, and hope and love.

In these respects as it is the earliest, so too it is the most unique and attractive of all Church Histories.

F. W. FARRAR

THE UNFOLDING DRAMA OF REDEMPTION

ACT II SCENE 2

THE PROGRESS OF CHRISTIANITY IN THE WORLD
TO THE END OF THE FIRST CENTURY A.D.

THE HISTORICAL EXPANSION OF CHRISTIANITY
THE DOCTRINAL EXPRESSION OF CHRISTIANITY

ACTS TO JUDE

THE APOSTOLIC PERIOD

THE Apostolic period lasted for seventy years, A.D. 30-100, and no two generations in all history have proved to be so momentous. During this period Judaism was superseded by Christianity, and what this meant is stated on p. 284 where is considered the need for Paul.

Also, during this period Jerusalem and its temple were destroyed by the Romans, and this event marked the complete rupture of the Christian Church with the Jewish synagogue and temple. And further, the Christian Church spread throughout the whole Roman world, and was established beyond the possibility of destruction. It was also in this period that the inspired literature of the Church was written, the twenty-one Epistles of the New Testament.

As events in the intellectual, moral, and spiritual realms are to be accounted for by personalities, we naturally expect to find these behind and in the events of this great period. We see on page 179 (*Biographical Value*) that crowds of personalities helped in one way or another to create this story, but there are four that stand out from all the others as having given direction and complexion to the early Church, namely, *James*, *Peter*, *Paul*, and *John*. These represent aspects of Christianity, and lay emphasis on different elements of Christian truth. For this contribution to the total result each of these men was endowed temperamentally and experimentally, as we shall see under the *Doctrinal Expression of the Church*.

ACT II

Of the Unfolding Drama, ACT I relates to the Mosaic Dispensation, and ACT II, to the Christian Dispensation. The former treats of the Law, and the latter, of the Gospel. In the former the Nation of Israel is the medium of expression, and in the latter it is the Church of God. The former was a preparation for the latter; and while all that is vital in Judaism is preserved in Christianity, the latter vastly transcends the former.

In this Second Act there are two Scenes. The First presents the *Introduction of Christianity into the World by Jesus the Messiah*, and the Second unfolds the *Progress of Christianity in the World to the Close of the First Century A.D.*

Scene 2

THE PROGRESS OF CHRISTIANITY IN THE WORLD TO THE CLOSE OF THE FIRST CENTURY A.D.

Scene 1 covers a period of about thirty-five years; and Scene 2, a period of about seventy years (bearing in mind that the first five years are not reckoned as A.D. in our chronology).

Scene 1 is presented in four historical Writings, without anything epistolary; and Scene 2 is presented in one historical Writing, and twenty-one epistolary.

The following chart indicates what is meant.

CHART 129

ACT II		
THE HISTORICAL AND EPISTOLARY WRITINGS		
	HISTORICAL WRITINGS	EPISTOLARY WRITINGS
SCENE 1	MATTHEW. MARK. LUKE. (JOHN)	NONE
SCENE 2	ACTS	ROMANS. 1-2 CORINTHIANS GALATIANS. EPHESIANS PHILIPPIANS. COLOSSIANS 1-2 THESSALONIANS 1-2 TIMOTHY. TITUS PHILEMON. HEBREWS JAMES. 1-2 PETER 1-2-3 JOHN. JUDE

This fact is worthy of consideration. The historical had to precede the epistolary because that could not be contemplated and interpreted which did not exist in fact. Interpretation requires something or someone to be interpreted, and so the advent, and life, and death, and resurrection of Christ had to precede the interpretation of Him. Only when He had been historically revealed could the minds of men turn to the consideration of His significance. The Evangelists present the facts, and make no attempt to explain or apply them, and later the Apostles, without recording the facts (except occasionally), set forth the meaning and value of them theologically and experimentally.

We should see the relation to one another of three things—*revelation*, *interpretation*, and *apprehension*. The first was in the pre-apostolic age; the second was in the apostolic age; and the third in the post-apostolic age. Since the close of the first century there has been no historical revelation, and no inspired interpretation, but only spiritual apprehension of the revelation which has been interpreted.

In the period represented by the Gospels is revelation without interpretation or apprehension. In the period of the Apostles are apprehension and interpretation of the revelation already made. And in the period from the close of the apostolic age until now has been neither divine revelation nor inspired interpretation, but only apprehension of the truth.

CHART 130

REVELATION	INTERPRETATION	APPREHENSION
B.C. 5–A.D. 30	A.D. 30–100	A.D. 100–
The Life and Ministry of Christ	The Period of the Apostles	The Christian Church for over 1900 Years
The Gospels	The Acts and the Epistles	No Canonical Writings
A PERSON	A Group of Inspired Men	Church Councils and Systems of Theology
Consummated	Concluded	Continuous

'Councils and doctors have claimed a right to be heard, only as asserters and witnesses of apostolic teaching. No later communications from heaven are supposed or alleged. What has been handed down—what is collected out of the Writings of the Apostles—is the professed authority for all definitions and decrees; and all reference to (what may appear to be) other authority is based upon the fact, asserted or implied, that in the quarters appealed to there was reason to recognise some special connection with the apostolic teaching'. (T. D. Bernard, *The Progress of Doctrine*: Lect. i.)

It is important to recognise that when we speak of the *Progress of Christianity in the World to the Close of the First Century*, it is implied, indeed affirmed, that the close of the first century marks the close of the divine revelation of which the Bible is the record. Christianity from then until now is the superstructure which rests on that foundation.

CHART 131

ACT II	
100 YEARS. B.C. 5—A.D. 95 (100)	
SCENE I	SCENE 2
Introduction of Christianity into the World by JESUS the MESSIAH	Progress of Christianity in the World to the end of the First Century A.D.
THE CHRIST. B.C. 5-A.D. 30	A.D. 30-95 (100). THE CHURCH
The Founder	The Foundations	The Historical Expansion	The Doctrinal Expression

The progress of Christianity from A.D. 30-100 will, therefore, be considered along two lines: the *Historical Expansion*, which the Acts records; and the *Doctrinal Expression*, which is found in the Epistles. The *Expansion* points to the Church's activities, and the *Expression*, to the Church's beliefs. The one is factual, and the other is doctrinal. The one tells of the promulgation of the Good News, and the other, of the apprehension of it. These two lines are not consecutive but concurrent. Paul's letters, for example, belong to, and do not follow his missionary activity, but it will be best to consider each of them separately.

These New Testament Writings, shown in chart 129, relate to the activities and thought of the Christian Church for about two generations, from A.D. 30 to A.D. 100, and together they tell a story of thrilling interest and profoundest significance.

Although many of the Letters were written before the Evangelic Records, with the possible exception of 'Mark', it should be remembered that they are all rooted in the content of the Oral Tradition. It is the historical Jesus who stands behind all the New Testament Writings, and apart from Him, His Person, His Teaching, and His Work, these could have had no existence. He was the Fact that made possible 'The Truth' (John xvi. 13, R.V.), and He was also 'The Truth' (John xiv. 6) that explained the Fact.

Beneath all the diversity of these Writings unity is given them by 'a common relation to Christ', on the part of the writers, 'a common faith in them involving common religious convictions about Him'. (Denney).

ACT II   SCENE 2

THE HISTORICAL EXPANSION OF CHRISTIANITY
THE BOOK OF THE ACTS

INTRODUCTION

Although we do not propose to enter upon a critical examination of the Acts, it will be well to consider certain introductory matters, because this Book is the sole remaining historical work which deals with the beginnings of Christianity and Church history.

1. TITLE

The Book never had any one title which commanded general acceptance; in some manuscripts being called 'Acts', and in others 'The Acts', 'Acts of Apostles', 'Acts of the Apostles', 'The Acts of the Apostles'. It is now commonly known by the last of these, although it is not an account of the doings of all the Apostles, but, in the main, of two of them only, nor is it a record of all the acts of these two. A negro convert has called it, not unsuitably, 'Words about Deeds'. Perhaps the most comprehensive title we could give to it would be '*The Acts of the Holy Spirit through Apostles and others, during the first generation of the Christian Church*'.

2. AUTHOR

From earliest days tradition has ascribed to Luke the authorship of this Book, and there is no reason to call that tradition into question. We may summarize the evidence for the Lucan authorship as follows:

(1) The Third Gospel and the Acts are clearly from the same hand, for the same style, language, and method characterize them both.

(2) The author was a medical man, for in his narrative he uses a number of medical terms in a technical sense. A valuable and interesting book on this subject is, *The Medical Language of St. Luke*, by Hobart. See also Harnack's *Luke the Physician*, Appendix I, pp. 175-198.

(3) The author of the Acts was one of Paul's companions. This is shown in what are called the 'we' sections of the Book (xvi. 10-17, xx. 5-15, xxi. 1-18, xxvii. 1-xxviii. 16). Whoever the author was, he joined Paul at Troas, and went with him to Philippi (xvi. 8-12), and he appears to have remained there until Paul returned thither on his third missionary journey (xx. 5, 6). Ramsay thinks that the '*man of Macedonia*', whom Paul saw and heard in the vision at Troas, was Luke (*St. Paul the Traveller*, pp. 202, 203), and it has been conjectured that he and Paul may have met in student days when Luke was a medical student in the university of Tarsus (Knowling, *Expositor's Greek Testament*). If this were so, Paul, because of the condition of his health, may have sought out Luke that he might have the benefit of his professional skill.

(4) The fact that Luke's name does not occur in the Acts. If it be thought a mere conjecture that Luke should be read into the 'we' of the above sections, the fact that his name does not occur in this Book must be accounted for. We know that he was one of Paul's companions, much beloved by him, and that he stood by him in days of darkness and danger (Philemon 24, Col. iv. 14, 2 Tim. iv. 11). Is it likely, then, that anyone else writing this record would have failed to mention him? But if Luke himself is the author, the suppression of his name is easily understood, as is the suppression of John's name in the Fourth Gospel.

(5) The author of the Acts was with Paul at Rome (xxvii. 1-xxviii. 16), and Luke was with him there at that time (2 Tim. iv. 11).

(6) An author writing this Book at a late date would certainly have used Paul's Epistles as sources for his work, for they are 'the most weighty documents for the history which he professes

to describe', but the Acts is written independently of them, and, as Knowling says, 'it cannot be said that any one letter in particular is employed by the writer'. But if Luke is the author, this silence cannot surprise us, for his knowledge would not need to be obtained from the Apostle's letters. All these considerations make it certain that the author of the Acts was 'Luke the beloved physician.'

3. DATE AND PLACE OF WRITING

We may confidently set aside the view that the Acts was written early in the second century; and also the view that it was written after the destruction of Jerusalem in A.D. 70; and we will assume that A.D. 63 best suits all the facts and requirements, and that the place of writing was Rome.

4. UNITY

It is practically certain that the author of the 'we' sections of the Book is also the author of the rest of it, and that he was controlled by a definite object in writing. The idea of a number of redactors or editors working over a number of sources can scarcely be taken seriously. The impression left upon one from reading the Book is that it is a story coherent and progressive, and a detailed study of it confirms this impression.

5. SOURCES

But when we speak of the unity of the Acts, we do not mean that the author had no recourse to sources of information, oral or written. In the 'we' sections such were not necessary, as the writer was a witness of what he relates, but this is not the case in the other parts of the Book. For information concerning events of which Luke was not an eye-witness, he must, of course, have been dependent on others, and his method of investigation is stated in his Gospel (i. 1-4). The question is not therefore, did Luke use sources? but, what sources did he use? Those who would know in detail what has been said on this subject are referred to Knowling on the Acts, *Expositor's Greek Testament*, pp. 17-33, or to a good Bible Dictionary, but very briefly we would indicate the line of investigation.

(1) As already said, chapters xvi. 10-17; xx. 5-15; xxi, 1-18; xxvii. 1.-xxviii. 16, are accounted for, Luke being an eye-witness.

(2) For the remainder of the record Luke was dependent on persons who had knowledge of the events he records. First and foremost of these, of course, was Paul. Luke was much with him, and during times of enforced inactivity, as at Caesarea, Malta, and Rome, nothing is more natural than that the great missionary should have communicated to his beloved friend the records of his work and experience in great heathen centres of commercial or intellectual life, like Corinth, Ephesus, and Athens. This would account for everything in the Acts from chapter xiii.

(3) What is related in chapter xii he might well have got from Mark, to whose home Peter went after his release from prison, and who was with Luke in Rome (2 Tim. iv. 11).

(4) Cornelius, who lived at Caesarea (x. 1) could have given Luke the information for the major part of chapters ix-xi, for Luke was at Caesarea with Paul.

(5) The details of chapters vi-vii he could have got from Paul, who witnessed the martyrdom of Stephen; and also from Philip.

(6) Chapter viii he could have got from Philip and his daughters, who lived at Caesarea. Philip was one of the seven (vi. 5, xxi. 8).

(7) This accounts for chapters vi-xxviii of the Acts, in a highly reasonable and probable way. The sources of chapters i-v are not so clear, but Peter, Barnabas, and Philip, who enter into this history, and who were known to Luke, might well have supplied him with the details which he records. The Acts, however, is not a collection of reports from various sources, but the work of one 'thoroughly independent in style', and who 'assimilated his materials like a true historian.' (A. T. Robertson).

There is no evidence that Luke draws upon Josephus.

6. CHRONOLOGY

The chronology of the Acts is a vexed question for which in detail the student must consult Bengel, Wendt, Zahn, Ramsay, Harnack, Holtzmann, Lightfoot, Turner, and others; but the following details should be of interest and of some help.

TWELVE DATES IN OUR PRESENT SCHEME

A.D. 30   -   Death of Jesus.

37   -   Conversion of Paul (ix).

44   -   Death of James, son of Zebedee (xii).

44-46   -   Paul and Barnabas at Antioch (xii. 24, 25).

47-49   -   First missionary journey (xiii-xiv).

50   -   Conference at Jerusalem (xv).

50-53   -   Second missionary journey (xvi-xviii).

54-58   -   Third missionary journey (xviii-xxi).

58   -   Paul's arrest in Jerusalem (xxi).

58-60   -   Caesarean imprisonment (xxiv-xxvi).

61-63   -   First Roman imprisonment (xxviii).

67-68   -   Martyrdom of Paul and Peter, and perhaps of Luke.

POINTS OF JEWISH AND PAGAN HISTORY
WITHIN THE PERIOD OF THE ACTS
WHICH MAY BE REGARDED AS PROBABLY CORRECT

1. A.D. 44   Death of Herod Agrippa I.
Acts xii. 20-23.

2. A.D. 45-46   Famine in Jerusalem in the time of Claudius.
Acts xi. 28-30; xii. 25.

3. A.D. 47   Sergius Paulus, Proconsul in Cyprus.
Acts xiii. 7.

4. A.D. 49   Expulsion of the Jews from Rome.
Acts xviii. 2.

5. A.D. 49-50   Proconsulship of Gallio in Achaia.
Acts xviii. 12.

6. A.D. 52   Appointment of Felix as Procurator of Judaea.
Acts xxi. 38; xxiii. 24; xxiv. 10, 27.

7. A.D. 57   Festus, Procurator in Judaea.
Acts xxiv. 27.

CHART 132

Here can be seen at a glance how fourteen scholars date twelve important events in the Acts

Event	USSHER	BENGEL	EICHHORN	OLSHAUSEN	EWALD	WORDSWORTH	ALFORD	HARNACK	TURNER	RAMSAY	LIGHTFOOT	H. A. W. MEYER	D. SMITH	RACKHAM
The Ascension	33	30	32	33	33	30	30	29-30	29	30	(30)	31		29
Conversion of Saul	35	31	37-38	35	38	34	37	30	35-36	33	34	35	33	32
First visit to Jerusalem	38	33	40-41	38	41	37	40	33	38	35-36	37	38	36	34
Second visit to Jerusalem	44	41-44	44	44	45-46	44	44	(44)	46	46	45	44	46	43
First Missionary Journey	45	45-46	45	to 49	48-51	45	45	45	47	47	48	45-51	47-49	46
Council at Jerusalem	52	47	52	52	52	49-50	50	47	49	50	51	52	50	48
Second Missionary Journey	53	47	53	52	52	51	51					52	50-53	48
Fourth visit to Jerusalem	56	49	56	55	55	54	54	50	52	53	54	55	53	51
Third Missionary Journey	56	49	56	55	55	54	54					55	53-57	
Fifth visit to Jerusalem and imprisonment at Caesarea	60	53	60	60	59	58	58	54	56	57	58	59	57	55
Paul's imprisonment in Rome	63-65	56-58	63-65	63-65	62-64	61-63	61-63	57-59	59-61	60-62	61-63	62-64	60-62	58-60
Paul's Martyrdom	67							64	64-65	65	67		67	64

175

Into whatever scheme is adopted must be worked the various references particularly in the Acts to Paul's sojourn in various places. For example:

The three years in Arabia and Damascus (Gal. i. 18);
The sojourn with Barnabas at Antioch 'for a whole year' (xi. 26);
The stay at Antioch for 'no little time' upon the return from the first missionary journey (xiv. 26-28);
The Jerusalem Conference (xv);
The waiting at Athens (xvii. 16);
The eighteen months at Corinth (xviii. 11);
The interval between the second and third missionary journeys, which is spoken of as 'some time' (xviii. 22, 23);
The three years in Ephesus (xix. 10; xx. 31);
The three months in Corinth (xx. 3);
The 'many days' at Caesarea (xxi. 10);
The sojourn at Jerusalem (xxi. 15-xxiii. 22);
The two years in Caesarea (xxiii. 23-xxvi. 32, cf. xxiv. 27);
The journey to Malta (xxvii);
The 'three months' in Malta (xxviii. 11);
The 'two whole years' in Rome (xxviii. 30).

These notes of time show that somebody must have kept a diary, and that journeys and sojourns were carefully recorded. Back of that was the belief of these men that their lives were God-planned. When we all believe that, the calendar will be consecrated.

7. Purpose and Plan

Various views have been held regarding the purpose of the Acts, and divers tendencies have been alleged, political, biographical, and missionary.

But undoubtedly the last of these is the right view. In the others the theories are brought into the Book, but in this one the Book supplies the theory (i. 1-8). In this introduction the writer plainly indicates both the purpose and the plan of the record.

As to *purpose*, it is to show that He Who did and taught on earth is now doing and teaching from heaven (1); and as to the *plan*, it is to show how Christianity developed and spread from Jerusalem, through Judaea and Samaria, to 'the uttermost part of the earth' (8).

It is true that the record shows that opposition to Christianity came rather from the Jews than from the Romans; and it is also true that there are some striking parallels between the work of Peter and of Paul, such as the healing of a lame man (iii. 2, and xiv. 8), the raising of the dead (ix, 37, 40, and xx. 9, 10), and the pronouncement of a judgment (v. 1-6 and xiii. 9-11). These particulars, however, do not indicate a 'tendency', but naturally fall within the scope of the writer's main purpose, which is to show how the Christian missionary movement spread from Jerusalem to Rome in a single generation, mainly through the instrumentality of two men, Peter and Paul.

This progress of Christianity is clearly traced throughout, as the following passages show:—

'The Lord added to the Church day by day them that were being saved' (ii. 47).

'Believers were the more added to the Lord, multitudes of men and women' (v. 14-16).

'The Word of the Lord increased and the number of the disciples multiplied in Jerusalem exceedingly, and a great number of the priests were obedient to the faith' (vi. 7).

'So the Church throughout all Judaea and Samaria and Galilee had peace, being edified, and walking in the fear of the Lord, and in the comfort of the Holy Spirit, was multiplied' (ix. 31).

'The Word of the Lord grew and multiplied' (xii. 24).

'So the churches were strengthend in the faith, and increased in number daily' (xvi. 5).

'So mightily grew the Word of God and prevailed' (xix. 20).

These seven of many summaries amply indicate the author's purpose, a purpose which is carried out in the whole plan of the Book.

8. Values

The Book of the Acts inevitably has many and great values, of which the following are outstanding:—

(i) *The Historical Value*

It was fashionable at one time to call its historical accuracy into question, and even to deny it, but that day has passed, and never more so than now has this Book been regarded by scholars as of the highest historical value, thanks largely to Lightfoot and Ramsay.

RAMSAY says that he began the study of the trustworthiness of the Acts 'with a mind unfavourable to it', and he ended that study by 'placing this great writer on the high pedestal that belongs to him'. HARNACK, in his '*The Acts of the Apostles*', says, 'The book has now been restored to the position of credit which is its rightful due.' HEADLAM says, 'the investigators of the last twenty or thirty years have tended more and more to confirm the accuracy of the writer. In almost every point where we can follow him, even in minute detail, he is right'. A. T. ROBERTSON says that Luke's veracity has been triumphantly vindicated where once it was challenged, and that 'his character as a historian is firmly established in the passages where outside contact has been found.'

(ii) *The Dispensational Value*

Suppose we had not this record, would it be possible for us to understand the Epistles on the background of the Old Testament? In the Epistles we have Christianity, and in the Old Testament we have Judaism, but without the Acts we could not know how the one came to supersede the other, how the Church displaced the Temple and synagogue, and how national privileges yielded to world-wide blessing.

The Acts is probably the most important dispensational book in the Bible, for it tells us how the great change-over was made. In its pages we see that one dispensation is going, and that another is coming; that Judaism is less and less, and Christianity more and more; it is a story both terminal and germinal; it is the hinge on which the two ages swing, one out and the other in.

One has only to study side by side Peter's sermon at Jerusalem on the day of Pentecost, and Paul's at Antioch in Pisidia (ii; xiii), to see the change of viewpoint. Mark carefully what happened between these two sermons, the manifold preparation for the wider witness (see Analysis).

The Jewish element dominates in the first part of the Book (i-vii); the Gentile element in the last part (xiii-xxviii); and the way from the one to the other is explained in the middle part (viii-xii).

(iii) *The Doctrinal Value*

We may not look for any development of doctrine in this brief record of Christianity within the limits of a single generation, and that, following immediately on the Ascension of Jesus; that came later; but, on the other hand, we are not to suppose that the Church at the beginning was without doctrine. The time for the formulation of creeds had not arrived, but in the apostolic preaching is found the very essence of any Christian Creed. It is not necessary for one to know much in order to become spiritually strong and powerful, but what is known must be of vital significance.

What, then, was it that the Apostles believed and preached which made them such a power, and wrought such a change within so short a time?

In the main,* four things—that *Jesus was the Messiah*; that *His death was redemptive*; that *He rose from the dead*; and that, *by His Spirit, He was present with His people*. That is a very simple but a very powerful creed.

There are some seventeen discourses in the Acts, longer or shorter, and these facts and truths are the substance of them all. Not all at once did even the Apostles grasp the far-reaching implications of these truths, but what they did see they held firmly and preached boldly.

(iv) *The Biographical Value*

Like the *Pilgrim's Progress*, this Book is crowded with characters of all kinds, and the originals of some of Bunyan's characters are here. The outstanding personalities are, of course, Peter and Paul, and these are in the fellowship of a host of Christians, most of whom are unnamed. And there are foes here as well as friends, and women as well as men. What a gallery!

Aeneas, Agabus, Agrippa, Alexander, Ananias, Andrew, Annas, Apollos, Aquila, Aristarchus, Augustus;
Bar-Jesus, Barnabas, Barsabas, Bartholomew, Bernice, Blastus;
Caesar, Caiaphas, Candace, Claudius, Cornelius, Crispus;
Damaris, Demetrius, Dionysius, Dorcas, Drusilla;
Erastus, Eutychus;
Felix, Festus;

Gaius, Gallio, Gamaliel;
Herod;
James, Jason, John, John Mark, Justus;
Lucius, Lydia;
Manaen, Mary, Matthew, Matthias, Mnason;
Nicanor, Nicolas, Niger;
Parmenas, Priscilla, Prochorus, Publius;
Rhoda;
Sapphira, Sceva, Secundus, Sergius Paulus, Silas, Simeon, Simon,
    Sopater, Sosthenes, Stephen;
Tabitha, Theophilus, Theudas, Timon, Timothy, Trophimus,
    Tychicus, Tyrannus, and possibly others.

This is a crowded platform and a crowded scene. To know
these people is to know the history of the Christian Church from
A.D. 30-63.

(v) *The Missionary Value*

Having all the circumstances in view, it is not too much to
say that this is the greatest missionary story that has ever been
told, and it must ever remain the authorised Missionary Manual
of the Church. There has been a great development of missionary
activity since that day, but still all that is vital for effective service
throughout the world is found in the pages of the Acts.

It shows, to begin with, that the Christian Church is missionary,
that Christianity is necessarily a self-propagating religion; that it
cannot be localized anywhere in a sense in which it cannot be
be localized everywhere; that if it did not spread it would die.

Palgrave has said that Mohammedanism flourishes wherever
the palm grows, and that is about the scope of it, but Christianity
flourishes wherever human beings are. We have only to run
over the names of the places mentioned in the Acts to be convinced of the missionary character of Christianity.

Here are some of them:

Amphipolis, Antioch, Antipatris, Appollonia, Assos, Athens, Attalia,
Azotus; Beroea; Caesarea, Cenchreae, Chios, Clauda, Cnidus, Corinth,
Cos, Crete, Cyprus; Damascus, Derbe; Ephesus; Gaza; Iconium;
Jerusalem, Joppa; Lydda, Lystra; Malta, Miletus, Mitylene, Myra,
Mysia; Neapolis; Paphos, Patara, Perga, Philippi, Ptolemais, Puteoli;
Regium, Rhodes, Rome; Salamis, Samaria, Samos, Samothrace,
Seleucia, Sidon, Syracuse; Tarsus, Thessalonica, Troas, Tyre, and
other places, every one of which tells something of the beginnings of
Christianity.

The loss of the Acts would be irreparable.

Surely we feel the thrill of these names, which represent so much of the intellectual, political, and commercial life of the ancient world. Look at a map of Paul's travels long enough and steadily enough to be deeply impressed by the fact that because God loved all the world He commanded His disciples to 'go into all the world and preach the Gospel to every creature'.

But when we come from the broad facts to the details, we still find that the Acts is a Text Book of first rate importance. For instance, we see from it that this great enterprise had a home base.

It was at Antioch in Syria that Barnabas and Saul were called to the work of world evangelism, and it was to Antioch that they returned and 'rehearsed all things that God had done with them' (xiii. 1-3; xiv. 26-28). Furthermore, it was the whole Church in Antioch that sent them out, because, in fact, the whole Church was a Missionary Society.

Then, we see that in his journeyings Paul chose strategic places for the delivery of his message—*Antioch, Philippi, Thessalonica, Corinth, Ephesus, Athens,* and other places of like importance—in the belief that if Christianity were established in the centre it would spread to the circumference, that if the cities were captured the villages would be evangelized from there.

Again, wherever the missionaries went, churches were established which became self-governing and self-supporting. Christian Jews were not sent out from Jerusalem or Antioch to take charge of these indigenous churches, but elders were ordained, instruction was given, and they were left to build up and extend the good work (xiv. 21-23).

Also, these churches were taught the great principle of Christian giving, and especially to care for their poorer brethren (*cf.* Acts xxiv. 17; 2 Cor. viii-ix).

The message and the manner, as well as the method of these missionaries, are full of instruction for the present-day enterprise. Wherever they went they preached the Gospel, and did so tactfully. Their first care was for the souls of the heathen, and not for their physical or temporal welfare. We may be sure that if Paul lived to-day he would rejoice in Medical, Educational and

Industrial Missions, but we may be equally sure that he would be vigorously opposed to any of these taking precedence of Evangelistic Missions. Those days had their temporal problems as well as these, but the missionaries always put first things first.

(vi) *The Spiritual Value*

The Acts discloses the true character of the Christian Church, and the secret of her life and service. More and more it came to be seen that the Church was not something grafted on to the Temple or the Synagogue, but was a Spiritual Institution, a Holy Society, indwelt, empowered, and guided by the Holy Spirit.

The Book is, really, the Acts of the Holy Spirit; He dominates the record. He is the Spirit of Promise (i), of Power (ii), of Healing (iii), of Boldness (iv), of Judgment (v), of Administration (vi), of Steadfastness (vii), of Evangelism (viii), of Comfort (ix), of Guidance (x), of Prophecy (xi), of Deliverance (xii), of Missions (xiii), of Protection (xiv), of Councils (xv), of Restraint and Constraint (xvi), of Opportunity (xvii), of Revelation (xviii), of Purpose (xix), of Ordination (xx), and so forth to the end.

> It was about the Spirit that Jesus spoke to His Apostles just before He ascended (i. 2, 4, 5, 8);
>
> It was the Spirit that came upon them at Pentecost (ii. 4);
>
> It is the Spirit that is promised to all who believe (ii. 38, 39);
>
> It was to the Spirit that Ananias and Sapphira lied (v. 3, 4, 9);
>
> It was with the Spirit that the apostles witnessed (v. 32);
>
> The first deacons had to be filled with the Spirit (vi. 3, 5);
>
> Philip was instructed by the Spirit to speak to the eunuch (viii. 29);
>
> The Spirit bade Peter go to Cornelius (x. 19; xi. 12);
>
> The Spirit instructed the Church to send forth Barnabas and Saul on missionary work (xiii. 2, 4);
>
> It was the Spirit with the Apostles Who settled the Jewish-Gentile controversy (xv. 28);

and so is it all through the story. The Acts is the record of a Spirit-begotten, Spirit-filled, Spirit-guided Church, and that accounts for what she accomplished in those days. It is when the

Church finds substitutes for the Holy Spirit that she is ineffective and defeated.

9. OUTLINE

The story of the Acts reaches from Jerusalem to Rome, and, as we have said, the purpose of it is to show that the Christian Church is essentially a witnessing agency, and to relate how, why, where, and through whom it witnesses, and with what effect. This is done in three distinct parts.

CHART 133

ACT II.	SCENE 2	
THE HISTORICAL EXPANSION OF CHRISTIANITY		
The Book of the Acts. A.D. 30–63＝33 Years		
Subject: WITNESS. Key—ch. i. 8		
Period 1	**Period 2**	**Period 3**
JEWISH	TRANSITION	GENTILE
i. 1–viii. 4	viii. 4–xii. 25	xiii–xxviii
JERUSALEM	ANTIOCH	ROME
Jewish Christianity	Gentile Christianity	Universal Christianity
PETER	PETER and BARNABAS	PAUL
The City	The Provinces	The World
A.D. 30–37	A.D. 37-47	A.D. 47-63
7 Years	10 Years	16 Years
DEPTH	BREADTH	LENGTH

It is an amazing movement, carried forward with unresting and untiring energy to the great achievement of erecting the Gospel standard in the Capital of the Empire.

Christianity being the one universal religion must advance, and it is essentially missionary, self-propagating, and self-authenticating.

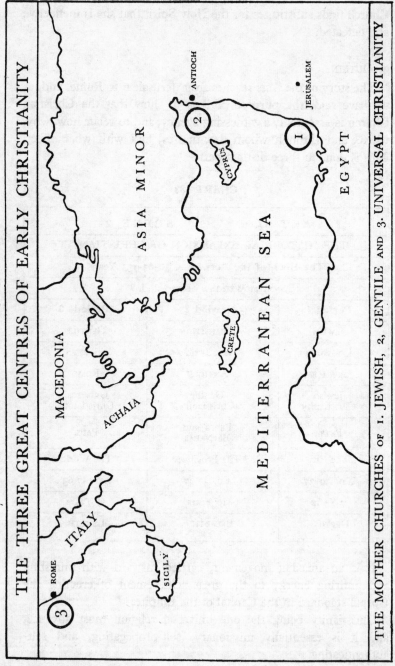

MAP 14

THE THREE GREAT CENTRES OF EARLY CHRISTIANITY

THE MOTHER CHURCHES OF 1. JEWISH, 2, GENTILE AND 3. UNIVERSAL CHRISTIANITY

W. G.S.

Copyright

184

From the abrupt conclusion of the Acts one may reasonably infer that it was the intention of the author to continue the story, but for some reason he was prevented doing this, and so it eventuates that of the seventy years from the ascension of Christ to the close of the first century we have in the New Testament a historical record of less than a half of that period. Of the years A.D. 63-68 some particulars may be gathered from the Epistles, but there is no New Testament history of the period A.D. 68-100; and only dimly from the Apocalypse may we see what was the situation at the close of the century (if the late date be accepted). For the historical events of this period we must turn to extrabiblical sources, both Jewish and Gentile.

I. THE JEWISH PERIOD OF THE CHURCH'S WITNESS
The Church Established
ITS DEPTH

Chs. i. 1-viii. 4. A.D. 30-37: 7 Years.

Central City	-	-	JERUSALEM
Leader	-	-	- PETER

1. Founding of the Church	- - -	i. 1-ii. 13
2. Testimony of the Church	- - -	ii. 14-47
3. Opposition to the Church	- - -	iii. 1-iv. 31
4. Discipline in the Church	- - -	iv. 32-v. 16
5. Testing of the Church	- - -	v. 17-42
6. Administration in the Church	- - -	vi. 1-6
7. Persecution of the Church	- - -	vi. 7-viii. 4

II. THE TRANSITION PERIOD OF THE CHURCH'S WITNESS
The Church Expanded
ITS BREADTH

Chs. viii. 4-xii. 25. A.D. 37-47: 10 Years.

Central City	-	-	- ANTIOCH
Leader	-	-	BARNABAS

1. Philip's Preparation	- - -	viii. 4-40
2. Saul's Preparation	- - -	ix. 1-31
3. Peter's Preparation	- - -	ix. 32-x. 48
4. The Apostles' Preparation	- - -	xi. 1-18
5. The Church's Preparation	- - -	xi. 19-xii. 25

III. THE GENTILE PERIOD OF THE CHURCH'S WITNESS
The Church Extended
ITS LENGTH

Chs. xiii-xxviii. A.D. 47-63: 16 Years.

Central City	-	-	- ROME
Leader	-	-	- PAUL

186

1. Paul's Tireless Activities

Chs. xiii-xxi. 16. A.D. 47-58

(i) The First Missionary Journey

Chs. xiii. 1-xiv. 28

A.D. 47—49-50. 2 Years

(a) The Call and Consecration at Antioch. Ch. xiii. 1-3.

(b) The Circuit in Asia Minor. Chs. xiii. 4-xiv. 28
(The Conference at Jerusalem. Ch. xv. 1-35)

(ii) The Second Missionary Journey

Chs. xv. 36-xviii. 22

A.D. 50-54. 3-4 Years

(a) Apostolic Labours in Asia Minor. Chs. xv. 36-xvi. 10.

(b) Apostolic Labours in Macedonia. Chs. xvi. 11-xvii. 14.

(c) Apostolic Labours in Achaia. Chs. xvii. 15-xviii. 22.

(iii) The Third Missionary Journey

Chs. xviii. 23—xxi. 16

A.D. 54-58. 4 Years

(a) Paul's Activities in Asia. Chs. xviii. 23-xix. 41.

(b) Paul's Experiences in Europe. Ch. xx. 1-6.

(c) Paul's Journey to Jerusalem. Chs. xx. 6-xxi. 16.

2. Paul's Fruitful Captivities

Chs. xxi. 17-xxviii. A.D. 58-63.

(i) At JERUSALEM

Chs. xxi. 17-xxiii. 30
A.D. 58

(ii) At CAESAREA

Chs. xxiii. 31-xxvi.
A.D. 58-60

(iii) At ROME

Chs. xxvii-xxviii
A.D. 60-63

Released from first Roman imprisonment, A.D. 63-67.

Rearrested, taken to Rome, retried, and martyred, A.D. 67-68.

CHART 134

ACT II	SCENE 2
THE PROGRESS OF CHRISTIANITY IN THE WORLD TO THE END OF THE FIRST CENTURY A.D.	
(i) **The Historical Expansion of the Church**	
Stage One A.D. 30–67	*Stage Two* A.D. 67–95
THE RAPID ADVANCE	THE SEEMING ARREST
CHRISTIAN WITNESS The Jewish Period Ac. i. 1–viii. 4	The Martyrdom of Paul and Peter A.D. 66–68
The Transition Period Ac. viii. 4–xii. 25	The Destruction of Jerusalem A.D. 70
	The Long Silence A.D. 70-95
The Gentile Period Ac. xiii–xxviii	The Last Voice. A.D. 95
(ii) **The Doctrinal Expression of the Church**	
THE PAULINE EPISTLES Romans to (Hebrews?)	THE CATHOLIC EPISTLES James to Jude

THE ACTS

THE BEGINNINGS OF CHURCH HISTORY

The Apostle Peter

As Peter was the dominating personality throughout Parts One and Two of this Story, it will be best at this point to present a survey of the life of this great Apostle.

The stories of Peter and Paul constitute the history of Christianity during forty years of the New Testament period (A.D. 27-67). The material relative to Paul is abundant, but, having regard for the importance of Peter in the story, comparatively little information has survived. With the Peter of Jewish legend, and of Christian tradition we are not here concerned, but we must briefly outline what is said about him in the Gospels, the Acts, and the Epistles.

This material is divisible into two distinct periods, namely, Peter before, and Peter at and after Pentecost, and the sources for these periods are respectively the Gospels, and the Acts and Epistles. One may say that the dividing line was the day of Pentecost.

I. PETER BEFORE PENTECOST

1. The surface details of his life are soon told. His name was Simon. His father's name was Jonah, or John. He had a brother whose name was Andrew. He was married, and lived with his wife, brother, and mother-in-law in Capernaum. By trade he was a fisherman, and owned a fleet of fishing boats, which he worked with his brother. The sons of Zebedee, John and James, were his partners. He was known by his Jewish name, Simon. He was one of John the Baptist's disciples, and probably his first contact with Jesus was at the latter's baptism (Acts i. 22).

2. Peter became related to Jesus in three stages. First, he was *invited to friendship* (John i. 35-42); secondly, he was *called to discipleship* (Luke v. 1-11); and finally, he was *made an apostle* (Mark iii. 13-19. Luke vi. 12-16). In all the lists of the Twelve Peter holds the first place, and he was one of the three Apostles

who on three occasions were chosen from among the Twelve to witness a divine mystery: at the raising of the daughter of Jairus; on the Mount of Transfiguration; and in the Garden of Gethsemane.

3. Outstanding events in Peter's story in this period were—his confession of Jesus' divine Messiahship; his witness of the Transfiguration; his emphatic denial of his Master; Jesus' appearance to him in resurrection life; and Jesus' final commission of him after He had risen.

4. When Jesus said to Peter, 'When you are converted', that is, 'when you turn again to Me', surely He was referring to characteristics in His disciple's temperament which should not be cultivated, and which some day would be exchanged for their opposites. Among such were the following:—

(i) *He had a great love of self-distinction*: 'Lord, if it be Thou, bid me come unto Thee on the water' (Matt. xiv. 24-31).

(ii) *He was influenced largely by worldly policy*: 'Lord, spare Thyself' (Matt. xvi. 21-23).

(iii) *He was afflicted with spiritual short-sightedness*: 'Lord, let us make here three tabernacles'. (Matt. xvi. 27-xvii. 7).

(iv) *He was characterized by over-weening self-confidence*: 'Though all should be offended because of Thee, I will never be offended. Though I should die with Thee, yet will I not deny Thee' (Matt. xxvi. 30-35).

(v) *He placed confidence in carnal methods of defence*: 'He struck a servant of the high priest, and smote off his ear' (Matt. xxvi. 46-54).

(vi) *He was guilty of the basest cowardice*: 'I know not the man' (Matt. xxvi. 67-74).

These incidents are in chronological order, and in them we discern a development of self which makes Peter less and less a pattern and guide.

Yet this is the man to whom Christ said: 'Blessed art thou, Simon Bar-Jonah'; the only occasion when the Lord pronounced a beatitude on an individual. Also, 'Thou art Peter, and upon this rock I will build my church; and the gates of Hades shall not

prevail against it'. And again, 'I will give unto thee the keys of
the Kingdom of Heaven; and whatsoever thou shalt bind on earth
shall be bound in heaven; and whatsoever thou shalt loose on
earth shall be loosed in heaven' (Matt. xvi. 13-19). ˉSurely before
these promises could be fulfilled a great change would have to be
wrought in Peter; and this change was wrought in him on the
day of Pentecost. Peter was sifted, and though Satan operated
the sieve no true grain was lost (Luke xxii. 31, 32).

II. Peter After Pentecost

1. After forty days of resurrection life on earth the Lord Jesus
ascended to heaven, where He will remain until the second advent.
But before His departure He spoke to His Apostles of the spread
of Christianity and the growth of His Church. This was to be
in three stages:

(a) 'In Jerusalem'; (b) 'in Judaea and Samaria'; and (c) 'unto
the uttermost part of the earth' (Acts i. 8).

The record of the Church in Jerusalem is in Acts i-vii; of the
Church in the provinces, in chapters viii-xii; and of the Church
throughout the world, in chapters xiii-xxviii.

Peter dominates the first two periods (chapters i-xii), and
Paul, the third (chapters xiii-xxviii).

2. In the references to Peter in the Acts the matters of outstanding
importance—in addition to his strong leadership throughout the
period covered by chapters i-xii—are his contact with Cornelius
(x-xi), and his statement at the Jerusalem Conference (xv. 6-11).

(i) Peter and Cornelius
(Acts x-xi)

In Gal. ii. 8, 9 Paul says: 'He that wrought for Peter unto the
apostleship of the circumcision, wrought for me also unto the
Gentiles'; also, to Barnabas and himself, when in Jerusalem,
James and Peter and John 'gave the right hand of fellowship
that we should go unto the Gentiles, and they unto the circumcision'. This just means that Peter was commissioned to evangelize Jews, and Paul, to evangelize Gentiles, and, in the main,
this is what each of them did.

But it must be remembered that these commissions were not mutually exclusive. Peter ministered to Gentiles, and Paul ministered to Jews. When Peter went to Samaria to confirm Philip's work there, he went to a people who were only nominally Jews, and whom the Jews hated (John iv. 9); and when he lodged with 'Simon a tanner' at Joppa (Acts ix. 43), he took a long step towards eating with Gentiles. But the great event for Peter was his going to Caesarea to preach the Gospel to a gathering of Gentiles, an event which ran counter to his upbringing and inclination (Acts x. 9-16, 28). This was the formal opening of the door of the Christian Church for Gentiles to enter, and it was Peter and not Paul who opened the door; and furthermore, this momentous event was endorsed by the Jerusalem Apostles (Acts xi. 18).

Whatever may be the true interpretation of 'the keys of the kingdom' in Matt. xvi. 19, certain it is that it was Peter and not Paul who first used them, and which made available to Gentiles the full privileges of Christianity.

(ii) *Peter at the Jerusalem Conference*
(Acts xv. 6-11)

1. In Acts vi. 1-6 is recorded the *first* Church business meeting, and in chapter xv the *second* is put on record. The first concerned a matter of administration, and the second related to the conditions, if any, on which Gentile believers were to be admitted to the full fellowship of the Christian Church.

There were those who held that before Gentiles could be admitted they must be circumcised, that is, that in order to become Christians they must first become Jews. Was Christianity, which began in Judaism, to be but an extended form of the latter, or was it to be something quite different? Must Gentiles become subject to the Mosaic Law in order to be saved? The Hellenist side of the Church said 'no' to these questions, and the Hebrew side said 'yes'.

This situation called for a conference, and Acts xv is the record of what happened, and it must be read with Gal. ii. 1-10. After an open debate (xv. 7), Peter spoke (xv. 7-11). He was followed by Paul and Barnabas (xv. 12); and James summed up the debate and gave his verdict (xv. 13-21).

2. We are concerned here only with what Peter said. He was against imposing the Mosaic Law upon Gentile believers, and appealed to his experience in the house of Cornelius in Caesarea (ch. x.). Without being circumcised these believing Gentiles were saved and were given the Holy Spirit. Jews and Gentiles alike were saved by grace on God's part, and by faith on their own part. And Peter added that the yoke which the Judaisers urged should be put on the Gentiles they themselves were not able to bear.

From this utterance, which, no doubt, is just a summary of what Peter said, it is clear that he had learned the lesson of the vision recorded in Acts x. 9-16, and while he continued to be the Apostle of the circumcision he endorsed the verdict of the Jerusalem finding which is epitomised in Acts xv. 19, 20.

With this event Peter passes from the scene, so far as Luke's record is concerned, but if tradition be correct there remained to him about seventeen years before his death about A.D. 67. What was he doing during this period?

(iii) *Peter Rebuked by Paul*

1. In Galatians ii. 11-21 is recorded one of the most remarkable scenes in sacred history. The place was Antioch in Syria; the occasion was a gathering of Jewish and Gentile Christians; and the persons concerned were the two outstanding Apostles, Peter and Paul. The circumstance was this: for some reason or another Peter was at Antioch, and acting in harmony with his experience in Acts x and with his declaration in Acts xv he met the Gentile converts in the city in social friendship and ate with them. Certain strict Jews who had come from Jerusalem criticised Peter's conduct, and, yielding to their scruples, 'he withdrew and ate separately from the Gentiles—out of sheer fear of what the Jews might think' (J. B. Phillips). Peter's example was followed by others, and even Barnabas was influenced.

2. When Paul saw what had happened he courageously and publicly rebuked Peter for his inconsistency.

'If you, who are a Jew, do not live like a Jew but like a Gentile, why on earth do you try to make Gentiles live like Jews?' (J. B. Phillips). Then Paul, in a luminous and dynamic statement, contrasted Judaism and Christianity, and showed that the Law and the Gospel embodied mutually exclusive concepts relative to salvation; and he concluded by saying: 'I refuse to stultify the grace of God by reverting to the Law. For if righteousness were possible under the Law then Christ died for nothing' (Phillips).

3. We are not told what the reaction was of Peter and the others to this challenge, but we know that it did not result in animosity on Peter's part to Paul, for, towards the end of the seventh decade, probably between 65-67 A.D., he wrote: 'Account that the long-suffering of our Lord is salvation; even as *our beloved brother Paul* also, according to the wisdom given to him, wrote unto you; as also in all his epistles . . .'; and these epistles included the one in which his own censure was recorded (2 Pet. iii. 15, 16). This has rightly been characterized as 'an eminent triumph of Christian humility and love'.

(iv) *Peter's Travels and Writings*

1. All we know of Peter as a missionary is that he went to *Babylon*. (1 Peter v. 13). 'The co-elect here in Babylon greet you'. But the question naturally arises as to what is meant by 'Babylon', and three answers have been given to the enquiry.

First, that by Babylon is meant *Rome*. This is the belief of those who hold that Peter went to the imperial Capital, and was martyred there. This was the unanimous belief of the Christian Church at the close of the second century. Secondly, that by Babylon is meant the *Chaldean Capital* on the Euphrates. When Paul went westward it is not unlikely that Peter went eastward, and it is known that in the East was a large Jewish population, and, no doubt, many Gentile believers. (Josephus *Antiq.* xviii. 8; xv. 2. 2). The nations to which Peter's first letter was sent (i. 1) are, in the main, from East to West, which would be natural if he wrote from the Chaldean Capital. Thirdly, that by Babylon is meant a military station near Cairo in Egypt. This would explain the early tradition that Mark was appointed bishop of Alexandria; but few have accepted this interpretation of the name.

In the second view the name is understood literally, and in the first view it is understood mystically.

Whether or not Peter was ever in Rome we do not here discuss, but cannot forbear to quote three statements made by Foakes-Jackson in his *Peter: Prince of Apostles*.

> 'It must be acknowledged that the evidence of the New Testament, of the Apostolic Fathers, and of the Christian writers before Irenaeus does not support the view that Peter was ever at Rome' (p. 156).

> 'Despite the great names by which it is supported, the literary argument for Peter's visit to Rome is certainly unsatisfactory, although the probability that he visited the city is strong' (p. 161).

> 'The fact (that Peter visited Rome) is not as unquestionable as is often assumed.' . . . 'The evidence for this cannot in honesty be pronounced to be unquestionable' (pp. 162, 163).

The point of the reference in our survey is that Peter did travel either far East or far West.

From 1 Peter i. 1 it has been believed that 'he had preached far and wide in the peninsula of Asia Minor', but the words do not necessarily imply this.

2. As to the Apostle's writings, we assume that he wrote the two Epistles which bear his name, but reserve further reference till we consider the New Testament Epistles.

3. It is appropriate, however, to say here that relative to Mark's Gospel, two things are held almost unanimously, (*a*) that it was the first of the Gospels to be written, and (*b*) that it represents the preaching of Peter; so though he was not the author of this priceless record, he was the originator of it (see the writer's *A Guide to the Gospels*), and by it he is immortalized.

CHART 135

THE APOSTLE PETER	
BEFORE PENTECOST	**AFTER PENTECOST**
THE GOSPELS	THE ACTS AND THE EPISTLES
A.D. ?-30	A.D. 30-67(?)
His Home and Trade *Capernaum. Fisherman*	His Leadership in the Early Church
His Calls *to* *Friendship. Discipleship. Apostleship*	His Proclamation of the Gospel to Gentiles
His Character *Intense. Impulsive. Injudicious*	His Share in the Jerusalem Conference
His Commission *To lead and to feed believers young and old.* John xxi. 15-17	His Vacillation, and Paul's Rebuke (Gal. ii)
	His Travels and Writings *Babylon* 1-2 *Peter*
His Predicted End *A violent death* John xxi. 18, 19	His Responsibility for Mark's Gospel
	His Martyrdom

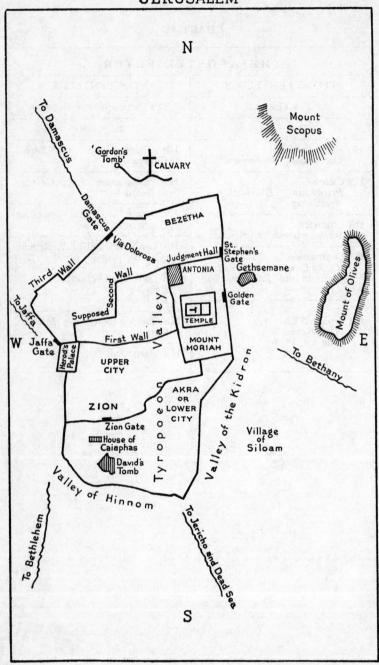

JERUSALEM

N

Mount Scopus

To Damascus

'Gordon's Tomb'

✝ CALVARY

Damascus Gate

BEZETHA

Via Dolorosa

Judgment Hall

St. Stephen's Gate

ANTONIA

Gethsemane

Third Wall

Second Wall

Golden Gate

Mount of Olives

Supposed

TEMPLE

To Jaffa

First Wall

MOUNT MORIAH

W

Jaffa Gate

Herod's Palace

UPPER CITY

To Bethany

E

ZION

AKRA OR LOWER CITY

Valley of the Kidron

Village of Siloam

Zion Gate

House of Caiaphas

Tyropoeon

David's Tomb

Valley of Hinnom

To Bethlehem

To Jericho and Dead Sea

S

MAP 15
196

JERUSALEM

As this City figures so largely in apostolic history it may be useful to present here a few facts concerning so famous a place.

FORMS OF THE NAME:

Hierosolyma; Hierousalem; Hierusalem; Ierousalem; Solyma; Urusale(i)m; Yerushalaim; Yerushalem.

DERIVATION: 'Almost impossible to descry' (G.A.S.). 'Shalem casts the lot'; 'Secure lot'; 'Hearth of peace.' (*Jerusalem.* Vol. I, Chap. ix. George Adam Smith).

OTHER DESCRIPTIONS:

Ariel. *City* of Judah, of God, of our God, of the Great King, of Jahweh of Hosts, of David. The Holy City. The City of Righteousness. *Daughter* of Zion, of Jerusalem, of My people. Virgin daughter of Sion.
(*Jerusalem.* Vol. I, Chap. x. George Adam Smith).

ELEVATION:

2,593 feet above sea level.

GATES (main):

Damascus; Double; Dung; First; Fish; Fountain; Garden; Golden; Herod's; Horse; Jaffa; Sheep; Single; Sion; St. Stephen's; Valley; Water; Zion.

TEMPLES:

Solomon's, B.C. 1012; Zerubbabel's, B.C. 520-516; Herod's B.C. 20-19—A.D. 27 (John ii. 20).

VALLEYS:

Hinnom; Kidron; Tyropoeon.

HILLS

The City was built on four hills: Zion, Moriah, Acra, and Bezetha. The chief of these was Zion, the city of David (2 Sam. 5. 7-9), and was distinguished from the temple hill called Mount Moriah (Gen. xxii. 2; 2 Sam. xxiv. 18; 2 Chr. iii. 1). Among "the mountains round about" was the Mount of Olives which is so sacred in Christian story.

REVERSES

No city has had so chequered a history as has Jerusalem. The city of to-day is not that of 2,000 years ago, which lies far beneath it.

Joshua took part of the city nearly 1,500 years B.C. David conquered the Jebusites and took it all, more than 1,000 years B.C. Shishak, King of Egypt, conquered the city in the 10th century, B.C. In B.C. 586 Nebuchadnezzar destroyed Jerusalem and brought the Hebrew monarchy to an end.

Under Zerubbabel in B.C. 536 the Temple was rebuilt, and the restoration of the City began, and was continued by Nehemiah in B.C. 445.

Ptolemy Soter, King of Egypt pillaged Jerusalem in the 4th century B.C., and Palestine was annexed to Egypt.

In B.C. 175 Antiochus Epiphanes plundered the City and destroyed its walls; and by his outrages he roused the revolt of the Maccabees (B.C. 165), which lasted for nearly a century.

In B.C. 63 Pompey of Rome took Jerusalem, and from that time until its final destruction by Titus in A.D. 70, the Jews were under the dominion of the Romans. This last overthrow of the City and Temple differed from all others in that it ended the nationhood of the Jews, and the system of Judaism. From this disaster there has, as yet, been no recovery.

The modern city is divided between Jews and Arabs, and awaits the fulfilment of the 'latter day' prophecies.

THE BOOK OF THE ACTS

PART ONE

THE JEWISH PERIOD OF THE CHURCH'S WITNESS

Chapters i. 1—viii. 4

A.D. 30-37 -   - 7 Years

THE CHURCH ESTABLISHED - -   ITS DEPTH

THE JEWISH PERIOD OF THE
CHURCH'S WITNESS

IN Part One of this entrancing story there are seven distinct sections which, step by step, trace the development of the early Church from its coming into being to the scattering of its members in consequence of the persecution which arose over Stephen. The record is compressed, yet it is a very graphic account of the first seven years of the Church's history.

Each of these sections is of vital importance for an understanding of the beginnings of Church history.

Six of these seven are alternating, as follows:

I. FOUNDING OF THE CHURCH

II. TESTIMONY OF THE CHURCH

III. OPPOSITION TO THE CHURCH

IV. DISCIPLINE IN THE CHURCH

V. TESTING OF THE CHURCH

VI. ADMINISTRATION IN THE CHURCH

VII. PERSECUTION OF THE CHURCH

Sections II, IV, VI relate to matters *inside* the Church, advancing it, and sections III, V, VII, relate to activities *outside* the Church, and against it.

The following is a detailed summary of these sections (i. 1-viii. 4).

I. FOUNDING OF THE CHURCH (i. 1-ii. 13)
　　　　1. The Days of Preparation, i. 1-26.
　　　　2. The Day of Pentecost, ii. 1-13.

II. TESTIMONY OF THE CHURCH (ii. 14-47)
　　　　1. Their Simple Creed, 14-41.
　　　　　　The Discourse of Peter.
　　　　2. Their Sanctified Conduct, 42-47.
　　　　　　A Description of the First Church.

III. OPPOSITION TO THE CHURCH (iii. 1-iv. 31).

1. The Occasion of it, iii. 1-26.
2. The Expression of it, iv. 1-22.
3. The Sequel to it, iv. 23-31.

IV. DISCIPLINE IN THE CHURCH (iv. 32-v. 16).

1. The Originating Circumstances, iv. 32-37.
2. The Specific Occasion, v. 1-10.
3. The Salutary Effects, v. 11-16.

V. TESTING OF THE CHURCH (v. 17-42).

1. The Detention and Deliverance of the Apostles, 17-21a.
2. The Trial and Triumph of the Apostles, 21b-42.

VI. ADMINISTRATION IN THE CHURCH (vi. 1-6).

1. The Complaint of the Disciples, 1.
2. The Conference of the Apostles, 2-4.
3. The Choice of Deacons, 5-6.

VII. PERSECUTION OF THE CHURCH (vi. 7-viii. 4).

1. The Reason for it, vi. 7.
2. The Focus of it, vi. 8-viii. 1a.
3. The Issues of it, viii. 1b-4.

The following is a detailed analysis of section one:

FOUNDING OF THE CHURCH (i. 1-ii. 13)

1. *THE DAYS OF PREPARATION* (i. 1-26)

    (i) THE FORTY DAYS: i. 1-11.

        (a) MANIFESTATION (1-3)
        (b) INSTRUCTION (4-8)
        (c) ASCENSION (9-11)

    (ii) THE TEN DAYS: i. 12-26

        (a) SUPPLICATION OF THE DISCIPLES (12-14)
        (b) ELECTION OF AN APOSTLE (15-26)

            (1) FIRST NECESSITY (ver. 16) Past
            (2) SECOND NECESSITY (ver. 21) Present

2. *THE DAY OF PENTECOST*: ii. 1-13

    (i) THE ADVENT OF THE PROMISED SPIRIT: ii. 1-4a

(a) TIME	1a
(b) OCCASION	1b
(c) MANNER	2
(d) EVIDENCE	3
(e) RESULT	4a

I. FOUNDING OF THE CHURCH
(i. 1-ii. 13)

1. The Days of Preparation
(i. 1-26)

(i) THE FORTY DAYS (i. 1-11)

The first verse of this chapter shows that the Acts is a sequel to and continuation of the Evangelic Records. Verse 3 connects with the *Resurrection* at the end of Matthew's Gospel; verses 9, 10 connect with the *Ascension* at the end of Mark's Gospel; verses 7, 8 connect with the *Promise of the Spirit* at the end of Luke's Gospel; and verse 11 anticipates the *Second Advent* at the end of John's Gospel. A period of 2000 years is envisaged in these few verses: Christ's Life (1), Death (3), Resurrection (3), Kingdom (3, 6, 7), Spirit (4, 5, 8), Ascension (9-11), and Second Advent (11).

Luke says that the Gospel he wrote told only of what '*Jesus began to do and to teach*' and the natural inference is that in the Acts he is about to record what Jesus, now the risen Lord, is continuing to do and to teach; and as this record is only the first chapter of Church history it is clear that Christ is still doing and teaching. The difference between the *beginning* and the *continuing* is that *then* He wrought in person here on earth, and *now* He is working from heaven by His Spirit, in and through His Church. Christ's departure was not a sunset, but a sunrise.

Verse 8 is the key to the Book, telling as it does of CHRISTIAN

WITNESS: the Central Subject, *Christ*; the Widening Sphere, *from Jerusalem* to the' *uttermost part of the earth*'; the Exclusive Source, '*ye*', the Christian Church; and the Unfailing Secret, '*the Holy Spirit.*'

Swiftly and impressively are these forty days summarized in the manifestation (1-3); instruction (4-8); and ascension (9-11) of Christ.

(ii) THE TEN DAYS (i. 12-26)

A Momentous Prayer Meeting

The Founding of the Church was prepared for, not only by Christ's ascension (9-11), but by prayerful waiting on the part of the disciples (12-14). The '*upper room*' (13), and '*one place*' (ii. 1), was, without doubt, where they had kept the Passover nearly six weeks before (Luke xxii. 12). The prayer-meeting lasted for ten days (i. 5; ii. 1) which with the forty days after the resurrection made the fifty between the Passover and Pentecost (Lev. xxiii. 15), and it was attended by all the Apostles, except Judas Iscariot, who was dead; by certain women, including the mother of Jesus, of whom we never read again; and also by Jesus' brothers, who now at last believed (John vii. 5). What were they waiting for? See verses 4, 5. The Father's promise was fulfilled 1900 years ago, so that our duty now is, not to *wait*, but to *take*.

Now follows a most important event. The divinely appointed number of the Apostles was *Twelve*, and the number of the Tribes of Israel was *Twelve*, which, together are represented by the *Four and Twenty Elders* of Revelation iv. 4. Judas was dead (16-20), and so it was necessary that some one be appointed to take his place (21, 22), which was now done (23-26).

The Death and Doom of Judas (16-20, 25)

Peter's explanation in verses 16, 17, is for the information of the 'hundred and twenty' (15) and not of his brother apostles. Verses 18, 19 are a parenthesis added by the historian Luke. Read this with Matt. xxvii. 3-8. The accounts are not contradictory, if we assume that *the rope broke* with which Judas hanged himself. Make a note of Peter's interpretation of Psalm lxix. 25.

The Appointment of a New Apostle (21-26)

Mark the necessary qualification (21, 22): '*All the time . . .
beginning from . . . unto*'. Observe '*put forward*', not '*appointed*',
in verse 23. It says, '*Thou hast*', not, '*Thou wilt*', in verse 24.
'*Part*' in verse 25 should be '*place*', then we see the place Judas
forfeited, and the place he acquired. Matthias was elected.
Did God appoint you to the office which you hold? Then, don't
talk about resigning. Our place in eternity is determined in
time (25).

2. The Day of Pentecost
(ii. 1-13)

The Jews had three great annual Feasts: *Passover*, in April,
celebrating the deliverance of the Israelites from Egyptian
bondage; *Pentecost*, in June, commemorating the completed
harvest of the ground; and *Tabernacles*, in October, in remembrance of the sojourning of the Israelites in the wilderness. These
Feasts were typical and prophetical. We know that the *Passover
Feast* was fulfilled by the death of the Lamb of God; and the
Feast of Pentecost, by the creation of the Christian Church.

After the ten days comes the Great Day, the Birthday of the
Christian Church (1-13). There were *Christians* before Pentecost
(i. 13, 15. 1 Cor. xv. 6), but on this day they were constituted
the Christian Church by the Descent and Baptism of the Holy
Spirit: Christian believers became Christ's Body. In our portion
are two main particulars.

(i) THE ADVENT OF THE PROMISED SPIRIT (1-4a)

Observe carefully the *day*, the *company*, the *place*, the *sound*,
the *light*, the *power*, and the *endowment*—seven things. A new
dispensation was inaugurated on this day. True, all the members
of the Church were Jews during the first seven years (cf. vi. 5,
Nicolas), but yet this was Christianity, and not Judaism.

We may say that the *wind* symbolizes the spiritual constitution
of the Church; the *fire*, the individual possession of the Spirit;
and the *tongues*, the universal commission of the saved. Distinguish between the *Baptism* and the *Infilling* of the Spirit.

Both blessings were vouchsafed on the Day of Pentecost; but, whereas the Baptism is once for all, the Filling is oft repeated (cf. iv. 31. Eph. v. 18). Baptism and Filling are opposite figures. In the former, the vessel is in the element; in the latter, the element is also in the vessel. We are made Christians and members of Christ's Body by the Baptism; but we are made Christ-like by the Filling.

(ii) THE EFFECT OF THE SPIRIT'S ADVENT (3-13)

Let us clear up two popular misunderstandings here. First, the *speech* is not the same throughout this passage (1-8). '*Tongues*' in 3, 4 is *glossai*, whence our word *glossolalia*; but in 6, 8 it is *dialektoi*, whence our word *dialects* (in the Acts only). It is clear that the 'tongues' of 1 Cor. xiv were not known languages. Secondly, these Christians were not preaching the Gospel (11). They did not speak because the crowd was there; the crowd came there because they were speaking (6). The utterance was one of adoration, and such will always be variously interpreted (12, 13).

The Diaspora

We have already seen that the widespread scattering of the Jews was a preparation for Christianity (see p 60), and this passage (ii. 7-11) illustrates the fact. Sixteen countries are named from which Jews had come to Jerusalem to celebrate the Feast of Pentecost. (Map 16). These, no doubt, would be brought into the blessing of this memorable occasion, and would return to their adopted countries to tell the story of what had happened, and to share the blessing with their brethren.

In this way was the Church Founded.

MAP 16

THE JEWISH DISPERSION ILLUSTRATED AT PENTECOST

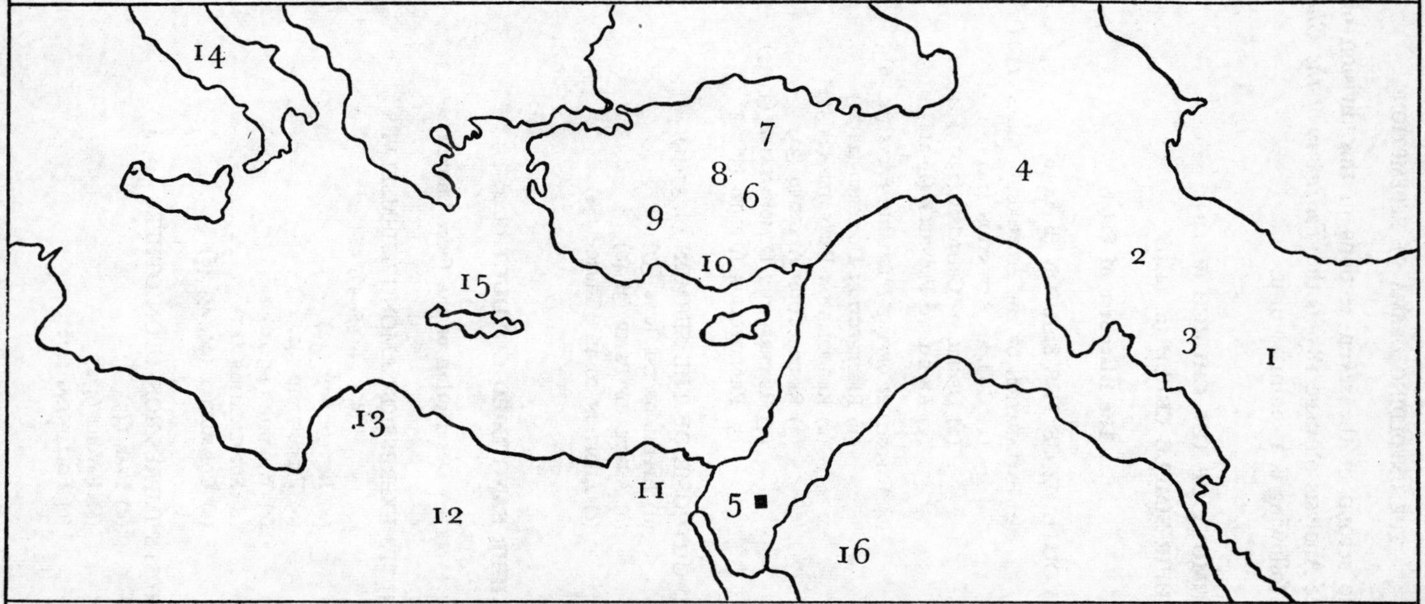

The Jewish Dispersion represented at the Pentecostal Feast at Jerusalem. (Acts ii. 9-11)

■ Jerusalem; 1, Parthia; 2, Media; 3, Elam; 4, Mesopotamia; 5, Judaea; 6, Cappadocia; 7, Pontus; 8, Asia; 9, Phrygia; 10, Pamphylia; 11, Egypt; 12, Lybia; 13, Cyrene; 14, Rome; 15, Crete; 16, Arabia.

Copyright   W.G.S.

In the second of the seven sections in this division of the Acts (see Analysis on page 185) is the *Testimony of the Church*, and the following is a summary of it.

II. TESTIMONY OF THE CHURCH (ii. 14-47)

1. THEIR SIMPLE CREED (ii. 14-41)

The Discourse of Peter

(i) OUTLINE OF THE SERMON (ii. 14-36)

    (a) EXPLANATION OF THE PENTECOSTAL SIGNS (14-21)
        (1) CALL TO ATTENTION (14)
        (2) DENIAL OF CRITICISM (13-15)
        (3) APPEAL TO PROPHECY (16-21)

    (b) EXPOSITION OF THE MESSIANIC FACTS (22-36)
        (1) RESURRECTION DECLARED (22-24)
        (2) RESURRECTION PREDICTED (25-31)
        (3) RESURRECTION ATTESTED (32)
        (4) RESURRECTION DEMONSTRATED (33-35)
        (5) RESURRECTION APPLIED (36)

(ii) OUTCOME OF THE SERMON (ii. 37-41)
    (a) APPEAL OF THE JEWS (37)
    (b) ANSWER OF PETER (38-40)
    (c) ADDITION TO THE CHURCH (41)

2. THEIR SANCTIFIED CONDUCT (ii. 42-47)

A Description of the First Church

(i) ITS EXPRESSION AMONG THEMSELVES
        (42, 44, 45, 46, 47a)
    (a) INSTRUCTION (42)
    (b) FELLOWSHIP (42, 46)
    (c) WORSHIP (42, 46)
    (d) SUPPLICATION (42)
    (e) COMMUNITY (44, 45, 46)

(ii) ITS IMPRESSION UPON OTHERS (43, 47)
    (a) FEAR (43)
    (b) FAVOUR (47a)
    (c) FOLLOWING (47b)

II. TESTIMONY OF THE CHURCH
(ii. 14-47)

1 The Church's Simple Creed (ii. 14-41)

The Discourse of Peter

(i) OUTLINE OF THE SERMON (ii. 14-36)

The Sermon of Peter is in two main parts: an *Explanation* (14-21), and an *Exposition* (22-36). In the Explanation there is first a *Defence* (14, 15), and then a *Declaration* (16-21). In the first he quashes, and in the second he quotes.

Explanation and Exposition

Drunk! No Jew on the Sabbath, and that a Feast Day, would either eat or drink before nine in the morning (15). The suggestion was preposterous. Peter's explanation, '*this is that*', and the remainder of his introduction, is a quotation from Joel ii. 28-32. The original passage is spoken only of Judah, but the scope of the prophecy is here enlarged (ii. 14-21). Yet, it is not on this occasion fulfilled, but still awaits a day to come.

In the body of the Sermon, Peter takes his stand boldly on the *resurrection of Jesus*. If that can be proved, all is proved. If He who seven weeks before expired on Calvary is now alive, then, the Church is established and must be triumphant (ii. 22-36)

Defence and Declaration

Jesus Christ *lived*, and *died*, and *rose again* (22-24). *He* lived His life (22); *men* compassed His death (23); and *God* raised Him from the dead (24). How great a word is this '*it was not possible that He should be holden of death*' (24). Why, *not possible?* Because He was God as well as man. Because He trusted His Father to raise Him up. Because the Scriptures cannot be broken. Because it is unthinkable that death and the devil should triumph. '*Thou wilt not leave my soul in Sheol, neither wilt Thou suffer Thy Holy One to see corruption*'. 'IT WAS NOT POSSIBLE'. The resurrection of Christ is the very heart of the Christian Gospel.

Peter shows that *the Resurrection was predicted* (25-31). He just makes a quotation (25-28), and draws a conclusion (29-31).

It is all very simple, and very powerful. Read Psalm xvi. 8·11.
Observe that reference is made in the prediction to the Messiah's
soul, which went to Sheol (Hades), and to His *body*, which was put
in the tomb, but not to see corruption. The conclusion is conclusive. David's body did see corruption, so that it could not
have been himself that he referred to in the Psalm. Only One
fulfilled these words, therefore David was a *prophet* (30),
and a *seer* (31), and foretold an event which did not take place
until 1,000 years later. As Abram looked for the CITY, David
looked for the KING.

The preacher declares that the resurrection of Christ is well
attested: '*we all are witnesses*' (32). 'All', at least one hundred and
twenty (i. 15), and probably many more. Would any Court of
Law refuse the testimony of one hundred and twenty eye-witnesses?
No event in human history is better attested than the resurrection
of Jesus Christ from the dead.

The proof of this great fact is the Christian Church (33-35)
consequent upon the gift of the Spirit, which 'gift' was bestowed
when Christ ascended, which He could not have done if He had
not risen, which last fact is predicted in another Davidic
Psalm (cx).

The only rational and logical upshot of the matter is: '*Let
every house of Israel therefore know assuredly*'—what? '*that
God hath made Him both Lord and Christ, this Jesus whom ye
crucified*' (36). Observe carefully the designation. *Jesus* is His
human name; *Christ* is His official title; and *Lord* is His Divine
designation. Jesus is both CHRIST and LORD, He is therefore the
LORD JESUS CHRIST. That truly is a wonderful sermon; and we
shall see that it had a mighty effect.

Truth spoken with power is something to reckon with.

This Sermon represents the apostolic 'preaching' long before
any Gospels or Epistles were written (cf. iii. 12-26; x. 34-43;
xiii. 16-41).

(ii) OUTCOME OF THE SERMON (ii. 37-41)

We are not through with this Sermon yet, for so powerful was
it that there had to be an after-meeting. 'They were *pierced* in
their heart' hearing of Him whom they had *pierced*, and conviction

stimulated inquiry (37). Only they will ask 'what shall we do?' who are conscious to some extent of what they have done. Peter plainly points out to them the way of salvation: first of all, the TERMS of it (38), and then the SCOPE of it (39).

In the TERMS two things are required of us, repentance and confession (38a), and one thing is promised by God, the bestowment of the Holy Spirit (38b). As to the SCOPE, the offer of salvation is personal, 'as many as'; universal 'to all that are afar off'; and age-abiding, 'to you and to your children'. Peter testified and exhorted, two things preachers should do every time they preach (40); and the proof that Christ has saved us will be that we shall 'save ourselves' (40).

At the first proclamation of the Law, three thousand souls were slain (Exod. xxxii. 28); but at the first proclamation of the Gospel, three thousand were saved (41). They were not 'added' in order to be saved, but because they were saved. Is that how you joined the Church?

Those whom 'the Lord added' (47) were 'added to the Lord' (v. 14). If you have been added by any other person, or in any other way, it is time you were subtracted.

Only a pure Church can be powerful and permanent.

Testimony is borne, not only by its Simple Creed (ii. 14-41) but also by

2. The Church's Sanctified Conduct
(ii. 42-47)

This description of the life of the early Church is very brief, but profoundly impressive.

'They were constant in listening to the teaching of the Apostles and in their attendance at the Communion, that is, the Breaking of the Bread, and at prayer (at the prayers).

'Fear came upon every one, and many marvels and signs were done by the Apostles. And all the believers kept together, and had everything in common. They sold their lands and other property, and distributed the proceeds among all, according to everyone's necessities.

'And day by day, attending constantly in the Temple with one accord, and breaking bread in private houses, they took their meals with great happiness and single-heartedness, praising God and being regarded with favour by all the people. . . . Also, day by day, the Lord added to their number those whom He was saving.' (Weymouth).

This passage cannot be read too often, and it should not be difficult to separate the local and temporary in it from the universal and abiding. The five dominating notes are *doctrine*, *fellowship*, the *Lord's Supper*, *prayer*, and *public worship*. These things abide in the life of the Church, whereas miracles and the community of goods in their original forms were temporary.

The Breaking of the Bread in the early Church was very different from what it is to-day in Christendom. There was nothing sacerdotal about it at the beginning, and should never have been. It was frequent and was celebrated in private houses, and the occasion was characterised by joyfulness and single-heartedness. Sectarianism and sacerdotalism have dashed all this, alas; so that what then was unifying is now divisive.

The third of the seven sections in this part of the Acts (see p. 202) is *Opposition to the Church*, and the following is an analysis of it.

III. OPPOSITION TO THE CHURCH (iii. 1-iv. 31)

1. THE OCCASION OF IT (iii. 1-26)

(i) THE MIRACLE OF HEALING (1-10)

(*a*) THE CIRCUMSTANCES (1)
(*b*) THE CASE (2, 3)
(*c*) THE CURE (4-7)
(*d*) THE CONSEQUENCES (8-10)

a. To the healed man (8)
b. To the people (9-10)

(ii) THE DISCOURSE ON THE MIRACLE (11-26)

(*a*) AN EXPLANATION (12-16)

(1) Correction (12)
(2) Accusation (13*b*-15)
(3) Declaration (13*a*, 16)

(*b*) AN EXHORTATION (17-26)

(1) The action of man, and the purpose of God (17, 18)
(2) A call to repentance, and a promise of blessing (19-21)
(3) The light of the past on the events of the present (22-24)
(4) The application of the whole argument to the people of Israel (25, 26)

2. THE EXPRESSION OF IT (iv. 1-22)

(i) THE ARREST (1-4)

(ii) THE TRIAL (5-12)

(1) **The Inquiry of the Court** (5-7)
(2) **The Reply of the Apostle** (8-12)

(*a*) THE FACT (8, 9)
(*b*) THE MEANS (9, 10)
(*c*) THE TRUTH (11, 12)

(iii) THE RESULT (13-22)

(1) **As affecting the Sanhedrin** (13-18)

(*a*) THEIR EMBARRASSMENT (13, 14)
(*b*) THEIR CONSULTATION (15, 16)
(*c*) THEIR DECISION (17, 18)

(2) **As affecting the Apostles** (19-22)

(*a*) THEIR DETERMINATION (19, 20)
(*b*) THEIR LIBERATION (21, 22)

3. THE SEQUEL TO IT (iv. 23-31)

(i) THE REPORT TO FRIENDS (23)

(ii) THE PRAYER OF FAITH (23-30)

(*a*) GOD IN CREATION: HIS POWER (24)
(*b*) GOD IN HISTORY: HIS WISDOM (25-28)
(*c*) GOD IN EXPERIENCE: HIS GRACE (29, 30)

(iii) THE ANSWER IN FULNESS (31)

III. OPPOSITION TO THE CHURCH
(iii. 1-iv. 31)

1. The Occasion of the Opposition
(iii. 1-26)

(i) THE MIRACLE OF HEALING (iii. 1-10)

In this story four things claim attention.

The Circumstances (iii. 1)

It is interesting to find Peter and John together: opposites often agree well. Peter was practical; John was mystical; each had something which the other lacked, and so they could help one another; and they did. Let us cultivate an interest in people who are different from ourselves, and so enrich ourselves. These two men were on the way to the Temple. The Christian Church did not at once break away from the Jewish Temple. There are no sudden ruptures in the Kingdom of God. These men were going to public prayer at 3 p.m. Private prayer is not instead of, but in preparation for, public prayer. What we call the Prayer Meeting will be better attended and maintained when we all pray more and better in private.

The Case (iii. 2, 3)

A man, forty years of age (iv. 22), and lame from his birth, was lying at the Gate Beautiful of the Temple, having been carried there, and was begging, asking for alms who needed legs. Mark these particulars. In his helplessness he illustrates the inability of us all in our unregenerate state to walk with God.

The Cure (iii. 4-7)

The Apostles looking on the man, bade him look on them. His expectation was aroused, but it did not rise higher than to his physical need. Our need is always greater than we imagine it to be, and God's grace is also greater. He does for us 'exceeding abundantly above all that we ask or think'. '*Silver and gold have I none*' (6). The true wealth of the Church is not material, but spiritual. Peter was poor, and yet, how rich! Can he ever be poor who has led a soul to Christ! (ii. 41).

'*Such as I have*'—and that was vastly more than he, at this time, imagined: see his Epistles. Well, what should we do with what we have? What Peter did—'*give I thee*'. He who *has*, and *keeps*, will *lose*. Give what you have, and you will get. '*In the Name . . . rise up and walk*'. There was and is power in the Name. Plead it, and then lend a helping hand (6, 7).

The Consequences (iii. 8-10)

The healed man was delirious with joy (8), and the people were dumb with wonder (9-10). No doubt this miracle is introduced here because of its consequences for the Apostles and the Church (iv). No event ends with itself. It is better to leap up than to lie about (iii. 2).

(ii) THE DISCOURSE ON THE MIRACLE (iii. 11-26)

An Explanation (12-16)

This is Peter's *third address*, with which compare the first, i. 15-22; and the second, ii. 14-36. The audience gave Peter a great opportunity (11, 12a); he saw the situation, and seized it. Always be on the look-out for opportunities; they are all around us.

What did Peter '*answer*'? (12). The people's state of mind. We can often answer when there is no verbal question; eyes as well as mouths can ask questions. Peter answers by asking two questions, and in doing so he corrects two mistakes. The people *marvelled*; but why should they? Surely a great God can do great things. But they thought that the miracle was the work of the apostles, whereas Peter and John were but the agents (12).

Now follows some plain speaking: the people are charged with murder (13-15), but man's ruling God over-ruled: He whom they crucified, God glorified; He whom they rejected, God raised. When Peter charged these people with *denying* Jesus, he cannot but have remembered that he had done the same (13, 14).

An Exhortation (iii. 17-26)

There is power in Christ's Name, but it must be trusted to become operative (16). The solemn charge of verse 15 is somewhat softened by verse 17, yet the people were responsible and are called upon to repent (19). Though men act with perfect freedom Divine sovereignty runs through human history; the wicked as well as the worthy are employed for the working-out of eternal designs (18, 24). And the end is not yet (19, 21).

Christ is the subject of all prophecy (24), and *salvation* is the greatest of all themes (26). Here is a striking word—'*God sent Him to bless you*'—God, Him, you; and the blessing is in being turned from our sins, and turned to the Saviour (26). Only the Crucified can convert (18, 19).

2. The Expression of The Opposition
(iv. 1-22)

(i) THE ARREST (iv. 1-4)

Three things combined served as occasion for the Apostles' arrest—religious intolerance, political animosity, and rationalistic unbelief. These are represented by the priests, the captain, and the Sadducees (1), and the fact of Christ's resurrection condemned them all (2), as it continuously condemns the corruptions of the Church, the despotism of the world, and the pride of unbelief.

And so it was thought best that these men should be '*put in ward*' (3). However, you do not cow the lion by caging it, or break an eagle's spirit by breaking its wing. In spite of all opposition, many will believe (4). The five thousand here referred to, were all *men* (*andrōn*; not *anthrōpōn*; cf. Lu. xi. 31. Matt. xiv. 21), and were in addition to the three thousand on the Day of Pentecost.

(ii) THE TRIAL (iv. 5-12)

Mark, first of all, *The Council's Inquiry* (5-7). Take a good look at these people: rulers, elders, scribes, Annas, Caiaphas, John, Alexander, many! What they lacked in moral weight they made up for in numbers (5). '*By what power? or by what name?*' (7). See ch. iii. 6, 12, 16, and also iv. 12. The emphasis is upon 'ye' (Gr.), meaning 'such as you' unlearned and contemptible men. That has always been the way with the highbrows, but abuse is never an argument. Contempt is always contemptible, except when we 'pour contempt on all our pride.'

Now mark *The Apostle's Reply* (8-12). Here is first, an affirmation (8-9), and then, an interpretation (10-12) of the miracle-fact. Christ, killed by them, but raised by God, is the sufficient explanation of this man's cure (10). *Builders* should be good judges of *stones*, but, as often, the experts were mistaken (11). However, in spite of it all, there is salvation by a Name, by one Name only, and for all (12). That is the Gospel—*One for all*. This is Peter's *fourth* discourse.

Confidence in Christ begets courage for the conflict.

(iii) THE RESULT (iv. 13-22)

Peter and John and the healed man are led out to an ante-room, whilst these authorities discuss their case behind closed doors (14. 15). The scene and sound would be laughable if it were not so sad. Here is a crowd of men up against a fact: '*we cannot deny it*', they say, it is '*indeed a notable miracle,*' and '*is manifest to all in Jerusalem*' (16). Very well, what's the difficulty? The difficulty is this, that they do not wish it to be a fact! That's awkward; but facts are stubborn things. So they say, '*What shall we do to these men?*', not, 'What shall we do with the facts'? 'How shall we escape dealing fairly with them?' Think of it! There you see not only malice, but also cowardice. Infinitely better be *unlearned* and *unschooled* like Peter and John, but with their courage, than be learned and schooled like these authorities, with their cowardice (13). It was as evident that they had not '*been with Jesus*' as that these Apostles had been. Do we present to all men the indisputable evidences that we are *in the habit of being with Jesus*?

Look now at *The Decision of the Court* (17-18). In secret conclave they arrived at a course of action (17), and they must see it through with as much dignity as they are capable of carrying, and that was not much. They had not learned that red-tape can never be a substitute for rectitude. Have you? So Peter and John and the healed man are marched in again (18). They had been having a fine time in the ante-room, a prayer-meeting, no doubt. They receive the solemn charge (17, 18). But the Council might as well have told the sun not to shine, and the tides not to move, and the winds not to blow, as to tell these men not to talk about Jesus.

The Apostle's answer is magnificent (19, 20). '*Whether it be right*', should always be our first consideration. 'Right' is one of the words we ought to restore to its proper place in our thinking, and what it means, to its rightful place in our practice. Settle every question on principle. 'Right is right if God is God, and right the day must win; to doubt would be disloyalty, and to falter would be sin'.

Verses 21, 22 show the utter impotence of ungodly powers. What dignified ineptitude! What asinine pomposity! This sort of thing has happened a thousand times in history, but the Church goes marching on.

3. The Sequel to the Opposition
(iv. 23-31)

The Apostles are '*let go*'. What will they do now? '*They went to their own company*' (23). What did you do when you were 'let go', or what would you do if you were 'let go', that is, how do you use your freedom? There are many '*let go*' crises in life; when we leave school and home; when we get aboard an ocean liner; when we go to some other land. What do we do then? We have to choose our own company, and we always do so according to what we essentially are. What these men *choose* to do now, Judas *had* to do at last (i. 25). What sort of '*company*' is yours? In this passage mark three things:

Praise. (24-28)

Verses 25, 26 are from Psalm ii, and probably were *sung*. If so, it is the beginning of singing in the Christian Church. They address *God the Creator* (24), and acknowledge Him to be *the sovereign Ruler* (25-28). He is back alike of nature and history. His eternal decrees and man's free actions interlock (27, 28). That is a mysterious fact: ponder it. We all have something for *which to offer praise*, and there, like the apostles, we should begin.

But inevitably, the next thing will be—

Prayer (29, 30)

Having reviewed *the past*, they naturally come to the *present*: and mark the connection between past and present. What God has done, He can do. From days gone by we should draw encouragement for the present hour. The apostles point to the danger (29a), confess their need of courage (29b), and ask for vindication (30). Their prayer is brief, but comprehensive.

The reference here to God in three relations is noteworthy: in relation to *creation*, revealing His power (24); in relation to *history*, displaying His wisdom (25-28); and in relation to *experience*, disclosing His grace (29, 30).

And now follows—

Power (31)

'*When they had prayed*' something happened. That is when things do happen, for 'more things are wrought by prayer than this world dreams of'. Mark carefully the three things which did happen: first, an earthquake; then, a soul-quake; and finally, a tongue-quake.

The fourth of the seven sections of this division of the Acts (see p. 202) is *Discipline in the Church*, and the following is an analysis of it.

IV. DISCIPLINE IN THE CHURCH (iv. 32-v. 16)

1. THE ORIGINATING CIRCUMSTANCES (iv. 32-37)

   (i) COMMUNION IN GOD (32*a*)

   (ii) CONFESSION OF CHRIST (33*a*)

   (iii) CONSECRATION OF PERSON (33*b*)

   (iv) COMMUNITY OF GOODS (32*b*, 34-37)
       (*a*) THE GENERAL PRACTICE (32*b*, 34, 35)
       (*b*) A PARTICULAR EXAMPLE (36, 37)

2. THE SPECIFIC OCCASION (v. 1-10)

   (i) THE OFFENDERS AND THE OFFENCE (1, 2)
       (*a*) ANANIAS AND SAPPHIRA
       (*b*) AN ACTED LIE

   (ii) THE CHARGE AND THE CONSEQUENCE (3-10)
       (*a*) THE CASE OF ANANIAS (3-6)
           (1) PETER'S INDICTMENT (3, 4)
           (2) ANANIAS' DEATH (5, 6)

       (*b*) THE CASE OF SAPPHIRA (7-10)
           (1) PETER'S INQUIRY (7, 8*a*)
           (2) SAPPHIRA'S REPLY (8*b*)
           (3) PETER'S SENTENCE (9)
           (4) SAPPHIRA'S DEATH (10)

3. THE SALUTARY EFFECTS (v. 5*b*, 11-16)

   (i) FEAR AMONG THE PEOPLE (5, 11)

   (ii) PROGRESS OF THE CHURCH (12-16
       (*a*) DIVINE POWER (12*a*)
       (*b*) CHRISTIAN FELLOWSHIP (12*b*)
       (*c*) OFFICIAL ALOOFNESS (13*a*)
       (*d*) POPULAR RECOGNITION (13*b*)
       (*e*) INCREASE OF CONVERTS (14)
       (*f*) WIDESPREAD HEALINGS (15, 16)

IV. DISCIPLINE IN THE CHURCH
(iv. 32-v. 37)

1. **The Originating Circumstances** (iv. 32-37)

This is a passage which may easily be misinterpreted and mis-applied, as indeed, it has been. But there is nothing here comparable to modern communism. The reference, to begin with, is not to the *State*, but to the *Church*; in the second place, the *social community* was based on and sprang from *spiritual unity*; and once again, quite obviously, *the measure was exceptional and transitory*, and disappeared within the apostolic age. But the spirit and principle remain. All for each, and each for all, is the ideal of the Heavenly Commonwealth, for such is the Christian Church. Never, when the heart has been open, has the pocket been closed. The great generosity of these Christians issued from their '*great grace*' (33).

2. **The Specific Occasion** (v. 1-10)

Two concrete examples of the working of this enterprise are now given, that of Barnabas (iv. 36, 37); and that of Ananias and Sapphira (v. 1-10); the one for commendation, and the other for condemnation. Study carefully what is said of Barnabas, for we are to hear of him again. He is one of a few who rendered great service to the Church in its formative period.

What a contrast we have in Ananias and Sapphira! Alas, early was darnel sown among the wheat. What was the sin of this man and his wife? *An acted lie.* They were under no compulsion to sell their property; and having done so they were under no compulsion to hand over to the Church the entire proceeds (4a); but when they made out that the part was the whole, they lied to the Holy Spirit (4, 9), being actuated by Satan (3). The conviction of Ananias was expressed by Peter, felt by himself, and confirmed by God. The wife, who helped in the sin, shared in the judgment. We must never suppose that the element of good in our actions can counter-balance the element of evil therein. Be straight. Hate hypocrisy as you would the devil.

The sin of Ananias was greed of gain. He wanted part of his money, and he also wanted credit for having given his all. This

love of money lay at the bottom of most of the sins and failures
in the Acts—of Simon Magus, of Elymas, of the Philippian
'masters', of the Ephesian silversmiths, and of Felix—and it is a
sin widespread in Christendom to-day.

Ananias belonged to the Achan, Gehazi and Judas group.
This is the first outbreak of evil in the Christian Church, and it
called for, and got, summary judgment. What we 'conceive in
our heart' (4) indicates our real state. Ananias and Sapphira
must have discussed this matter together, and decided to act
together deceitfully. There are occasions when a husband and
wife should disagree.

3. The Salutary Effects (v. 5b, 11-16)

The salutary effects of this discipline were twofold, in the main,
arresting and *advancing* the growth of the Church (13, 14). There
are two ways in which a church may grow—*like a building*, by
adding stone to stone; and *like a plant*, by development from the
root. The one is an *organization* and the other is an *organism*.
It is never safe to judge of the success of a church by the length
of its members' roll. Subtraction is sometimes strength. Only
a pure church is powerful.

One minister said to another, 'I've had a great blessing in my
church'. 'Oh,' said the other, 'How many members have you
added?' 'None,' said the other, 'but I've lost two'.

If Ananias and Sapphira had been allowed to remain, this
passage would never have been written, and winter instead of
summer would have settled down on the Church's life. It is
abidingly true that that in the Gospel which attracts some,
repels others; but not on this account should the Church lower
her standards, or widen her doors. The outflow of judgment
may be a preparation for the inflow of grace. Observe what are
the elements which entered into this rich experience in the Church's
history: *fear* (11), *harmony* (12b), *reverence* (13b), *faith* (14),
and *works* (12a, 15, 16).

In verse 11 is the first occurrence in the Acts of the word
Church. In chapter ii. 47 it is omitted by the R.V., but, up to
this point no one is left in doubt as to what the Church is. To-
day it badly needs to be defined in the light of the New Testament.

In verse 14 believers were added 'to the Lord', and in ii. 47 it is the Lord who added them. This shows the vital and intimate connection between the Lord and the Christian Church.

The miraculous activity of the early Church should be contemplated (cf. ii. 43).

After the first opposition (iv. 1-21) the Apostles were released, but now they are imprisoned. Opposition is growing in intensity. The 'indignation' of verse 17 is 'jealousy' (zelos). This quality may be good or bad, and as bad it has characterised religious factions from the beginning until now.

> Stone walls do not a prison make,
>   Nor iron bars a cage;
> Minds innocent and quiet take
>   That for a hermitage;
> If I have freedom in my love,
>   And in my soul am free;
> Angels alone, that soar above,
>   Enjoy such liberty.   (Lovelace).

One of these free Angels delivered these imprisoned men, as later on this Messenger delivered Peter (chapter xii). Angels are not impersonal forces, but celestial intelligences, who, from the time of Gen. xvi. 7, have been the Agents of Jehovah.

The fifth of the seven sections of this division of the Acts (see p. 202) is the *Testing of the Church*, and the following is an analysis of it.

V. TESTING OF THE CHURCH (v. 17-42)

1. DETENTION AND DELIVERANCE OF THE APOSTLES
(v. 17-21*a*)

(i) THEIR DETENTION (17, 18)
(*a*) INDIGNATION OF THE AUTHORITIES (17)
(*b*) IMPRISONMENT OF THE APOSTLES (18)

(ii) THEIR DELIVERANCE (19-21*a*)
(*a*) BROUGHT OUT OF THE PRISON (19)
(*b*) SENT INTO THE TEMPLE (20, 21*a*)

2. TRIAL AND TRIUMPH OF THE APOSTLES (v. 21b-42)

(i) THE CONSTERNATION OF THE SENATE (21b-26)

(a) THE ASSEMBLING OF THE COUNCIL (21b)
(b) THE REPORT OF THE OFFICERS (22-25)
(c) THE REARREST OF THE APOSTLES (26)

(ii) THE COURSE OF THE TRIAL (27-39)

(a) THE SPEECH OF THE HIGH PRIEST (27, 28)
(b) THE SPEECH OF THE APOSTLES (29-32)
(c) THE SPEECH OF GAMALIEL (33-39)

(iii) THE CONCLUSION OF THE MATTER (40-42)

(a) PUNISHMENT OF THE APOSTLES (40)
(b) JUBILATION OF THE APOSTLES (41)
(c) BOLDNESS OF THE APOSTLES (42)

V. TESTING OF THE CHURCH
(v. 17-42)

1. The Detention and Deliverance of the Apostles
(v. 17-21a)

Prosperity brought persecution, but it is the persecutors who are made to look ridiculous, for the forces are unequal, as they always are when God is on one of the sides. Authority is always weak when it has not moral support, and no amount of gold braid and brass buttons can make up for the want of such support. The apostles were delivered not that they might be *safe*, but that they might be *used* (20). Their commission was to '*speak to the people*', and their message was '*all the words of this Life*'.

2. The Trial and Triumph of the Apostles
(v. 21b-42)

(i) THE CONSTERNATION OF THE SENATE (21b-26)

This bit of narrative is not wanting in humour. See those self-conscious and self-important soldiers safe-guarding something that was not there! What a sell to be protecting so empty a cell! Omnipotence can make earthly powers look very ridiculous. The Old Testament likens godless potentates to 'grasshoppers'. All over the world to-day are proud grasshoppers, but God will keep them on the hop.

In this connection read what Peter wrote long after: I Peter ii. 20-24; iii. 14, 17; iv. 1, 12-19; v. 10.

Their punishment did not, however, have the intended effect, for they went back to their preaching and teaching, and in an intensified way. Mark 'daily', 'in every house', and 'ceased not'. That is the spirit that conquers. Again and again in the history of God's people the worst that the world could do proved to be— no thanks to the world—the best thing that could have happened. Out of the eater has come forth meat, and out of the strong, sweetness (cf. viii. 1).

(ii) THE COURSE OF THE TRIAL (27-39)

There are here three speeches which should be carefully studied.

(a) What the High Priest said to the Apostles (27, 28)

'Did we not charge you by a charge?' Certainly. 'Ye have filled Jerusalem with your doctrine'. Well done; and the sufficient explanation and warrant are to be found in 'this man,' 'this name', 'this life', 'this counsel', and 'this work' (28, 20, 38). Charging with charges is of no use here.

(b) What the Apostles said to the Sanhedrin (29-32)

Both times the highest note was struck: 'Whether it be right', in iv. 19; and 'we ought', here. He is lost who in such a crisis as this consults his comfort or convenience, but he is saved who does his duty. The one only true determining principle for us all is, GOD FIRST. Let us ever do what we ought to do in the face of fear, envy, and hate. The apostolic gospel has for its foci the Cross and the Crown on the one part, and repentance and remission on the other part (30, 31). 'We are his witnesses of these things.' Are we? The Holy Spirit is (32). 'When they heard, they were sawn through' (33; vii. 54). Resist the truth and it will cut you; yield to it and it will crown you.

(c) What Gamaliel said to them all (34-39)

This man was Paul's teacher, and, no doubt, greatly influenced him. His speech is a model of its kind, and contains much shrewd common sense. We may learn from him—that there is always

danger in repression; that time is required for the true nature
of a movement to be clearly seen; that movements which have
no spiritual vitality in them come to an end, sooner or later,
if left alone; that the past has much to teach the present; and
that it is useless to antagonise the truth. These are great lessons.

Three possible attitudes towards God are here in view—
hostility, 'fight against God'; *neutrality*, 'let these men alone';
and *co-operation*, 'teaching and preaching Jesus Christ' (39, 38, 42).

(iii) THE CONCLUSION OF THE MATTER (40-42)

The Apostles were 'beaten' (40), presumably for not having
obeyed the order of chapter iv. 18. This was the usual Jewish
penalty, 'forty stripes save one', and it must have been a painful
experience. Nevertheless, the Apostles were joyful (41), and
carried on with their work of preaching and teaching (42).

How much do we know of joy in the fellowship of shame? (41).
There is no enterprise where there is no enthusiasm.

The sixth of the seven sections of this division of the Acts
(see p. 202) is *Administration in the Church*, and the following
is an analysis of it.

VI. ADMINISTRATION IN THE CHURCH (vi. 1-6)

1. THE COMPLAINT OF HELLENISTS (1)

(i) THE OCCASION OF IT—DISCIPLES MULTIPLYING
(ii) THE FOCUS OF IT—GREEK-SPEAKING JEWS
(iii) THE NATURE OF IT—APPARENT TEMPORAL
NEGLECT

2. THE COUNSEL OF THE APOSTLES (2-4)

(i) THE DISCIPLES SUMMONED (2a)
(ii) THE APOSTLES' STATEMENT (2b-4)
  (a) THEIR RESPONSIBILITY (2b)
  (b) THEIR RECOMMENDATION (3)
  (c) THEIR RESOLVE (4)

3. THE CHOICE OF DEACONS (5, 6)

(i) AGREEMENT WITH THE APOSTLES (5a)
(ii) SELECTION OF SEVEN MEN (5b)
(iii) ORDINATION OF THE CHOSEN (6)

VI. ADMINISTRATION IN THE CHURCH
(vi. 1-6)

1. THE COMPLAINT OF THE HELLENISTS (1)

One of the earliest Christian institutions was an Order of Widows, who were maintained at the common cost, and who gave themselves to prayer and works of mercy (ix. 41. 1 Tim. v. 3, 9, 10, 11, 16). Greek-speaking Jews complain against Aramaic-speaking Jews, that the fund was not being fairly administered. What a lot of murmuring there has been over money. Of course Church funds should be properly used, and all complaint is not contrariety.

2. THE COUNSEL OF THE APOSTLES (2-4)

The Apostles did well to call together the disciples.

This is the first Church Business Meeting on record, and it was proposed and carried that a new office be created to handle the *temporalities* of the Church, so that the Apostles might continue to care for the *spiritualities* (2, 4).

3. THE CHOICE OF DEACONS (5, 6)

Co-operation by distribution of labour is a fundamental principle of success in the Church, and out of it. The supreme work of the minister is defined in verse 4: supplication in private, and ministration in public, and always in that order; to these, such should '*give themselves*'.

It is worth while to observe, in the light of the complaint (1), that all the deacons bear Greek names (5). What qualifications are required of a Church deacon? He must be reputable, wise, and Spirit-filled (3). Do all deacons foot that line? The chosen are then consecrated (6); and the Church continues to prosper (7).

The procedure was thoroughly democratic.

(See *On Deacons*, 3, 1 Tim. iii. 8-13).

The last of the seven sections of this division of the Acts (see p. 202) is *the Persecution of the Church*, and the following is an analysis of it.

VII. PERSECUTION OF THE CHURCH (vi. 7-viii. 4)

   1. **THE OCCASION OF IT: The Progress of the Church** (vi. 7)

   2. **THE FOCUS OF IT: STEPHEN** (vi. 8-viii. 1a)

      (i) THE DOINGS AND TEACHINGS OF STEPHEN (vi. 8-10)
     (ii) THE ARREST AND CHARGE AGAINST STEPHEN
         (vi. 11-vii. 1)
         (a) SPEAKING AGAINST MOSES AND GOD (vi. 11)
         (b) SPEAKING AGAINST THE TEMPLE AND THE LAW (vi. 13, 14)
    (iii) THE ADDRESS OF STEPHEN TO THE SANHEDRIN
         (vii. 2-53)

         (A) The Charge Confronted (2-50)

         (a) THE PERIOD BEFORE THE LAW AND THE TEMPLE (vii. 2-16)
             Time of the Patriarchs
            (1) Abraham (2-8)   (2) Joseph (9-16)
         (b) THE PERIOD OF THE LAW (vii. 17-43)
             Time of Moses
            (1) His Birth (17-21)   (2) His Training (22-29)
            (3) His Call (30-34)   (4) His Work (35, 36)
            (5) His Prediction (37) (6) His Rejection
                                   (38-43, 35)
         (c) THE PERIOD BEFORE THE TEMPLE (vii. 44-46)
             From Moses to David
            (1) The Tabernacle in the Wilderness (44)
            (2) The Tabernacle in the Land (45, 46)
         (d) THE PERIOD OF THE TEMPLE (vii. 47-50)
             From Solomon onward

         (B) The Counter Charge (vii. 51-53)

His hearers are the followers of the persecutors and rebels of the past.

    (iv) THE FINAL TESTIMONY AND DEATH OF STEPHEN
         (vii. 54-viii. 1a)
         (a) THE RAGE OF THE SANHEDRIN (54)
         (b) THE VISION OF STEPHEN (55, 56)
         (c) THE STONING OF STEPHEN (57-59a)
         (d) THE PRAYER OF STEPHEN (59b, 60a)
         (e) THE DEATH OF STEPHEN (60b)
         (f) THE INTRODUCTION OF SAUL (58, viii. 1a)

   3. **THE ISSUES OF IT: Widespread Evangelism** (viii. 1b-4)

      (i) THE ASSAULT UPON THE CHURCH IN JERUSALEM
         (1b)
     (ii) THE SCATTERING OF THE CHRISTIANS FROM
         JERUSALEM (1c)
    (iii) THE BURIAL OF STEPHEN (2)
    (iv) THE ENMITY OF SAUL AGAINST THE CHURCH (3)
    (v) THE SCATTERED DISCIPLES PREACHED EVERY
         WHERE (4)

VII. PERSECUTION OF THE CHURCH
(vi. 7-viii. 4)

1. The Occasion of the Persecution

THE PROGRESS OF THE CHURCH
(vi. 7)

The condition of things in the Church at Jerusalem makes it evident that there was an interval of time between chapter v and chapter vi. The Church had grown in numbers; Hellenists were prominent among the disciples; and there was an organized body of 'widows'. With growth comes need for adjustment and increase of machinery; and so, as we have seen in vi. 1-6, a new office was created which occasioned the first apostolic ordination.

That 'a great company of the priests' joined the Church should not be overlooked, for it indicates a transference of allegiance, and, no doubt, helped to stir up the persecution now about to break out. Decaying institutions are always jealous of new and vigorous enterprises; but resort to physical force is never an argument in the realm of the spiritual—or in any realm for that matter. Truth is never hysterical; and reality is ever sovereign.

2. The Focus of the Persecution

STEPHEN
(vi. 8-viii. 1)

STEPHEN IS INDICTED (vi. 8-vii. 1)

The persecution which now arose was directed, first of all, against Stephen. Of the seven appointed deacons only Stephen and Philip survive in the record, and of these two Stephen was a great maker of history, for he was the link between Peter and Paul, and, it is safe to assume, he began in Saul of Tarsus the struggle which ended in the latter's conversion.

The brunt of the battle falls upon its leaders; it is the front line which feels the full force of the attack. I doubt not the other six deacons were quite loyal, but it is Stephen who draws the enemy (vi. 8, 9). Having been charged (vi. 13, 14), he is now put on his defence (vii. 1). How does he reply? By reviewing the history of his people (2-50). But is that a reply? Yes, rightly understood it is, for the true view of Jesus and His mission rests on the whole past history of the Hebrew people.

Stephen's day of ministry had scarce begun when it was violently ended, but the greatness of one's life must not be looked for in length of days. What the writer of the book of *Wisdom* said is true of Stephen,

'he, being made perfect in a short time, fulfilled a long time; for his soul pleased the Lord; therefore hasted He to take him away from among the wicked' (iv. 13, 14).

Stephen means *crown*, and early did he receive his. The charge brought against him was that he spoke against Moses and God (11), and against the Temple and the Law (13, 14). No doubt it is true that he perceived clearly the incidental and temporary character of the Mosaic Law, and also of the Temple and all its worship, and in doing so he was but indicating that Judaism must give way to Christianity.

So, now, Stephen faces his accusers, but what a contrast! Faithfulness and fanaticism, power and weakness, truth and error, deeds and lies, one and many!

STEPHEN'S SERMON (vii. 2-50)

We cannot here examine in much detail, Stephen's sermon, but it should be compared with Peter's before (chapter ii), and with Paul's after (chapter xiii). All three appeal to the Old Testament, which shows its Messianic character, and all three see in Jesus the promised Messiah, though Stephen does not mention Him.

We cannot but be impressed by the fearlessness of Stephen: his courage born of deep conviction, his freedom from Jewish prejudice, and his knowledge of the Scriptures; also his skill in argument, rhetorical power, spiritual insight and self-command.

In his sermon he traces four periods in the history of the Israelites, and he would have gone on to relate the history to the time of Jesus Christ, but he was interrupted.

In scope the sermon reaches from ABRAHAM to SOLOMON (2-47), and here the history is followed chronologically, those events in it being selected which best served the purpose of Stephen's defence. The two main divisions are—(a) THE HEBREW FAMILY (2-16), and (b) THE ISRAELITISH NATION (17-50).

THE HEBREW FAMILY
(vii. 2-16)

(a) The Period before the Law and the Temple

This period covers the Book of Genesis.

The Time of the Patriarchs (vii. 2-16)

Two figures stand out in the scene. ABRAHAM, the father of the Hebrews (2-8), and JOSEPH, the saviour of his people (9-16). The former illustrates *divine election*, and the latter, *divine providence*. Both these run through all history, and give to it its real significance and worth; for what matters in history is what God is doing in it. 'Through the ages one increasing purpose runs.' In heaven's light much success is seen to be failure, and much failure is seen to be success.

The second main part of this sermon is a review of

THE ISRAELITISH NATION
(vii. 17-50)

This is contemplated in two great periods of its history, the Theocracy, and the Monarchy.

The line followed is chronological, geographical, and biographical. If in the previous part, ABRAHAM and JOSEPH dominate, here MOSES dominates.

(b) The Period of the Law

The Time of Moses (vii. 17-43)
The Birth and Training of Moses (vii. 17-29)

This takes the story to the sojourn of Moses in Midian, embracing eighty years of his life. A number of important truths and lessons crowd in here, among which observe—that God's

Q

promise is his purpose, and it is never lost sight of (17); that
struggles always precede freedom; that permanent good must
sooner or later be struggled for (18, 19); that in the hour of our
greatest need, God draws near to help us, in some way or through
someone; that when the hour comes the man is not wanting, and
no movement is ripe until the leader appears (20); that those whom
God would use, He carefully prepares (20-22); that an insignifi-
cant event may at any time precipitate a momentous crisis (24);
that a trifling circumstance may stimulate to energetic action—
thus, the act of Moses in delivering the individual Israelite from
his oppressor greatly promoted his national design. Do the thing
that lies nearest to thee; the second will have already become
clearer.

A further lesson is, that we must remain true to the highest
we know, though we be misunderstood (25). Read, 'Now he
supposed his brethren would understand how that God, by his
hand is giving them salvation; but they understood not.' If we
are in God's will, we must not allow misunderstanding on the
part of foe or friend to chill our enthusiasm or arrest our behaviour.
Better be an exile for the truth than a craven at home (29).
Suffering is the price of leadership.

The Call and Work of Moses (vii. 30-36)

Moses was for forty years in the Egyptian Court (20-28);
for forty years he was in Midian (29, 30a); and now he enters
upon the third period of forty years (36, 42). In these periods
respectively, he was Prince, Pastor, and Prophet: first, learning
that he was somebody; then, that he was nobody; and finally
that God was all.

For his great task he had been in preparation for eighty years.
Youth is in too much of a hurry, and generally is impatient of
training days. Remember Moses: and also that for three and a
half years' service, Christ had over thirty years of preparation.
Training days are tremendous days, and once past they do not
come again; so be patient and diligent.

Before Moses saw the *vision*, and heard the *voice* (30, 31),
God saw a *vision*, and heard a *voice* (34). He always sees and
hears before we do; and we see and hear only because He does.

Note this also: He says '*I am come . . . come thou*' (34). He Himself does what He sends us to do (34). '*I will send thee* into Egypt' (34), that is the place where our task begins. He sends, but we must go.

The Prediction and Rejection of Moses (vii. 37-43)

Stephen's point in these verses, though he does not plainly say so, is that the people to whom he is speaking are now rejecting the Messiah as their forebears had rejected Moses. '*Like unto me*' (37). How? Each had a special preparation; each had a Divine call; each founded a dispensation; each was a new spiritual force; each was a great religious teacher; each claimed a hearing on Divine authority; and each was rejected by his own generation. But Messiah was greater than Moses.

Much in this review is passed over by Stephen, but he fixed on Israel's idolatry (39-43), the sin which brought them into a new captivity; for observe that after *exit from Egypt* (36), is *entrance into Babylon* (43). Let the delivered beware of further bondage.

(c) The Period before the Temple

From Moses to David (vii. 44-46)

Stephen now passes from the Law to the Tabernacle of the Testimony, showing that it was this and not the Temple which God appointed, a pattern of which was shown to Moses in the Mount.

(d) The Period of the Temple

The Time of Solomon (vii. 47-50)

It was Solomon and not David who built the Temple, and it was only a material shadow of a spiritual reality.

(1 Kings viii. 27f. Isaiah lxvi. 1. Matt. v. 34, 35)

This speech presents difficulties in certain statements (e.g., vii. 2; see Gen. xii. 1), and also as to its general drift; but several things are clear: (*a*) so far from being guilty of blasphemy (vi. 11) Stephen glorified God, and began his address by calling Him 'the God of Glory' (vii. 2); (*b*) he did not speak against Moses (vi. 11) but showed that he looked for One to come who would be greater than himself, namely, the Messiah (vii. 37)

(c) nor did he speak against the Law and the Temple (vi. 13, 14), but he did imply that they would be displaced by institutions which would be spiritual (vi. 14).

'The whole speech becomes a proof of the Messiahship of Jesus as against those who appealed to the authority of Moses, and saw in Jesus a twofold cause of offence: (1) that He was rejected by His people and crucified; (2) that He had treated with impiety that which they held most sacred—the Law and the Temple' (Knowling)

It must be assumed that the line of Stephen's argument was the one he had adopted previously (vi. 9, 10), and must have had the same end in view. As already said, he was not allowed to complete his argument (vii. 51).

The true view of Jesus and His mission rests on the whole past history of the Hebrew people. Divine revelation is progressive, and it was fatal for the people of Israel not to follow it to its consummation in the life and sacrifice of Christ.

That Stephen in his speech was working towards this is clear from his final testimony which follows (vii. 52, 55, 56, 59, 60).

THE FINAL TESTIMONY AND DEATH OF STEPHEN (vii. 54-viii. 1)

Part of the charge brought against Stephen was that he spake 'blasphemous words against this holy place' (vi. 13, 14); and he has replied to that, passing from the *Tabernacle* (44) through the *Temple* (47) to the *Universe* (49, 50). At this point it would appear, he was interrupted, and he turns from his survey to characterize and countercharge these people (51-53). Stephen was the most gracious of men, but he could speak with words which bit and burned. In both these respects he was like his Master (cf. 51, 60). What a picture of moral depravity verses 54, 57, 58, present! And what a picture of moral and spiritual nobility verses 59, 60 present! In Stephen's hour of anguish he was vouchsafed a vision: 'Jesus standing' (55). (Compare Hebrews x. 12.) Did He *rise* to welcome the first Christian martyr? How often in the history of God's people suffering and sight have gone together! How stupid and useless a thing it is for men to persecute those who do not think and act as they do. Stephen could be got rid of by means of stones, but not the Truth.

Here that saying has its first illustration, that 'the blood of the martyrs is the seed of the Church'.

It is difficult to see what in Stephen's speech could have aroused the Council to such anger, unless indeed they were cute enough to discern its implications; but the speaker, facing these angry men, argues no more, though much more could have been said, but immediately passes on to Jesus the Messiah, and charges the Council with His murder (52, 53). The Name he had not mentioned so far he now boldly utters, 'the Righteous One', 'Son of Man', 'Lord Jesus' (52, 56, 59).

Saul saw Stephen die, after having heard him preach, and I, doubt not, Stephen is Saul's spiritual father; the sacrifice of the one led to the salvation of the other. See how a Christian can die (59, 60)! Only a godlike soul can pray as Stephen did.

Compare Samson's prayer in Judges xvi. 28.

Compare also, 'with one accord' (57), with ii. 1. Is your agreement with heaven, or with hell?

Precious in God's sight is the death of His saints.

This is the third death recorded in the Christian community, and what a contrast (chapter v. 5)! Ananias and Sapphira died for a lie; Stephen died for the truth. The two were condemned by the Holy Spirit; the third was welcomed by the Son of Man.

Jesus' death and Stephen's were both illegal. The Jews admitted that they had no right to put any man to death (John xviii. 31), and yet members of the Sanhedrin stone Stephen, and Saul was in charge of the operation (viii. 1 and xxii. 20).

He who was so prominent at Stephen's martyrdom was to die in like manner after suffering far in excess of anything that Stephen endured (2 Cor. xi. 23-28).

The effects of what was done that day have continued to the present time through Paul and his letters, and in the Christian Church.

3. The Issues of the Persecution

WIDESPREAD EVANGELISM
(viii. 1-4)

Individual believers had suffered for the Faith before this event (iv. 1-22; v. 17-42), but this is the first organized and widespread *persecution* of the Church; the first, but not the last, for the next 300 years were to be characterized by such experiences.

These few verses tell us of the assault upon the Church in Jerusalem, of the scattering of the Christians, of the burial of Stephen, of Saul's enmity against the Church, and of the spread of the Gospel in consequence of this scattering. This is another illustration of the truth that 'except a grain of wheat fall into the earth and die, it abideth by itself alone; but if it die, it beareth much fruit' (John xii. 24).

We know of the reactions of this persecution upon only one of those who were responsible for it—upon Saul. He says: 'I persecuted this way unto the death, binding and delivering into prisons both men and women'. 'I said, Lord, they know that I imprisoned and beat in every synagogue them that believed on Thee; and when the blood of Thy martyr Stephen was shed, I also was standing by, and consenting unto his death, and kept the raiment of them that slew him'. 'Many of the saints did I shut up in prison . . . and when they were put to death I gave my voice against them. And I punished them oft in every synagogue, and strove to make them blaspheme and being exceedingly mad against them, I persecuted them even unto strange cities'. 'Beyond measure I persecuted the Church of God, and wasted it'. 'I am the least of the apostles, that am not meet to be called an apostle, because I persecuted the Church of God'. 'Who was before a blasphemer, and a persecutor, and injurious'. (Acts xxii. 4, 19, 20; xxvi. 10. 11; Gal. 1. 13. 1 Cor. xv. 9, 1 Tim. i. 13). But this ravaging wolf became God's best sheep-dog.

> Saint, did I say? with your remembered faces,
> Dear men and women, whom I sought and slew!
> Ah, when we mingle in the heavenly places
> How will I weep to Stephen and to you!
>
> Oh, for the strain that rang to our reviling
> Still, when the bruised limbs sank upon the sod,
> Oh, for the eyes that looked their last in smiling,
> Last on this world here, but their first on God!

(F. W. H. Myers)

A Summary of Part One of the Acts
ACTS i. 1-viii. 4

We should take time to be impressed by certain salient facts in this FIRST PERIOD OF THE CHURCH'S HISTORY.

1. It is a period of seven years only, A.D. 30-37. That is not long in the history of any institution, yet how much may be accomplished within it!

2. The scene of what is here related is JERUSALEM which had been the religious capital of Judaism since the time of David.

3. The story begins with the last words of the Messiah to His Apostles, after which He was 'taken up' into heaven; and it ends with a persecution which drove all the Christians out of Jerusalem, except the Apostles.

4. The outstanding fact is that at the beginning of this period, and what made the period possible, all the followers of Jesus were constituted a spiritual Body. They became a multiple unit, henceforth to be known as the Church.

5. This momentous event was accomplished by the Holy Spirit, Who, in fulfilment of a promise descended ten days after the Messiah ascended.

6. The Christian Church, in this first period, was Jewish in its composition. We read of only one 'proselyte' (vi. 5). This was inevitable because Gentiles could enter Judaism only by proselytism. It is not until we reach the event of chapter x that the barrier between Jew and Gentile is removed (cf. Eph. ii. 11-22).

7. The presence at Jerusalem for the Feast of Pentecost of Jews from many countries resulted, no doubt, in many conversions, and these would spread the Gospel in the lands from which they came.

8. There was in this period no departure from the institutions of the Jews. Temple and synagogue were still frequented (iii. 1; v. 12, 20, 25, 42; vi. 9, 10). But it was not long before distinctly Christian institutions began to appear.

9. Distinct progress is discernible in the events of these seven years. Following the Founding of the Church (i. 1-ii. 13), the six narratives (p. 201) divide into three and three, alternating. Numbers 2, 4 and 6 relate to events within the Church, Testimony (ii. 14-47), Discipline (iv. 32-v. 16), and Administration (vi. 1-6); and numbers 3, 5 and 7 relate to events without the Church, though in relation to it, Opposition (iii. 1-iv. 31); Testing—the imprisonment and flogging of the Apostles (v. 17-42), and Persecution—organized hostility to all Christians (vi. 7-viii. 4).

The early Church had her growing pains, but her pains did mean growth as these years show. 'Out of the eater came forth meat, and out of the strong, sweetness'. 'Through much tribulation we enter the Kingdom'. 'Knowledge by suffering entereth, and life is perfected by death'. (E. B. Browning)

FURTHER NOTES ON STEPHEN

For an understanding of the Section from vi. 7 to viii. 4, the following points must be regarded:—

1. That this persecution was not against the Apostles, but against a Christian layman (vi. 5).

2. That Stephen, appointed to administer the Church's funds, also wrought miracles and preached (vi. 8-10).

3. That what he preached is not recorded, and can be inferred only from the charge of those who had argued with him (vi. 9, 11).

4. That from the charge it is clear he had spoken about 'Moses and God'; about the 'holy place, and the law'; and he is accused of having said that 'Jesus of Nazareth shall destroy this place (the Temple), and shall change the customs which Moses delivered unto us' (vi. 11, 13, 14).

5. That these charges no doubt are true, for he does not deny them.

6. That, therefore, in the new age, he was the first to apprehend and to teach that Christianity was not an adjunct of Judaism, but something quite new, involving the end of the former order of things.

7. That this was not the view, as yet, of the Apostles, who came to it slowly, and only under the pressure of events (chs. viii-xii).

8. That his address to the Sanhedrin is designed to show that this is so; that God had a people before there was either Law or Temple (vii. 2-16); that Moses had predicted the Messiah (vii. 37); that the 'fathers' of old did not receive Moses (vii. 35, 39-40); that the chosen people became idolators (vii. 41-43); that the Temple was

not in existence before the time of Solomon (vii. 44-46); that after
that, Isaiah declared that the dwelling-place of the Most High was
not in any earthly place (vii. 48-50); that those whom he addressed
were the murderers of the Messiah (vii. 51-53)

9. That while the Sadducees accepted nothing outside the Pentateuch,
   the Pharisees accepted the Prophets also, and so were confronted
   with what Isaiah had said about the Temple (vii. 48-50).

10. That, apparently, this interpretation of the Old Testament was new
    to Saul, who, after his conversion, became the great exponent of it.

11. That, therefore, Stephen was really the spiritual father of Saul.

12. That also, in advance of all the Apostles, he grasped and taught the
    real significance of the Church, and of the Christian dispensation.

THE BOOK OF THE ACTS

PART TWO

THE TRANSITION PERIOD OF THE CHURCH'S WITNESS

Chapters viii. 4-xii. 25

AD 37-47—10 Years

THE CHURCH EXPANDED - - ITS BREADTH

THE TRANSITION PERIOD OF THE CHURCH'S WITNESS

(Chapters viii. 4-xii. 25)

It must be apparent even to the casual reader of the ACTS that chapters i. 1-viii. 4 are dominantly *Jewish*, and that chapters xiii.-xxviii. are dominantly *Gentile*, and naturally one asks how, in thirty-three years, this was made possible. The answer is to be found in chapters viii. 4-xii. 25. The first and second periods cover seventeen years (A.D. 30-47); and the third period covers sixteen years (A.D. 47-63).

Much was accomplished in the first seven years of the Church's history, but its area of activity was limited to Jerusalem. From chapter xiii. there was a great movement outward, the missionaries travelling to Rome the Capital of the Empire, and perhaps as far as Spain. But if chapters viii. 4-xii. 25 were eliminated it would be difficult—if indeed possible—to account for a witness restricted to a single city suddenly becoming a universal movement, and the converts of it, being only Jews, suddenly becoming chiefly Gentiles.

Movements in history—intellectual, moral and spiritual—do not come about abruptly. There is no sudden conclusion of old processes, followed by sudden commencement of new processes. It is this fact which makes Acts viii. 4-xii. 25 of such importance. These few chapters tell of a series of events which made the expansion and extension of the Christian Church possible, and indeed inevitable. These events we speak of as *The Transition Period of the Church's Witness*

The Church which has been established must now be expanded and then extended, and the whole movement is spiritually organic. Transference, as to its content and forms, from Judaism to Christianity could not be made suddenly or quickly. The new outlook could come only gradually, and old revered institutions could give place only slowly to new orders of worship. The proclamation of the Gospel by Jews to Jews is one thing, and its proclamation by Jews and Gentiles to Jews and Gentiles, and chiefly to Gentiles, is another thing, and this change required a period and process of re-education, and this is found in the record of Acts viii-xii. Preparation for the wider witness is in five stages. First of all Philip, one of the Seven, is prepared; then, Saul, by his conversion; then Peter, the leader of the Jewish-Christian Church; then, the body of the Apostles; and finally, the growing and spreading Church with its increasing Gentile element.

I. PHILIP'S PREPARATION FOR THE WIDER WITNESS
Ch. viii. 5-40

II. SAUL'S PREPARATION FOR THE WIDER WITNESS
Ch. ix. 1-31

III. PETER'S PREPARATION FOR THE WIDER WITNESS
Chs. ix. 32-x. 48

IV. THE APOSTLES' PREPARATION FOR THE WIDER WITNESS
Ch. xi. 1-18

V. THE CHURCH'S PREPARATION FOR THE WIDER WITNESS
Chs. xi. 19-xii. 25

Chapter viii. 1-4 tells us that Stephen was buried and greatly mourned; that from this centre of suffering was described a wide circumference of persecution. The Jerusalem Christians were scattered abroad, and that scattering was as seed which was to produce a great and golden harvest. It ever has been so. The devil's breath has fanned the flames of the Gospel. The bruised tree has filled the air with perfume.

Coming now to the second main division of this Book, we have first of all Philip's preparation for the Wider Witness.

The expanding movement is indicated in the two sections in chapter eight, verses 5-25, and 26-40; the one tells of Work in Samaria, and the other, of the Word towards Africa.

The following is an analysis of this section:

I. PHILIP'S PREPARATION FOR THE WIDER WITNESS
(viii. 5-40)

1. The Gospel in Samaria
(viii. 5-25)

This work was commenced by Philip, and was confirmed by the Apostles.

(i) PHILIP AT SAMARIA (viii. 5-13)

This is not the Apostle, but Philip the *deacon* (vi. 5), and *evangelist* (xxi. 8). How was it that he met with such good success at Samaria? Read John iv. 39-42. A woman sows, and a man reaps; and the reaper himself becomes a sower for other reapers. No one can fail who goes forth with Philip's message (5), and this great message believed, is productive of *great joy* (8). '*But;*' yes, there is always a 'but' (9)—some fly in the ointment, some drag on the wheel. Here is Christianity's first collision with sorcery and superstition (9-13), and Christianity won. So far from the sheep being devoured by the wolf, the wolf aped the sheep. Simon was a humbug. Make quite sure that you are not. In every good work there are disappointments.

(ii) APOSTLES AT SAMARIA (viii. 14-25)

We should remember as we read the Acts, that one dispensation is ending, and another is beginning: Judaism is setting, and Christianity is dawning. This means that, as in all transition periods, there necessarily are factors and features which, as to their particular manner and manifestation, are transitory and not permanent. An illustration of this is in our portion (15-17). In one sense every one, in the hour of his regeneration, receives the Holy Spirit. In another sense, in the hour of one's deliberate and full dedication to God, he appropriates the divine Gift; but there is *now* no such communication of the Spirit as there was at Samaria. Modes, methods, and manners change, but spiritual realities remain.

Simon the Sorcerer

What at first (13) seemed to be a great triumph, is later seen to have been a veritable tragedy: the believer is found to be a blasphemer. '*He offered them money*' (18). There have not been wanting in the Church since then those who would have taken it, but they could not have 'delivered the goods'. This unenviable man has left a mark on literature, and on ecclesiasticism. Shakespeare uses his name in the line, 'simony was fair play'; and in the Church, simony is the act, practice, or crime of trafficking in sacred things, and especially in the buying and selling of ecclesias-

tical preferments, of the corrupt presentation of any one to an
ecclesiastical benefice for money or reward. 'But,' says Black-
stone, 'the law has established so many exceptions that there is no
difficulty whatever in avoiding the forfeiture' which is imposed
for such practice.

But there are some things which, though they may be imitated,
cannot be counterfeited, and foremost of these is *the power of the
Holy Spirit*. Fleshly energy can pass for spiritual power only
among those who are wholly lacking in discernment. You ask—
but was Simon not truly saved? (13). Certainly not (21-23).
Every professor is not a possessor; every Church member is not a
Christian; every communicant is not 'born again'. Are you?
Hypocrites should be spoken to as Peter spoke to Simon. Such
occasions are not for 'bated breath, and whispering humbleness,'
but for courage and firmness, not unmingled with hope (22).
Pretence can never pass for power.

2. The Gospel Towards Africa
(viii. 26-40)

With this ends Philip's preparation for the wider witness. The
portion is full of interest. A man in the midst of a flourishing
mission in a city is commanded to leave it and go to a desert road
to talk to a single soul. Was that worth while? The Lord thought
so (26), and so it proved to be, for by leaving the city he reached
a continent; through the eunuch Philip gave the Gospel to Africa.
Was it worth while for a simple preacher to have delivered his
brief message in a little chapel in Colchester one snowy day?
A thousand times worth while, for there and then Charles
Haddon Spurgeon was saved, and he became the greatest Gospel
preacher of the Christian Age. May the Lord deliver us from
counting heads in such matters; from measuring success by the
arithmetic table. The Lord said, *'arise and go'*. Philip *'arose and
went'*. No one who acts thus, is unblessed.

Now look at this eunuch. We see first (a) *a dissatisfied man*
(27), notwithstanding that he had position, power, and possessions.
Then, we see (b) *an enquiring man* (28-35), diligent, humble and

R

teachable. And finally, we see (c) *a converted man* (36, 38, 39: verse 37, is not in R.V.), believing, confessing, and rejoicing. In that chariot were a high official of an African Royal Court, and a simple evangelist of the Jerusalem Church; the one reading, and the other explaining Isaiah liii. The Ethiopian would be reading 'Isaiah' in the LXX Version. It is clear that Philip did not regard the Suffering Servant of this Old Testament chapter to be Israel, but JESUS (35). There is a scholarship in insight which we are too apt to overlook, or to despise. I wonder what the eunuch said to the Queen when he got back! I wonder what Philip would say if he could see missions in Africa to-day! Perhaps he can. Christianity discovered and disclosed the worth of the soul.

This was Philip's special contribution to the advance of Christianity, but he does not yet drop out of the narrative. We learn that he made a missionary tour, proclaiming the Gospel in all the cities of the Shephelah, the low coastline, which contained large Gentile populations. Eventually he settled in Caesarea which was the Roman capital of the province of Judaea, and here we find him twenty years later entertaining Paul and Luke; and probably it was on that occasion that he supplied Luke with the present narrative. In all likelihood he was head of the local Church. The Evangelist, we are told, had four daughters who prophesied.

THE MISSION OF PHILIP THE EVANGELIST (Acts viii)

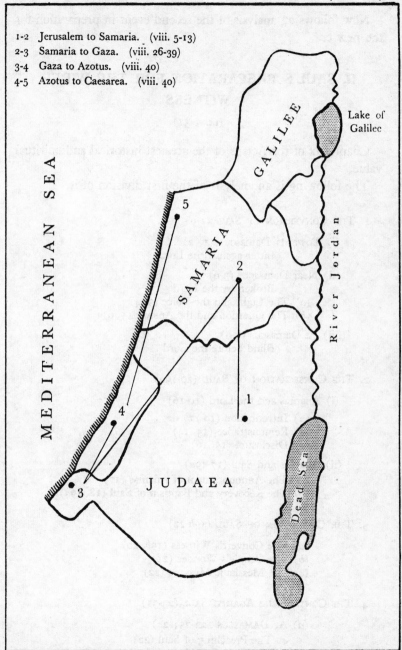

1-2   Jerusalem to Samaria. (viii. 5-13)
2-3   Samaria to Gaza. (viii. 26-39)
3-4   Gaza to Azotus. (viii. 40)
4-5   Azotus to Caesarea. (viii. 40)

Lake of
Galilee

GALILEE

MEDITERRANEAN SEA

SAMARIA

River Jordan

JUDAEA

Dead Sea

Now follows an analysis of the second event in preparation for the new era.

II. SAUL'S PREPARATION FOR THE WIDER WITNESS

(ix. 1-31)

Chapter ix of the Acts is of the greatest historical and spiritual value.

The following is an analysis of the first division of it.

1. THE CONVERSION OF SAUL (1-9)

    (i) Towards Damascus (1, 2)
            Bitter against the Lord

    (ii) Near Damascus (3-6)
            Broken by the Lord
      (a) The Light and the Voice (3, 4)
      (b) The Question and the Answer (5, 6)

    (iiii) At Damascus (7-9)
            Blind before the Lord

2. THE CONSECRATION OF SAUL (10-19a)

    (i) Ananias and the Lord (10-16)

      (a) Introduction (10-12)
      (b) Remonstrance (13, 14)
      (c) Disclosure (15, 16)

    (ii) Ananias and Saul (17-19a)
      (a) The Announcement of Ananias (17)
      (b) The Recovery and Baptism of Saul (18, 19a)

3. THE CONFESSION OF SAUL (19b-22)

      (a) The Convert's Witness (19b, 20)
      (b) The People's Wonder (21)
      (c) The Messianic Message (22)

4. THE CONSPIRACIES AGAINST SAUL (23-31)

      (a) At DAMASCUS (22-25; 24)
          The Preaching of Saul (22)
          The Plot of the Jews (23, 24)
          The Escape from the Danger (25)

Later we must say more about Paul's character and ministry, but the events of a few years from his conversion, recorded in chapter ix, together with references to these events recorded elsewhere, cannot be too carefully pondered. The four principal matters, relative to Paul, are his conversion, his consecration, his confession, and the conspiracies against him.

1. The Conversion of Saul
(ix. 1-9)

Of all the remarkable events in the history of the soul, probably the most remarkable is the conversion of Saul of Tarsus, the memory of which is continuously celebrated on the 25th of January. This most remarkable event is recorded three times: in ix. 1-9, in xxii. 6-16, and in xxvi. 12-18. We are shown how the fierce persecutor became the foremost preacher of the apostolic age.

What made Saul so fierce? Stephen's sermon. Never is a man madly irritated against an opinion, violent against a cause or a person, except as evidence of a struggle within. The man is really at war with himself. A conviction is reluctantly forcing its way upon him; he feels the goads of conscience, and vents his resentment upon objects outside of himself.

Who was he so mad against? The people of *The Way* (2). This was the earliest name for what we now call Christianity; and very significant it is, for Christianity is a way of thinking, of feeling, of living, and of serving. Christ apprehended this man who was determined to apprehend the Christian (Acts. ix. 1, 2; Phil. iii. 12). It was all very sudden.

> Between the stirrup and the ground,
> He mercy sought, and mercy found.

If the Christian witness was to become world-wide someone would have to be raised up who was competent to initiate and carry out such a project. Such a person would have to be richly endowed, and also would have to be divinely commissioned. None of the apostles was equal to this task, and so God apprehended (Phil. iii. 12) and appointed Saul of Tarsus, who by temperament, training, and contacts, who religiously, politically, and intellectually had the equipment necessary for such a mission. No greater thing happened in this Transition Period than the Conversion of Saul.

The late Earl of Birkenhead, in his *Turning Points in History*, gives a prominent place to The Conversion of St. Paul (pp. 24-36). Introducing the subject he says: 'Of all men who may claim to have changed the course of the world's history, St. Paul must surely take the first place. He altered the basic ideas of Western civilisation; the whole of our history bears the marks of that busy career of impassioned teaching which the Jewish tent-maker undertook after his conversion to faith in Jesus Christ'.

Such an estimate from such a quarter should send us again to Acts ix. to contemplate once more the beginnings of it all.

It was the answer to Stephen's prayer (vii. 60), and the first-fruits of his blood. This conversion was the beginning of something quite new in religious history; it was the opening of a door into a much larger world than was known to Judaism. It meant ere long the admission of Gentiles into the Church of God, the Church which up to this point was Jewish. Saul would have been about 35 years of age at this time, which means that he would have been about 28 at the time of Jesus' death; but it is not certain that he ever met the Messiah (cf. 2 Cor. v. 16).

Damascus had a large colony of Jews, and there were several synagogues. Also there must have been in the city a considerable body of Christians, and it was this fact which explains why Saul was sent thither by the Sanhedrin. Saul's accounts of what happened just outside Damascus on that day are obviously factual, and make Renan's explanation of the event fatuous. Paul ascribed his whole after life to this experience, and he had no doubt as to what actually happened.

2. The Consecration of Saul
(ix. 10-19a)

Two men are now introduced of whom we know nothing beyond what is here stated. It was at the house of a Jew named *Judas* that Saul stayed for three days, blind and fasting. What could Judas have made of his strange guest, and what conversation, if any, passed between them? All we know of Judas is that he lived in Straight Street.

The other person is *Ananias*, who is mentioned in this passage only, but to good purpose. He was a Christian Jew, and was told by the Lord to go to the house of Judas and to impart to Saul a threefold blessing—his sight, the Holy Spirit, and baptism.

Ananias had heard bad news of Saul, and was hesitant about making contact with him, but the Lord reassured him. The value of this paragraph is in what the Lord said to Ananias about Saul (11, 15, 17). He told him that Saul was praying; that in a vision he had seen Ananias coming to him and giving him back his sight; that Saul was a chosen vessel, to bear the Lord's name before the Gentiles, and Kings, and the Children of Israel; and that He, the Lord, would show Paul that he would have to suffer much for his Saviour's sake.

This is a key to the whole of Saul's future career.

3. The Confession of Saul
(ix. 19b-22)

A point of chronology is of interest and importance here. From Galatians i. 17, 18, we learn that Saul went into retreat in Arabia at this time, which event we must place between verses 19, 20, or verses 22, 23, or verses 25, 26, of our lesson. If after verse 22, 'many days' (23) would point to this period. Saul's conversion was so astounding an experience that he needed time to get the new perspective of his life and thought. During that period of retreat he would read the Old Testament again, and understand it as he had never done before. With every new spiritual experience we come into possession of a more wonderful Bible.

The retirement in the desert and the ministry in Damascus must have lasted for more than two years, but it is not said what proportion of time was spent in each place.

Little did Saul imagine that he was to become the Church's theologian, and was to write thirteen of the New Testament Epistles! But his theme from the beginning was *Christ, the Son of God* (20), which fact he 'proved' (22). The people were '*amazed*' (21), not only at the ability and power of the preacher, but at his being a preacher at all, who until now had been so bitter a persecutor.

Saul believed that the predicted Messiah would come, but what, until now, he did not believe was that Jesus who had been crucified was the Messiah. It was for this belief that Stephen had died; on this belief the Church was founded; and on account of this belief the great persecution arose in which Saul took so prominent a part.

What was revealed to him during the three days of his blindness in Damascus and during the period in Arabia, is the truth that Jesus whom he was persecuting was indeed the promised Messiah (ix. 4, 5). The light of this truth flashed on the Old Testament gave Saul a new Bible, and it was this change of front that amazed both the Christians and the non-Christian Jews.

Returning to Damascus Saul 'proclaimed Jesus, that He is the Son of God' (ix. 20). This is the first mention of Him as such in the Acts (viii. 37 is not in the R.V.), and it indicates the relationship of the Messiah to the Father.

In the Damascus synagogues Saul also 'proved' that Jesus is the Christ (ix. 20, 22). The word 'proved' is *sumbibazō*, which means *put-together* (cf. ch. xvi. 10. 1 Cor. ii. 16. Col. ii. 2, 19). What he *put-together* were Messianic Old Testament passages (cf. Luke xxiv. 26, 27). It is little wonder that the people were amazed.

4. The Conspiracies Against Saul
(ix. 23-31)

There was antagonism as well as amazement, and it was in both Damascus and Jerusalem.

Both pleasure and pain enter into the texture of our life; but it is never all pain, as it is never all pleasure. Men may kill the preacher, but they cannot kill the Gospel (23). Nothing is so utterly absurd as to suppose that what is true and right can be got rid of by killing people who proclaim it. Yet this insanity has been practised ever since Cain killed Abel. With verse 25 read 2 Cor. xi. 32, 33. The fear of the Jerusalem disciples was quite natural, but Barnabas became Saul's sponsor (26, 27).

At this time Saul stayed with Peter for a fortnight (28, Gal. i. 18). Try and imagine how Peter would have talked, and how Saul would have listened, and think of the places in and around the City they would have visited together! But Saul was too hot for the hypocrites (29), and so God told him to get away, (30, with ch. xxii. 17-21), and he returned to Tarsus. There are times when one should remain and fight, and there are times when one should flee. Now that a fierce foe had become so faithful a friend, the churches had peace and prosperity (31).

The Church at Rest

(ix. 31)

This verse stands between Saul's preparation and Peter's for the wider witness, and its significance is great. After persecution came peace in the Church, and this was the result of Saul's conversion.

The three districts of Palestine are named—Judaea, Samaria, and Galilee, the only time that Galilee is mentioned in connection with the Church. The peace which the scattered but unified Church enjoyed resulted in a twofold blessing; *within* it was upbuilt, and *without* it was multiplied, and this must always be the course of the Church's growth, from within outward.

The third great event in preparation for the wider witness relates to the Apostle Peter, and it is of tremendous importance. The following is an analysis of this section:

III. PETER'S PREPARATION FOR THE WIDER WITNESS

(ix. 32-x. 48)

1. PETER AT LYDDA (ix. 32-35)

   (i) Saints Edified (32)
   (ii) Sick Healed (33, 34)
   (iii) Sinners Saved (35)

2. PETER AT JOPPA (ix. 36-x. 23a)

   (i) The Restoration of Tabitha (ix. 36-43)

       (a) The Occasion (36, 37)
       (b) The Miracle (38-41)
       (c) The Result (42, 43)

   (ii) The Communication with Cornelius (x. 1-8)

       (a) What he was (1, 2)
       (b) What he saw (3)
       (c) What he heard (4-6)
       (d) What he did (7, 8)

   (iii) The Illumination of Peter (x. 9-16)

       (a) The Vision (9-12)
       (b) The Voice (13-16)

   (iv) The Deputation from Caesarea (x. 17-23a)

       (a) The men to the tanner (17, 18)
       (b) The Spirit to Peter (19, 20)
       (c) Peter to the men (21)
       (d) The men to Peter (22)
       (e) All together for a night (23a)

3. PETER AT CAESAREA (x. 23b-48)

   (i) *The Salutation* (23b-33)

       The Jew and the Roman meet.

       (a) The party journey (23b, 24)
       (b) The obeisance of Cornelius (25, 26)
       (c) Peter's greeting (27-29)

           (1) A Prejudice (27, 28a)
           (2) A Correction (28b, 29a)
           (3) An Inquiry (29b)

       (d) The reply of Cornelius (30-33)

           (1) He tells of the Vision (30-33a)
           (2) He asks for the Message (33b)

(ii) *The Sermon* (34-43)
> The universal message of Salvation
>> (*a*) The Scope of the Gospel (34, 35)
>> (*b*) The Word of the Gospel (36-41)
>>> (1) Anticipation of it (36, 37)
>>> (2) Substance of it (38-41)
>>> JESUS OF NAZARETH
>>> His Ministry (38, 39*a*)
>>> His Death (39*b*)
>>> His Resurrection (40*a*)
>>> His Manifestation (40*b*, 41)
>> (*c*) The Offer of the Gospel (42, 43)
>>> (1) The Charge (42)
>>> Christ the Judge
>>> (2) The Promise (43)
>>> Christ the Saviour

(iii) *The Sequel* (44-48)
> The Spirit outpoured upon the Gentiles.
>> (*a*) The Enduement (44-46*a*)
>> (*b*) The Baptism (46*b*-48)

It was imperative that Peter should be prepared for wider witness because his outlook was exclusively Jewish, although he had quoted in his Pentecostal sermon, 'I will pour out of my Spirit upon *all flesh*' (ii. 17).

But it is clear in Acts x that only a special revelation could bring Peter to see that the Gospel was for all men, and that the Church could not consist of Jewish believers only.

In this portion of the narrative we see Peter in three places, in Lydda, Joppa, and Caesarea.

1. Peter at Lydda (ix. 32-35)

'Rest' (*Peace*, R.V.) is variously regarded and interpreted (31). Peter interpreted it in terms of *work*. He always was a man of energy and enterprise. The leader of the Jerusalem Church made excursions from time to time, and these were fruitful, not only for the places visited, but also for the home church left meanwhile.

A man who had been in bed for eight years got up and rose out of weakness into strength, by *power* on God's part, and *faith*

on his own.   In the absence of either of these factors there is
no transition from one state to another.   A bodily-absent Christ
may be a spiritually-present Power.   Physical healing may lead to
spiritual life: '*all that saw turned to the Lord.*'

2. Peter at Joppa (ix. 36-x. 23a)

This narrative falls into two parts.   The first tells of a miracle
which the Apostle performed, and the other, of two revelations
which he received.   These events, especially the latter, have given
a permanent place historically to Joppa, Jaffa, the modern Tel
Aviv now the capital of re-nationalized Israel.

(i) THE MIRACLE (ix. 36-43)

It is interesting to contrast the previous narrative with this
one.

There a *man* (33), here a *woman*; there, *healing* (34), here,
quickening; there '*all*' believed (35), but here, '*many*' (42).   God
was the power and Peter was the agent in both cases.   Both
events were miraculous, but they differ widely.

Dorcas is delivered from death.   She was missed and mourned
because she had been merciful.   The people would not have
grieved if Dorcas had not been good; the wicked are not wailed,
or should not be.   Back of this woman's labour was her love.   If
she came back to earth to-day, imagine her surprise to find
everywhere *Dorcas Societies*.   From a little seed well sown comes
a rich harvest.   Surprises await many an unselfish woman.   God
sees what is obscure, and will reward all that is done for Him.   I
was going to say that Dorcas deserved to live again, but, upon
reflection, was it not a sad thing that she should come back into
such a world as this?   Not for her own sake was she brought back,
but for the Gospel's, and the Church's.   The Bible tells us of
nine persons who were raised from the dead, but not one of them
has told us of his or her experience in the other world.

(ii) THE TWO REVELATIONS (x. 1-23a)

One of these was vouchsafed to Cornelius, a Gentile; and
the other, to Peter, a Jew, but they were both related to the same

thing, which was one of the most momentous events in the history of Christianity. This event is doctrinally unfolded by Paul in Eph. ii. 11-13.

That Peter lodged with Simon *a tanner* is evidence of the breaking down of Jewish prejudices, and it helped to prepare Peter for what was soon to follow.

This is a chapter of incalculable importance alike for the Church and the world. It records nothing less than the formal opening of the Door of Grace to the Gentiles. Peter, the apostle of the circumcision, preached the Gospel to a Roman official at the latter's house, and this was the Apostle's great preparation for the wider witness. Here are two revelations, and both are preparations. Remember, every revelation is a preparation for something beyond itself.

(a) *The Revelation to Cornelius the Gentile* (x. 1-8)

This is a fine illustration of the distinction between religion and Christianity. Christianity is religion, but all religion is not Christianity. Cornelius was a religious man, but he was not yet a Christian man. Note his piety, reverence, liberality, prayerfulness, receptivity, and obedience. He was living up to the light he had; but that was not enough; it never is. Yet, do not this man's moral earnestness, simple faith, and genuine humility put many a Christian to shame?

(b) *The Revelation to Peter the Jew* (x. 9-16)

His preparation for wider witness had already begun, but there were barriers yet to be broken down. It was natural, perhaps inevitable, that the subject should be raised relative to food (cf. 1 Cor. x. 23-33), because the question of clean and unclean meats was fundamental. The Lord had spoken about it, but the Jews were slow to learn.

It would be a great thing if every Christian in the world prayed for two minutes every day at 12 o'clock (9). Two details here contributed to weaken Peter's Jewish prejudices: first, his residing with a *tanner* (ix. 43), involving contact with dead animals; and secondly, the wide view he had over the Mediterranean may have led him to think of the regions beyond.

Well, while they were getting a meal ready, Peter fell asleep, and he got a vision which was better than the best victuals. Read verses 11-16 with Leviticus xi, and you will understand Peter's point of view. Read also Daniel i. 8-16, Ezek. iv. 13, 14, Matt. xv. 10-20, Mark vii. 14-23.

Nowhere in language is so flagrant and fearful a contradiction fixed in three words as in Ch. x. 14: 'NOT SO, LORD'; Whoever says '*not so*', should never add '*Lord*'; and whoever truly says '*Lord*', will never say '*not so*'. It is not for the servant to dictate to the Master. Say to-day whether you will part with the first two words, or with the third.

(c) *The Two Revelations Meet* (x. 17-23a)

This is a profound passage, revealing as it does, the activity of God in the minds and hearts of men, separated by distance from one another, with a view to their being brought together.

Because God is sovereign over men He is the director of events. How long Peter would have continued to be 'perplexed' (x. 17) we cannot say, but light was to dawn suddenly from an unexpected quarter. While Peter was thinking, three men were travelling, and soon seven Jews and three Gentiles would be on the road together, bound for Caesarea twenty miles away to the north (x. 19; xi. 12). I wonder what was the substance of their conversation on the way!

3. **Peter at Caesarea** (x. 23b-48)

The record of this section falls into three parts—the salutation the sermon, and the sequel.

(i) THE SALUTATION (x. 23b-33)

History records many interviews between great men: e.g. DIOGENES with ALEXANDER; LUTHER with CHARLES V; MILTON with GALILEO; GARIBALDI with VICTOR EMMANUEL; and LIVINGSTONE with STANLEY; but none of them was so momentous as that of PETER with CORNELIUS (25). This was one of those hinges upon which, small as they may seem at the moment, vast interests turn. It was one of those moments when revolutions in the whole state of human society are at the birth; when that is being unconsciously enacted by the doers which will powerfully affect mankind to the end of time, and beyond it.

Christ had given to Peter '*the keys of the kingdom*' (Matt. xvi. 19), and Peter with them opened the gates for the entrance of countless millions of Gentile believers. *An Israelite shows an Italian the way.* There are wheels within wheels in Divine Providence; events mesh; and '*in everything God works for good with those that love Him*' (Rom. viii. 28). The order here is— revelation, commission, action; the *vision* is followed by the *voice*, and the *voice* by the *venture*.

The man who in ch. v. 40 was whipped, is now worshipped (25), but he will have none of it (26). There they are, the Peter party, and the Cornelius party (27). Peter speaks first (28, 29), and then Cornelius (30-33). The heart of Peter's speech is in the words, '*God hath shewed me*'; and the heart of Cornelius' speech is in, '*we are all here present before God, to hear all things that are commanded thee of God.*' This whole thing was a *Godly* affair.

There is always an open door for the open heart.

(ii) THE SERMON (x. 34-43)

Here is the universal message of salvation, in which we see: (a) *The Scope of the Gospel* (34, 35); (b) *The Word of the Gospel* (36, 41); and (c) *The Offer of the Gospel* (42, 43).

Under (b) *The Word of the Gospel* (36-41) mark the *anticipation* of it (36, 37), and the *substance* of it (38-41); *Jesus of Nazareth*: His ministry (38, 39a); His death (39b); His resurrection (40a); and His manifestation (40b, 41).

And under (c) *The Offer of the Gospel* (42, 43) mark the *charge* —Christ the Judge (42), and the *promise*—Christ the Saviour (43).

Peter's word 'I perceive' is of great importance. It is an emphatic word for seizing or grasping (cf. Phil. iii. 12. John i. 5, *katalambanō*), and what Peter really says is, 'I am getting a firm grasp of the truth that God is no respecter of persons'; that is, he had begun to understand Deut. x. 17. The dividing wall was beginning to crumble. Peter knew and said that for him to enter into Cornelius' house was a distinct breach of Jewish custom, but he was now beginning to 'apprehend' that many Jewish customs were doomed.

This portion is of profoundest importance, not only because here is *the sermon*, by which the middle wall of partition between Jew and Gentile was broken down, but also because in it we have the fullest specimen which the Church possesses, of a 'primitive Gospel', which was widely preached at least a quarter of a century before any of our Gospel Records was committed to writing; and in this sermon is summarized the leading thought of each of the Four.

Mark's Gospel, which was written at Peter's instigation, is but an expansion of verse 38, in Peter's sermon; indeed we may say that this, his sixth address, is Mark's Gospel in germ. It is wonderful that within fifteen years of Jesus' death, this staunch Jew had got the length of telling an Italian congregation that Jesus 'is Lord of ALL,' and 'the Judge of quick and dead' (36, 42). Note, it does not say that all *religions* are alike in God's sight, but all *nations* (34, 35).

This is the first trumpet-sound of the Gospel in the heathen world, and its great notes are: the personal Redeemer, the witnessing Church, and the universal invitation. Jesus is more than a philanthropist, He is a Propitiation. He is more than a reformer, He is a Redeemer. Never let these facts go, for if you do, everything else that matters will go with them. There is no use of any one preaching to anybody at home or abroad, who cannot preach—the Christ who lived, the Christ who died, the Christ who lives again, and the Christ who can save any one and every one from sin now and for ever.

(iii) THE SEQUEL (x. 44-48)

This is the first Gentile Church, resting on the same *Rock*, and receiving the same *Seal* as the Jewish Church on the Day of Pentecost. The Gospel is needed by all, is sufficient for all, is accessible to all, and may be received by all. Oh, grand and glorious Gospel! The gift of the Spirit and speaking with tongues were closely associated in the early Church, but never anywhere does it say that 'tongues' is evidence of the gift.

Tradition must give way to truth.

This, then, was Peter's preparation for the wider witness, and by the events here recorded the Christian Church took a long stride forward.

Now follows the fourth stage of preparation for the new age.

IV. THE APOSTLES' PREPARATION FOR THE WIDER WITNESS

(xi. 1-18)

1. **The Complaint against Peter (1-3)**

2. **The Circumstances of Gentile Blessing Rehearsed (4-17)**

    (i) The Vision and the Voice at Joppa (4-10)

    (ii) The Summons and Response of Peter (11, 12)

    (iii) The Events in the House of Cornelius (13-15)

    (iv) The Effect of the Experience on Peter (16, 17)

3. **The Conclusion of the Apostles (18)**

So far we have followed the preparation for the next great movement of the Church of three individuals—Philip, Saul, and Peter—but now the whole body of the Apostles at Jerusalem is to enter into a larger conception of the meaning of Christianity. This is brought about strangely enough by way of an *indictment of Peter* for going to Cornelius (1-3). But they had to learn, and so have we, that where there is revelation there must be enlargement, and that what at first is censured, may have at last to be commended. How did Peter meet this charge and censure? I think I know how he would have met it *before* Pentecost, but he was another man now. Has the Holy Spirit made any difference in your life?

In this his seventh address Peter simply narrates the facts of ch. x. 5-17, declaring that he had done all under Divine direction (5, 9, 12, 15, 16). A fact is a great argument (see iv. 14); it is more than abuse ever can be, though this too often is resorted

s

to in debate. But, remember, abuse is the refuge of the weak. Peter just tells the story. He does not go behind the facts and try to explain them; he is content to affirm them, and to point to the result of his so-called lawless action (x. 28). He considers that if an *angel* could stand in the house of a Gentile, an apostle might well do so (13).

Relating the effect upon himself of what had happened, he says, '*then remembered I*—' Here is a lesson on *getting* memory-stores, *keeping* memory-stores, and *using* memory-stores. The first effect, then, was one of *memory*; the second, was one of *conviction* that this was God's work, and therefore not to be opposed (17). Here let us see God's purpose, so striking; God's plan, so simple; and God's power, so sufficient. The argument of fact convinced the Apostles (18). Criticism was silenced when conviction was reached. Complaint (1-3) is followed by a rehearsal of the circumstances of Gentile blessing (4-17), and this leads the Apostles to conviction and a sound conclusion (18).

Let us tell what we know of God's doings.

The final stage in preparation for the new age is now reached; and the following is an analysis of it.

V. THE CHURCH'S PREPARATION FOR THE WIDER WITNESS

(xi. 19-xii. 25)

1. *Progress of the Church at Antioch* (xi. 19-30)
    - (i) The Spread of the Gospel among Jews and Gentiles (xi. 19-21)
    - (ii) The Ministry of Barnabas at Antioch (xi. 22-26)
        - (*a*) His Success (22-24)
        - (*b*) His Associate (25, 26)
    - (iii) The Bounty of the Church at Antioch (xi. 27-31)
        - (*a*) Anticipated Need (27, 28)
        - (*b*) Generous Supply (29, 30)

2. *Persecution of the Church at Jerusalem* (xii. 1-23)

   (i) The Martyrdom of James (1,2)

   (ii) The Imprisonment of Peter (3-19*a*)
      (*a*) The Intention of Herod (3, 4)
      (*b*) The Prayers of the Church (5)
      (*c*) The Visit of an Angel (6-8)
      (*d*) The Deliverance from Prison (9-11)
      (*e*) At the Home of Mary (12-17)
      (*f*) The Death of the Guards (18, 19*a*)

   (iii) The Visitation upon Herod (19*b*-23)
      (*a*) His Displeasure (19*b*, 20)
      (*b*) His Oration (21, 22)
      (*c*) His Death (23)

3. *Prosperity of the Church in General* (24, 25)

There remains one more stage in the Transition Period of Witness, and this is the preparation of the Church itself. Everything that preceded led up to this, and nothing beyond this was possible, for now the conditions were ripe for the next great advance, for the world-wide enterprise of Christianity. The first three stages centred in individuals—Philip, Saul, and Peter; the fourth stage embraced the circle of the Apostles, without whose concurrence in principle with the broadening of the Church to admit Gentiles it would have been difficult, if indeed possible, for the world-movement to get started. But by the time it could be said of them: 'When they heard these things, they held their peace, and glorified God, saying: "Then hath God also to the Gentiles granted repentance unto life",' the conditions were present for the whole Jewish Church to catch this vision, and, when the hour arrived, to move forward.

Towards this final movement three things recorded in this section contributed: the progress of the Church at Antioch; the persecution of the Church at Jerusalem; and the prosperity of the Church in general.

It has been said of Syrian Antioch that 'In no city of antiquity was the enjoyment of life so much the main thing, and its duties so incidental'. 'The brilliant civilization and perfect art of the Greek failed to redeem the turbulent, fickle, and dissolute character of the Syrian. Instead of either race being improved by the contact, each rather infected the other with its characteristic vices.'

After Rome, and Alexandria, Antioch was the third great city in the Empire, and it was the capital of the east. The Church there had a position half-way between the Hebrew Church of Jerusalem and the Gentile churches which Paul founded. Also, as we shall see, it became the first missionary Church.

One other fact at this point must not be overlooked, namely the reintroduction of Saul into the history (xi. 25). He had returned to Tarsus when his life was jeopardised in Jerusalem (ix. 26-30), and he was there when Barnabas went to Antioch (xi. 22), who, when he saw the need and scope of the work in this northern capital, realized that he would need help, and himself went to Tarsus and persuaded Saul to go to Antioch, that together they might organize and instruct the Gentile-Jewish Church there. This Saul did, and these two great men remained for a year in the city (xi. 22-26). What is not here stated, but which nevertheless was the fact, is that now Peter begins to disappear from the narrative, and Paul begins to dominate it. At first Barnabas and Saul are named in this order, but soon Saul takes precedence and Barnabas eventually disappears, being mentioned for the last time in the Acts in chapter xv. 39; a regrettable farewell.

1. The Progress of the Church at Antioch

(xi. 19-30)

It should be observed that verse 19 connects directly with viii. 1-4, and what follows (19-21) is independent of what happened between these passages, namely, viii. 5 to xi. 18.

The establishment of a Christian Church in Antioch in Syria was a momentous event. The city is said to have had a population 500,000. It was one of the three largest cities in the Roman

Empire, was famed for its commerce, art, and literature, and was infamous for its vice and frivolity. That was just the place for a Christian Church.

The founding of this Church was in three stages, marked by the arrival of *travelling preachers* (19-21), of *Barnabas* (22-24), and of *Saul* (25, 26).

The men of Cyprus and Cyrene who went to Antioch (xi. 20) were Hellenists, that is, Greek-speaking Jews, but the people they evangelized in the city were 'Greeks', God-fearing Greeks and heathen Greeks. This was an entirely new departure, and indicates how definitely the door was opening for the entrance of Gentiles into the Christian Church.

Barnabas seems to have had an unusual power of doing the right thing at the right time (cf. iv. 36; ix. 27; xi. 23, 24). This is something we should all covet and cultivate. The advice of Barnabas to those people we may well take to ourselves: '*With purpose of heart to cleave unto the Lord*' (23). We need tenacity in the hour of temptation.

Mark the new name '*Christians*' (26), given to the disciples by the heathen at Antioch in jest or mockery. But what a superb jest, containing, as the word does, *Hebrew thought*, the equivalent of *Messiah*; *Greek language* in the substantive *Christ*; and a *Latin element* in 'ians', and in this way reflecting the universality of the Gospel. (Compare Luke xxiii. 38.)

Life is energetic, and love is sacrificial, and so a collection is taken up (27-30). By the raising in Syria of a collection for the Christian Jews in Judaea we see the two great parts of the Church drawing together—Christian Gentiles and Christian Jews (27-30). This is the first instance of one Church raising an offering for the members of another Church. Soon the ideas *Gentile* and *Jew* would die, and only *Christian* be left.

2. The Persecution of the Church at Jerusalem
(xii. 1-23)

This persecution was not general, but was directed against the leaders as 'certain of the Church', as the account which follows shows.

In this portion of the narrative are three particulars: the martyrdom of James (xii. 1. 2); the imprisonment of Peter (xii, 3-19a), and the visitation upon Herod (xii. 19b-23).

(i) THE MARTYRDOM OF JAMES (xii. 1, 2)

Here are the execution of one murder, and the contemplation of another. For what reason? To please the Jews (3). This is a chapter of sharp contrasts. Over against the love of the Gentiles (xi. 29, 30) is the hate of the Jews (3); over against the death of one apostle is the deliverance of another; over against a king's power is his subjects' weakness; over against armed security is angelic salvation; and over against cruel purpose (4) is Divine protection.

James was a son of Zebedee, an apostle, a brother of John, one of the Three, and the first of the apostles—so far as we know— to die. It is astonishing that the martyrdom of this man is recorded in two words only, *aneilen machairē*!

Before bidding farewell to him, review his history (Matt. iv. 21. Matt. x. 2. Matt. xvii. 1. Mark v. 37. Mark x. 35; xiii. 3; xiv. 33. Luke ix. 54. John i. 41. Acts i. 13; ii. 4. Acts xii. 2. 1 Cor. xv. 7). The second martyr goes. Blessed are the dead who die, not only '*in*' but '*for*' the Lord.

(ii) THE IMPRISONMENT OF PETER (xii. 3-19a)

Herod intended to make a great spectacle of Peter's death after the Passover Feast (4), but he reckoned without God. Observe, however, what precautions he took to keep his victim secure (4, 6). 'BUT PRAYER' (5). Yes, that alters the whole situation. Does your case seem hopeless? '*But prayer!*' Are the odds all against you? '*But prayer!*' And observe that this prayer was (a) *without ceasing*; (b) *of the church*; (c) *unto God*; (d) *for him* (5): that is, it was persistent, united, worshipful and definite. In reply God brought deliverance; but He waited until the last night (6), and the last moment (18), between three and six o'clock in the morning. He never is before His time, and He never is behind.

Verses 6-10 are very graphic. Sixteen soldiers (4), two chains, keepers (6), an iron gate, and two wards (10), and a prisoner off

to see some friends of his (12). Heaven has played a trick on
Herod: an angel has made him look foolish. But though miraculously delivered, Peter must exercise common sense; he must
think quickly and act promptly, or it will be 'as you were' (11, 12).
Think of the leisureliness of God (8).

The delivered Peter, *having grasped the situation*' (12), resolved
to go to the home of Mary, the mother of John Mark. No doubt
Peter had often stayed there. Now, remember, these people
were praying for Peter's deliverance (12), yet when he turned up
at the house, they did not believe that it was he, and called the
maid *'raving mad'* for saying he was there (15); and as she
'kept confidently asserting' the fact, they then concluded that it
was *'his angel'*; and when the door was opened, Peter having been
kept standing there knocking, they beheld him, and *'were
amazed'*.

What a way to pray! It may be well to remind ourselves that
prayer is not an end in itself, but a means to an end, so that when
the means is made the end, the end is never reached. If God
answered your prayers, would *you* be astonished? Let us frankly
acknowledge that the answers we get to our prayers are not of
our merit, but of His mercy. God does better for us than we
deserve.

But what has become of Peter? (18). Peter was a problem.
Christians often are to the world. And there is another, a moral
problem here. These 'keepers' were not responsible for either
Peter's imprisonment, or his escape; yet, they were 'put to death'
(19). That is part of an age-long and world-wide problem, the
sufferings of the innocent, and we must just leave it.

(iii) THE VISITATION UPON HEROD (xii. 19b-23)

This is Agrippa I, the grandson of Herod the Great. Tyre and
Sidon, cities which had displeased Herod, and from whom
Herod had cut off supplies of food, sent a deputation to him to
ask for peace. The King was celebrating at Caesarea a festival
in thanksgiving for the safe return of the Emperor Claudius from
his expedition against Britain. Herod 'made an oration' to the
assembled crowd, and they shouted, 'The voice of a god, and not
of a man'. But pride goes too far when it reaches to the throne

of God, and in that hour Herod was smitten by 'an angel of the Lord'. Rebellion and retribution are never far apart. The same angel that saves believers (xii. 7) smites blasphemers.

> The theatre is thronged. The orb of day
> Sheds its bright radiance from a cloudless sky.
> The monarch on his throne, in proud array,
> Glistens with silver—dazzles every eye,
> And drinks the fulsome draughts of flattery.
> "A god! a god!" they shout; "behold a god!"
> He swells with pride, and apes the Deity.
> Up, Nemesis, with thy avenging rod!
> She smites, and down he sinks, a livid, lifeless clod!

3. The Prosperity of the Church in General
(xii. 24, 25)

Brief though this record is, it is very significant. 'The word of God grew and multiplied'. The progress of the Church has been, and will continue to be, like a river which runs vigorously to the sea, meeting with many obstacles in the way, but over-leaping them and rushing on; slowing down at times, and winding about, but still set for the sea. This is the record so far:

'Added (to the Church) about three thousand souls' (ii. 41).

'The Lord added to the Church daily such as should be saved' (ii. 47).

'Many of them that heard the word believed; and the number of the men was about five thousand' (iv. 4).

'The multitude of them that believed were of one heart and of one soul' (iv. 32).

'Believers were the more added to the Lord, multitudes both of men and women' (v. 14).

'The word of God increased, and the number of the disciples multiplied in Jerusalem greatly, and a great company of the priests were obedient to the faith' (vi. 7).

'The people with one accord gave heed unto those things which Philip spake' (viii. 6).

'There was great joy in that city' (Samaria. viii. 8).

'They believed Philip preaching the things concerning the Kingdom of God, and the name of Jesus Christ; they were baptized both men and women' (viii. 12).

'Then had the Churches rest throughout all Judaea and Galilee, and Samaria, and were edified; and walking in the fear of the Lord, and in the comfort of the Holy Spirit, were multiplied' (ix. 31).

'All that dwelt at Lydda and in Sharon . . . turned to the Lord'
(ix. 35).

'Many (in Joppa) believed in the Lord' (ix. 42).

'On the Gentiles also was poured out the gift of the Holy Spirit'
(x. 45).

'Much people was added unto the Lord' (xi. 24).

Let us remember that this is the record of only sixteen or
seventeen years of the Church's history, and almost entirely in
Jerusalem. The same record in any Church to-day would be regarded as outstanding.

There had been setbacks, failures, disappointments, oppositions,
persecutions and martyrdoms, but these notwithstanding the
Church went forward to wider and deeper triumphs as the
remainder of the Acts shows (xiii-xxviii). God's workmen pass
away, but His work continues.

Another thing of importance in this brief statement is the
introduction of John Mark; John his Jewish name, and Mark or
Marcus his Roman name; and it is worth while observing that
he became and is known by his Roman name. Barnabas and he
were cousins.

This ends the second of the three periods of the Church's
history in the first generation; and the way is now wide open for
a great extension of its activities and conquests.

It is agreed that Herod Agrippa I died in A.D. 44 (chapter xii),
but there is no common agreement as to the date of the opening
events of chapter xiii though the chronologers place the beginning
of the first missionary journey in A.D. 45, or in A.D. 47. If the
former date be correct the Journey started in the year after
Herod's death; but if the latter date be correct—which we are
assuming—then Paul and Barnabas remained with the Church
at Antioch for fully two years before setting out on their missionary
enterprise. This appears to be a reasonable conjecture, in which
case they would be largely responsible for the prosperous condition of the Church (xii. 24).

THE UNFOLDING DRAMA OF REDEMPTION

ACT II

SCENE 2

THE BOOK OF THE ACTS

GOD'S APPOINTED MESSENGERS

BARNABAS

MARK

PAUL

GOD'S APPOINTED MESSENGERS

In Acts xii. 25, we read: 'BARNABAS and PAUL returned from Jerusalem when they had fulfilled their ministry, and took with them JOHN, whose surname was MARK'.

The period referred to is after the death of Herod in A.D. 44, and before the commencement of the first great missionary journey in A.D. 47.

It will be well, before entering upon the third and chief division of this Book (xiii-xxviii), to consider the history of these three men, and especially that of Paul who from now on dominates the record.

Barnabas

This name, which means 'son of exhortation', occurs twenty-four times in the Acts, and five times in the Epistles (1 Cor. ix. 6. Gal. ii. 1, 9, 13. Col. iv. 10). His original name was Joses. He was a Levite, and his home was in Cyprus. He had removed to Jerusalem and acquired property there, the law of Num. xviii. 20, 23; Deut. x. 9, having fallen into abeyance (cf. Jer. xxxii. 7). The practice of community of goods in the early Church led Barnabas to sell his property and to put the proceeds into the common fund.

Being a Hellenist it is likely that he had visited the University at Tarsus—Cyprus not being far away—and there he may have met Paul. At any rate the incident of ch. ix. 26, 27 favours the view that these two men had met before. The success of gospel-preaching to Gentiles in Syrian Antioch led the Apostles at Jerusalem to send Barnabas thither. He found a great work in progress, and needing help in the ministry of the Word, he himself went to Tarsus, where Paul was (ix. 30), and brought him to Antioch, and the two of them ministered there for a year (xi. 25, 26).

When 'in the days of Claudius Caesar' famine broke out, the disciples at Antioch sent relief to the disciples in Judaea by Barnabas and Paul. This ministry completed, these men returned to Antioch, taking with them John Mark.

Later, the Church at Antioch, by the Spirit's command, sent Barnabas and Paul on a missionary journey which took them about two years to accomplish. This journey belongs to the history of Paul, but it should be noted that it began in Cyprus, the home of Barnabas. At Lystra the natives called Barnabas *Zeus*, 'the king of gods and men,' and Paul they called *Hermes*, 'the interpreter and prophet of the gods'. From this journey these brethren returned to Antioch and 'rehearsed all that God had done with them, and how He had opened the door of faith unto the Gentiles.' This, probably, was in A.D. 49; and in A.D. 50, when a Council was convened in Jerusalem to decide whether or not believing Gentiles were to be subject to circumcision and the ceremonial law, Barnabas was one of a deputation which the Church at Antioch sent to Jerusalem, and he and Paul contended there for freedom of the Gentiles from these restrictions. This was agreed to, and these brethren returned to Antioch with the Council's verdict.

The last time we read of Barnabas in the Acts is when a second missionary journey was proposed. Barnabas wished Mark, his cousin, to go with them as before, but Paul would not agree to this, as Mark had left them on the first journey. Consequently Paul and Barnabas separated, and the latter, with Mark, went to Cyprus.

The most important reference to Barnabas in the Epistles (Gal. ii) tells of a temporary yielding on his part in favour of Peter's inconsistent conduct relative to the status and freedom of the believing Gentiles at Antioch. This links up with the Jerusalem Council in A.D. 50.

Tradition has regarded Barnabas as one of the Seventy (Luke x); as the author of the Epistle to the Hebrews; and as the writer of the Epistle of Barnabas.

Luke's estimate of Barnabas is simple and satisfying:

'he was a good man, and full of the Holy Spirit and of faith' (xi. 24).

His goodness and faith were fruits of the Spirit, and are in evidence in the part he played in the first two periods of the Church's history. The previous misunderstanding recorded in ch. xv. 36-41 was between two good men, and responsibility for what happened was not the fault of either of them alone; but more of this later.

Mark

Though Mark is not in the front line of the Christian personalities to which the New Testament introduces us, he, nevertheless, occupies a prominent and important place in the Church of the first century.

The name MARK occurs eight times in the New Testament (Acts xii. 12, 25; xv. 37. 39. Col. iv. 10. Philem. 24, 2 Tim. iv. 11. 1 Peter v. 13). He is commonly known by this his Roman name, but his Jewish name was John. We assume that the Mark of the Gospel, of the Acts, of Paul's Epistles, and of 1 Peter v. 13 is the same person. To view him in his several relations will help us to assess his importance.

1. *Mark and Mary*

Mary was Mark's mother. She was a prominent member of the Church at Jerusalem, and legitimate inference would show that she was a woman of ample means, for she kept a slave girl, and her house was the meeting-place of many believers, and not improbably was the scene of the Last Supper, and of the events of Pentecost. When Peter was released from prison in A.D. 44, he went at once to Mary's house, and perhaps, it was his Jerusalem home. It is not unlikely that Barnabas and Paul stayed there when they went to Jerusalem as the bearers of help from the Christians in Antioch to the Christians in Judaea in a time of famine (Acts xi. 27-30; xii. 12-17; i. 12-14; ii. 1). These details show what was Mark's early environment; that he had a Christian upbringing, and that in impressionable years he met the leaders of the Christian Church.

2. *Mark and Barnabas*

These two men were cousins (Col. iv. 10, R.V.) and the relationship helps to account for the elder man's attitude towards the younger on several occasions (Acts xii. 25; xv. 36-39). Barnabas was a Levite, a native of Cyprus, and was well-to-do (iv. 36, 37). Mark, probably, had Cyprian blood in his veins, and it may be that his first home was in Cyprus.

When in A.D. 44 Barnabas and Paul returned to Antioch from

Jerusalem 'they took with them John, whose surname was Mark' (xii. 25). It may be that he had shown industry and ability in the distribution of the funds, and the elder brethren, especially Barnabas, felt that he could help them much in Antioch. He went with the Apostles on the first missionary journey, and later, about A.D. 50-51, when Paul suggested a second missionary tour, Barnabas agreed and willed to take with them, as on the first journey, his cousin Mark; but Paul definitely refused to do so, because Mark had left them at an early stage of the previous enterprise. Paul got his way, and Barnabas with Mark went to Cyprus. Here, the thread of Mark's story is broken. We do not read of him again in the Acts, and from ten to twelve years pass before he again appears in apostolic history (Col. iv. 10. Philem. 24).

3. *Mark and Paul*

So far as we can see from the record Mark's first contact with Paul—then called Saul—was when he and Barnabas went to Jerusalem with the gift which the Church at Antioch sent to the Christians in Judaea. When that ministry was fulfilled these brethren returned to Antioch, and took Mark with them. This would be in A.D. 44, and during the next two years, apparently, he with the elder brethren served the Church in Antioch. Only by inference can we say what the nature of his service was. Then, about A.D. 47, when Barnabas and Paul set out on the first mission-ary journey, they had John with them as an assistant or helper (xiii. 5). The word here is *hupēretēs*, literally an *under-rower*. Half-a-dozen Greek words are translated *servant* in the New Testament, and the general significance of this one is *subservience to another's will*, which means, in this context, that Mark served the two Apostles in some ways not defined, and was at their dis-posal. There were many things which needed somebody's special attention on such a journey—the selection of routes, arrangements for hospitality, times of sailing, provision of food, and so on—in which case he was like the secretary of an evangelistic campaign. But the word may well indicate that he interviewed inquirers, baptized converts, and did a certain amount of preaching (Acts xxvi. 16. 1 Cor. iv. 1. Gr.). In the light of this it is easy to see how serious a matter it was for him to leave the Apostles when they reached Perga in Pamphylia (xiii. 13).

This brings us to the next and last reference to Mark in the Acts (xv. 36-39). The sorry scene should be carefully pondered. What concerns us at this point is Paul's attitude toward and estimate of Mark when it was proposed by Barnabas that he should again accompany them on their missionary tour.

> 'Paul did not approve of taking with them a man who had deserted them in Pamphylia instead of going on with them to their work' (xv. 38). (Goodspeed).

Instead of going on Mark had gone away, and in Paul's view that disqualified him for so responsible a task. The result of Mark's defection was deplorable. How deplorable two words in the text indicate (xv. 39): 'sharp contention', *paroxusmos*, paroxysm, which occurs again only in Heb. x. 24; and 'departed asunder', *apochōrizō* occurs again only in Rev. vi. 14. Paul and Barnabas quarrelled and separated, and never worked together again although, it would appear, they were reconciled (1 Cor. ix. 6).

Naturally we ask, 'why did Mark apostatize'? (this is the word Paul uses in xv. 38). This question can never be answered, though there have been not a few guesses: homesickness, anxiety for his mother's safety, home duties, the desire to rejoin Peter, the fear of future perils on such a journey, the growing precedence of Paul over Barnabas, and the nature of the mission which had become clearer at Paphos (xiii. 7, 12). These suggestions only show that what is not revealed cannot be discovered, and so we must leave the matter where it is, keeping in mind only the fact that Mark defaulted when the first great test came to him.

It is, however, gratifying to know that Paul and Mark were reconciled, and that the young man once again served the dauntless veteran (2 Tim. iv. 11). The word here for 'ministry' is not the same as in ch. xiii. 5.

4. *Mark and Peter*

Mark had much more to do with Peter than with Paul. He is spoken of as Peter's 'son', which may mean that the Apostle was the means of his conversion, or it may be, as Swete says, 'the

T

affectionate designation of a former pupil', who 'had come to look upon his mother's old friend and teacher as a second father, and to render to him the offices of filial piety'.

It would seem, as we have already said, that Mary's home was the headquarters of Peter when he was in Jerusalem, and it was thither that he turned when miraculously delivered from prison (xii. 12). Mark, then, must have seen much of Peter, and was later to see more of him.

Almost certainly Mark was at Antioch at the time when Peter and Barnabas dissembled and were rebuked by Paul (Gal. ii. 11-14), and may then have shown sympathy with his old friend and with his cousin, and this too may have been in Paul's recollection when he refused to take him on the second missionary journey.

Between the last mention of him in the Acts (xv. 39) and Paul's reference to his co-operation in Rome (2 Tim. iv. 11) a period of ten to twelve years elapsed. What was Mark doing in those years? Dr. F. H. Chase says: 'A constant tradition in the early Church, reaching back to the confines of the apostolic age and harmonizing with the notices of the N.T. certifies us that Mark was a companion of St. Peter (i.e. in his missionary labours), was with him towards the end of his life, and wrote the Gospel to preserve his master's teaching'. (H.B.D. vol. III. p. 247).

We do not here debate the question whether or not Peter was ever in Rome, but Lightfoot says that the evidence for his having been there, and having been martyred there, is overwhelming; and tradition is almost unanimous that Mark wrote the Gospel attributed to him at Rome, and that this Gospel represents the substance of Peter's preaching (See the writer's *Guide to the Gospels*).

Certain it is that Mark was associated for a long time with Peter in the ministry of the Gospel, and was at Rome when Paul, and probably Peter, died. His life was rich in contacts and varied in ministry.

5. *Mark and Timothy*

In Paul's last letter to Timothy (iv. 11), detailing his circumstances he says 'Get Mark and bring him with you, for he is of great assistance to me'. Probably Timothy had met Mark before, but, in any case, it strikes the imagination to see these two young men together, and one wonders what they talked about as they journeyed towards Rome. The scene at the meeting with Paul must have been wonderful!

6. *Mark and the Church*

The Gospel which bears Mark's name is his value to the Church. The first of the Synoptic Gospels, it is re-issued almost bodily in the other two, and it represents the earliest oral Gospel. Matthew and John were sources in themselves, being of the Twelve; Luke was a collector and student of sources, and has given us in his Gospel and in the Acts the results of his inquiries— and in the Acts in places what he knew firsthand—but Mark differs from them all in that his Gospel is in a real sense Peter's, another of the Twelve, so that in the New Testament Peter contributes three Writings; but it is Mark, early called Peter's 'interpreter', who preserved for the whole Church the preaching of this Apostle, and who, in doing so, has deeply and richly influenced the life and thought of Christians for nineteen hundred years.

Mark was not a great leader and thinker, but he so served great leaders and thinkers as to be worthy of some of the credit for what they accomplished.

7. *Mark and Tradition*

This need not detain us, but tradition says: that he was one of the disciples who turned back (John vi. 66); that he was the man 'bearing a pitcher of water' (Mark xiv. 13); that he was the young man who followed and fled on the night of the betrayal (Mark xiv. 51); that he was the first to found churches in Alexandria, and was the first bishop there; that he had been a priest, and after becoming a Christian amputated a finger to disqualify himself for priestly service, and received the nickname of *Kolobodaktulos*, stump-fingered; and that he died a martyr's death.

PAUL

Summary of his story.

A. THE NEED FOR PAUL THE APOSTLE

I. The Work to be Done

1. Christianity meant the expansion from a national to a universal privilege in God.
2. Christianity meant the transference from a sensuous to a spiritual form of worship.
3. Christianity meant the proclamation of a Mystical Body instead of an Earthly Kingdom.
4. Christianity meant the presentation of a Crucified Christ instead of a Messianic King.

II. The Man for the Task

1. PAUL, A MAN OF RICH PERSONALITY
   (i) Intellectual Power.
   (ii) Splendid Courage.
   (iii) Determined Perseverance.
   (iv) Tender Sympathy.
   (v) Perfect Integrity.
   (vi) Consummate Tact.
   (vii) Lateral Humour.

2. PAUL, A MAN OF UNIQUE PRIVILEGES
   (i) His Hebrew Nature.
   (ii) His Greek Environment.
   (iii) His Roman Citizenship.

B. PAUL'S PRE-CONVERSION PREPARATION FOR HIS TASK

1. The Time of his Coming.
2. His Home City, Tarsus.
3. His Early Education.
4. His Trade.
5. His Training in Rabbinism.

C. THE PROCESS AND CRISIS OF PAUL'S CONVERSION

1. The Judaean Persecution.
2. Stephen's Sermon and Death.
3. Paul's Inward Struggle.
4. The Sanhedrin Commission.
5. The Heavenly Vision.
6. The Divine Voice.
7. Paul's Capitulation.

D. PAUL'S POST-CONVERSION PREPARATION FOR HIS TASK

1. His contact with Ananias.
2. His retreat to Arabia.
3. His proclamation in the synagogue at Damascus.
4. His introduction as a Christian to the Apostles at Jerusalem, and his ministry there.
5. His return to Tarsus.
6. His ministry with Barnabas at Antioch in Syria.
7. His visit to Jerusalem and his return to Antioch.

E. PAUL'S MISSIONARY CAREER FROM ANTIOCH TO ROME

1. The First Journey.
2. The Second Journey.
3. The Third Journey.
4. The First Imprisonment.
5. The Fourth Journey.
6. The Second Imprisonment.
7. The Martyr-Death.

PAUL

This man figures so largely in the history of the Church during the thirty years A.D. 37-67, and his influence upon the thought of the Church for nineteen hundred years has been so great, that any summary of his life, work, and teaching must be inadequate, and may easily be misleading.

At this distance Paul must be judged, not by any part of his character and work, but by the whole man and the whole task, and this view is not easy to get. Libraries have been written on this subject, and more will come, but our first duty is to see this Apostle and his task as these are presented authoritatively in the Acts and Epistles.

To understand the New Testament revelation of Christianity we must study this man *Paul*, for to him it was given as it was to none other. For this reason it will be well at this point to learn what we may about this extraordinary personality.

We shall be concerned at present not with Paul's theology but with what he was and did, and even this can be only in outline, but sufficiently full, it is hoped, to indicate the great scope of the subject. With this before us we shall better be prepared to follow this great missionary on his journeys till martyrdom brought them to an end. Consider, then, the above outline.

A. THE NEED FOR PAUL THE APOSTLE

Here let us think of the work to be done, and of the man to do it.

I. THE WORK TO BE DONE

This work was nothing less than the apprehension and interpretation of Christianity which was to supplant Judaism as the medium of divine revelation.

The significance of this change in religious history is fourfold.

1. Christianity Meant the Expansion from a National to a Universal Privilege in God

As to Israel's privilege in God, contemplate:

(i) The Fact of it.

> (Deut. vii. 6.   Matt. x. 5, 6.   Mark vii. 27.
> Rom. iii. 1, 2; ix. 4, 5).

(ii) The Purpose of it.

> (Genesis xii. 2, 3; xxii. 17, 18).

(iii) The Abuse of it.

Israel was first fenced round to be instructed, and then scattered abroad to be used; but they misread the meaning of their history and cultivated a spirit of religious exclusivism and self-righteousness. The Book of Jonah illustrates this (iv. 2). The correction of this attitude is recorded in Acts viii-xii.

(iv.) The Withdrawal of it.

In consequence of Israel's blindness, which led them to crucify their Messiah, they have been cast off by God as a nation, though their rejection is neither total nor final (Rom. ix.-xi.).

2. Christianity Meant the Transference from a Sensuous to a Spiritual Form of Worship

Israel's Form of Worship

(i) The Character of it.

It was material, sensuous, visible; laying emphasis on places, offices, times and seasons, objects and acts.

> (Col. ii. 16.   Heb. i. 1).

(ii) The Origin of it.

It was divinely revealed and commanded, as Exodus, Leviticus, and Deuteronomy show.

(iii) The Necessity for it.

It was designed to meet the need and to suit the capacity of Israel in preparation for another and higher form of worship. This higher form of worship was anticipated by Psalmists and Prophets.

(Matt. v-vii. John iv. 24. Col. ii. Hebrews).

iv. The Abolition of it.

Christ by His incarnation, life, death and resurrection is the fulfilment of the history, types and prophecies of the Old Economy, so that for these there is no more need or use. This is the teaching of Galatians iii.-iv. (cf. v. 1-4).

3. Christianity Meant the Proclamation of a Mystical Body Instead of an Earthly Kingdom

(i) An earthly Kingdom was that for which Israel looked, for it was promised.

(2 Sam. vii. 12-16. Jer. xxiii. 5. Joel iii. 1, 16, 17).

(ii) The Old Testament promises of blessings for the Gentiles assured it.

(Isa. xi. 10; xlii. 6, 7; lxvi. 10-13. Rom. xi).

(iii) These hopes and promises, as yet unrealized, must be fulfilled.

(Psa. ii. 6-9; lxxii. Daniel. Revelation).

(iv) But the revelation of Paul's Epistles is an entirely new thing.

(Gal. iii. 26-28. Col. iii. 11. Eph. ii. 11-22; iii. 1-12).

The incorporation into one Body, with Christ as Head, of Jews and Gentiles on equal terms, is the Good News of the Church, which Paul speaks of as *his* Gospel.

(Rom. ii. 16; xvi. 25. 2 Tim. ii. 8).

4. Christianity Meant the Presentation of a Crucified Christ instead of a Messianic King

(i) The hope of Israel centred in a promised King.

This is involved in all passages which tell of a Messianic Kingdom, which is plainly predicted.

(Hos. iii. 4, 5.   Mic. iv. 7.   Psa. ii. 6; xxiv; lxxxix. 34-37).

(ii) This predicted King was also typified.

(2 Sam. vii. 12-17.   Luke i. 30-33).

(iii) But there came a Man of Sorrows who was crucified.

He too was predicted, but Israel did not see in Him the Messiah.

(Isa. liii.   1 Peter. i. 10, 11.   John xix. 14, 15, 19-21).

(iv) The New Testament declares this Man to be the King of Israel's hopes, and the Saviour of the world.

This was a 'stumbling-block to the Jews' (1 Cor. i. 22-24), but to all of them who believed it proved to be 'the power of God' (Acts xvii. 2, 3).

This, then, is the change which was wrought in the first two generations of the present era.

Universal blessing took the place of Jewish exclusivism. Spiritual worship took the place of sensuous worship. The Church of God suspended the realization of the earthly Kingdom. The Messianic King became the crucified Christ.

For the effecting of such a change as this an agent or agents were necessary who could guide the thoughts of men from Judaism to Christianity; who could teach that the Old must give place to the New, and teach it in such a way as to ensure for the truth a large measure of acceptance among the Jews; and who could usher in a change of dispensation, but with such consummate skill as to establish the new ideal in the heart of the saved ere they scarce had apprehended that the old ideal had been superseded.

There was only one man in the first century, of whom we have any knowledge, who was equal to such a task, and that man was PAUL.

II. THE MAN FOR THE TASK

No man could accomplish the foregoing task who was not at once a man of rich personality and unique privileges, and Paul alone of the apostolic circle possessed these qualifications.

1. Paul, a Man of Rich Personality

By personality let us understand the collective attributes or qualities which characterize personal as distinguished from impersonal existence. It is the sum total of traits necessary to describe what it is to be a person. Of personality temperament is a large part, being that combination of qualities in a person by which his manner of acting and feeling and thinking is permanently affected. One's temperament is the sum of his intellectual and emotional tendencies.

Some knowledge of Paul's personality and temperament will show how eminently fitted he was to define Christianity and to spread it throughout the Roman Empire.

In him there met a variety of great qualities which, under God, constituted his fitness to fulfil that immense task which has already been outlined; and these qualities being found in such variety and proportion in no other man means that no other man was equal to such a task; in other words, God made this man for this work.

(i) Paul's Intellectual Power

When all has been said that can be said for the part which divine revelation plays in the marvellous originality of the Pauline Letters, the fact yet remains that that revelation was made through a heart and intellect of unusual capacity and of eminent power.

This quality is reflected in his recorded addresses in the Acts. (xiii. 17-41; xvii. 22-31; xx. 18-35; xxii. 3-21; xxiv. 10-21; xxvi. 2-23).

> 'He could never be listened to with indifference. His preaching excited warm assent or contradiction. He set all minds astir and in debate around him. His presence and discourse acted like an electric current that drives to opposite poles the mingled elements through which it passes.'
>
> (Acts xiii. 42-45; xiv. 4. 2 Cor. ii. 14-17).

Paul's intellectual power is seen also in those features which make his Epistles so unique—their grasp, profoundness, sanity, penetration, vigour, depth, refinement and fervour; the soaring reason and forceful logic of *Romans*; the lofty mysticism of *Colossians* and *Ephesians*; the clear and wide vision of *Thessalonians*, and the insight and grasp of *Corinthians*.

Other facts which point to Paul's intellectual strength are, that of the twenty-one Epistles of the New Testament he wrote thirteen, and that the unique distinction was given to him most fully to interpret his Master, and to formulate for all time the terminology of Christian theology.

(ii) *Paul's Splendid Courage*

The three forms of courage—physical, intellectual, and moral, are all found in Paul. *Physical courage* can be passive as well as active; it can exhibit itself in endurance as well as in accomplishment, and both forms of it are seen in Paul. (Acts xiv. 19-21; xix. 29-31; xxi. 10-14, 34-40; xxvii. 2 Cor. xi. 23-28.) His *intellectual courage* is exemplified in his proclamation of Christianity as distinct from Judaism; of grace as distinct from the law; and of the freedom of believing Gentiles from the Mosaic ritual. (Acts xv. Galatians). Paul's *moral courage* is seen in his loyalty to Christ in the presence of his foes (Acts ix. 20, 21, 27-29), and in his fearless testimony before Felix, Festus, Agrippa, and Nero. This quality is exhibited also in Paul's frankness and faithfulness with his friends; with Barnabas, and with Peter at Antioch. (Acts xv. 36-40. Gal. ii. 11-14).

The Apostle was not a stranger to weakness and fear (1 Cor. ii. 3. 2 Cor. vii. 5), but he knew how to conquer both. (Eph. vi. 18-20)

(iii) *Paul's Determined Perseverance*

Nothing less than his whole Christian career can adequately illustrate this quality. His missionary journeys covering twenty years (A.D. 47-67) are evidence enough of this. The Apostle had his times of physical and mental fatigue, like the rest of us, but he was indefatigable and unremitting in the prosecution of his great calling. In the face of many infirmities, giant difficulties, and cruel opposition, he plodded on until, his task completed, he rested at his Master's feet.

(iv) *Paul's Tender Sympathy*

A superficial reading of the Acts and Paul's Epistles might lead one to think that the Apostle was stern and forbidding, but a closer reading will show that this was not so. The Epistle to the Corinthians is evidence of this quality in the Apostle. With tenderness he seeks to win them back to the truth, and with reluctance he censures and warns them. Frequently we read of his tears (Acts xx. 19, 31, 37; xxi. 13. 2 Cor. ii. 4; Phil. iii. 18), and writing to the Thessalonians he speaks of his gentleness and affection (1 Thess. ii. 7, 8). The number and variety of Paul's friendships are evidence of his sympathetic nature, and so are his discriminating messages to individuals, and his specific prayers according to the necessity and character of each. (Rom. xvi. 3-16. Col. iv. 7-15)

He longed for the company of his friends, and felt being left 'alone' at Athens. To the Thessalonians he wrote, 'I had no rest in my spirit because I found not Titus my brother'. Reluctantly did he part with Onesimus. He grieved that Demas had forsaken him; and to Timothy he wrote, 'do thy diligence to come unto me before winter'. Another evidence of this quality in Paul's character is his genuine gratitude to all who ever showed him any kindness. (Gal. iv. 14. Phil. iv. 10. 2 Tim. i. 16-18) Tender sympathy is never so attractive as when it is seen in a strong character.

(v) *Paul's Perfect Integrity*

Integrity is uprightness of character, soundness of moral principle, and this characterized Paul in an eminent degree. This is seen in his frequent reference to his own *conscience*. (Acts xxiii. 1; xxiv. 16. Rom. ix. 1. 2 Cor. i. 12. 1 Tim. 1. 5, 19; iii. 9; iv. 2. 2 Tim. i. 3)

The Apostle also refers to the consciences of others with a view to the direction of conduct. (Acts xxiv. 16. 1 Cor. i. 8; x. 25-29. 2 Cor. iv. 2; v. 11).

He was also most conscientious in money matters:
(Rom. xiii. 8. Phile. 18, 19. 1 Cor. xvi. 3, 4. 2 Cor. viii. 16-21).
He enjoins orderly and systematic giving to the Lord. (1 Cor.
xvi. 1, 2. 2 Cor. viii. 11-13). It was a principle with him never
to go into debt, except spiritually (Rom. i. 14; viii. 12; xiii. 8);
and also to maintain an attitude of independence in the matter
of earning his own bread, while recognizing the privilege and
obligation of others to minister materially to those who serve
them spiritually. (Acts xx. 33-35. 1 Cor. ix. 7-15. 2 Cor. xi.
7-12. Phil. iv. 10-19).

(vi) *Paul's Consummate Tact*

This is an exceedingly useful but all too rare a quality. The
elements of it are sensitiveness of feeling, insight into the motives
of others, experience as to the consequences of conduct, and
subtlety of reasoning especially with reference to details. Tact is
sensitiveness of touch, adroitness in adapting words and actions
to circumstances, and so it is often more valuable than either
talent or knowledge.

Within the limits of the literature available perhaps no writer
or speaker has supplied us with so many illustrations of tact
as has the Apostle Paul. The two accounts of his conversion are
examples of this quality.

In the first of these (Acts xxii), addressed to Jews he emphasises what was calculated to allay their fury and lead them to the
understanding of his message and motive. In the second account
(Acts xxvi), addressed to Festus and Agrippa, his courteous
address, his noble restraint, and his moving appeal are noteworthy
(verses 24-29). We observe the Apostle's tact also in his habit
of giving credit for something to those whom he would conciliate.
(Acts xvii. 22-R.V. margin. 1 Cor. i. 4-8. Phile. 4-7).

Another illustration of Paul's tact is in the fact and aptness of
his quotations from heathen sources. To the Athenians he
quotes one of their own poets in regard to a principle of natural
religion: 'For we are also his offspring'. (Acts xvii. 28). On the
Corinthians he urges a lesson of morality from one of their own
comic writers: 'Be not deceived, evil communications corrupt
good manners' (1 Cor. xv. 33). He judges the Cretans by quoting

one of their own sages: 'The Cretans are always liars, evil beasts, slow bellies' (Tit. i. 12).

In this way Paul wings his controversial shafts with feathers borrowed from their own plumes. In 1 Cor. ix. 19-23 Paul's habitual tactfulness is again illustrated, and the whole of his letter to Philemon is a perfect example of it, every word being chosen with this particular end in view—his naming Apphia and Archippus; stressing the fact that he was old and a prisoner; speaking of Philemon's *love* rather than of his faith; congratulating and encouraging Philemon; not naming Onesimus at the beginning; then speaking of him as his own *son*, not as Philemon's *slave*; and giving no hint as to what Christianity would do ultimately with slavery.

(vii) *Paul's Lateral Humour*

To question this quality in the Apostle may be due to a want of humour in the objector, or to a misunderstanding of what humour is, or to a feeling that any such thing must be inconsistent with the seriousness of the Bible. But humour is in both Testaments, and in Paul. The Apostle is fond of playing upon words. For example: 'He heard unutterable utterances, which it is not lawful for a man to utter' (*arrēta rhēmata*, 2 Cor. xii. 4).

Onesimus means *profitable* or serviceable, and Paul, fearing lest the mention of the name might cloud Philemon's brow, immediately makes the effort to bring a smile to his face by a play on the name (10, 11); 'Who in the past was to thee unserviceable (*achrēston*), but now to thee and to me serviceable (*euchrēston*)'.

Occasionally Paul has humour with sarcasm, for illustration of which see 2 Cor. x. 10-12. Gal. ii. 6; vi. 3.

In two passages in 2 Corinthians an exalted sense of humour is displayed. Dr. Arthur Way calls ch. iv. 8-11 a Hymn of Tribulations.

> On every hand hard-pressed am I—yet not crushed!
> In desperate plight am I—yet not in despair!
> Close followed by pursuers—yet not abandoned by Him!
> Beaten to the earth—yet never destroyed!
> Evermore bearing about in my body
> The imminence of such a death as Jesus died,
> So that the life too of Jesus may be shown forth
> In this body of mine.

Always, always, while yet I live,
Am I being handed over to death's doom
For Jesus' sake!
So that in this mortal flesh of mine may be shown forth also
The very life of Jesus.

And the same translator calls ch. vi. 4-10 a Hymn of the Herald
of Salvation.

In many-sided endurance—
Amid afflictions, sore straits, and privations,
Amid scourgings, prison-cells, and riots,
Amid toils, night-vigils, and fastings:—

    In purity, in spiritual illumination,
    In long-suffering, in kindness,
    In the Holy Spirit's presence,
    In love unfeigned,
    In uttering the Message of Truth,
    In using the might of God:—

Bearing the sword of righteousness in my right hand,
    the shield on my left;
Compassed with glory and infamy,
With praise and defaming;
    Branded as a deceiver—vindicated as true;
    Ignored by men—recognized by God;
    Ever at point to die—yet lo, I live on!
    Chastened by suffering, yet never done to death;
    Sorrowing ever, yet evermore glad;
    Poor myself, yet bestowing riches on thousands;
    Having nothing, yet holding all things in sure possession!

These two passages are incomparable examples of rich humour
deep emotion, and unconquerable faith. And once, at least,
Paul's humour turns to fun. Autographing the letter to Galatia,

'his trembling hand shaped the words with more than the accustomed
uncouthness, and he playfully apologized for the ungainly scrawl'
(David Smith).

'See,' he says, 'with what large letters I am writing to you with
my own hand' (vi. 11).

2. Paul, a Man of Unique Privileges

Lightfoot has said: 'We are accustomed to look to three
countries especially, as the teachers of the modern world—
Rome, *Greece*, and *Judaea*. *Rome*, the foremost of all nations

in the science of government, has handed down to us the principles of law and order. *Greece*, setting before us her rich treasures of thought and imagination, has been a school-mistress in art and literature. And above all from *Palestine* we have learnt our true relation to God, which gives higher significance to art and literature, and an eternal value to the principles of law and order.

> 'If *Rome* supplied the bone and sinew of our colossal man, while *Greece* clothed him with flesh, and gave him grace and beauty, it was *Judaea* that breathed the breath of life into him.
>
> Now all these three influences were combined in the great Apostle of the Gentiles. He was a citizen of Rome; his native place, Tarsus, was the great university of Greece; and he was brought up in the Jews' religion in its most rigorous and most typical form.'

The newly-established faith had to face three all-important factors—Judaism, Hellenism, and Imperialism, and it is evident that in order to present Christianity in a manner suitable to these world factors, a character many-sided, versatile, and cosmopolitan was required.

> 'To be the herald of a religion which had its origin in Judaism, a Jew was essential. To possess sympathy with, and insight into, all the manifold details of Hellenistic life, it was necessary that this Jew should have been born and bred in a Hellenistic city. And to enable such an one to take full advantage of the unique opportunities afforded by the Imperial system for the expansion of Christianity, it was of the highest importance that he should belong to the ruling class, and possess the citizenship of the Empire. All these three conditions met in Paul.' (Maurice Jones).

It was no accident that Paul had a Hebrew nature, a Greek environment, and a Roman citizenship, and there can be little doubt that he refers to these privileges when he says: 'It pleased God to mark me out from my birth'. (Gal. i. 15). Of this statement Ramsay says: 'If that be not the meaning of Paul's words the historian may abandon altogether the task of interpreting them, for they cease to have any historical application ' (cf. 1 Cor. ix. 20-22)

(i) *Paul's Hebrew Nature*

He was a Hebrew by parentage, creed, language, tradition, and education. He sat at the feet of Gamaliel, the foremost theologian at Jerusalem, and was instructed according to the strict manner of the law of the Jews (Acts xxii. 3. Phil. iii. 5, 6. Gal. i. 14). This meant, among other things, a thorough acquaintance with the Hebrew language (Acts xxii. 1, 2), and with the Old Testament Scriptures, of which his speeches and writings are full. It also involved a knowledge of the Septuagint Version (Greek) of the Old Testament, which the Apostle quotes. The use that Paul made of this knowledge is evident in his speeches (Acts xvii. 2, 3).

'Paul brought with him to the Christian camp the resources of a trained Jewish jurist, a skilled rabbinical scholar and disputant. He was the one man qualified to effect the transition in doctrine and institutions from the old faith to the new; to transplant Christianity, without destroying any of its roots, from the ancient soil of Judaism, into the wide and rich field ready for it in the Gentile world'. (G. G. Findlay)

(ii) Paul's Greek Environment

Ramsay has shown in *The Cities of St. Paul* that Tarsus was a great commercial, religious, and educational centre. There the products of East and West met; there the manifold corruptions of idolatry were to be found; and there the widest learning was represented.

It was there that Paul was born, spent his early years, and was numbered among its citizens (Acts xxi. 39). This fact he regarded as of great importance for his work, and he did not fail to make use of it.

It was in Tarsus that he learnt the trade of tent-making, a craft which stood him in good stead in after years, and to which he makes frequent reference. (Acts xviii. 3; xx. 33-35. 1 Cor. ix. 6-18. 1 Thess. ii. 9. 2 Thess. iii. 8-10)

What Paul saw and heard at Tarsus went to augment his stock-in-trade for the great future that lay before him. The many peoples he would see in its streets would 'stir in an impressionable child thoughts and dreams of the wide world, and impart an instinctive aptitude for mixing with all sorts of men, and from such a theatre of mental activity, he could not but receive intellectual stimulus if only by way of aversion'. (G. G. Findlay)

It is clear that the Apostle had some knowledge of Stoic philosophy, and some acquaintance with Grecian literature. In 1 Cor. xv. 33 is an obvious maxim of practical life from Menander. In Acts xvii. 28 a religious sentiment is quoted from Cleanthes, which was repeated by Aratus. In Titus i. 12 is a bit of pungent satire from Epimenides.

> 'It was fitting that he whose life-work lay among strange people, in many unfriendly cities, should have begun his life and spent his boyhood in a place where so many opposing influences met, and so many diverse interests were at stake, and so many kinds of people were to be seen.
>
> 'It was fitting also that he who was to be the bearer and the messenger of a religion suited to all men, fitted to meet and satisfy all human needs, should have seen with his own eyes, and felt in his own life the pressure of pagan religions, as all who lived at Tarsus must have felt them.
>
> 'Before his eyes throughout his boyhood Paul saw a living picture of the intellectual, moral, and social effects which spring from heathenism. How disastrous these results were, and how keenly he felt them, may be gathered from a perusal of Romans i. Even in his boyhood he must have longed to turn men from idols to the service of the living God'. (J. Iverach).

It was no accident that Paul was born and bred at Tarsus. God's foreknowledge saw what equipment he would need for the task to which He was appointing him.

(iii) Paul's Roman Citizenship

Saul was his Hebrew name, and Paul, his Roman name. 'The chief captain came and said unto Paul, "Tell me, art thou a Roman?" He said, "Yes".' (Acts xxii. 27)

'To the Jewish student, and the Greek cosmopolitan in Paul, there was added the Roman gentleman'. (Findlay). Paul's father, or an ancestor, may have obtained the Roman citizenship in several ways: by being exempted from slavery; as a reward of merit, bestowed by the Emperor; by being born of two Jewish Roman citizens united in marriage; by purchase (Acts xxii. 27, 28).

The privileges attached to the Roman franchise were considerable. It meant exemption from all degrading punishments, such as scourging and crucifixion. (Read Acts xxii. 24-29; xxiii. 26, 27.) It meant the right of appeal to the Emperor after sentence

(Acts xxv. 9-12). It meant the right to be sent to Rome for trial before the Emperor if charged with a capital offence (Acts xxv. 11). Paul did not always use this privilege, nor always enforce his rights, nor always claim redress when they were violated (Acts xvi. 37-39). Think of what would have been lost if he had done so at Philippi (Acts xvi. 27-34).

Paul could and did on important occasions use the franchise to secure himself from treatment which, no doubt, would have cut short his life (Acts xxii. 24-29; xxiii. 26, 27). It also secured for him the freedom of the world. It

'superseded all other privileges before the law, and in the general opinion of society, and placed Paul amid the aristocracy of any provincial town.' (Ramsay).

'In Syria, in Asia, in Greece, wherever he went, he bore about with him this safeguard of his liberties. How valuable such a protection must have been to St. Paul! How often he must have invoked its aid in a life spent in travel, and in the midst of enemies, we can well imagine.' (Lightfoot).

It enabled him to fulfil the great ambition of his life—to plant the Gospel in the Imperial Capital (Rom. i. 10-15). But the enjoyment of this liberty exercised a yet wider influence upon Paul—it entered into his teaching in such passages as speak of the unity of the Church, and of the believer's heavenly citizenship. (Eph. ii. 19. Phil. iii. 20)

Thus wonderfully were Jew and Gentile mingled in Paul, equipping him for his unique and world-wide mission. Hebrew tenacity, Greek versatility, and Roman facility combined to fit this man for his life's work. Let all the foregoing facts be considered, and it will be impossible to resist the conclusion that Paul in all the circumstances of his birth, inheritance, education, and experience was a plan of God for the accomplishment of the most momentous task ever alloted to a human being.

B. PAUL'S PRE-CONVERSION PREPARATION FOR HIS TASK

There is a sense in which a man begins to live at the moment of the great change-over in conversion, but from this fact we must not draw the inference that his past was all blank and waste. Fuller knowledge of the past of any converted person will generally show that, in many ways, it was a preparation for the great change, and in the change became sublimated. This certainly was so in the case of the great Apostle.

1. THE TIME OF PAUL'S COMING

God's messages and messengers come when the time is ripe for them. Paul and Moses could not have changed places. Each of them was prepared for his age, and the age was prepared for each of them.

For Paul and the message entrusted to him the world had been prepared in four ways at least: by having a universal language, Greek; by being under one sovereign authority, Roman law; by the dispersion of the Jews; and by the widespread decay of religion. By these events God was ordering the course of history in preparation for the Redeemer and Christianity.

(a) Without a *universal language* it would have been impossible for the earliest preachers to have made their message understood in the many lands which they visited; but everywhere Greek was spoken, and in this tongue the New Testament was written.

(b) The rise of the Roman Empire created a *world political unity* which was of inestimable value for the spread of the Gospel. The Roman Government unwittingly advanced that religion which it persecuted. Roman law is the best the world has ever known, and repeatedly in the course of his travels Paul was succoured and shielded by it alike from Jewish and heathen violence.

The *Roman roads* also made possible the missionary activities of Paul. Constructed originally for the transit of troops, they served afterwards the happiness of civilisation and rendered travel easy.

(c) Again, preparation was made for Paul's mission and message by *the dispersion of the Jews*, known as the *Diaspora*. We have already seen how widespread this scattering was (pp. 60, 61). It is recorded that there were 'infinite myriads' of Jews beyond the Euphrates. No fewer than 10,000 perished by massacre in Damascus in the reign of Nero. Alexandria, the Egyptian capital, was mapped out into five divisions, two of which were designated Jewish, and the total Jewish population in Egypt was not less than a million.

The value of this dispersion to Christianity is obvious. It supplied the first Christian missionaries—who were themselves Jews—with a point of contact wherever they went, and their mission was not to overthrow the ancient faith but to proclaim its fulfilment. On arrival in a city they first repaired to the Jewish synagogue and there preached the glad tidings.

(d) Another way in which preparation was made for Paul and the missionaries was by the *widespread decay of religion* in the Roman Empire. Both Paganism and Judaism were decadent.

The religious mythology of Homer and Hesiod had lost its hold upon the people; the philosophers made but a limited appeal; the state-appointed and regulated religion gave no satisfaction, and men were left with hungry hearts. Their quest was for God, and widespread the custom had arisen of erecting altars to 'The unknown God'.

Nor was the case much better with Judaism. For 400 years no prophet-voice had been heard. Religious externals had been multiplied, but the inner spirit had disappeared.

In these four ways preparation was made for the Christian Gospel, and for Paul and the Christian missionaries. These conditions made straight in the desert a highway for our God.

2. PAUL'S HOME CITY, TARSUS

That a boy's geographical surroundings make impressions on his unfolding mind which may easily give direction to his future will not be disputed. It certainly was so with Paul. Tarsus, the city in which he was born, stood about half-way between Jerusalem and Istanbul. The Cydnus river, issuing from the Taurus, flowed rapidly down to and through Tarsus, and within the town its banks were lined with wharves on which was piled the merchandise of many countries. That Tarsus, which was only ten miles from the sea (Ramsay), was navigable is proved by the fact that it floated the gorgeous galley of Cleopatra on her coming from Egypt to Anthony's camp in Cilicia (see Shakespeare's *Anthony and Cleopatra*, II. ii. 195-223).

The city in which Paul's boyhood was spent greatly influenced him alike by way of attraction and repulsion. Students of many lands flocked to its University, and, said Strabo, 'So deeply are the people there imbued with zeal for philosophy that they have surpassed Athens and Alexandria and every other place that can be mentioned'. The city has a long list of distinguished names to her credit of philosophers, grammarians, and poets, and one of Paul's mental alertness and ability could not but feel the stimulus which living in a university city supplies.

But if he was attracted by the learning of Tarsus, he was repelled by its heathenism. What was true of Cilicia generally was true, of course, of its chief city, that over the deep stagnancy of moral degradation was drawn the shimmering film of an intellectual culture.

Sensuality and superstition characterised the worship by which Paul was surrounded, and these were quite enough to awake the indignant loathing of every true-hearted Jew. Living in such a city as Tarsus Paul would easily learn that 'error in the intellect involves an ultimate error in the life and in the will, and that earthly knowledge has no necessary connection with heavenly wisdom' (Farrar). These convictions found expression later in his letters (Rom. i. 21, 22. 1 Cor. i. 18-29), and formed a fundamental part of his theology.

That Paul was born and brought up in a city and not in a village proved to have been a matter of great consequence. He who was to live and minister in cities, such as Antioch, Ephesus, Corinth, and Rome, needed to know men and cities, and needed 'to encounter men of every class and race; to sympathise with human nature in all its varieties; and to look with tolerance upon the most diverse habits and customs.' (Stalker).

There is much significance then in Paul's having said, 'I am a Jew of Tarsus in Cilicia, a citizen of no mean city' (Acts xxi. 39 xxii. 3); and in the Lord's command to Ananias in Damascus to 'inquire for one named Saul, a man of Tarsus' (Acts ix. 11).

3. PAUL'S EARLY EDUCATION

The Apostle's word to Agrippa that he had lived after the straightest sect of the Jews' religion; his saying before the Sanhedrin: 'I am a Pharisee, a son of Pharisees'; and his entire life before his conversion, show that his father, though living among Gentiles was a zealous observer of the Law. He who lived in a Greek city was reared in a Hebrew home. Greek ideas did not haunt his childhood, but he grew up an Israelite, nurtured in the history of his nation, and from earliest days was made familiar with the visions of Hebrew prophets, the songs of Hebrew poets, and the wisdom of Hebrew proverbs. What was true of Timothy was true of himself, 'that from a babe thou hast known the sacred 'writings' (2 Tim. iii. 15). This knowledge of the Scriptures is reflected in the Apostle's quotations from them in his letters, of which references there are about ninety, and it is probable that the most of these were cited from memory.

The heroes of Paul's childish thought and imagination would not be Hercules and Achilles, but Abram, and Joseph, and David. His religious instruction was given him first at home, and then in the school attached to the Synagogue. At an early age he would thoroughly know his Bible—the Old Testament—and was able to think and speak in three languages, Hebrew, the Aramaic vernacular, and the colloquial Greek. The curriculum of the Jewish child's education until manhood was reached has been thus defined:

'At five years old he comes to the reading of Scripture; at ten, to Mishnah, that is, oral repetition of the Law; at thirteen, to the practice of the commands; at fifteen, to Talmud, that is, doctrine; and at eighteen to marriage.'

It is clear, then, that Paul's religious education laid the foundation on which he built so heavily and well after his conversion. When he was divinely illumined he saw in the history of Israel the purpose of God for them and for all men which Christianity was to fulfil.

4. PAUL'S TRADE

Every Jewish boy had to learn a trade whatever his profession was to be. This was specially necessary in the case of Rabbis who exacted no fees and received no gifts; and so we learn that these teachers were millers, bakers, shoemakers, clerks, tailors, potters, smiths, and so on. Such labours were not looked down upon

It was a maxim that one who did not teach his son a trade taught him robbery. One of the Rabbis said: 'Excellent is the study of the Law together with worldly business, for the practice of them both puts iniquity out of remembrance, and all Law without work must fail at length, and occasion iniquity'.

Paul learned the trade of tent-making, which was a thriving industry at Tarsus. It is said that the staple manufacture of the city was weaving, first, into ropes, then into tent-covers and garments, of the hair which was supplied in unlimited quantities by the goat flocks of the Taurus. As Paul left school at the age of thirteen, and went to the Rabbinical College when he was about fifteen, there was time in the interval for him to learn his trade. The value of this to him in after life no one could have foreseen, but it was in the providence of God that when on his missionary journeys he was able to earn his own living.

To the Thessalonians he was not 'burdensome', but 'working night and day' that he might not be a charge on them, he preached the Gospel (I Thess. ii. 6, 9). And later, writing to these people he said: 'Neither did we eat bread for nought at any man's hand, but in labour and travail, working night and day, that we might not burden any of you'. (2 Thess. iii. 8). Writing to the Corinthians he says that he who ministered to them spiritually was entitled to be helped by them materially, but, he adds, 'I have used none of these things', for, he says, it were better for him to die than that he should be dependent on them for temporal support (I Cor. ix. 12, 15). And when addressing the Ephesian Elders he said: 'Ye yourselves know that these hands ministered unto my necessities, and to them that were with me'. (Acts xx. 34). Writing about this occupation Farrar says: it 'had one advantage in being so absolutely mechanical as to leave the thoughts entirely free. While Paul plaited the black, strong-scented goat's hair, he might be soaring in thought to the inmost heaven, or holding high converse with Apollos or Aquila, with Luke or Timothy on the highest themes which can engage the mind of man'.

5. Paul's Training in Rabbinism

There were many Rabbinical Colleges, but Paul chose, or was sent to, the most celebrated of them, the College at Jerusalem where Gamaliel was teaching (Acts v. 34). The age of fifteen seems early to enter upon such a course, but there are not a few parallels. John Knox entered Glasgow University at the age of sixteen. Calvin went to the University of Paris when he was fourteen. Thomas Chalmers matriculated at St. Andrew's University when he was scarcely twelve years of age.

It would appear that Paul was at College for about four years, and Gamaliel's influence on him was great (Acts xxii. 3). At the end of his curriculum at Jerusalem he would return to Tarsus, and in all likelihood he married there; but the next time we meet with him is in A.D. 37 during the persecution recorded in Acts vii. During these unrecorded years it is probable that Paul exercised the ministry of a Rabbi in Tarsus, or, at any rate, in Cilicia. If this be so he could not have been in Jerusalem while Jesus was there.

From what has been said we can see that the whole of Paul's life to the time of his conversion was a preparation for the great ministry he exercised after his conversion. This opens a large and fruitful subject for study. The tangled skein of human life, as we see it, represents a pattern which we do not see, or see only imperfectly in this life.

C. THE PROCESS AND CRISIS OF PAUL'S CONVERSION

Paul's attitude to Christianity is explained by himself, and we must thoroughly understand his position or we shall greatly misjudge him. He says, 'I did it ignorantly in unbelief' (1 Tim. 1. 13). 'I verily thought with myself that I ought to do many things contrary to the name of Jesus of Nazareth' (Acts xxvi. 9), and what he did was 'with pure conscience' (2 Tim. i. 3).

Paul was not a cruel monster like Nero, but was 'zealous toward God', and 'exceedingly zealous of the tradition of (his) fathers' (Acts xxii. 3. Gal. i. 14).

The first time we read of Saul is in connection with the martyrdom of Stephen: 'The witnesses laid down their clothes at a young man's feet, whose name was Saul'; And 'Saul was consenting unto his death' (Acts vii. 58; viii. 1). He had a Rabbi's mastery of the Old Testament Scriptures, but as he listened to Stephen's sermon he saw them in a new light, and from that moment he began to lose confidence in his interpretation of them, and an inner struggle was commenced which expressed itself in restless persecution of all Christians (Acts ix. 1, 2; xxii. 4, 5, 19-21; xxvi. 9-11). It was Stephen who shot light into Saul's darkness which resulted very soon in his conversion.

Saul's conversion was both a process and a crisis, as most probably every conversion is. We have followed the process in his pre-conversion years, and the crisis was sudden and decisive about noon one day just outside of Damascus. There are three accounts of it, one by Luke (Acts ix. 3-18), and two by Paul himself (Acts xxii. 1-21; xxvi. 1-18). No psychological theory is valid that calls in question this sudden and momentous change in the experience of this man. In an instant he became a new creation; old things passed away and all things became new. It is little wonder that he went into retreat for a while to think through the new situation and to see clearly the new perspective (Gal. i. 16, 17).

The essence of what he learned is that Jesus of Nazareth who had been crucified on Calvary was the promised Messiah, and the Redeemer of mankind (Acts ix. 20-22). This truth is the foundation both of his sermons and his letters, and it was his profound belief in it which led him into thirty years of devoted and sacrificial service.

It would seem that about ten years passed between Paul's conversion and his first missionary journey, and they were very fruitful years, spent in Arabia, Damascus, Jerusalem, Tarsus and Antioch in Syria.

D. PAUL'S POST-CONVERSION PREPARATION FOR HIS TASK

It will not be necessary to do more than summarise this period as our information here is scanty; yet much is said in few words.

1. PAUL'S CONTACT WITH ANANIAS (Acts ix. 10-19; xxii. 11-16)

The period of the early Church was a time of *visions*. These were vouchsafed to Saul, and Ananias, and Cornelius, and Peter, and later again to Paul.

In the Acts there are three men who are named Ananias, and what a study in contrasts they present. The first to be named is the Ananias who, with his wife, lied to the Holy Spirit, and was visited with death (v. 1-11). The third to be named is Ananias the high priest, who Paul called a 'whited wall' (xxiii. 2; xxiv. 1). The second to be named is the one before us, who was told by the Lord to go to Straight Street in Damascus, and take to the now converted persecutor the temporal and spiritual blessings of sight, the Holy Spirit, baptism and Christian fellowship.

What the Lord told Ananias of Saul and his future is of great importance (ix. 15, 16). Saul was a *vessel*, divinely *chosen*, to *bear* God's *Name*, that is, to bear witness to Him, before *Gentiles*, *kings*, and the *children of Israel*; and this ministry would involve as we know it did, great *suffering*.

Was there ever in the experience of anyone else such a transformation as this!

2. PAUL'S RETREAT TO ARABIA (Gal. i. 15-17)

We learn of this from Paul himself in a letter which he wrote: '(I did not go) up to Jerusalem to them which were apostles before me; but *I went away into Arabia*, and again I returned to Damascus'. It would appear that the place of this statement is between verses 19 and 20 of Acts ix. After his amazing experience it was necessary for Paul to get away from places and people he knew to some quiet place where, without interruption, he could rethink his beliefs in the light of all that had happened. Moses, and Elijah, and our Lord Himself had retired to a wilderness, and it might have been better for the whole Church if many a servant of the Lord had done the same.

Paul does not say what wilderness he retired to, but it may have been to the Mount of God (Gal. iv. 25). Nor does he say how long he was away, but we know that the retirement and the ministry in Damascus did not exceed three years (Gal. i. 18).

3. PAUL'S PROCLAMATION IN THE SYNAGOGUE AT DAMASCUS
(Acts ix. 20-22)

The result of Paul's contemplation in the wilderness became evident at once when he returned to Damascus. Without delay he began to preach, and began in the synagogue—which after wards was his custom whenever possible—and his message related to the Person of Jesus (R.V.). In retirement he had come to the conclusion that the man *Jesus* of Nazareth who had been crucified a few years before, outside the wall of Jerusalem, was the *Son of God*, and the promised *Messiah*. This fact is the foundation and root of Christian theology; it is the central truth of Paul's belief and teaching. What had now become his implicit faith was revealed in his explicit statement. Any teaching which does not proceed from this truth is not Christian teaching.

Paul's theology confused and confounded the Jews and they plotted 'to kill him'. How utterly senseless! The head of truth cannot be cut off with a chopper, though the head of the proclaimer of it may be; yet this killing business has been going on for nineteen hundred years.

4. PAUL'S INTRODUCTION AS A CHRISTIAN TO THE APOSTLES AT JERUSALEM, AND HIS MINISTRY THERE.
(Acts ix. 26-30. xxii. 17-21).

Three years before this visit to Jerusalem Paul had been sent to Syria with the authority of the Sanhedrin, to exterminate the Christians, and now he returns, himself a Christian. The Jews regarded him as a renegade, and the disciples, as a hypocrite; but Barnabas believed his story, and secured the confidence of Peter and James, and Paul stayed with Peter for a fortnight (Gal. i. 18).

At Jerusalem Paul did what Stephen had done, 'he spake and disputed against the Grecian Jews', the Hellenists (Acts vi. 9, 10; ix. 29), and they resolved to deal with him as they had dealt with Stephen, but Christians who knew of their design got him to leave the city, which he was the more ready to do as he had had a command from the Lord to go (Acts xxii. 17-21).

5. PAUL'S RETURN TO TARSUS (Acts ix. 30)

This was a great event, the details of which are not given to us, but it is clear that Paul ministered in the provinces of Syria and Cilicia, and established Churches there (Gal. i. 21. Acts xv. 23, 41). What the effect was upon his own family of his changed self we are not told, but Dean Howson suggests that some of them, possibly his sister and her son, were converted (Rom. xvi. 7, 11. Acts xxiii. 16).

The Apostle must have come into contact with many whom he had known in earlier years, and there must have been much controversy. How long he remained in these parts is not known, but it could scarcely have been less than four years, during which time great events had taken place (Acts x., xi).

6. PAUL'S MINISTRY WITH BARNABAS AT ANTIOCH IN SYRIA
   (Acts xi. 25, 26)

Barnabas appears again in a very important rôle. At Antioch in Syria many converts were being gathered into the Church, and to keep in touch with this movement the mother-church at Jerusalem sent Barnabas to Antioch to guide and encourage the growing Assembly.

He soon found that more help was needed, and, as has been said, 'he knew of one exactly suited for this development of Church work—a Hebrew, yet full of Roman sympathies, intimate with Greek thought, and familiar with the neighbourhood' (Rackham). This person was Saul, and so he went to Tarsus to search for him, and having found him he returned to Antioch, and the two of them, with other teachers (xiii. 1), ministered there 'for a whole year'.

7. PAUL'S VISIT TO JERUSALEM AND HIS RETURN TO ANTIOCH
   (Acts xi. 27-30; xii. 25)

Famine arose in the days of Claudius, and the rich Church at Antioch decided to raise a public collection to aid the poor Church at Jerusalem. This was done, and Barnabas and Paul took it to the Jewish capital. Among several things of considerable importance in this account should be noticed—the beginning of collections in the church; the obligation of churches to help one another; the first mention in the Acts of *prophets* in the church; and the introduction of John Mark in a service capacity (xii. 25).

For fully two years from now Barnabas and Paul continued their work at Antioch, and then began the great missionary movement which is the subject of the remainder of the Acts.

E. PAUL'S MISSIONARY CAREER FROM ANTIOCH TO ROME

This is recorded in Acts xiii-xxviii, but we should try to get a conspectus of this amazing ministry, remembering that this first and greatest of all missionaries had none of the travel facilities which abound to-day. Paul must have been in middle age when he started on his journeys, and during the twenty years that followed he suffered as few have done, and had ill-health to contend with most of the time. Yet he travelled considerably more than 12,000 miles by land and sea, and the land journeys were mostly on foot.

Comparing himself with his detractors he says:

'In toils I have immeasurably surpassed them, in imprisonments immeasurably; in endurance of scourging there is no comparison. Many a time I have been face to face with death. From the Jews alone I have five times received the nine-and-thirty stripes (i.e. 195 lashes). Three times have I been beaten with the Roman rods. Once I suffered stoning; three times I have been shipwrecked; for a whole night and day have I drifted on the fathomless sea. I have been incessantly travelling; have been exposed to perils from rivers in flood, to perils from bandits, to perils from my countrymen the Jews, to perils from the heathen, to perils in the city, to perils in lonely places, to perils on the sea, to perils from traitors disguised as fellow-believers.

'I have endured toil and travail, sleepless nights—ay, often!—hunger and thirst, fastings—yes, many a time—cold and nakedness.

'And besides all the rest, there is the daily haunting insistence of anxiety for all the churches.' (2 Cor. xi. 23-28. Arthur S. Way).

To this appalling catalogue of sufferings must be added all that the Apostle endured during the last ten years of his life, A.D. 57-67, after this record of sufferings was written.

It seems almost incredible that a human body and mind could have survived all this!

People who belittle Paul only advertise their mental, moral, and spiritual degeneracy.

THE BOOK OF THE ACTS

PART THREE

THE GENTILE PERIOD OF THE CHURCH'S WITNESS
Chapters xiii-xxviii

A.D. 47-63—16 Years

THE CHURCH EXTENDED - - ITS LENGTH

PAUL'S TIRELESS ACTIVITIES

PAUL'S FRUITFUL CAPTIVITIES

PAUL'S FINAL ACTIVITY AND CAPTIVITY
(After the ACTS record)

THE PROGRESS OF CHRISTIANITY IN THE WORLD
TO THE CLOSE OF THE FIRST CENTURY A.D.

This second Scene of Act II of the Drama is divisible into two distinct parts, namely, the *Historical Expansion* of Christianity, and the *Doctrinal Expression* of it.   The first of these is recorded in the Book of the ACTS, and the second, in the EPISTLES of the New Testament.

The relation of these two parts to one another must be obvious. History is not a product of literature, but literature, of history. Events precede expressions; historical facts precede thought-formulations.   The Elizabethan Age, viewed historically, was not the product of Shakespeare and Milton, but the occasion for them.   The history was the root, and the literature was the fruit.

In like manner, the New Testament Epistles did not occasion the history of the Acts, but were the product of it; the history necessitated the literature, and the literature reflects the history. This will become more evident when we consider in detail the Doctrinal Expression of Christianity.

We have seen that the HISTORICAL EXPANSION, of which the Acts is the record, divides clearly into three parts relative to the Church's Witness: firstly, the *Jewish Period*; secondly, the *Transition Period*; and thirdly, the *Gentile Period*. Peter dominated the first two periods, which represent seventeen years (A.D. 30-47); and Paul dominated the third period, which, in the Acts, covers sixteen years (A.D. 47-63); in all, thirty-three years, a single generation.

These three periods emerge from one another, the second from the first, and the third from the other two.

x

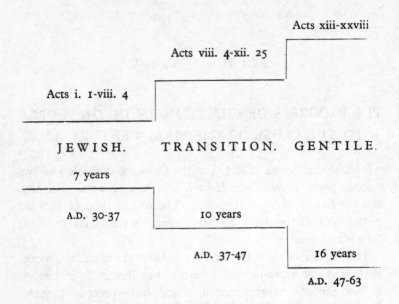

Of course the Gentile period did not end where Luke ends his narrative, but has continued from that day until now, and will continue until the Lord returns; but it is incorrect to speak of the Gentile Church. The first Church was composed of Jews only (cf. ch. vi. 5), but it has never been composed of Gentiles only (Gal. iii. 28)

The movement from the first half of the Acts (i-xii) to the second half (xiii-xxviii), though prepared for, is an astonishing religious phenomenon. Almost suddenly a door opened upon the whole world. The story passes from the mission of *Peter* to the mission of *Paul*, and the basis of action is removed from *Jerusalem* to *Antioch*. By the time we reach chapter xiii of the Acts, the stage had been set and the actors prepared for the scene for which the world had waited for over 2000 years; God had told Abram that in him all the families of the earth would be blessed. Early in his Pentecostal ministry Peter referred to this promise (Acts iii. 25), and Paul did the same when he wrote to the Galatians (iii. 8); and now a tremendous stride is about to be taken toward the fulfilment of this covenant. The Church which had been *established* (i. 1-viii. 4), and *expanded* (viii. 4-xii. 25), is now to be *extended*; what already had depth and breadth, is now to be given length. (Chart 133: p. 183).

First of all we must get a synoptical view of this third and greatest part of the Book of the Acts.

CHART 136

PAUL'S WORLD MISSION	
HIS TIRELESS ACTIVITIES	HIS FRUITFUL CAPTIVITIES
ACTS xiii-xxi. 16	ACTS xxi. 17-xxviii
A.D. 47-58. 11 Years	A.D. 58-63. 5 Years
THE FIRST JOURNEY Acts xiii. 1-xiv. 28. A.D. 47-49	AT JERUSALEM Acts xxi. 17-xxiii. 30. A.D. 58
THE JERUSALEM CONFERENCE Acts xv. 1-35. A.D. 50	AT CAESAREA Acts xxiii. 31-xxvi. A.D. 58-60
THE SECOND JOURNEY Acts xv. 36-xviii. 22. A.D. 50-54	To and At ROME Acts xxvii-xxviii. A.D. 60-63
THE THIRD JOURNEY Acts xviii. 23-xxi. 16. A.D. 54-58	Release from First Imprisonment at Rome. A.D. 63
THE FOURTH JOURNEY Phil. ii. 24. Phile. 22. 1 Timothy. Titus. 2 Timothy A.D. 63-66	Recapture Second Imprisonment at Rome. Trial. Death A.D. 66-68

PAUL'S TIRELESS ACTIVITIES

All that we attempt in our survey of the Acts is to indicate, in what detail may be necessary, the progress of the Gospel in the Gentile world, and the outstanding events from stage to stage. This purpose will be served by the help of charts and maps, which should be carefully followed.

Let us first of all look at the facts, and then make certain observations on them.

Paul's First Missionary Journey

Acts xiii. 1-xiv. 28. A.D. 47-49

The following map will indicate the scope of this journey.

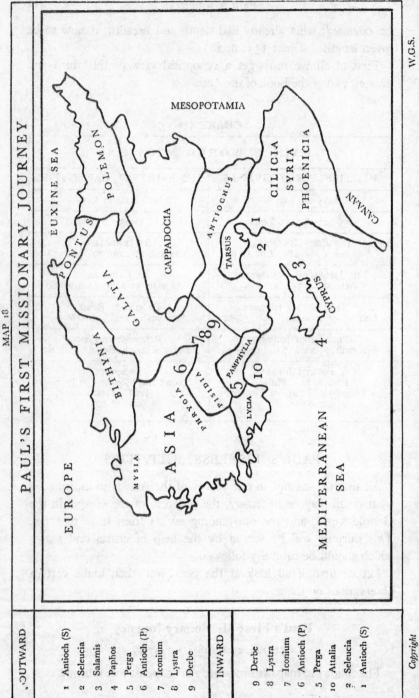

MAP 18

PAUL'S FIRST MISSIONARY JOURNEY

EUROPE

EUXINE SEA

PONTUS

POLEMON

BITHYNIA

GALATIA

CAPPADOCIA

MESOPOTAMIA

ANTIOCHUS

TARSUS

1

2

CILICIA

SYRIA

PHOENICIA

CANAAN

3

CYPRUS

4

MYSIA

ASIA

7 8 9

PHRYGIA

PISIDIA

5

10

PAMPHYLIA

LYCIA

MEDITERRANEAN
SEA

W.G.S.

OUTWARD	
1	Antioch (S)
2	Seleucia
3	Salamis
4	Paphos
5	Perga
6	Antioch (P)
7	Iconium
8	Lystra
9	Derbe

INWARD	
9	Derbe
8	Lystra
7	Iconium
6	Antioch (P)
5	Perga
10	Atalia
2	Seleucia
1	Antioch (S)

Detailed Analysis of the First Journey.

I. THE FIRST MISSIONARY JOURNEY
xiii. 1-xiv. 28. A.D. 47-49 2½ Years

1. THE CALL AND CONSECRATION AT ANTIOCH
(xii. 24, 25; xiii. 1-3: A.D. 47)

Prophets and Teachers (1)
The Word of the Spirit (2)
Dedication and Farewell of Barnabas and Saul (3)

2. THE CIRCUIT IN ASIA MINOR
(xiii. 4-xiv. 28)

(i) The Outward Journey (xiii. 4-xiv. 20)
The Evangelization of sinners

ANTIOCH in Syria	Starting Point
SELEUCIA	Port of embarkation (4)
SALAMIS, Cyprus E.	Preaching in synagogues (5)
PAPHOS, Cyprus W.	Interest and inquiry of Sergius Paulus (7)
	Opposition of Elymas (6, 8)
	Judgment on Elymas (9-11)
	Conversion of Sergius Paulus (12)

From this point:—
(*a*) The name 'Saul' is exchanged for 'Paul'.
(*b*) Paul takes precedence of Barnabas
(xiii. 2, 7, 13, 43; cf. xiv. 14; xv. 12, 25)

PERGA (Pamphylia 13)

John Mark returned home

ANTIOCH (Pisidia 14-51*a*)

FIRST SABBATH (xiii 14-43)
Paul and Barnabas in the Synagogue

(1) Paul's First Message (16-41)

I. SUMMARY OF THE HISTORICAL PREPARATION FOR CHRIST'S COMING (16-25)

1. From the Call of Abram to the Deliverance from Egypt (17)
2. From the Deliverance from Egypt to the Death of Moses (18)
3. The Period of Joshua (19)
4. The Period of the Judges (20)
5. The Reign of Saul (21)
6. The Reign of David (22)
7. The Advent of Jesus, announced by John Baptist (23-25)

II. CHRIST HAVING COME IS DECLARED TO BE THE FULFILMENT OF A DIVINE PROMISE (26-37)

1. His Death (27, 28)
2. His Burial (29)
3. His Resurrection (30-37)
   - (a) Evidence of it (30, 31)
   - (b) Fulfilment of Promise (32-35)
   - (c) The Prediction did not relate to David (36, 37)

III. THE IMPORTANCE, TO ALL WHO HEAR, OF THE TRUTH ABOUT CHRIST (38-41)

1. The Nature and Offer of the Gospel (38, 39)
2. A Warning against refusing the Gospel (40, 41)

   (2) **The Effect of the Message** (42, 43)
   - (a) Request for more instruction (42)
   - (b) Exhortation to steadfastness (43)

SECOND SABBATH (xiii. 44-51a)

Paul and Barnabas in the Synagogue

   (1) **Paul's Second Message** (44)
       (unrecorded)

   (2) **The Effect of the Message** (45-51a)
   - (a) Opposition of the Jews (45)
   - (b) Paul's indictment and decision (46, 47)
     A turning-point in the history of Christianity.
   - (c) The Gentiles receive the Gospel (48, 49)
   - (d) The Jews persecute the missionaries, and so they leave the city (50, 51a)

ICONIUM (Phrygia: xiii. 51- xiv. 6)	Ministry in the Synagogue (1)
	Trouble Brewing (2)
	Continued Ministry (3)
	A Divided Multitude (4)
	Contemplated Assault (5)
	Flight of the Missionaries (6)
LYSTRA: (Lycaonia: xiv. 6-20)	A Cripple Healed (8-10)
	Reaction of the Crowd (11-13)
	Protest of the Missionaries (14 18)
	Stoning of Paul (19, 20)

DERBE (Lycaonia: The Gospel Preached
     21)   Many Disciples Made

(ii) The Inward Journey (xiv. 21-28)
The Organization of saints

1. From DERBE to ANTIOCH P. (xiv. 21-23)
                     Confirming (22)
                     Exhorting (22)
                     Intimating (22)
                     Ordaining (23)
                     Praying (23)
                     Fasting (23)
                     Commending (23)

2. From ANTIOCH P. to ANTIOCH S. (xiv. 24-28)

PERGA (25)   Preached (cf. xiii. 13)

ATTALIA (25)   Port of embarkation

SELEUCIA   Port of disembarkation

ANTIOCH S. (26-28) Report to the church on the missionary
                   journey (27)

Ministry at Antioch, for about $1\frac{1}{2}$ years: A.D. 49, 50

Approximate Distances

Outward	miles	Inward	miles
Antioch S. to Seleucia	16	Derbe to Lystra	30
Seleucia to Salamis (Sea)	100	Lystra to Iconium	30
Salamis to Paphos	100	Iconium to Antioch P.	85
Paphos to Perga (Sea)	175	Antioch P. to Perga	100
Perga to Antioch P.	100	Perga to Attalia	20
Antioch P. to Iconium	85	Attalia to Seleucia (Sea)	320
Iconium to Lystra	30	Seleucia to Antioch S.	16
Lystra to Derbe	30		
	636		601

TIME: More than Two Years: A.D. 47-49
DISTANCE: Over 1,200 miles

PAUL'S FIRST MISSIONARY JOURNEY

Acts xiii. 1-xiv. 28

A.D. 47-49. About $2\frac{1}{2}$ Years

Acts xiii records the beginning of an entirely new movement in the history of revealed religion. This movement had been anticipated, and, indeed, was the substance of God's covenant with Abram (Gen. xii. 1-3), but here the promise begins to be fulfilled on the world-scale. 'The middle wall of partition' which had begun to crumble (Acts x-xii) was now to be demolished, not instantly and suddenly, but progressively and surely. The new centre was the Syrian Antioch, and the new leader was Paul.

THE CALL AND CONSECRATION

(xiii. 1-3)

The call and consecration of Barnabas and Saul is briefly but impressively narrated. What was the work of the Spirit as the authority, was the work of the Church as the agent. These verses reflect the beginning of public worship which was independent of the synagogue. It is clear also that the government of the Church was not hierarchic, but democratic. The command of the Spirit was emphatic: 'Separate me *now at once*, or *indeed* (cf. 1 Cor. vi. 20. Lu. ii. 15. Acts xv. 36, Gr.). The hour had been reached for the work to begin. The calling of these men was not to Christian service, for in that they had been for long engaged, but to the apostleship of Gentile evangelization.

It is worth while noting that evangelists worked in pairs: Peter and John, Paul and Barnabas, Paul and Silas, Titus and Trophimus, and of the Seventy it is said that the Lord 'sent them two and two before His face into every city and place whither He himself would come' (Luke x. 1).

In verse 5 it says that John Mark went with them, but it is not said that he had been separated to the work by the Spirit and the Church as Barnabas and Saul were. Does this have any bearing on what happened a little later? (verse 13).

The word '*minister*' (5) means '*under-rower*', and suggests that he was the attendant of the missionaries, relieving them of

the details of the journey, and serving them in other practical
ways. We do not read of any baptisms in Cyprus.

THE OUTWARD JOURNEY
(xiii. 4-xiv. 20)

Cyprus
(xiii. 4-12)

This was and is a considerable island, its coast-line measuring
nearly 400 miles. It is from 30 to 60 miles in breadth from north
to south, and about 100 miles in length from east to west, between
Salamis and Paphos. It had produced several distinguished men,
—Aristos the historian, Zeno, the founder of the Stoic philosophy,
and Apollonius the physician. It was the native country of
Barnabas, and this fact would give to the mission a promising
start.

MAP 19   W.G.S.

Modern Cyprus

Because of the importance of Cyprus to-day, in the light of the administrative controversy started in 1954 between Britain and Greece, a few particulars about the island will be of general interest.

It is 3,572 square miles in area. Its estimated population in 1952 was 497,788, about 81 per cent. of whom were Greek-Orthodox, and 18 per cent. Moslems. During the school year 1951-52 there were 489 Greek schools; 204 Turkish; 4 American; 5 Maronite; 4 Latin, and others 3; with a total enrolment of 64,668; and these schools are under the general control of the Government.

Modern Greek and Turkish are the common languages, English and French being spoken only by the educated classes.

The chief towns are NICOSIA, the capital; FAMAGUSTA, LARNACA, LIMASSOL, PAPHOS and KYRENIA. The chief industries of the island are agriculture and mining.

It is of considerable interest that the Mediterranean Islands of Cyprus, Crete, and Malta, which are prominent in the Pauline story, are still living centres of regard and influence.

Salamis

(xiii. 5)

The missionaries began their work in the synagogues at Salamis where there was a large Jewish population—though the inhabitants in general were Greeks—and probably Barnabas took the lead here. It is probable also that there were Christians at Salamis (Acts xi. 19). The evangelists then *worked their way through* the island, preaching in the principal towns—of which there were fifteen of considerable note (cf. xiv. 24; xv. 3, 41; xvi. 6; xviii. 23; xix. 1. 21; xx. 2), until they reached Paphos the capital. This journey must have occupied several weeks, but there is no record of their having accomplished anything.

Paphos
(xiii. 6-12)

Salamis was the chief city in the east of the island, and Paphos was the chief city in the west, a hundred miles away; and it was also the administrative capital, and the residence of the Roman Proconsul, Sergius Paulus.

Here things began to happen. The Proconsul sent for the missionaries that he might learn what their message was. His range of interest is seen in that he had at Court a Jew who was an astrologer and a false prophet, whose proper name was Barjesus, and whose official title was Elymas, 'the Wizard'.

Saul seems to have been the spokesman, and Barjesus, apprehending that if Sergius Paulus became a Christian his own power was at an end, kept interrupting and contradicting Saul, who turned upon him, and by the Holy Spirit said: 'You mass of trickery and rascality!' You 'son of the Devil', you enemy of all righteousness, will you not stop twisting 'the Lord's straight ways'?' (David Smith). And he continued:

'See, now! The hand of the Lord will fall on you, and you will be blind, not seeing the sun for a time.'
'And at once a cloud and darkness fell on him, and he went about trying to find someone to lead him by the hand.' (11, 12). (C. K. WILLIAMS).

We cannot but recognise in this a repetition of Saul's own experience, first, in his opposition to the truths of Christianity, and secondly, in the judgment of temporary blindness which was visited upon him (Acts ix. 1-9). The physical judgment answered to the spiritual condition (Acts xxviii. 26, 27).

Sergius Paulus was greatly impressed by what he heard and saw, and it is recorded that he 'believed'. Exactly how much this means it is difficult to say, but it is evident that he was not baptised.

This was the first presentation of 'the word of God' to the Roman world. Also, it was at this time that Saul took the name of Paul. He was called by his Hebrew name until his first circuit among the Gentiles, but from now forward he assumed this

Roman name, to be more in keeping with his mission, and more acceptable to his audiences.

Barjesus represents sorcery; Sergius Paulus represents intellectualism; and Paul represents Christianity. The last judged the first, and saved the second. From now onward Paul takes precedence of Barnabas, except at Jerusalem (xv. 12. 25; but cf. xiv. 14).

Compare Peter and Simon Magus with Paul and Barjesus (chapters viii. 18-24; xiii. 6-12).

The judgment on Barjesus is the first record of a miracle wrought by Paul.

Perga
(xiii. 13, 14a)

Having completed the initial stage of their work Paul and his party sailed from Paphos to Perga, a distance of about 175 miles. They did not land at the Pamphilian port Attalia, but continued up the Cestrus river which was navigable to Perga, about seven miles from the sea.

Two things confront us in this brief record of 27 words (Gr.): first, that the Apostles did not preach here; and secondly, that on reaching Perga John Mark left them and returned to Jerusalem.

It is more than likely that these events are related in some way. Ramsay thinks that Mark left the party because of a change of plan with which he did not agree, and that this change of plan was due to Paul contracting malarial fever, which made it necessary that without delay he should go to higher country, which he did by going to Galatia. Ramsay's theory is supported by the reference in Gal. iv. 13, 14 to Paul's physical condition in Galatia, and frequently in 2 Cor. xii. 1-10. Mark himself may have fallen ill with mosquito malaria, and Paul may have felt that if *he* himself could carry on, the younger man could have done so also. The Day will declare. (See p. 279).

Antioch in Pisidia
(xiii. 14-52)

THE JOURNEY

Paul was ill, and it was necessary that the party—minus Mark— should leave the miasmal lowlands of Pamphylia, and journey to the bracing highlands of Galatia. *Pisidian Antioch* was a hundred miles distant from Perga northward, and it was about 3,600 ft., above sea-level. The journey across the steep and rugged range of the Taurus was fatiguing and dangerous. Brigands infested the mountains, and swollen torrents swept the ravines. Probably Paul refers to these dangers in 2 Cor. xi. 26. The journey was made on foot, and at the rate of about 20-25 miles a day, they would be about a week on the way.

On arriving, Paul at any rate would be exhausted, and in all likelihood it would be about a fortnight before the missionaries could begin their work of witness.

There were many Antiochs, but the two which have Christian significance are *Antioch in Syria*, and *Antioch in Pisidia*. These should be definitely distinguished and carefully compared. One matter of importance in this connection relates to LUKE.

The Syrian Antioch, the Pisidian Antioch, and Philippi respectively have been regarded as his native city. We cannot discuss the matter here, but that he was a native of Antioch in Pisidia is not unlikely. The record of what happened there after the missionaries arrived, and later on, appears to be the work of an eye-witness. Luke displays intimacy with Southern Galatia, and the record of Paul's sermons in the synagogue (xiii. 14-44) almost certainly is made by someone who heard them.

Paul and Luke may have met before, perhaps at the University in Tarsus, but almost certainly they were together in Antioch of Pisidia.

THE SERMONS

The first of Paul's recorded sermons is the one he preached in the synagogue in Antioch. Though all his utterances had certain foundational truths in them it is clear that they were adapted in form to the audience he was addressing. Compare this sermon with the one he preached at Athens (xvii. 22-31).

See the analysis on pp. 315, 316 of the discourse at Antioch. It is seen to have been in three parts, each beginning by addressing his audience (xiii. 16, 26, 38).

It should be compared and contrasted with Stephen's sermon,

which Paul heard (ch. vii), and also with Peter's Pentecostal discourse (ii. 14-41).

A week later Paul delivered another message, which is not recorded, but the final result of his ministry in the city constituted a crisis in the history of Christianity. This is the determining utterance: 'Paul and Barnabas spoke out plainly, and said:

'God's message had to be told to you first, but since you thrust it off and judge yourselves unworthy of eternal life, we now turn to the heathen. For these are the orders the Lord has given us: "I have made you a light for the heathen, to be the means of salvation to the very ends of the earth".'

The crisis was precipitated by the Jews themselves. They *pushed away* the offer of salvation, and in doing so *passed judgment on themselves.*

PERSECUTION AND PROSPERITY

The rejection of Paul's message had the same result as had the rejection of Stephen's: God was glorified, many were converted, the Gospel was spread abroad, and the disciples were filled with joy and with the Holy Spirit (xiii. 48-52).

Ramsay says, 'The first thoroughly Gentile congregation, separate from the synagogue, was established at Pisidian Antioch'.

Iconium
(xiii. 51-xiv. 6)

Being expelled from Antioch and the district the missionaries went 85-90 miles S.E. to Iconium, the metropolis of the Lycaonian district. Let us remember all the time that these men walked these distances, and this journey would take them four or five days. Where did they get food, and where did they sleep?

On reaching Iconium, an important city, the missionaries followed the procedure which they had adopted at Antioch. '*Together*' (ver. 1) means '*in the same way*'. They attended the synagogue and addressed the people who were assembled there. The results were most encouraging. But the Jews made trouble by rousing the Gentiles against the Apostles.

It is not unlikely that the missionaries were taken to the Law

Court, and if so they were discharged. This would seem to be the connection between verses 2 and 3 of chapter xiv. The legal proceedings gave them a fine opportunity, and they used it for some months—perhaps six or seven, adding 'signs and wonders' to their messages (3).

But the Gospel is divisive. It makes evident vital distinctions, dividing people into the categories of believers and unbelievers, and placing them in light, and in darkness. Uncompromising Christianity has never sought and has never had the friendship of the world; and it has never been so effective as when it was persecuted.

So, the citizens of Iconium were divided for and against the missionaries, and what the dissentients had failed to do legally they now proposed to do illegally (5). It is clear that their contemplated purpose was not accomplished for Paul was 'stoned' only once, and that was not at Iconium (2 Cor. xi. 25).

Paul and his party heard of the design, and they 'fled unto the cities of Lycaonia, Lystra, and Derbe, and the region round about' (6, 7).

There are times when a Christian should stand firm, and times when he should run (cf. Neh. vi. 11; Matt. x. 23). A Christian should have caution as well as courage, sense as well as loyalty.

Here, for the first time in the Acts, Paul and Barnabas are called Apostles (4-14). The legend of Paul and Thekla has its scene in Iconium. (See H. V. Morton's *In the Steps of St. Paul*, pp. 218-225.)

Lystra
(xiv. 6-20)

What happened at Lystra is told in fifteen verses, whereas the events at Antioch in Pisidia are given thirty-nine verses. If, however, the visit of Paul to each of these places gives to it its distinction in the Christian story, then, the visit to Lystra was the more important.

A HEATHEN CITY

Travelling 30-40 miles S.E. from Iconium, the missionaries arrived for the first time at a purely heathen city. There was no synagogue there, from which it must be inferred that there were few resident Jews.

The inhabitants were worshippers of gods, the Roman *Jupiter* and *Mercury*, the Greek *Zeus* and *Hermes*.

A MIRACLE

As there was no synagogue in Lystra the preaching must have been done in the open-air—perhaps the beginning of open-air preaching. Paul must have spoken in Greek, but the people were more familiar with their native Lycaonian. Nothing happened, however, until Paul healed a man who had been a cripple from his birth, and then the crowd became alive with interest, and their excitement was due to their superstition.

INCARNATE GODS

The idolatrous population concluded that their deities had become incarnate; that Barnabas was Jupiter, and that Paul was Mercury, and they felt that they must offer them a sacrifice. With this purpose they hastened to the temple of Jupiter which was outside the city's walls. The missionaries must have greatly wondered what the people were doing, as they had not understood what had been said (11).

When the purpose became evident the Apostles dramatically protested (14), and Paul delivered his first message to a purely pagan audience (cf. xvii. 21-32) Rom. i. 18-23).

PAUL'S ADDRESS

His messages were always adapted to the audiences he was addressing, and as he had not had such a congregation before, it is important to observe what line he took.

After repudiating divine honours and condemning idolatry Paul proclaimed 'the living God' as the Creator (15), the Controller of nations (16), and the Giver of all good (17), the God of Nature, of History, and of Providence.

REVULSION OF FEELING

An illustration is now given of the superficial character of religious excitement, which was witnessed before, during the Passion Week. Jews from Antioch and Iconium arrived at

Lystra and incited the populace against the missionaries, and what at Iconium they had planned to do they actually did here, they stoned Paul (xiv. 5, 6, 19. 2 Cor. xi. 25), and dragging him out of the city they left him for dead. What in chapter vii. 58 Paul saw, he here felt.

DISCIPLES

How dramatic a scene followed! As Paul lay there 'disciples stood round about him' (20). Who were they? Certainly Barnabas, and probably Lois and Eunice, and a boy in his teens named Timothy. Maybe with this Jewish family the missionaries had been lodging. While the sorrowing souls beheld the prostrate figure of Paul, and perhaps, thought about burying him, he rose up and went back with them to his lodging.

Luke does not say that Paul had been killed, but he does give the impression that his recovery was more than natural. The party remained that night in Lystra, and the next day they left.

Derbe
(xiv. 20, 21)

How much can be said in a few words! One verse is given to record the visit of the missionaries to Derbe, but in it much is implied.

Derbe was the Roman frontier town of the Province of Galatia, from 25-35 miles East or South East of Lystra. It was a small town, for the record implies that all the inhabitants heard the Gospel, and it is evident that enemy Jews did not pursue them thither. How long Paul and Barnabas were there we are not told, but their stay was both pleasant and profitable. The Apostles had been expelled from Antioch, threatened with stoning at Iconium, and Paul was actually stoned at Lystra, and these experiences are referred to nearly twenty years afterward, but Derbe is not mentioned (2 Tim. iii. 11).

SUCCESSFUL EVANGELISM

Surely in Christian history no evangelistic effort was ever recorded in so few words and in so satisfying a way as it is here! Only eight words! But they tell us that the Gospel was preached, and that souls were saved, and from a later reference we learn that one of the converts was Gaius (xx. 4), who later travelled with Paul.

WHICH WAY NOW?

Another matter occupied the minds of these two men while they were at Derbe, and it was just this: 'Where do we go from here?' The alternatives were (a) to go eastward to the Cilician Gates, and so by Tarsus to Antioch in Syria; and (b) to go back, visiting again the places to which they had been.

There were seasonal and circumstantial difficulties in their going home by Tarsus; and Cilicia had already been evangelised by Paul (Gal. i. 21); but for the other alternative there were strong reasons. In Antioch, Iconium and Lystra there were converts to Christianity who in each city constituted the nucleus of a Christian Church; but they were ignorant, unorganized, and would be persecuted. The treatment of the Apostles in these places had not allowed of their gathering the converts into organized societies, and because much remained to be done they resolved to retrace their steps, and in some sense to complete what they had commenced.

THE INWARD JOURNEY
(xiv. 21-28)

The object of the outward journey had been the evangelization of sinners, but the object of the inward journey was the organization of saints. This is an important point, because it accounts for the fact that on the journey homeward they had not, as formerly, to face opposition and persecution. On the outward journey they created churches, and on the inward journey they confirmed them. This order and necessity are as imperative in the promulgation of Christianity as in the building of houses. Nothing can be continued which has not been commenced, but, in this realm, what has been commenced should be continued. He who has begun a good work in us will perfect it until the day of Jesus Christ (Phil. i. 6). Foundations are useless without superstructures, and superstructures are impossible without foundations, that is, if they are to stand.

Cities Revisited

We can well believe that with a spring in their step Paul and Barnabas retrod the road to Lystra, and Iconium, and Antioch, and had their conversation and devotions been reported the record would have been a religious classic. As they came in sight again of Lystra Paul could not but recall the stoning, but over against that was the glad prospect of meeting again Lois, Eunice, Timothy, and others who on his first visit had experienced the grace of God. This would not be the last time he would visit Lystra (xvi. 1), though Barnabas would not be there again, but it was a momentous visit, as we shall see. On re-entering Iconium the missionaries would have many memories of the months they spent there, and of the converts that were made. And, of course, the recollection of their previous visit to Pisidian Antioch stirred deep thoughts and feelings in them. There Paul's mission to the Gentile world was finally determined upon, and there he met Luke who was to mean so much to him in years to come.

A Mission to Christians

The record makes it quite clear that these return visits were not for the purpose of preaching, but of teaching. Paul's evangelistic work in these places was done, and he would now prepare his converts to carry it on.

The programme consisted of seven items—confirming, exhorting, intimating, ordaining, praying, fasting, and commending (xiv. 22, 23). These verses are of vital importance for early Church history. By *confirming* is meant that the Apostles gave much needed strength to these Christians who were ignorant and persecuted. They were urged to stand fast in the faith, that is, in the Christian truths which the Apostles had already taught them. They intimated that persecution was inevitable, and that it brought to them who endured it an enriching reward. Paul himself was illustration enough of this truth. The central item on the programme is, probably, the most important of all. *Elders were appointed in each of the churches.* This was the beginning of church organization, and the two things to note are, *what was done*, and *how it was done*.

Lewin says, 'They now ordained priests to take charge of the churches'; but they did nothing of the kind. The word *priest* does not occur in Paul's Epistles ('Hebrews' omitted), and only thrice in the Acts, but not in connection with Christians. *Elder* and *bishop* are inter-changeable terms, *elder* being the Jewish, and *bishop* the Greek designations of the same office (Titus i. 5, 7).

In 1 Tim. v. 17, 19 '*priests*' in the modern translation, *Letters to Young Churches*, is entirely without authority. The word is *presbuteros*, which never means *priest*. This is an illustration of tradition displacing authority.

Paul knew nothing of sacerdotalism. Overseers were appointed in each church to counsel and guide, though, at this time, with little or no experience for the responsible task. The way in which it was done was by *appointment*. The word used in verse 23 originally meant *to vote by show of hands*, and then came to mean *by the choice of an assembly*. Both meanings indicate that the elders were appointed by the body of the believers, showing that early church organization was not autocratic, but democratic, and was indigenous, and not exotic. Each assembly was self-constituted and self-governed.

This solemn matter was accompanied by prayer and fasting, and then the Apostles 'commended the believers to the Lord'. Of this A. T. Robertson says, 'They had "trusted" in Jesus, and Paul now "entrusts" them to Him with confidence'.

Homeward Bound

When it says that the missionaries 'passed through' Pisidia it may mean that they preached wherever they could on the way. At any rate they did so at Perga which they had so hastily left on the outward journey, and where Mark had broken away from them. They did not embark at Perga but went on to Attalia the seaport of Pamphylia, and one version adds that they preached the Gospel there. At Attalia they went aboard a ship which, passing Cyprus by, took them to Seleucia their home port. To these two men that sea voyage of over 300 miles would be memorable. Their first mission in Asia lay behind them, and their home Church, awaiting their return and report, lay before them. In the two years of their absence so much had happened, and it must have been wonderful to hear Paul and Barnabas relate the story (xiv. 27, 28). So ends the first great mission to the heathen in the history of the Christian Church.

Impression

Looking back over this journey, and having regard for the fact that there were no trains, no motor cars, no aeroplanes, and very different sea transport from what we are used to in our time, and that, in consequence, travel by land, for these men at any rate, was made on foot, in circumstances that were perilous for several reasons; and remembering that these travellers could not go to comfortable hotels but had to be put up privately, or go to some Inn; and knowing further that they were not financed by their home Church, but had to earn their living by working with their hands; and recalling also Paul's physical maladies, and sufferings from persecution—bearing all these things in mind it is astonishing that these men travelled over 700 miles on foot and over 500 miles by sea, preaching from city to city, making converts and organizing churches over a large part of eastern Asia Minor, and all within a period of about two years. No wonder they reported that these things 'God had done with them' (xiv. 27). No doubt Barnabas was a comfort and welcome companion to Paul, but it was the latter who did the major part of the work and suffered the onslaughts, and, probably, earned the money which fed them both.

THE JERUSALEM CONFERENCE

(ACTS xv. 1-35.   A.D. 50)

THE JERUSALEM CONFERENCE
(Acts xv. 1-35. Gal. ii. 1-10)

The Time of It

In the Book of the Acts five visits of Paul to Jerusalem are recorded. 1. After his conversion (ix. 26. A.D. 37). 2. With the Antiochene contribution for the brethren in Judaea in a time of famine (xi. 27-30. A.D. 45). 3. To consult the Apostles about the necessity of circumcision for Gentile believers (xv. A.D. 50). 4. After the second missionary journey (xviii. 22. A.D. 54). 5. Before his imprisonment at Caesarea (xxi. 15. A.D. 58).

It may be assumed that 1 and 2 were too early for the Conference, and that 4 and 5 were too late. Therefore Paul's visit to Jerusalem recorded in Acts xv. and Gal. ii. 1-10 must have been about A.D. 50. As Farrar well says: 'In the two narratives the same people go up at the same time, from the same place, for the same object, in consequence of the same interference by the same agitators, and with the same results.'

The Cause and Course of It

The following is a summary outline of this event:

(i) **The Dissension concerning Circumcision** (1-5)

    (*a*) The question raised and debated (1, 2*a*)
    (*b*) A deputation appointed to go to Jerusalem (2*b*)
    (*c*) The journey, and the ministry by the way (3)
    (*d*) The arrival of the deputation, and their report (4)
    (*e*) The insistence of certain Judaizers (5)

(ii) **The Discussion of the Problem at Jerusalem** (4-12)

    (*a*) The Debate of the Apostles and Elders (6, 7)
    (*b*) The Speech of Peter (7*b*-11)
        (1) Declaration (7-9)
        (2) Interpolation (10)
        (3) Affirmation (11)
    (*c*) The Testimony of Barnabas and Paul (12)

(iii) **The Decision of the Church and her Leaders** (13-29)

    (*a*) The Verdict of James (13-21)

    (*b*) Choice of a Deputation to visit Antioch (22)

    (*c*) A Letter Embodying the decision of the Council (23-29)

        (1) Salutation (23)

        (2) Repudiation (24)

        (3) Commendation (25-27)

        (4) Prohibition (28, 29)

(iv) **The Delight of the Gentile Christians** (30-35)

    (*a*) The return to Antioch (30*a*)

    (*b*) The delivery of the Letter (30*b*)

    (*c*) The joyful reception of the news (31)

    (*d*) The exhortation of Judas and Silas (32, 33 (34))

    (*e*) The ministry of Paul and Barnabas (35)

        (about one year)

(v) **The Defection** of Peter and Barnabas (Gal. ii. 11-14, or to 21).

We shall follow the event under five captions: 1. Dissension; 2. Discussion; 3. Decision; 4. Delight; and 5. Defection.

(i) THE DISSENSION (xv. 1-5)

This chapter is of incalculable importance in Church history, recording, as it does, the proceedings of the *First Great Christian Council*. Some idea of its importance may be gathered from the fact that Peter, and Paul, and James the Lord's brother attended it, the last of these presiding. Here also, we have *the earliest example of a Christian Letter*, and it contains the *Charter of Gentile Christian Liberty*. Read verses 1-35 carefully, together with Galatians ii. 1-10. The majority of commentators consider that these passages are complementary narratives, describing different aspects of the same event. What, then, is it all about?

For background we should read again chs. viii., x., xi., xiii. 46-48, and Gal. i. During the early years of the Christian Church its members were converted Jews only, and not until the dispersion from Jerusalem, which followed on the martyrdom of Stephen, was the Gospel preached to the Gentiles. We have seen that in chs. viii. to xii., Philip, Saul, Peter, the Apostles, and the whole Church were prepared for a wider witness, that is, for a mission to Gentiles. Following that came Paul's first missionary journey

(xiii. and xiv.), from which, at this time, he has returned. But for all this, the event of ch. xv would never have occurred. The problem arose out of the conversion of Gentiles. A great blessing precipitated a grave crisis, and often since then problems for the Church have been occasioned by her successes.

The point at issue here is whether or not Christian Gentiles should be circumcised. '*Certain men from Judaea*' had gone to Antioch in Syria and were teaching that circumcision was essential for salvation (1), and that the Mosaic Law, ceremonial as well as moral, must be obeyed by the Gentiles if they would attach themselves to the Church. This, of course, raised a matter of vital importance. Was Christianity to be but a Christianised Judaism? Could the Christian Church have existence only within the Jewish Church? These implications of the present demand were firmly opposed by Paul and Barnabas, and *not a little commotion and discussion* ensued (2a); and as there seemed no prospect of the parties coming to an understanding, it was agreed that the matter be submitted to the authorities in Jerusalem (2), and so the company went south, at the expense of the Church.

On the way these messengers travelled by Tyre, Sidon, and Samaria, and everywhere caused great joy by '*declaring the conversion of the Gentiles.*' No doubt they chose this theme because of its bearing on the matter about which they were going to Jerusalem.

(ii) THE DISCUSSION (xv. 4-12)

Three things here should be clearly distinguished.

1. The Church's reception of the deputation on their arrival in Jerusalem; the rehearsal of missionary experience by Paul and Barnabas; and the objection of the Judaic party to the liberty which was being granted to the Christian Gentiles (xv. 4, 5).

2. Between verses 5 and 6 of Acts xv. there is a gap which is accounted for in Gal. ii. 1-10. What happened between verses 5 and 6 is the interview which Paul and Barnabas had *privately* with James, Peter, and John, in which were discussed the missionaries' attitude to the demand that Christian Gentiles should be

circumcised; the case of uncircumcised Titus, who was one of the party; and the apostleship of Paul.

There is a division of opinion as to whether Titus was circumcised in Jerusalem at this time; but the apostleship of Paul was granted by the Jerusalem Apostles, and they agreed with the missionaries on the question of Gentile circumcision.

3. The gathering of the Church a second time to discuss the subject for which the deputation was there (xv. 6).

On their arrival at Jerusalem Paul and Barnabas were formally received by the Church, the apostles, and the elders there, and without delay they *'rehearsed all things that God had done with them.'* That must have been a profoundly interesting report, the substance of which we have in chs. xiii., xiv. We can imagine how astonished and thrilled the listeners would be as Paul and Barnabas related their experiences, and told of the founding of churches throughout Galatia, in which were both Jews and Gentiles who confessed the name of Christ.

'But' (5). Almost certainly, where good work is being done, there will be somebody who has an objection to raise, a criticism to offer, or some word of discouragement to speak. These people are Christians, but they are great in *'buts'*. So here, *'certain of the Pharisees who believed'* expressed themselves to the effect that this good work needed safeguarding; these Gentile converts must toe the line of the Law (5). These men were so rooted in tradition that they had not felt the thrill; they were so loyal to the Law as to imagine that there was an element of danger in the Gospel. At any rate, their view raised the whole question at Jerusalem which had been discussed at Antioch.

For the private meeting of the missionaries and the Jerusalem Apostles see Gal. ii. 1-10.

In Acts xv. 6-21 Luke records the final discussion of the matter in dispute.

Church Members

Observe the constitution of this assembly. There were present Paul and Barnabas and *'certain other'* from Antioch (2); there were those objecting *'Pharisees who believed'* (5), *'the apostles and elders'* (6), and a *'multitude'* of the Jerusalem Church members

(12). And now here, as at Antioch, there was much '*discussion*' (7, 2), in which, it appears, the members of the Church joined, for at a later moment they '*kept silence*' (12), a reference which would be pointless if they had been silent all the time.

Peter

After this general discussion *Peter* rose to address the assembly (7). That was an interesting and critical moment. How all eyes would be turned upon him who was recognized as the apostle of the circumcision (Gal. ii. 7, 8), and how specially anxious Paul would be, wondering what line Peter would take.

What line he did take is told in verses 7-11, which read again carefully. Of course, this is not the full address, but Luke's notes, which are adequate for the purpose of the record. The speech is in two parts. In the first (7-9) is a *statement of facts*. The speaker takes his stand on *an event*, the conversion, through his instrumentality, of Cornelius and other Gentiles (ch. x.), and on *their knowledge of it* (7; ch. xi.). He reminds them that these Gentiles had received the great evidence of conversion, the Holy Spirit (8), and that in this experience they were in no respect inferior to Jewish believers; they had exercised saving faith, and their hearts had been cleansed (9). These were the facts, and, of course, no one was prepared to deny them.

In the second part of his speech, Peter makes an appeal based on the preceding facts (10, 11). It is very impressive, leaving his hearers no alternative. He says in effect, 'We Jews were not saved by circumcision, so why should we impose this rite upon the Gentiles as a condition of salvation? These were saved by grace, and we Jews can be saved in no other way'.

No doubt Peter had discussed the whole subject with Paul, and had been finally convinced, if any doubt lingered in his mind after the Joppa—Caesarea experience, that Christianity was not a something added to Judaism, but was a new revelation and a Gospel.

Barnabas and Paul

This address completely silenced the whole gathering (12a), and gave *Barnabas* and *Paul* a fine opportunity. They made use of this, not by adding any argument to Peter's, but by simply *'rehearsing what signs and wonders God had wrought among the Gentiles by them.'*

They illustrated the argument, and thus greatly advanced the end they had in view.

Barnabas' name precedes Paul's here, as the better known of the two, and as the leader of the Antioch party.

(iii) THE DECISION (xv. 13-29).

James

The Lord's brother, austere, dignified and devout was, twenty years after the crucifixion, President of this Conference at Jerusalem. He, with Peter and John, had received Paul and Barnabas privately, and had agreed with their point of view relative to the matter in dispute, but at this public debate he listened patiently to the noisy vehemence of the Hebrew party, to the speech of Peter, and to the testimony of Barnabas and Paul; and now, everyone who wanted to speak having had the opportunity (the Apostle John was silent) the moment had arrived when the Chairman had to sum up and state his verdict on the subject. This he does in the words of xv. 13-21.

The speech is Judaic in tone, brief, wise, conciliatory and convincing, and was listened to in tense silence. Accepting Peter's testimony he affirms that it was in keeping with ancient prophecy. He quotes Amos ix. 11, 12, and it should be noted that he does so, not from the Hebrew, but from the Septuagint which differs considerably from the former; but his statement concedes the main point at issue, namely that Gentile believers were under no necessity to be subject to the Mosaic ceremonial law (19), but he advises that the Gentiles observe certain restrictions. He names four things which were abhorrent to the Jews, and which, if practised by the Gentiles, would make social intercourse impossible. In giving his judgment James speaks for the whole Church, and his verdict is masterly in conception and expression. He recognised that the Jews had a claim as well as the Gentiles, and that it would not be fair to give everything to either the one or the other, and so he proposes a middle course.

He would not have the Gentiles 'troubled' with the Mosaic ceremonialism, he would not have imposed on them the 'yoke' which Peter had said the Jews themselves were *not able to bear* (10); but, on the other hand, they must so conduct themselves as not to outrage Jewish sensitiveness on certain matters of observance. He suggests that a letter be written, setting forth this verdict for the guidance of both elements in the Christian Church. The proposition moved by the Chairman was put to the meeting and was unanimously adopted, though probably the Judaic objectors did not vote. Peter now disappears from the history of the Acts.

(iv) THE DELIGHT OF THE GENTILES (xv. 30-35)

Having discussed thoroughly this Gentile matter, it was now resolved that a deputation be sent to Antioch, with a letter which would put their minds at rest who were troubled about the attitude of the Judaizers. Two men, *Silas* and *Judas*, were chosen by '*the whole church*', to accompany Paul and Barnabas.

The letter was drafted under the immediate direction of James, it would appear, for only once again in the New Testament does the salutation '*Greeting*' occur, and that is in James i. 1.

The text of this famous letter is as follows:

'The Apostles and Elders and Brethren send greetings unto the brethren which are of the Gentiles in Antioch and Syria and Cilicia: forasmuch as we have heard, that certain which went out from us have troubled you with words, subverting your souls, saying, Ye must be circumcised, and keep the law: to whom we gave no such commandment: it seemed good unto us, being assembled with one accord, to send chosen men unto you with our beloved Barnabas and Paul, men that have hazarded their lives for the Name of our Lord Jesus Christ. We have sent therefore Judas and Silas, who shall also tell you the same things by mouth. For it seemed good to the Holy Spirit, and to us, to lay upon you no greater burden than these necessary things; that ye abstain from meats offered to idols, and from blood, and from things strangled, and from fornication: from which if ye keep yourselves, ye shall do well. Fare ye well.' (Acts xv. 23-29).

22. Then it pleased the apostles and elders, with the whole church, to send chosen men of their own company to Antioch with Paul and Barnabas; namely, Judas surnamed Barsabas, and Silas, chief men among the brethren. 30 So when they were dis-

missed, they came to Antioch: and when they had gathered the multitude together, they delivered the epistle: 31 which when they had read, they rejoiced for the consolation. 32 And Judas and Silas, being prophets also themselves, exhorted the brethren with many words, and confirmed them. 33 And after they had tarried there a space, they were let go in peace from the brethren unto the apostles. 34 Notwithstanding it pleased Silas to abide there still (not in R.V.). 35 Paul also and Barnabas continued in Antioch, teaching and preaching the word of the Lord, with many others also.

This is the first Epistle of the Christian Church, and its importance is out of all proportion to its length. Read it carefully, and mark the *Salutation* (23), the *Repudiation* (24), the *Commendation* (25-27), *Prohibition* (28-29), and the *Conclusion* (29).

Do not overlook that expression in the *Salutation,* '*the brethren which are of the Gentiles.*' That registers a tremendous stride forward towards the realization of what we call the Holy Catholic Church, towards the enjoyment of that fellowship which rises high above all racial and social distinctions. Christian Gentiles are now regarded as parts of one indivisible Church, together with Christian Jews.

The *Repudiation* is impressive. The Church takes no responsibility either for the visit to Antioch of 'certain men' (1), Jews, nor for what they had said when they got there (24). They had '*troubled*' these Gentiles 'with words'. What a lot of trouble words can give, and what a lot of help. A dictionary never yet hurt any one, but selections from it have broken many a heart. Watch and winnow your words.

The *Commendation* is very hearty. One can feel the warmth of the words, '*our beloved Barnabas and Paul*', and can appreciate the justice as well as the generosity of the acknowledgment of the risks they had taken for love of Christ and the souls of men. We should not withhold praise when and where it is due. We are generally very generous with blame.

Judas and Silas are given ample authority, and, when they read the letter to the Church in Antioch, and commented on it, they would be listened to with respect and eagerness (27).

It is noteworthy that in this letter of one hundred and nine words (Greek), only thirty-one deal with the matter in hand (28, 29). We can frustrate a purpose by too great emphasis: there is power in restraint.

And now mark carefully what are called *The Decrees* (xvi. 4). They are introduced on the assumption that the verdict of the Jerusalem Church was the verdict of the Holy Spirit, that He and they, that they and He came to this decision. They had taken upon themselves the duty of determining what the mind of the Spirit was. This must have been done by discussion and prayer together, and it was done by the *whole church*, and not by a Clerical Council. Bishop Wordsworth wisely says, 'It cannot be held that councils of the Church now are entitled to adopt the words of the text in the framing of canons.' But, we must add, the Church has still the right to expect the guidance of the Holy Spirit in all her affairs.

And now for *the Decrees*. Four abstentions are enjoined. The Gentiles must abstain:

> 'from things sacrificed to idols; from blood; from things strangled; and from fornication.'

The first three concern ceremonial purity, and were of temporary importance, but the fourth concerns moral purity, and is of abiding obligation.

The first prohibition relates to food polluted by use at idol sacrifices, which was sent from the temples to the markets, and there bought and eaten. The second, 'blood', relates to the drinking of it; the third, is akin to this, but refers to blood which has not been 'poured out'; for both matters read Lev. xvii. 10-13. The fourth prohibition needs no explanation, further than to say that idol-worship and fornication have always been closely connected.

Looking again at these *Decrees* we cannot but appreciate the wisdom with which this difficult and delicate matter was satis-

z

factorily composed. The scruples of both parties had to be respected, and, by this settlement, were respected. The Pharisee party may well have said: 'If we may not demand of Gentiles what would please us but be an offence to them (circumcision), let us forbid what may please them but be an offence to us' (the four things). That is the compromise which this letter embodies, and it was acceptable all round, and brought joy to the Gentiles (31).

Thinking again about this Conference and its issue, we cannot but realise how wonderfully so grave a crisis was negotiated. If the decision had been given to the Judaizers, Christianity, if it had survived, would have become a mere adjunct of Judaism. Think about that. And more than once in the history of the Church since those days, narrow-mindedness and bigotry would have imposed upon believers a burdensome yoke (10), nor has good counsel always prevailed. There are still people who think more of a symbol than of the reality, who are sticklers for forms of godliness while, all the time, they are denying the power.

We should learn from this Conference that it is well for brethren to confer, and endeavour to see one another's view-point, and well is it, also, that we should be willing, in the interests of Christian concord, to yield something, whenever we can do so without sacrificing principle. Temporary arrangements may make for peace. It is not to be expected that all Christians will ever see alike on all matters, nor is it desirable; but it is always possible, while holding our particular view, to have the fullest fellowship with those from whom we differ, only in the Holy Spirit. (28). There can be no fellowship with wrong-doing.

Christianity is a religion of freedom and not of bondage, of peace and not of strife, of love and not of ill-will. No Christian and no church has a monopoly of either truth or wisdom.

(v). DEFECTION *of Peter and Barnabas* (Gal. ii. 11-14 or to 21)

Connected quite definitely with the subject of Acts xv. is the incident recorded in Gal. ii. 11-14 or to 21. Peter who had spoken at the Conference, and whose view on the subject of Christian Gentiles and the Mosaic ceremonial law was quite clear, acted upon his belief when, at Antioch, he had social fellowship with uncircumcised Gentiles; but when the Judaic troublers again visited the city, Peter, and it would seem Barnabas also, withdrew from fellowship with the Gentiles, and by so doing virtually denied his experience in the house of Cornelius, and his testimony at the Conference. This was a serious matter, and because of its possible consequences far and wide, Paul felt compelled to deal with it. This he did by publicly rebuking Peter for his inconsistency. He said, in effect:

> 'If you, being a born Jew are living Gentile fashion and not Jew fashion, how can you try to compel the Gentiles to Judaise?'

The logic of this left no room for escape, and evidently Peter did not try to escape, and 'the best proof that he regretted his weakness, and was too noble-hearted to bear any grudge, is seen in the terms of honour and affection in which he speaks of Paul and his Epistles' (2 Peter iii. 15. Farrar).

The moral strength of Paul was seen in this action of his. Peter was one of Christ's intimate friends, and was an apostle before Paul was converted. Also Paul had been Peter's guest for a fortnight not so long before; but from what he believed to be his duty Paul never shrank, and this collision with Peter saved a grave situation.

We are not so sure that Barnabas took it as Peter did. Lightfoot says: 'It may have prepared the way for the dissension between Paul and Barnabas which shortly afterwards led to their separation. From this time forward they never appear again associated together'.

PAUL'S TIRELESS ACTIVITIES

THE SECOND JOURNEY

ACTS xv. 36-xviii. 22

A.D. 50-53—3 Years

PAUL'S SECOND MISSIONARY JOURNEY

Acts xv. 36-xviii. 22

A.D. 50-53. About 3 years

Between the Conference and the New Venture

(xv. 36-39)

THE CONTENTION OF PAUL AND BARNABAS

The First Missionary Journey began in ch. xiii. 4 and ended in ch. xiv. 28. We are told that the returned missionaries *'tarried no little time'* with the disciples at Antioch. During this period the Jerusalem Conference was held (ch. xv. 1-35).

Thereafter Paul proposed a second missionary journey (36), which was begun without delay (40). But between the proposal and the start of the new venture a very sad incident occurred. Paul and Barnabas parted company, men who had known each other for ten years, and had lived and served together for about six of these years; nor did they part company agreeably.

What was the trouble? John Mark. This young man had gone with Paul and Barnabas on the first journey in the capacity of 'attendant' (xiii. 5), or assistant. In exactly what way he assisted them we are not told, but Paul especially would need some one to help him in many ways.

However, when the party reached Perga in Pamphylia, the place of first contact with Asia Minor, *'John departed from them and returned* to Jerusalem' (xiii. 13). This action is reported by Luke as a *withdrawal* (xv. 38), but the word is *apostanta*, apostatised. A terrible thing it is indeed for a young man and a Christian to have that said of him.

Why he left the party is not recorded, but the words *'withdrew'*, and *'went not with them to the work'* definitely denote blame. Perhaps Mark's courage failed him; perhaps there was a change of plan relative to the course they should take; perhaps Mark had more sympathy with Peter's conservatism than with Paul's liberalism; perhaps these, and other things combined, led to his deflection and defection. Anyhow, Mark was wrong (See p. 279).

And now, when Paul proposed a second journey, Barnabas (Col. iv. 10. R.V.) suggested that his cousin Mark should again accompany them. Paul, however, would not have it, and there was 'a sharp contention' (paroxusmos), an angry dispute, a paroxysm between them. This resulted in their parting company, Barnabas taking Mark and going to Cyprus (39, cf. iv. 36), and Paul taking Silas, and going through Syria, Cilicia and Galatia (36, 40, 41).

Here the question will inevitably arise, Which of these two good and great men was right, and which was wrong, in this dispute? Observation, if not experience, should have taught us that in affairs of this sort, rarely is one of the parties altogether wrong, and the other, altogether right; for generally a measure of blame attaches to each, and generally each is contending for a principle. It was so in this case.

Paul owed much to Barnabas (ix. 26, 27), and Barnabas owed much to Paul, and surely they could have come to some amicable arrangement in this matter without quarrelling and separating. Each was contending for something that was worthy. Paul would have Mark know that the work of the Lord must not be treated in that way; and Barnabas, who did not condone Mark's action, wished to give the young man a chance to retrieve his character.

Both these attitudes were worthy. Paul was intense, and Barnabas was kind, and each carried his virtue beyond the line of virtue. There are times when the Barnabas-like should be severe, and there are times when the Paul-like should be tender. No young man should be turned down for one mistake. There was good stuff in Mark, as subsequent events showed.

Chrysostom says that this strife was of great service to Mark, for the sternness of Paul brought a change in his mind, while the kindness of Barnabas suffered him not to feel abandoned. He made good at last, and Paul was reconciled. 'Get Mark, and bring him with you; for he is very useful in serving me' (2 Tim. iv. 11).

As we take leave of this story let us resolve that our tenderness shall not degenerate into softness, nor our severity into harshness.

'Barnabas went his way, and, dissevered from the grandeur and vehemence of Paul, passed into comparative obscurity, in which, so far from sharing the immortal gratitude which embalms the memory of his colleague, his name is never heard again, except in the isolated allusions of the letters of his friend'. (Farrar). (See on Barnabas, p. 276).

PAUL'S SECOND MISSIONARY JOURNEY
(xv. 36-xviii. 22. A.D. 50-53)

There are in this Journey three distinct stages—labours in *Asia Minor*, in *Macedonia*, and in *Achaia*.

The following is an outline of the first of these stages.

THE OUTWARD JOURNEY
(xv. 36—xviii. 17)

THE FIRST STAGE

1. APOSTOLIC LABOURS IN ASIA MINOR (xv. 36-xvi. 10)

   (i) *Contention of Paul with Barnabas* (xv. 36-40 pp. 349, 350)

   (ii) *Confirmation of the Churches in Syria and Cilicia*
   (xv. 41-xvi. 5; Gal. i. 21-23)

   ANTIOCH to TARSUS (not named, but cf. Antioch S. to the
                   ix. 30; xi. 25) Cilician Gates,
                                 about 130 miles

   TARSUS to DERBE (xvi. 1; cf. xiv. 20, 21) From the C.
                                  Gates to Derbe,
                                  about 100 miles

   DERBE to LYSTRA (xvi. 1-5; cf.   D-L, 28-30 miles
                   xiv. 6-20)
       The Call of Timothy (1-3)
       Delivery of the Decrees (4)
       Prosperity of the Churches (5)

   LYSTRA to ICONIUM (not named, but 30-40 miles
                   cf. xv. 36)

   ICONIUM to ANTIOCH P. (not named, 80-85 miles
                   but cf. xv. 36)

   (iii) *Continuation of the Journey into new regions* (xvi. 6-10).
       Through Phrygia and Galatia (6)
       Forbidden Bithynia (7)
       Mysia passed by (8)
       Troas reached (8)
       The Vision at Troas (9, 10)
       TROAS (8-10) (Antioch P. to Troas) 300-400 miles
       Paul's vision and decision

       Note.—THE HOLY SPIRIT (Restraining (6-8))
                                  (Constraining (9, 10))

1. Apostolic Labours in Asia Minor

(xv. 36-xvi. 10)

A GENERAL SURVEY

An examination of Map 20 and the accompanying key will show that the Second Journey embraced *Asia Minor*, and that the European part of the Journey included *Macedonia* and *Achaia*.

This is a great extension of the First Journey, and marks the westernmost limit of Paul's evangelistic tours, unless he went years afterward to Spain (Rom. xv. 24). It was as a prisoner that he worked in Rome (xxviii. 17-31).

GUIDANCE POSITIVE AND NEGATIVE

Paul had said: 'Let us return now and visit the brethren in every city wherein we proclaimed the word of the Lord, and see how they fare' (xv. 36). It was Barnabas he was addressing, and clearly he had in mind the places they both had visited, and in which they had preached on the first missionary journey; perhaps Cyprus, but certainly Pisidian Antioch, Iconium, Lystra, Derbe and Perga. Beyond this there was no plan at the time. But the rupture with Barnabas affected this programme. He and Mark went to Cyprus, and Paul and Silas went by land to Tarsus, and then on to Derbe, Lystra, Iconium, and Antioch in Pisidia.

This fulfilled the projected purpose and from this point Paul, and they who were with him, entered new territory without any definite idea as to where they were to go. It would appear that Paul's idea was to go to Ephesus, the capital of what is here called *Asia* (xvi. 6), but the Spirit prevented him from doing so. He then went North towards *Bithynia* where were a number of flourishing cities—Prusa, Nicaea, Nicomedeia, Chalcedon and Heracleia—but again the Spirit suffered them not to enter (xvi. 7).

Some scholars take the view that the party went to North Galatia, visited the three cities Pessinus, Ancyra, and Tavium, and established churches in these centres, and that it was to these Christians in the North that Paul wrote his Galatian Epistle. Into this discussion we cannot here enter, except to say that, going North from the Pisidian Antioch, he turned either east or west. For the missionaries it must have been a time of much perplexity. We believe that turning west, and passing through *Mysia* without preaching in that province, they journeyed some 200 miles to *Troas* the seaport of Mysia. It was not until they reached this city that they had any clear guidance as to what they should do; the only light they had was on what they should *not* do.

The path of Christian service is not always clear, and sometimes Christ's messengers are confronted with closed doors. At such times we should recognise that guidance can be negative as well as positive; and if our only will is to do God's will, light will break on our path, and we shall see what His plan for us is. It is well for us that the Spirit both restrains and constrains.

From this general view of the journey from Syrian Antioch to Troas, a distance of 800-900 miles (to which about 360 must be added if the missionaries traversed North Galatia), let us go back to consider some important details in the first part of the journey.

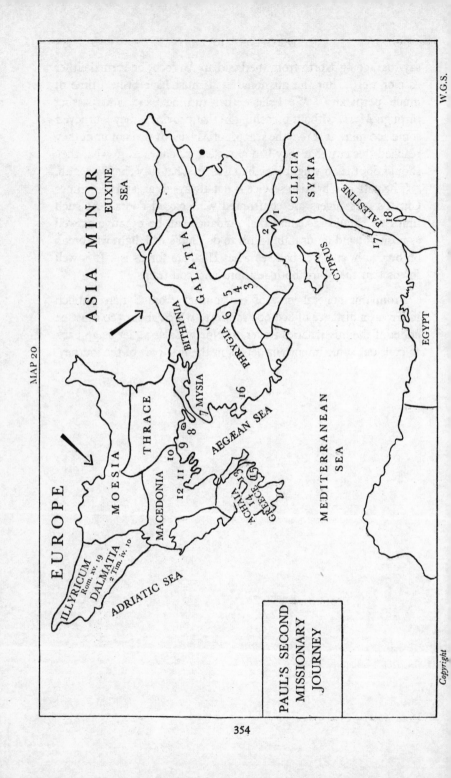

MAP 20

W.G.S.

EUROPE

ASIA MINOR

EUXINE
SEA

ILLYRICUM
Rom. xv. 19

DALMATIA
2 Tim. iv. 10

MOESIA

THRACE

MACEDONIA

BITHYNIA

GALATIA

PHRYGIA

MYSIA

CILICIA
SYRIA

PALESTINE

CYPRUS

ADRIATIC SEA

ACHAIA
GREECE

AEGÆAN SEA

MEDITERRANEAN
SEA

EGYPT

PAUL'S SECOND
MISSIONARY
JOURNEY

Copyright

KEY TO MAP 20

Paul's Second Missionary Journey

From	1.	Antioch (S)	xv. 35, 36	**Outward**
Through		Syria	xv. 41	1. Apostolic Labours
		Cilicia		in Asia Minor
To	2.	(Tarsus)	xv. 41	(xv. 36-xvi. 10)
	3.	Derbe	xvi. 1	
	4.	Lystra	xvi. 1	
	5.	(Iconium)	xv. 36.	
			xvi. 4	
	6.	(Antioch (P))	xv. 36	
			xvi. 9	
Through		Phrygia	xvi. 6	
		Galatia	xvi. 6	
By-Passing		Mysia	xvi. 7, 8	
		Bithynia	xvi. 7, 8	
To	7.	Troas	xvi. 8	
	8.	Samothrace	xvi. 11	2. Apostolic Labours
	9.	Neapolis	xvi. 11	in Macedonia
	10.	Philippi	xvi. 12	(xvi. 11-xvii. 14)
Passed		Amphipolis	xvii. 1	
Through		Apollonia	xvii. 1	
To	11.	Thessalonica	xvii. 1	
	12.	Beroea	xvii. 10	
	13.	Athens	xvii. 15	3. Apostolic Labours
	14.	Corinth	xviii. 1	in Achaia
				(xvii. 15-
	15.	Cenchreae	xviii. 18	**Inward**
	16.	Ephesus	xviii. 19	
	17.	Caesarea	xviii. 22	
	18.	Jerusalem	xviii. 22	
	1.	Antioch (S)	xviii. 22	

The cities in capitals are those of chief importance.
The cities in brackets are not named in the text, but must have been visited.
The references are to the Book of the Acts.

Some Details of Importance

Paul said: 'Let us return now and visit the brethren in every city wherein we proclaimed the word of the Lord, and see how they fare' (xv. 36). This is an echo of the word in the Song (vii. 12): 'Come, let us get up early to the vineyards; let us see if the vine flourish'.

Never were converts more dear to a pastor than Paul's were to him. His yearning instincts were great (1 Thess. ii. 17; iii. 10. Rom. i. 11; xv. 23).

Silas

Paul had lost two of his companions; first Mark, and then
Barnabas, and it was necessary for him to find substitutes. To
take the place of Barnabas he chose Silas. He was a recognised
prophet of Jerusalem and Antioch (xv. 22, 32), and there is some
ground for thinking that, like Paul, he was a Roman citizen
(xvi. 37). He was, therefore, eminently fitted for work in the
Roman Empire. References to him, other than in the Acts, are
in 2 Cor. i. 19. 1 Thess, i. 1. 2 Thess. i. 1. 1 Pet. v. 12. In the
Acts nothing is said of him until Philippi is reached, and there he
and Paul were beaten and imprisoned. He shared the Apostle's
ministry and sufferings in Macedonia and Achaia, and then he
drops out of Luke's story.

Tarsus

As the Decrees were not for Antioch only, but also for Gentile
Christians in Syria and Cilicia (xv. 23), Paul and Silas went
overland from Antioch to Tarsus, a distance of about 130 miles.
Here the Apostle was on familiar ground, for not only was Tarsus
his home town (xxii. 3), but three years after his conversion,
because of a plot in Jerusalem to kill him, fellow-believers sent
him out and off to Tarsus (ix. 30), and he was in those parts
evangelizing until Barnabas went thither from Antioch to persuade him to return with him to that capital of Gentile Christianity
(xi. 25, 26). This must have been a period of about four years
(A.D. 40-44), during which he was founding the churches referred
to in chapter xv. 23; and it may be that some of the sufferings
spoken of in 2 Cor. xi. 24-26 were endured at this time.

How precious would have been a record of these years, but we
are told only that there were Christian assemblies in these provinces, which now Paul and Silas visited, proclaiming the verdict
of the Jerusalem Conference, and, without doubt, widely preaching the Gospel.

Derbe

We are told that Paul planned to revisit the towns in which he
had ministered twice in his first missionary journey—Derbe,
Lystra, Iconium, and Pisidian Antioch, only this time he would

approach them from the east. To do this it is practically certain that he crossed the Taurus mountains by the Cilician Gates, and thence to Derbe, about 120-160 miles distant from Tarsus. The visit to the Church there was brief and uneventful, but Luke has something to say about Paul's return to

Lystra

It was there that he had healed a cripple; that he had been regarded by the heathen as an incarnate god; that he had made a restraining declaration; that he had been stoned; and that he had met the Jewesses Lois and Eunice, and the latter's son Timothy. This household he must have led to Christ, and, naturally, he would look forward to meeting them again, and probably they gave him and Silas hospitality. No doubt, also, they would want to know why Barnabas was not with him.

The event on which Luke concentrates relates to Timothy (xvi. 1-3), so here let us look at this young man's history.

Timothy

Viewing comprehensively all that is said about Timothy in the Acts and Epistles we may be left somewhat perplexed, because there are suggestions here and there that he had weak points of character—petulance, irritability, shyness, nervousness, a want of firmness, and doubtful courage. But it will be well for us to begin our consideration of him from another angle, that of Paul's estimate of him, assuming that Paul was a man of the highest ideals, and a great discerner of character.

What Paul thought of Timothy

It is not an exaggeration to say that Paul said more about this young man than about any other of his many friends and followers. Here are some of his expressions:

Timothy was 'like-minded' with himself; 'as a son with his father, he served with me in the Gospel'; 'minister of God'; 'fellow-labourer in the Gospel of Christ'; 'brother'; 'my beloved son'; 'faithful in the Lord'; 'my fellow-worker'; and 'my own son in the faith'.

These are striking expressions coming from such a quarter, and they are the more impressive when we find that Paul never rebuked Timothy as he had done Barnabas and Peter, and in the two letters he wrote to him he only hinted at certain possible defects. It may be said that Timothy did not reach the loftiest heights, but at any rate he left the valleys far behind.

> I know how far high failure overlaps
> The bound of low successes.   (Lewis Morris).

With this estimate of Timothy in our minds let us trace the story which the records supply.

Timothy's Home and Upbringing

On Paul's first missionary journey he went to Lystra, a purely heathen city, and the people who at first thought that he was a god eventually stoned him and left him for dead outside the city boundary And the record says:

'As the disciples stood round about him, he rose up, and entered into the city; and on the morrow he went forth with Barnabas to Derbe' (xiv. 20). Who were *the disciples*? We are not told, but we know that two Jewish women and the son of one of them lived there, Lois, Eunice, and Timothy, and it is not unlikely that the missionaries lodged with them on their visits outward and inward on that journey (xiv. 6. 21).

On the second missionary journey Paul again went to Lystra, and Luke tells us only one thing about the visit, and that relates to this Jewish household (xvi. 1-3). Eunice had married a Greek who, at this time, was dead, and she and her mother resolved that the boy should be brought up in the religion of the Jews as that was revealed in their Bible, the Old Testament, and they did this to good effect (2 Tim. i. 5).

It seems clear that Paul's preaching gave to this family a new understanding of their own Scriptures, so that instead of looking for the Messiah to come they realized that in Jesus of Nazareth He had already come, and this belief led them from Judaism to Christianity, and so they became *disciples*.

The influence of godly mothers upon their offspring is one of the richest things in human history. Think of what Susanna was

to John Wesley; what Mrs. Ruskin was to her son John; what
Margaret Ogilvy was to J. M. Barrie; what Mrs. Carlyle was to
Thomas; what Mrs. Smith was to her Gipsy Rodney; and what,
ultimately, Augustine's mother Monica was to him. The lack
of such women to-day goes far to account for the things in society
which we deplore.

A Young Missionary Recruit

When Paul first visited Lystra in A.D. 47-48, Timothy would
have been fifteen or sixteen years of age, for about twenty years
later he was still spoken of as young (1 Tim. iv. 12). From three
to four years later, when Paul was again in the city, Timothy
must have been bordering on twenty, yet, at that early age he
had been evangelizing, and 'was well reported of by the brethren
that were at Lystra and Iconium' (xvi. 2).

Silas had taken the place of Barnabas, but no one had taken
Mark's place, and Paul badly needed some young fellow to
whom he could turn for anything he wanted, and who would be
his understudy in the work which lay before him. For a year or
two he must have had Timothy in mind, so that at this time,
A.D. 51, it is not surprising to read: 'him would Paul have to go
forth with him' (xvi. 3). It is not difficult to imagine with what
mingled feelings Eunice learned of Paul's desire. It must have
gladdened her heart to see this fruit of her devout labours,
and yet there must have been a pang at the thought of losing him,
and we do not know that she ever saw him again. Constitutionally
Timothy was not strong (1 Tim. v. 23), and, having witnessed
the stoning of Paul, this loving mother could well imagine what
sufferings might await her boy in years to come; but when Paul
and Silas left Lystra Timothy went with them.

Timothy is Circumcised

In Acts xvi. 4 we read that as the missionaries 'went on their
way through the cities, they delivered them the decrees for to
keep, which had been ordained of the apostles and elders that were
at Jerusalem'. One term of this document was to the effect that it
was not necessary for Gentile believers to be circumcised (xv.
5. 19), and, according to one interpretation of Gal. ii. 3, Paul

had refused to circumcise Titus, who was a Greek. We can understand, that Paul exposed himself to the charge of inconsistency by circumcising Timothy.

But the cases were not the same. Titus was a pure Greek, but Timothy was half Greek and half Jew, and as frequently he would have to minister to Jews, Paul knew that he would not be acceptable to these if he remained uncircumcised. The decision of the Conference at Jerusalem had in mind Gentiles only, and Timothy was not a Gentile only. On grounds of expediency as well as of charity, when the sacrifice of principle was not involved, Paul was ready to become 'all things to all men' (1 Cor. ix. 20-23).

The Ministry of Timothy

We have not a complete record of this for there are gaps in the story unaccounted for. He does not appear in the inward part of Paul's second missionary journey; nor in the unhappy events which took place on Paul's arrival in Jerusalem at the end of his third journey; nor during the Apostle's imprisonment in Caesarea; nor on the voyage from Caesarea to Rome; but both before and after these events Timothy is seen to be responsibly engaged in the work of the Lord in Philippi, at Thessalonica, at Corinth, and at Ephesus.

After Paul's release from his first Roman imprisonment Timothy was with him; and when the end of his second imprisonment drew near he wrote and asked his young colleague to come to him quickly (2 Tim. iv. 9), for the veteran missionary knew that his martyrdom was at hand, and he wanted his dearest friend to be with him. Whether or not he arrived in time we cannot say, but Macduff in his *St. Paul in Rome* says:

'In the Church of San Paolo at Rome a gorgeous baldacchino surmounts the traditional tomb of Paul the Apostle. In immediate juxtaposition with it, in front of the high altar, is a shrine of more modest pretensions, on which is inscribed the one name, which tells its own touching story—

TIMOTHEI

Here the ashes of Timothy are said to rest. Strong is the temptation, for once, not too exactingly to demand and scrutinise authority for the truth of a legend in itself so beautiful, that these two honoured servants of Christ, who had loved and laboured, wept and prayed, sorrowed and rejoiced together, are now resting side by side, a true 'family burying-place', the father and his 'own son in the faith'.

Timothy and the Epistles

There are six Epistles in which Timothy's name is coupled with Paul's so closely in the opening sentence that he seems almost identified rather than associated with him; and of the only four letters which the Apostle wrote to individuals, two are to Timothy. These letters are very personal and intimate, and show us how strong was the bond which bound these two men together.

Timothy Exhorted

Dean Howson has spoken of Timothy as 'a character which is among the most faultless and charming in the Bible', but this surely is an exaggeration. Exhortations invariably indicate the need of them, and may well suggest weaknesses which should be watched and checked. There are not a few such exhortations in Paul's two letters to his young friend. He says:

> 'War a good warfare; Let no man despise thy youth; Give attendance to reading; Neglect not the Gift that is in thee; Take heed to thyself, and to thy teaching; Observe—things without prejudice, doing nothing by partiality; Keep thyself pure; Keep the commandment without spot, without reproach; Guard that which I committed unto thee; Be not ashamed; Suffer hardship; Hold the pattern of sound words; Consider what I say; Give diligence to present thyself approved unto God; Shun profane babblings; Flee youthful lusts; Foolish and ignorant questionings refuse; I charge thee.'

Let us remember that these exhortations were given, not when Timothy started out on his missionary career, but after he had been in it for sixteen years or more. We cannot imagine Paul saying or writing such things to Barnabas, or Silas. Yet every minister needs such reminders.

Troas

No details are given of the return to Iconium and Antioch, though we know that Paul and Silas went there (xv. 36). The probable and the certain details of the journey between Antioch and Troas are referred to on pp. 352, 353, but here the story again becomes definite (xvi. 8-10).

Paul often went over classic ground, but he has nothing to say about events and alleged happenings of times long since past. He may have walked over the site of ancient Troy, but if he thought of the immortal *Iliad* he makes no reference to it. His mind was full of other things.

Standing on the western verge of the Orient and looking towards Greece and Rome, his missionary heart must have been filled with longing to proclaim the Gospel to heathen multitudes. Troas itself was full of peoples of many nations, and what Paul saw and heard must have stirred his imagination. Tired, he fell asleep, and as in the case of Peter before him (chapter x), he had a vision and heard a voice. A Macedonian stood before him and said: 'Come over into Macedonia and help *us*'. 'It was the cry of Europe for Christ'. Paul and those with him had no difficulty in discerning that this was an indication of God's will for them, and so, without preaching in Troas, they boarded the next boat going West.

'*Luke, The Beloved*'

A matter of great importance emerges here. In xvi. 6-8 the third person plural is used by the historian, but from verse 10, the first person plural: 'we sought', 'we made a straight course'; 'we were in this city', *et. al.* The historian, who was Luke, now includes himself; he has become a member of the party, and, with but few breaks, he is the Apostle's companion to the end. From this point on, the record has what are known as 'we' passages which indicate the presence of Luke. They are xvi. 10-17; xx. 5-16; xxi. 1-18; xxvii. 1; and xxviii. 16; but we know that later than the date of the last chapter of the Acts (A.D. 63) Luke was with Paul, for it was in A.D. 67 or 68 that he wrote 'Only Luke is with me' (2 Tim. iv. 11).

We are not to suppose that Paul met Luke for the first time at Troas, for on several previous occasions there have been indications of his presence, but surely we are not wrong in thinking that it was at Troas that this good and gifted man definitely joined the party, and became the historian of the Church's first great missionary enterprise, as well as the author of the Gospel of the Messiah the Redeemer.

All that Luke meant to Paul we can never know. They were more of an age than were the Apostle and Timothy, and, unlike Timothy, Luke was highly cultured. Also his profession must often have come to the aid of Paul, who speaks of him as 'the beloved *physician*' (Col. iv. 14).

This was Paul's first visit to Troas, but not his last. He had there a friend, and probably a convert, in Carpus who later was to be his host (2 Tim. iv. 13).

As we hnve contemplated the second missionary journey so far, two lessons, at least, press themselves upon our attention.

1. What has been secured must be safeguarded. It was not enough for the Apostle to make converts; these must be instructed and protected. Their conversion was a foundation, and this was of no use without a superstructure. Paul's converts were organized in churches, and leaders were appointed for counsel and guidance. For want of such help many converts, through the centuries, must have relapsed into indifference and godlessness. The born must be bred. Where there is life there must be means of growth. Paul's yearning for those whom he led to Christ was as a mother's for her children. So must it be still. When there is no *follow-up* work, as we call it, there is bound to be waste, and worse.

Paul said: 'Let us go back . . . to see how they are doing' (xv. 36). Babes must be nourished, and children must be taught.

2. The second lesson relates to guidance.

What constitutes guidance it is not easy to say. Many have claimed guidance for what in reality was wilfulness or prejudice; and others have failed to see guidance where it really existed. The experience of Paul between Antioch in Pisidia and Troas makes it clear that the Holy Spirit both restrains and constrains; he prevents and compels.

Why should Paul not have entered Bithynia? We have not all the answers to this question, but surely one of them is to be

found in 1 Peter i. 1. And further, had Paul evangelized in
Pontus, Bithynia, and Mysia, is it not probable that he would
not have gone to Europe, at any rate at that time? If we are
really subject to God's will it is safe to believe that He is guiding us
when least we are conscious of it.

> So long Thy power hath blest me,
> Sure it still will lead me on.

Now follows the second movement in Paul's Second Missionary Journey, the move to Europe. The following is an outline of
it.

THE SECOND STAGE

2. APOSTOLIC LABOURS IN MACEDONIA (xvi. 11-xvii. 14)

TROAS (11). Port of embarkation from Asia Minor to
Europe. Paul, Silas, Luke, and Timothy board a
ship.

SAMOTHRACE (11). A large island in the Aegæan Sea,
off the coast of Thrace, between Troas and Neapolis.

NEAPOLIS (11). New Town. In Thrace. Sea Port
of Macedonia. Europe.

Troas to Neapolis about   125 miles

PHILIPPI (xvi. 12-40). From Neapolis   8-10 miles
Paul's first contact with Europe.

   (i) A Sabbath prayer-meeting by a river (12, 13).
On the Sabbath the company attend 'a place
of prayer' (*proseuchē*) 'by a river', the Gangites,
where a few women were assembled, with
whom the missionaries had conversation.

  (ii) Conversion and baptism of Lydia (14, 15*a*)

 (iii) The missionaries are given hospitality in
Lydia's house (15*b*)

 (iv) Healing of a Pythoness (16-18)

  (v) The arrest, flogging, and imprisonment of
Paul and Silas (19-24; 1 Thess. ii. 2)

 (vi) The midnight earthquake (25, 26)

(vii) Conversion and baptism of the jailor and his
household (27-34)

(viii) Departure of the missionaries from prison and
the city (35-40)

(Luke left behind. Third person resumed in xvii. 1)

AMPHIPOLIS (xvii. 1)   From Philippi   33 miles
 (*amphi-polis*=around the city, because the
 river Strymon flowed almost round the town)

APOLLONIA (xvii. 1)   From Amphipolis 30 miles

THESSALONICA (xvii. 1-9) From Apollonia 37 miles
Capital of Roman province of Macedonia.

 (i) Paul's ministry inside and outside the synagogue (1-5*a*)
  (*a*) Duration of it (2)
     (probably months: cf. 1 Thess.;
      Phil. iv. 16)
  (*b*) Subject of it (3)
    (the Lord's Return: 1-2 Thess.)
  (*c*) Effect of it (4, 5)
    (1) Upon the Gentiles (4)
    (2) Upon the Jews (5)

Distinguished converts: Aristarchus, Gaius, and
Secundus (xix. 29; xx. 4; xxvii. 2; Col. iv. 10;
Phile. 24)

Luke's record of the ministry in Thessalonica is
supplemented in many important respects in Paul's
two Letters to the Church there, written within a year
after his departure, and also from Phil. iv. 16.

 (ii) The assault upon Jason (5*b*-9)

  (*a*) The charges made (5*b*-7)
    (1) Harbouring the Missionaries (7*a*)
    (2) Treason against the Emperor (6, 7)

  (*b*) The decision reached (8, 9)

BEROEA (xvii. 10-14) From Thessalonica about 50 miles
 (i) Success of the ministry in the synagogue
  (10-12)

 (ii) Jews from Thessalonica create trouble (13)

 (iii) Paul sent away. Silas and Timothy remain
  (14)

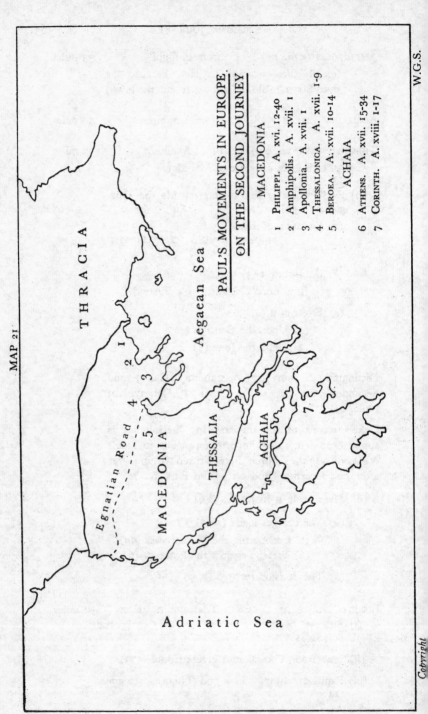

MAP 21

Copyright

W.G.S.

PAUL'S MOVEMENTS IN EUROPE
ON THE SECOND JOURNEY

MACEDONIA

1 PHILIPPI.   A. xvi. 12-40
2 AMPHIPOLIS.   A. xvii. 1
3 APOLLONIA.   A. xvii. 1
4 THESSALONICA. A. xvii. 1-9
5 BEROEA.   A. xvii. 10-14

ACHAIA

6 ATHENS.   A. xvii. 15-34
7 CORINTH.   A. xviii. 1-17

THRACIA

Aegaean Sea

Egnatian Road

MACEDONIA

THESSALIA

ACHAIA

Adriatic Sea

2. Apostolic Labours in Macedonia
(xvi. 11-xvii. 14)

Across the Aegaean (xvi. 8-11)

It must have been a thrilling moment for Paul when he with Silas, and Timothy, and Luke boarded the boat which, crossing the Aegaean Sea, was to take him to the great unknown world of the West. The 125 miles from Troas to Neapolis was accomplished in two days, a night being spent in the harbour of Samothrace. And it must have been a moment equally thrilling when Paul, and the others, stepped ashore at Neapolis, the port of Philippi; the East behind him, and the West before him. He knew what he had suffered, but little did he know what was to come. He had had wonderful triumphs in the past fifteen years of his converted life, but greater triumphs awaited him in the next fifteen years. Crossing the Aegaean was a crisis in Paul's life, but it was also a crisis in the progress of Christianity in the world.

Macedonia

Before proceeding to the details of Paul's ministry in Macedonia a word must be said about the province as a whole. A map should be before the reader. (Map 20, p. 354).

The Province was intersected by two great rivers, the Axius and the Strymon, and these determined its division into four districts, as Conybeare and Howson have shown. *Macedonia Prima* was the region east of the Strymon, of which Amphipolis was the capital; *Macedonia Secunda* lay between the Strymon and the Axius, and Thessalonica was its metropolis; and the other two regions were situated to the South towards Thessaly, and on the mountains to the west. *Macedonia Tertia* was between the Axius and the Peneus, with Pella—the birthplace of Alexander the Great—for its capital; and *Macedonia Quarta* had Pelagonia for its capital. Eventually the whole of Macedonia was made one province under the jurisdiction of a proconsul, who resided at Thessalonica, and it included Thessaly.

When the missionaries set foot on European soil at Neapolis they proceeded at once to Philippi.

The journey from Neapolis to Philippi, about ten miles inland, which would have been made on foot, presented a magnificent view of mountain, sea, and plain, but these men were not tourists, but Christian missionaries, who were going to the chief city of the district, not like Caesar and Antony to fight and conquer Cassius and Brutus, but, with the Gospel, to challenge paganism in its many forms, and not without success.

Philippi

(xvi. 12-40. 'Philippians')

Its Importance in History

This is a name of major importance in the Christian story: because it was the first place in Europe to which Paul and his party took the Gospel; because there he made his first convert in Europe; because there he and Silas were flogged and imprisoned, resulting from which their jailor and his household were converted; because of Luke's connection with the city and the Church there; because only the Philippian Church gave Paul financial help; and because he wrote to the Church there one of his most intimate and moving letters.

These facts are of far greater importance than the connection of Philip, Alexander's father, and of Augustus with the city, and than the fact that nearby had been profitable gold mines. Heaven's and earth's views of history can never be harmonized.

By the River (xvi. 13)

The population of Philippi was made up of native Macedonians, Roman colonists, an admixture of Orientals, and a few Jews. That the Jews were few in number is reflected in the fact that there was no synagogue in the city, and this accounts for the fact that on Sabbath mornings a meeting for worship was held by a river outside the town. Luke must have known of this, and probably it was he who took Paul, Silas, and Timothy thither on their first Sabbath in Philippi.

Paul's First Converts in Europe (xvi. 13-15)

It appears that only women were at the prayer meeting by the river, and Luke's record concentrates on one of them, whose name was *Lydia*. It would seem that she was not a Jewess but a 'God-fearer', and, therefore, devout. Her native town was Thyatira, in western Asia Minor (Rev. ii. 18-29), which was celebrated for its purple-dyeing. The sale of purple fabrics was Lydia's business in Philippi, and by this pursuit she was well-to-do, having a 'household', and was able to accommodate the four missionaries.

From paganism she had found a measure of satisfaction in Judaism, but her heart was still hungry, and when she heard Paul's Gospel she let the Lord open her heart, and she became a Christian and was baptized in the river, as were the members of her household who also believed and received the Good News. Was Lydia the true 'yoke-fellow' of Phil. iv. 3?

A 'Python' Expelled (xvi. 16-18)

The following statement by Marvin R. Vincent illumines these verses.

'"*A spirit, a Python.*" Python, in the Greek mythology, was the serpent which guarded Delphi. According to the legend, as related in the Homeric hymn, Apollo descended from Olympus in order to select a site for his shrine and oracle. Having fixed upon a spot on the southern side of Mount Parnassus, he found it guarded by a vast and terrific serpent, which he slew with an arrow, and suffered its body to rot (*puthein*) in the sun. Hence the name of the serpent *Python* (rotting); *Pytho*, the name of the place, and the epithet *Pythian*, applied to Apollo.

'The name *Python* was subsequently used to denote a prophetic *demon*, and was also used of *soothsayers* who practised *ventriloquism*, or speaking from the belly. The word *eggastrimuthos*, *ventriloquist*, occurs in the Septuagint, and is rendered *having a familiar spirit* (Lev. xix. 31; xx. 6, 27; 1 Sam. xxviii. 7, 8).

'The heathen inhabitants of Philippi regarded the woman as inspired by Apollo; and Luke, in recording this case, which came under his own observation, uses the term which would naturally suggest itself to a Greek physician, a *Python-spirit*, presenting phenomena identical with the convulsive movements and wild cries of the Pythian priestess of Delphi.'

Flogged and Gaoled (xvi. 19-24)

The heathen in Philippi were indifferent to the missionaries until their pockets were touched, and then they rose to action. On reading this account one cannot but wonder, on the one hand, that Silas was arrested, as it was Paul only who exorcised the demon, and, on the other hand, why Luke and Timothy were not arrested, as they were of the party. The indictment had little to do with the immediate circumstance but it served the purpose of the complainants. The proceedings were brief, and the results were brutal. The two missionaries were *stripped* in public, a shocking indignity; then they were *beaten* on the spot— one of three beatings which Paul suffered (2 Cor. xi. 25); and finally, with blood-stained backs, they were put into an inner prison cell, a dungeon, and their feet were put in the stocks, a wholly unnecessary refinement of cruelty, truly a terrible experience.

Why did they not claim their Roman citizenship? Perhaps they did, and were unheard in the tumult. Could Luke, Lydia, and Timothy do nothing about it?

God Acts (xvi. 25-34)

Nature is at God's disposal, and He has often used it in a crisis (cf. iv. 31). These verses (25-34) record an amazing event, or, rather, series of events!

The beaten missionaries prayed and sang at midnight (what would they sing?), and the other prisoners listened to them. A sudden great earthquake shook everything loose and open. The awakened governor of the prison, supposing that his charges had escaped, was about to commit suicide, but Paul reassured him. He, panic-stricken, brought out the two men, and asked them what he was to do to be saved (spiritually); and there, in the middle of the night, cold and sore, they preached the Gospel to him and his household, warders, slaves, and family, and they believed. The jailor bathed the wounds of Paul and Silas who then baptised them all, probably at the prison well or fountain. The governor then took the missionaries 'up into his house, and set a table before them, and rejoiced greatly, with all his house, having believed in God'.

It is reasonable to believe that the earthquake was regarded as a judgment for the gross injustice done to Paul and Silas.

We must linger a little longer with this great story.

Prison, midnight, wounds, songs, earthquake, fear, contemplated suicide, conviction, inquiry, the Gospel, faith, kindness, confession, joy, remonstrance, release, consolation; these are the notes of the story.

Suffering and Song

No suffering can still the Christian's song, and no night can hide his light. Christians are still singing their song in the night. These prisoners had an impromptu and free concert. Perhaps Paul would sing the 'air', and Silas, the 'part'. I wonder if it was a psalm they sang?

A Fruitful Earthquake

Well, there was a quake in the prison, and then in comes the jailor, but both were righted. Instead of the jailor keeping the prisoners, the prisoners saved the jailor (27, 28). 'He called for a light', and he needed it badly. He might have had it earlier, for Christians 'are the light of the world'. Some people never think about salvation until they are threatened by death (30). Here is the simplest expression of the Gospel (31). A Christian service is held on the spot (32), and everybody is 'washed', the stripes of the missionaries, and the sins of the jailor and his family (33). Look at these prisoners and their keeper having a gladsome and believing time together over a meal! (34). The change in the jailor expressed itself at once in love and joy, and Paul has told us that these are part of the 'fruit of the Spirit' (Gal. v. 22). Modernism has no such tale to tell.

Magistrates are Humbled.

When day dawned the rest of the drama unfolded itself. The authorities, who had heard the news, said that the prisoners might go (35, 36). But Paul said in effect, 'not at all; let them sup their own brew; they have humbled us, now they shall humble themselves; they attended personally to our degradation, and they shall attend personally to our vindication.' And they did (37-39). Mark the contrasts here (37, 20): 'publicly, privately,' 'cast out, conducted out,' and 'Jews, Romans.'

Because we are Christians, we are not to be soft. There is a meekness which is weakness. There should be iron in the Christian's blood. Don't be supine, but strong. 'Stone walls do not a prison make.'

Four Points

Was the Philippian jailor Epaphroditus? (Phil. ii. 25-30). The Christian Church had begun to meet in the house of Lydia (40), Luke says, 'they' departed (40), making it clear that he did not go with them.

Of the places visited so far by the Apostle, Philippi is the first named to which, later on, a letter was sent.

Amphipolis and Apollonia
(xvii. 1)

Paul's next place of ministry was to be Thessalonica, 100 miles S.W. from Philippi, but two places are mentioned which lay on his route, at each of which the party must have spent one night or longer, but in neither of which was the Gospel preached.

Amphipolis, so named because the river Strymon almost surrounded the city (*amphi-polis*), was 33 miles from Philippi. Herodotus tells us it was here that Xerxes crossed the Strymon, and offered a sacrifice of white horses to the river, and buried alive nine youths and maidens (Herod. vii. 114).

Apollonia, 30 miles distant from Amphipolis, was a place without distinction, except for the facts that not far from it were the birth-place of Aristotle, and the tomb of Euripides.

Probably it was because in these two places there were few Jews and no synagogue that Paul and his companions passed them by without preaching (for though Paul was the apostle to the Gentiles, it was his habit first of all to make contact with the Jews). Local conditions and Divine guidance interlocked to determine their course of action.

Thessalonica

The importance of Paul's visit to and ministry in this city makes it difficult to restrict oneself to severe limits of space such as are here necessary.

The City

Thessalonica was at one time called Thermae from the hot salt springs in the neighbourhood, but Cassander, one of Alexander's generals changed the name to Thessalonica in honour of his wife, a daughter of Philip and a sister of Alexander, whose name this was. It was the most populous of all the towns of Macedonia, and the capital of the whole province. It is still a large and prosperous city, called Salonica. In the middle of the 19th century it was estimated that 35,000 of its inhabitants were Jews, half the whole population at that time, and in 1940 its population was reckoned to be 226,147. In 1941 of the Second Great War the Germans took Salonica, and later it was liberated. We should remember these details of a very notable city. Thessalonica, Corinth, and Ephesus were flourishing commercial cities, and because of its situation Thessalonica's imports and exports were abundant. It was a 'free city,' and its magistrates were *Politarchs*, i.e. City-rulers (xvii. 6, 8).

The Missionaries

Having walked the 37 miles from Apollonia to Thessalonica, Paul, Silas and Timothy went, it would appear, to the Jewish quarter of the city, and became the guests of a fellow-countryman whose Greek name was Jason (xvii. 5, 7). For three Sabbaths Paul attended the synagogue, and on each occasion he accepted the invitation, usually given, to address the congregation. '*Three Sabbaths*' may mean 'three weeks', and this would imply that he attended the Monday and Thursday services between the Sabbaths, that is, that he conducted a three weeks' mission in the city. It must not be supposed from this statement that the Apostle was in Thessalonica for three weeks only. Supplementary details given in his letters to the Thessalonians, together with the fact that on two occasions, at least, he received a gift of money from the Church at Philippi, 100 miles distant, (Phil. iv. 16) require more time than 'three weeks' allow. The mention of this brief period of ministry in the synagogue may well imply that at its close, on account of the attitude of the Jews, he turned to the Gentiles, as he had done in other places. At Ephesus, after addressing himself to the Jews for three months, the Apostle left them, and continued to work outside for two years (xix. 8-10. cf. xiii. 45-48).

It is probable that the evangelizing party was here for some months.

Paul's Teaching

Here we must recognize two ministries, and not one only. There was, first of all, the ministry to the Jews and those who frequented the synagogue (xvii. 2-4); and then, the ministry to the Gentiles outside the synagogue, for the details of which we must go to the Thessalonian letters.

(a) THE JEWISH MINISTRY (xvii. 2-4)

Both the matter and the method of this are stated with precision.

> Paul 'argued with them from the Scriptures, explaining and proving that it was necessary for the Christ to suffer and to rise from the dead, and saying, "this Jesus, whom I proclaim to you is the Christ".'

Every word of this statement is heavy with meaning.

As to the Apostle's *method*, '*he reasoned from the Scriptures, opening and proving*' (xvii. 2, 3). Each of these four words is important. (1) The *graphōn* refer to the Old Testament, which was, and is, the Jews' Bible. Paul's ministry everywhere was essentially biblical. (2) By '*reasoned*' is meant *debated*, or *argued*, from which comes our word *dialectic*, the investigation of truth by argument. This is the first occurrence of the word in the Acts (cf. xvii. 17; xviii. 4. 19; xix. 8, 9; xx. 7, 9). The Christian Gospel—there is no other—is not *unreasonable*. (3) By '*opening*' is meant *to make plain, to open fully*, and is used with reference to the ears (Mark vii. 34), the eyes (Luke xxiv. 31), the heart (Acts xvi. 14), and the Scriptures (Acts xvii. 3). (4) '*Proving*' means setting forth alongside one another the Scriptures showing the relation of various parts.

The Apostle's entire argument was, as ever, based on the Bible, and in this he followed his Master (1 Cor. xv. 3, 4; Luke xxiv. 46). As to his *matter*, his subject was *The Messiah*, and about Him Paul had three things to say. First, that He who was foretold in prophecy was to be *a suffering Messiah*; secondly, that this Messiah *would die and be raised from the dead*; and thirdly, that this suffering, dead and risen Messiah was *Jesus of Nazareth*. The first two points rested on the Scriptures, and the third, on the preacher's experience.

What the result was of this teaching we are told in xvii. 4. A few Jews believed; a great multitude of 'God-fearers' among the Gentiles; and not a few women of high rank in the city.

(b) THE GENTILE MINISTRY
(1-2 Thessalonians)

It seems clear that a considerable interval must be allowed for between verses 4 and 5 of chapter xvii, the evidence of which will be found in Paul's letters to the Thessalonian Church which was predominantly Gentile. When, because of the hostility of the Jews, Paul transferred his ministry from Jews to Gentiles (cf. xiii. 45-48), his presentation of the truth changed. The Old Testament argument would be of no use among Gentiles, and it should be noticed that there is no reference to the Old Testament in either of the Thessalonian letters, and other subjects were the substance of his teaching among the heathen. Luke says nothing about this, but in 1-2 *Thessalonians* Paul frequently refers to what he had taught these Gentiles.

'Our gospel came unto you in power' (1. 5).

'Ye know our entering in unto you . . . to speak unto you the Gospel of God' (ii. 1, 2).

'Exhorting you, and encouraging, and testifying' (ii. 11).

'Yourselves know that hereunto (afflictions) we are appointed. For verily, when we were with you, we told you beforehand that we are to suffer affliction' (iii. 3, 4).

'Ye received of us how ye ought to walk and to please God' (iv. 1).

'We forewarned you and testified' (iv. 6).

'Yourselves know perfectly that the day of the Lord so cometh as a thief in the night' (v. 2).

'Stand fast, and hold the traditions which ye were taught, whether by word, or by epistle of ours' (II. ii. 15).

'Remember ye not, that, when I was yet with you, I told you these things?' (ii. 5).

Among other themes Paul gave the Thessalonians instruction on the Second Coming, the Kingdom of God, social purity, and daily industry, and in this last, he set them an example by earning his living at tent-making. For these various subjects see:

I. iv. 13-v. 11.   II. i. 7-10; ii. 1-12.   I. ii. 12.   II. 1. 5:
I. iv. 2-8.   I. iv. 11, 12.   II. iii. 6-15.

The earliest Pauline letters in our possession are 1-2 Thessalonians, and precious letters they are.

The Riot

When Christians are asleep the devil is quiet, but when they are awake he becomes active.

The action of the Jews against the missionaries was skilfully staged. It was instigated by *jealousy* which is always between people of the same profession. Actors are not jealous of footballers, but, too often, preachers are of preachers.

For their unholy ends the rabbis employed the rabble, because that course gave greater promise of success. In the market-place or *agora* there were always loafers, loungers, idlers, wharf-rats, 'bums', good-for-nothing fellows, hangers around, ready for any excitement and mischief. The rabbis made a selection of these to create a riot, and knowing that the preachers were the guests of Jason they broke into his house and searched for Paul and Silas, who, however, were already hidden. They then *dragged* Jason and some other Christians before the Politarchs.

The Charge

The strength of it was in the half-truth which it contained. The charge was that 'another king, Jesus,' was being proclaimed, and so the sovereignty of Caesar was challenged. The element of truth in this was that Paul had spoken of another kingdom and of a returning king (1 Thess. 11. 12. 2 Thess. 1. 5; ii. 6, 7), but not in the atmosphere of panic and riot can truth prevail or sense triumph. As the offenders were not present, the Politarchs took 'security' from Jason and the others, and let them go. What this 'security' was we are not told. Ramsay thinks that Jason promised that the missionaries would not return to the city. At any rate Paul and Silas left Thessalonica that night.

The Result

This looks like sad failure, but it was not. The Thessalonian Church had been created, and the quality of it is reflected in Paul's two letters to it (I. i. 7-10; ii. 13-20); and among the converts were Aristarchus and Secundus (xix. 29; xx. 4; xxvii. 2; Col. iv. 10; Phile. 24). The first two churches which Paul founded in Europe—at Philippi, and at Thessalonica—were dearer to him than any others, and the letters he wrote to them are more autobiographical than any of the others he wrote to churches.

Beroea

(xvii. 10-14)

A Journey by Night

On two occasions the movements of Paul were determined by others, in chapter ix. 25, 30, and here, in xvii. 10. He was in a difficult position, for to remain in Thessalonica would endanger all the Christians, and to leave it looked like abandoning them; but 'brethren' solved the problem. By night they hurried Paul and Silas out of the city, and we do not know if ever he returned to it (cf. xviii. 5; 1 Cor. xvi. 5), though he tried to do so (1 Thess. ii. 17, 18).

After the missionaries left the city the church there was severely persecuted (1 Thess. ii. 14; iii. 1-5; 2 Thess. i. 6).

The party went westward, from 40 to 50 miles, to Beroea which was a secluded but not unimportant city. Along that night journey Paul must have had a heavy heart as he thought of the dear people he had left behind him, and of the probability in front of him of the kind of treatment he had received at the hands of the Jews in Philippi and Thessalonica. However it was not his intention to go into retreat, but with vigour to continue the work to which God had called him.

The Beroean Jews

Without delay, therefore, they attended the synagogue, and there Paul got a glad surprise. The Jews here, unlike those of the two previous cities, were interested and earnest. Paul's theme was the same, relating Jesus of Nazareth to the Messianic

prophecies of the Old Testament, and the Jews, instead of re-
senting and resisting the subject, *examined* it *daily* to find out
if what Paul was saying was true. They critically scrutinized the
passages cited. The word means *from top to bottom, up and
down* as in legal research (Luke xxiii. 14; Acts iv. 9; xii. 19, *et. al*).
It is not irreverent thus to deal with the Scriptures. 'Paul's
preaching made Bible students of them all'. In this attitude of
the Jews consisted their *nobility* (cf. 1 Cor. 1. 26). One really
knows only what, by examination, he is convinced of. The result
of these synagogue sessions was most gratifying (xvii. 12).

Persistent Agitators

The devil is never off duty, and he never lacks agents to do
his work. The scorpion jealousy wriggled its way from Thessalonica to Beroea. Not content with their success in their own
city Paul's opponents repeated their tactics in Beroea. They
shook the crowds like an earthquake, and troubled them like a
tornado (iv. 31; xvii. 13); but they were too late; the good work
had been done; a Church was established, and Sopater (xx. 4)
was one of the converts.

Paul on the move again

Silas and Timothy who were not the victims of Jewish spite
remained in Beroea, but once more fellow-believers *sent* Paul
out and away, and went with him. The Apostle whose health
was so uncertain, and whose eyesight was so defective could not
have gone alone.

Interpreters differ as to how Paul went from Beroea to Athens.
There are two views: (a) that the party went to the port of Dium,
some 16 miles away, and there took ship to Athens; (b) that
appearing to go to the coast they turned and went overland in
order to dodge the Jews.

The journey from Beroea to Athens by either land or sea was
about 250 miles, and Farrar is probably right when he decides
for the sea route because of the distance, expense, danger and
fatigue of the land route.

With this departure from Beroea Paul's ministry in Macedonia
ended for the time being.

Paul's Second Missionary Journey lay in three distinct fields—
Asia Minor, *Macedonia*, and *Achaia*. The first two of these we
have considered, and we now come to the third. The following
is a brief outline of it, including the journey back to Antioch by
Ephesus and Jerusalem. (See Maps 20, 21, pp. 354, 366.)

THE THIRD STAGE

3. APOSTOLIC LABOURS IN ACHAIA (xvii. 15-xviii. 17)

ATHENS (xvii. 15-34)   From Beroea, by sea, about   200-250
(From Beroea to the Seaport, Dium, about 20 miles)   miles

    (i) Paul waits for Silas and Timothy (15-16)
   (ii) Paul disputes with Jews and Greeks in the
        synagogue and the market-place (17)
  (iii) Paul is taken by the philosophers to Mars Hill(?)
        to hear more of his teaching (18-21)
  (iv) Paul's Discourse to the philosophers (22-31)

       A.   THE PLEASING INTRODUCTION (22)

          (*a*) A Respectful Salutation (22*a*)
          (*b*) A Complimentary Ascription (22*b*)

       B.   THE PATHETIC INSCRIPTION (23)

          (*a*) A Tactful Intimation (23*a*)
          (*b*) A Startling Declaration (23*b*)

       C.   THE PROFOUND INTERPRETATION (24-31)

          (*a*) God and the Universe (24, 25)
          (*b*) God and Mankind (26-29)
          (*c*) God and the Ages (30, 31)

   (v) The Results of the Discourse (32-34)

CORINTH (xviii. 1-17)   West from Athens about   50 miles
    (i) Paul's association with Aquila and Priscilla (1-3)
   (ii) Paul's weekly ministry in the synagogue (4-6)
        (Silas arrives from Beroea (5; xvii. 14).
        Timothy arrives from Thessalonica
        (5; 1 Thess. iii. 6))
  (iii) Paul's break with the synagogue, and his wider
       ministry (6-8)
         JUSTUS (7)   CRISPUS (8)
  (iv) Paul, being depressed, is encouraged by the
       Lord (9-11)
               (1 Thess. iii. 1-8; 1 Cor. ii. 3)

1 Thessalonians. A.D. 52

2 Thessalonians. A.D. 53

(v) The Jews charge Paul before Gallio the Proconsul (12, 13)
(vi) Gallio summarily dismisses the case (14-16)
(vii) The Greeks beat Sosthenes, the ruler of the
synagogue (17)

THE INWARD JOURNEY
(xviii. 18-22)

CENCHREAE (18)   Eastern harbour of Corinth, about   8 miles
Paul cut his hair, having a vow.
Priscilla and Aquila accompany Paul.
(There was a church here, of which Phoebe was a
deaconess (Rom. xvi. 1))

EPHESUS (19-21). From Cenchreae, across the Aegean
Sea, about   240 miles
Paul reasoned with the Jews in the synagogue
Asked to remain in Ephesus Paul declined, but
promised to return.
Priscilla and Aquila remain in the City.

CAESAREA (22)   From Ephesus about   650 miles

JERUSALEM (22)   From Caesarea about   50 miles
Paul salutes the church.

ANTIOCH S. (22)   From Jerusalem about   300 miles
Paul spent 'some time' here

The Second Missionary Journey occupied from $2\frac{1}{2}$ to 3 years; and the
distance travelled was about 2,800 miles: 1,230 by sea; 1,570 by land.

3. Apostolic Labours in Achaia and the Journey Home
(xvii. 15-xviii. 22)

The disciples who accompanied Paul from Beroea took him to
Athens and immediately returned, with a message from Paul to
Silas and Timothy to join him at Athens as soon as possible
(xvii. 15). So Paul, for the first time in his missionary journeys
was left alone.

It would have been difficult for him to have taken the journey
from Beroea to Athens by himself as he was a tired and suffering

man, and his eyesight was defective, and it was this state of things which made his loneliness in Athens a real trial, one which he did not wish to endure longer than was necessary. However, if Silas and Timothy set out from Beroea as soon as they received Paul's message it would be at least a week before they could arrive in Athens. What was Paul doing meanwhile?

Athens

At one time this was one of the greatest cities in the world. Long ago *Jerusalem* was the religious capital of the world, *Rome* was its political capital, and *Athens* was its intellectual capital. It has been said that all the Old World's culture culminated in Greece—all Greece in Athens—all Athens in its Acropolis—and all the Acropolis in the Parthenon.

It is probably true to say that more people of eminent distinction have been associated with Athens than with any other city in the world. In the fields of history, poetry, tragedy, oratory, art, science and philosophy it was without a rival, though other university cities produced great names. One has only to mention *Homer*, and *Sappho*, and *Pindar*; *Aeschylus*, and *Sophocles*, and *Euripides*; *Herodotus*, and *Thucydides*, and *Xenophon*; *Socrates*, and *Plato*, and *Aristotle*; *Thales*, and *Anaxagoras*, and *Democritus*; *Plutarch*, and *Demosthenes*, *Pericles*, and *Alexander the Great*, to realise what is meant by 'The Glory that was Greece'.

Even in its ruins the Acropolis strikes the imagination, but what it was in the day of its glory who can say!

PAUL AT ATHENS

There is something fascinating about the conjunction of these two great names. The great person enters the great place. How long he was in the city we do not know, and opinions differ as to the value of what he accomplished while there. The Apostle did not go to Athens with the intention of preaching there. He was taken to the city in circumstances of flight, and had no recognizable plan. He would await the arrival of Silas and Timothy and then decide the next move. But meantime he took a look round the city and was sadly impressed by the evidence everywhere of superstition and idolatry. It is said that at one time Athens had over 3,000 public statues besides countless private ones, and Petronius is credited with saying that it was easier to find a god than a man in the city.

Paul was not a tourist but a missionary, and so was more concerned about the souls than the sights of Athens. He could not remain silent and inactive in the presence of such learned ignorance, and of such lifeless worship, and so he began a ministry the record of which is very slender.

Perhaps it is commonly overlooked that this ministry was three-fold: first among the Jews and 'God-fearers' in the synagogue; then, among the people who thronged the market-place; and finally, his discourse to the Epicurean and Stoic philosophers (xvii. 16-21).

Paul and the Jews

The substance of Paul's ministry in the synagogue we may gather from other such occasions, e.g. at Antioch in Pisidia (xiii. 14-41), and at Thessalonica (xvii. 1-3). He taught that Jesus of Nazareth in death and resurrection was the fulfilment of the Messianic prophecies of the Old Testament Scriptures.

There is no record of the result of this ministry.

Paul and the Crowd

All we are told is that 'he reasoned with those who met him in the market-place' (xvii. 17). This does not mean that he held what we call open-air meetings, but that, like Socrates more than four and a half centuries earlier, he moved in and out among the people and had conversation with any who would listen to him. What he would say to these Gentile heathen is indicated by such references as xiv. 7, 15-17, 21; xvi. 31, 32. This, we are told, continued daily (xvii. 17), but we are not told with what result.

The Market-place or Agora

Our present-day idea of a market-place gives no idea whatever of what that meant in Athens of old. This is how R. B. Rackham describes the *agora* at Athens, that is, the forum, or place of public assemblies, or trials (xvi. 19; xvii. 17).

'The agora was an open space in the centre of the city which served as the focus of the civic life. Around it were grouped the public buildings of the city—the temples of its patron gods, its senate-house, town-hall and law-courts. Besides these there were *stoas* or *porticoes*, i.e. *porches* or colonnades which were used for exchanges or places of concourse; and the rest of the circuit would be filled up with shops. Within this square beat the heart of the city. All the morning the agora was the scene of market, and crowded with country-people, buyers and sellers, merchants and business men. Hither also repaired all who had civic business, the magistrates and civic functionaries.

'Business over, it became the resort of the idle, the gossips and the newsmongers, whether loungers of fashionable society or lazy 'fellows of the rabble'. Being the resort of the citizens we should also find in the agora those who wanted an audience, whether philosophers and travelling rhetoricians, or charlatans or quacks. Such teachers or declaimers, if they came to stay, would take up their station in some porch and there gather round them a body of disciples.

'Of the agoras of Greece most famous was that of Athens. At this time among its sights were to be counted the Senate-house, the Temple of Zeus Eleutherius (the god of freedom), the Stoa Basilica (royal porch), where the Archon Basileus held his sessions and where the court of the Areopagus frequently met, a gymnasium built by Ptolemy Philadelphus, king of Egypt, a porch built by an Attalus king of Pergamum, and, more famous than all, the ancient Painted Porch, so called because it was adorned with frescoes by Polygnotus. This celebrated porch had been the scene of the labours of Zeno of Citium, and from it his disciples received the name of Stoics.' (*The Acts of the Apostles*, p. 309).

Paul and the Philosophers

This description will help us to understand the circumstances of Acts xvii. 16-21. As Paul held converse with one and another in the crowded agora, some philosophers overheard him, and got him to accompany them to the *Council of the Areopagus* to explain his teaching.

It is generally thought that Paul was taken to Mars' Hill (xvii. 22), but this is by no means certain, and, indeed would seem improbable. The Court of the Areopagus is much more likely to have been held in the Stoa Basilica which was in the agora, for there, not the philosophers only, but the public also would have been able to hear Paul, which they could not have done on Mars' Hill.

Two schools of philosophy are mentioned in the record, the *Epicurean* and the *Stoic*, the one derived from *Epicurus* (B.C. 342-270), and the other from *Zeno* (B.C. 362-260). The Epicureans were utilitarians; the Stoics were idealists. The Epicureans regarded the highest good as pleasure, and the Stoics taught that the highest good was virtue. The ruling principle of the one was *Pleasure*, and of the other, *Pride*.

Members of these ruling schools encountered Paul on the street, and probably it was the Epicureans who said, 'what would this babbler say?', and the Stoics who said, 'he seemeth to be a setter-forth of strange gods' (xvii. 18). The one attitude is impudent, and the other is respectful. The word 'babbler' (*spermologos*) means 'seed-picker', a picker up of the seeds, like a bird. A. T. Robertson says that the word has been used 'of a man hanging around in the markets picking up scraps of food that fell from the carts, and so also of mere rhetoricians and plagiarists who picked up scraps of wisdom from others'. The question was contemptuous and implied that Paul was just a quack.

The other view was that Paul by preaching Jesus and Anastasis was introducing new gods. So, bringing the Apostle to the Areopagus, they asked him to interpret his teaching (xvii. 18-20).

Paul's Sermon at Athens (xvii. 22-31)

This cannot be a verbatim record of what Paul said, yet, as a summary, it is complete. The discourse is both theological and philosophical, and was an indictment of and challenge to the false theology and shallow philosophy of the Athenians.

Paul proclaimed that

> God is sovereign in His own universe; is supreme in human history, and is the Redeemer and Judge of the world.

Paul thought imperially, as every Christian should, and spread before these philosophers an alpine-top vision of God in His manifold relations; a vision the truth and reality of which can never be affected by anything that religion may desire, that philosophy may imagine, or that science may discover.

The parts of the sermon are: the Approach (22, 23), the Affirmation (24-29), and the Appeal (30, 31).

Paul's Approach to His Subject
(xvii. 22, 23)

This is characterized by courtesy, resourcefulness, and tact. '*Men of Athens*' would at once arrest attention, for it was a classical form of address. We may be sure that Paul would not begin his address by saying that his listeners were 'too superstitious', which would have annoyed them, but by commending them, in a way, by saying that they were '*very religious*', which was true,

He then made a text of something he had seen as he looked about the city—an altar with the words on it *AGNŌSTŌ THEŌ*, to an *Unknown God*. From '*agnōstō*' comes our word agnostic, which in one form, appears in the next sentence, '*what you do not know*.' Paul's statement was designedly ambiguous. It could be understood in opposite ways. He did not say that his listeners were *ignorant* (A.V.), but, as the inscription witnessed, *they did not know*. The common denominator of the preacher and his audience was '*god*', and he went on to show that his God and their gods were not the same. There is nothing in this approach to his theme which could have aroused the indignation or anger of his hearers.

The Substance of the Sermon
(xvii. 24-31)

Neither the distinctive doctrines of Judaism, nor of Christianity are in this discourse. On the one hand there is no mention of the Messiah, and on the other hand, no mention of the crucifixion, but Paul did what he said he would do: 'Whom therefore ye worship in ignorance, Him set I forth unto you' (23). GOD is his theme, and the discourse is in three parts: *GOD and the Universe* (24, 25); *GOD and Mankind* (26-29); and *GOD and the Ages* (30, 31).

I. God and the Universe (24, 25).

1. THE FACTS

(i) *God is the Creator of the Universe*

'He made the world and all that is in it'.

Nothing is here said of processes, but only that God originated the universe.

(ii) *God is the Possessor of the Universe*

'Lord of sky and earth'.

He has not mortgaged any part of it, but sits upon the throne the sovereign owner and ruler.

(iii) *God is the Maintainer of the Universe*

'He Himself gives life and breath and all things unto all'.

The object of His rule is the well-being of His subjects, both angelic and human. From these facts proceeds

2. THE TEACHING

Three great truths emerge.

(i) *God is Uncreated*

He is '*the God*' (24). That could never be 'the' which once was not there.

(ii) *God is Universal*

'He does not dwell in shrines made by hand' (24).

He will not occupy a niche in any Pantheon. He cannot be localized.

(iii) *God is Independent*

'He does not receive service from human hands from need of anything' (25).

He has said: 'If I were hungry I would not tell you, for the world is mine and the fulness thereof' (Ps. 1).

This is not how the Greeks thought of either God or the universe, and but for the hold of sin upon their hearts and minds this revelation would have corrected their errors and dispelled their ignorance.

II. **God and Mankind** (26-29)

The reference is, first of all, to

1. MEN COLLECTIVELY (26, 27a).

Viewing mankind in this way Paul declares that

(i) 'God made out of one *every nation
of men to dwell on all the face of the earth*'.

To deny the unity of mankind is intellectual folly, and to ignore it is social folly. Athens thought that the race consisted of Greeks and Barbarians, and that the latter were of no account. Paul emphatically says 'No'. Beneath all nationalities the race is one.

(ii) God determined for the nations the seasons of
their prosperity, and the limits of their territory.

'Having fixed appointed seasons and the boundaries of their dwelling' (26).

This is a very profound statement, and is a philosophy of history which negatives every other. *'Determined'* is *to make a horizon.* God has revealed Himself in history as well as in creation; and, 'appointed seasons' refers not to fruitfulness of the earth, as in xiv. 17, but to the rise and fall of nations (Deut. xxxii. 8. Luke xxi. 24).

If the nations of the world had regarded the relation of geography to the will of God half their tragic history would never have been made. God would have nations respect the providence of mountains and rivers and seas.

(iii) God's design in history is that men
might seek God and find Him.

'That they should seek God, if haply they might feel Him and find Him' (27).

Conscious national need should lead to searching, and should issue in finding, but this is not the course which the nations have pursued. Where are ancient Egypt, Assyria, Babylonia, Greece, and Rome? The Apostle now turns to the consideration of

2. Men Individually (27b, 28)

This statement implies that only by individual salvation can social and national salvation be hoped for. No nation, as such, has ever been saved, and only the salt of Christianity in nations has preserved them from entire corruption. Salt does not make good what is bad, but it preserves the bad from getting worse (Matt. v. 13).

(i) *God is not infinitely far removed from us*

If this were so it would render our search for Him unavailing, but 'He is not far from each of us'. The transcendent God is also immanent. His nearness to us is not local but spiritual, and it is not general but particular. 'God is close to each of us'.

(ii) *In God each of us has his being*

'In Him we live, and move, and are'.

Paul does not say that God is in all men, but that all men are in God, which must be true if He is the source of all life.

It is in Him that we possess the gift of life; it is in Him that life functions; and it is in Him that we are what we are—personal beings.

(iii) *The foregoing statement is true of all men.*

'As certain even of your own poets have said: "For we are also His offspring".' These words are to be found in two heathen poets, *Aratus* of Soli in Cilicia (B.C. 270), and *Cleanthes*, a Stoic philosopher (B.C. 300-220). This life in God, which must not be confused with life in Christ, was not the exclusive privilege of the Hebrews. The reference of *Aratus* was to Zeus, but Paul lifted the conception to the level of the truth. The very breath with which, oftentimes, men curse God, and more often deny Him, is lent to them by God. We are entirely dependent on Him for our rational, animal, and physical life.

Here, then, is a profound philosophy of history. The race has sprung from a single Father. Nations have their rise in the will of God, and He ordains their sphere and mission. The underlying motive of all history is redemptive. God is spiritually near to each of us. Only by and in Him do we live. All this is true of all men in all ages.

History is not an agglomeration of fortuitous events, but is the expression, however feebly realized, of the wisdom, power, and love of God.

It is this revealed ideal in history which shows how fundamentally false is idolatry in thought and practice.

The final word of the preacher relates to

III. God and the Ages (30, 31)

1. GOD AND THE PAST

(i) During these ages the nations were
given over to the worship of idols (29)

The history of the world to the time of Christ's advent is the history of idolatry. The Hebrew people alone had the truth of monotheism, but even they were corrupted by idolatry.

(ii) During these ages God did not manifest
Himself in any special way to the nations.

'Times of ignorance'. Before Christ came the heathen acted in ignorance; spiritually they were in the dark. It will be well to remember this when we think of paganism in pre-Christian times. Many idolators were men of noble qualities.

(iii) During these ages God withheld from
the nations the punishment which
enlightenment would have rendered necessary.

'The times of ignorance God overlooked' (cf. Rom. iii. 25). This does not mean that the heathen world had no means of knowing God, and were without responsibility (cf. Rom. i. 18-32), but pagans had not the light which was vouchsafed to Israel, and so were not equally culpable; they were not judged for rejecting a God of whom they never had heard.

2. GOD AND THE PRESENT
'But now' (30b, 31).

(i) God has now, in Christ, manifested Himself to all nations as the *one true Object of Worship.*

'But now' is set over against 'the times of ignorance'. The advent of Christ has wrought a world-wide change, and by bringing enlightenment has taken all excuse from men, and has increased our responsibility.

(ii) *There is now a universal call to repent.*
'God commandeth men that they should all, everywhere, repent'.

There are few things that every man is called upon to do, but one of them is to repent, and this, because the relation of every man to God is fundamentally the same.

God being what He is, and we being what we are, and God and ourselves being related as we are, repentance is a moral necessity if man is to be saved from irretrievable ruin. And so last of all, attention is called to

3. GOD AND THE FUTURE (31)

There is an appointed Day of Judgment for all the world. 'He fixed a day on which He will judge the world in righteousness by a man whom He appointed, having given proof to all by raising Him from the dead'.

(i) *The criterion of this judgment will be righteousness.*
(ii) *The conduct of it is entrusted to Jesus Christ.*
(iii) *The certainty of it is witnessed to by the resurrection of Christ from among the dead.*

The Effect of the Sermon
(32-34)

This is stated simply and briefly: 'Some jeered; others said, "We will hear you again about this"; but some men joined him and believed'.

1. *Some Derided.* These, probably, were the Epicureans. People mock when they do not—and do not try to—understand. People mock when they cannot confute or silence what they hear. People mock when they will not yield to, and yet fear, what they hear. Ignorance, insincerity, and irrationalism have ever been hindrances to the progress of the Gospel.

2. *Some Deferred.* These, probably, were the Stoics.
Men procrastinate when their understanding is clear, but their
heart neither honest nor in earnest. Men procrastinate when they
know they should make a public confession of Christ, and yet
shrink from making it. Men procrastinate when their will
declines to endorse the verdict of their intelligence and conscience.

3. *Some Decided.* The Gospel does not call for hasty and ignorant
committals. It makes its appeal irrespective of caste or class. It
never has been, and never will be popular.

Among Paul's converts at Athens were, '*Dionysius the Areo-
pagite*' who was one of a college of twelve judges who had helped
to make Athens famous. '*A woman named Damaris*,' of whom
we know nothing else. '*And others.*' On the surface this seems
to be a poor result compared, for instance, with the 'multitude'
at Thessalonica (xvii), and the 'many' at Beroea (xvii. 12); but
of this we are not competent to judge.

Two views are held of this discourse: (*a*) that it is a 'masterful
exposition of God's place and power in human history'; a marvellous adaptation of message to audience; and (*b*) that Paul left
the simple gospel and tried the philosophic method with his
philosophic hearers, and found it to be ineffective, and that when
he went to Corinth he determined not to try excellency of speech,
or the persuasive words of wisdom, but to preach—what he had
not proclaimed in the Areopagus—Christ crucified. His disappointment at the failure of the former method to touch the
frivolous Athenians no doubt kindled the fire with which he
denounces the wisdom of the world in his first epistle to the
Corinthians' (1 Cor. i. 18-ii. 16), Rackham.

What we do know is that the Apostle 'went out from among
them', never to return, and that he sent no letter to the Christians
in this city.

Corinth
(xviii. 1-17)

Here is an illustration of Luke's selection and compression of
style. Paul was longer at Corinth than he had been at any other
place so far in his journeyings, and yet the record of his ministry

here is limited to seventeen verses. But not a little light is thrown upon this period of over eighteen months by the Apostle's two letters to the Church which he established in this city, letters written three or four years later.

ATHENS TO CORINTH

It was a great change to go from Athens to Corinth, though the cities were only 40-50 miles apart. 'It was', says Rackham, 'like passing from Oxford to London.' The one was intellectual, and the other was commercial. The one was proud, and the other was profligate. The one was a city of ancient fame, and the other, in Paul's time, was not a hundred years old. The one, like many University cities, was seclusive, and the other was for traffic the key-city between west and east.

It is not likely that Paul made the journey overland, which would have been tedious and expensive, but by sea, which was a day's sail.

THE CITY

Corinth was the capital of Achaia, and was the seat of Government. It was beautifully situated, and had two ports, Lechaeum in the Corinthian bay, and Cenchreae in the Saronic bay. Because of the dangerous navigation round the Peninsula the commerce by sea was carried across the Isthmus. Lechaeum was a mile and a half from the city, and Cenchreae was nearly nine miles.

Due to her enormous commerce and the Isthmian Games (1 Cor. ix. 24-27) Corinth was a wealthy city. At her marts were to be found Arabian balsam, Egyptian papyrus, Phoenician dates, Libyan ivory, Babylonian carpets, Cilician goats' hair, Lycaonian wool, and Phrygian slaves (Farrar). But side by side with magnificent buildings were wretched huts of wood and straw which sheltered the poor (1 Cor. iii. 12).

THE CORINTHIANS

These were notorious for immorality and drunkenness; so much so that a 'Corinthian' came to mean a profligate, a libertine. Their temple of Aphrodite possessed a thousand consecrated prostitutes. The city was a veritable Gomorrah, and it was from here that Paul dictated his frightful sketch of Paganism (Rom. i. 21-32). It was into this Vanity Fair of the Roman Empire that Paul entered alone and ill (1 Cor. ii. 3); and it was here that he was to spend nearly two years of his missionary ministry. But the deeper the degradation the greater was the need of the Gospel which Paul had to preach, and his preaching of it was not without effect. The moral depravity of the Corinthians, and the conversion of many of them, are often reflected in the two letters to this city (1 Cor. v. 1; vi. 9-20; x. 7, 8. 2 Cor. vi. 14; vii. 1; xii. 21).

AQUILA AND PRISCILLA

In this section (xviii. 1-17) there are two references to Imperial history; one in xviii. 2, and the other in xviii. 12. The former tells of an expulsion of Jews from Rome by an edict of Claudius. Suetonius says that this was caused by a series of disturbances 'due to the action of Chrestus.' Chrestus must mean *Christ*, and the trouble must have been occasioned by Christian propaganda in Rome.

Amongst those who left the capital, or were expelled, were Aquila and Priscilla, and, in all likelihood, they were already Christians, as we read of no such change after they met Paul. It may be that Aquila, a Jew of Pontus, had married a Roman lady of high rank. In six places where they are mentioned her name comes first four times. She appears to have been the more forceful personality.

Surely there is a providence of contact! There were several directions in which Aquila and his wife might have gone when they left Rome—for instance, to Pontus—but they went to Corinth, and when, after a few months, Paul also went there, he 'found' Aquila, perhaps in a Jewish Guild of Trades, and was at once attracted to him because he was a Jew, a Christian, and a tent-maker.

Aquila and Priscilla, who seem to have been well-off, invited Paul to stay with them, and 'he abode with them', probably for more than eighteen months, as later he was their guest in Ephesus (1 Cor. xvi. 19). It may be that Aquila carried on business in several capitals—Rome, Corinth and Ephesus (Rom. xvi. 3-5a.

1 Cor. xvi. 19), and that he was expert at his craft. Paul's fellowship with him in this must have been inspiring and enriching.

The friendship now formed was terminated only by the Apostle's death, and both Aquila and Priscilla jeopardised their lives for him (Rom. xvi. 3-5a).

PAUL'S INDEPENDENCE

The words *every Sabbath* in xviii. 4, in conjunction with verse 3, are significant, for they make it clear that Paul's ministry in the synagogue was only on Sabbaths, and that throughout the week he was busy tentmaking.

Two things he made quite clear to the churches he founded and served: first, that giving them spiritual help, he was entitled to their temporal help (1 Cor. ix. 1-14); and secondly, that from one church only had he taken such help, because he would not have it said that he was preaching for temporal gain (1 Cor. ix. 12, 15-18: cf. Phil. iv. 10-20). A famine in Greece made it difficult for Paul to earn a living, and at times he was actually in want, yet he refused aid from the Corinthians (1 Cor. ix. 7-17).

SILAS AND TIMOTHY

After Paul had been two or three months at Corinth these two brethren came from Macedonia—Silas from Beroea, and Timothy from Thessalonica—to share the ministry in this city with Paul. Their arrival had several important effects, and chiefly: the money they brought to him from the Church at Philippi (Phil. iv. 15) relieved him from the pressure of his manual labours; he was enabled for a time to give most of his time to preaching and teaching; and the good news which Timothy brought him about the Church at Thessalonica led him to write them a letter, which was, so far as we know, the first of all his Epistles (1 Thess. iii. 6-10).

The time referred to here is while Paul was still ministering in the synagogue, and Luke says that when Silas and Timothy arrived in Corinth the Apostle felt a divine constraint to proclaim to the Jews that Jesus was the Messiah, and to do so, not on Sabbaths only, but also during the week (xviii. 5).

PAUL'S SYNAGOGUE MINISTRY

'When Silas and Timothy came down from Macedonia, Paul began to be engrossed in preaching, protesting to the Jews that the Messiah was Jesus' (xviii. 5). (Lake and Cadbury).

'*Paul began to be engrossed in preaching*' indicates what took place at this time, and the context shows that the Apostle was occupied with the Jews. Wherever he went he began work in the synagogue, if there was one, and in substance his message to the Jews was always the same, namely, that Jesus of Nazareth was the promised Messiah (ix. 22; xvii. 2, 3; xviii. 5, 28). The implications of this contention were and are tremendous, affirming His divine Person, His atoning death, and His spiritual kingdom.

If '*the Messiah was Jesus*' is the correct reading (above, and Ramsay), it shows that Paul began with the 'known quantity' and led to the 'unknown', which is much more likely than the reverse argument.

It was when Paul connected Jesus with the Messiah that the Jews 'ranged themselves in hostile array' against him, and exclaimed '*Anathema Jesus*'. They had done this in Pisidian Antioch, and the result in both cases was the same—Paul left them and turned to the Gentiles.

1 Thessalonians

This is not the place to speak of this Epistle in detail, but we should now understand why two Epistles were written to this Church, and what, broadly, they are about. The report which Timothy brought to Paul about the Thessalonian believers was, on the whole, good, but there were some details which could not but give the Apostle some concern, and so, without delay, he wrote to them a message of *exultation* (ch. i), *explanation* (chs. ii.-iii.), and *exhortation* (chs. iv-v). In the first part he rejoices in the faith and witness of his converts. In the second part, he reminds them that his conduct while in their midst was not self-seeking or selfish, but that he was as a nurse and as a father to them, and earned his living by daily toil. He commends the Christians for their constancy under persecution. Also he tells them of his deep affection for them, how he longed to see them, and how great was his joy in the knowledge that they were standing fast. In the third part, he writes about the conduct which becomes Christians; he comforts them concerning those who were dying, and tells them of the Lord's return; and he exhorts them to Christian concord.

2 Thessalonians

Not long after Paul had written the first letter to the Thessalonians he heard that some things he had said in it, and in his teaching while with them, were being misconstrued, and that some members of the Church were so sure that Christ's advent was so near that they had ceased to work. Paul writes to correct these misapprehensions, and also to exhort the believers to prayerfulness and industry.

His main themes are: The Second Advent and the Recompense of Men (ch. i.); The Second Advent and the Course of Events (ch. ii.); and the Second Advent and the Present Duty (ch. iii).

By these two letters a correspondence was commenced which has enriched beyond estimate the whole Church of God for nineteen hundred years.

PAUL'S MINISTRY AMONG THE GENTILES

'From henceforth I will go unto the Gentiles' (xviii. 6; xiii. 46).

There are times when a religious assembly excommunicates an individual, but here an individual excommunicates an assembly. (cf. Rev. iii. 20)

NEXT DOOR

Any servant of God to-day would find it difficult, if indeed possible, to know when the time had come to leave the people who are rejecting his message, but Paul did this more than once—and his Master did it before him—and did it with God's approval.

When the Jews anathematized Jesus Paul left the synagogue and started a ministry next door (xviii. 7); an action which was both bold and provocative. He changed his residence from the house of Aquila to that of *Titus Justus*, a proselyte who had become a Christian. In this man's house meetings were held regularly and were attended by Jews and Gentiles, and among Paul's converts was *Crispus* 'the ruler of the synagogue', who was baptized by the Apostle (1 Cor. i. 14).

DEPRESSION

There was an occasion when the Lord said to His disciples 'Come ye yourselves apart and rest awhile'. Being a Christian does not release one from the laws which govern our physical and mental state. Our Lord himself was subject to these laws, and so we need not wonder that at Corinth Paul felt the strain of all he had gone through at Philippi, Thessalonica, Beroea and Athens, and now was experiencing at Corinth. He was a timid and shaken man; for a while he was in poverty; he had to work hard with his hands to earn a living; and his message was not acceptable to the Jews. All this reacted on his state of body and mind, and never did he come nearer to losing heart and acknowledging defeat (1 Cor. ii. 3; iv. 11. 12; 2 Cor. xi. 6-9). But 'dark is deepest before the dawn.'

ENCOURAGEMENT

When Paul was in this state the Lord appeared to him one night and said: 'Do not be afraid, but speak and do not be silent, because I am with you, and no one shall attack you, because I have much people in this city' (xviii. 9, 10).

That was of more use to Paul than all the doctors and drugs in the world; and Luke's next remark is that the Apostle 'dwelt there a year and six months, teaching the word of God among them'; a longer stay than he had made in any other place so far. The word 'dwelt' is, *'he sat down'* (cf. xiii. 14. Luke iv. 20; v. 3). The vision and the voice had calmed Paul's troubled spirit, and he settled down in Corinth.

Of the eighteen months spent in this city Luke has nothing to say, except that Paul taught the word of God; but much information can be gathered from the Apostle's letters to the Christians there.

THE CHURCH AT CORINTH

The members were many and came chiefly from the middle and lower classes (1 Cor. i. 26-29). There was a great display of divers gifts, especially 'tongues' (1 Cor. xii). Divisions (i-iv), disorders (v.-vi), difficulties (vii.-xiv.), and certain false doctrines (xv.) characterized the Assembly. There seems to have been little persecution, and there was a want of definitely organized ministry. This Church caused Paul much anxious thought, and he wrote to it at least three times (1 Cor. v. 9).

Yet his ministry here was fruitful in conversions, and of not a few influential persons. Of the latter we need only name Titus Justus, Crispus, and Sosthenes, who had been rulers of the synagogue; Erastus the treasurer of the city; Stephanas, Gaius, Chloe, Tertius, Fortunatus, Achaicus and Quartus (Acts xviii. 7. 1 Cor. i. 11, 14; xvi. 15-17; Rom. xvi. 22, 23). This was not a small harvest in eighteen months (cf. Acts xvii. 34).

SIGNS

It is noteworthy that at Corinth Paul performed miracles, which were the credentials of an apostle. Luke does not tell us this, but Paul does in two letters (2 Cor. xii. 12. Rom. xv. 18, 19). His references to 'signs and wonders and mighty works', and 'the power of signs and wonders', which he attributes to 'the Holy Spirit', indicate an outstanding feature of his ministry at Corinth.

OPPOSITION

The proconsulship of Gallio in Achaia was between A.D. 51-55, and it must have been in A.D. 53 that the Jews 'rose up against Paul', brought him before Gallio, and charged him with persuading men to worship God contrary to the law (xviii. 13). What law is referred to is not clear. Gallio's reply would seem to indicate that it was Jewish law, in which he had no interest, and he drove them from the judgment-seat (xviii. 14-16). By this precipitous action the Church has been deprived of a speech from Paul (ver. 14).

The Jews had made a tactical blunder, and the Gentiles took the opportunity of their discomfiture to thrash Sosthenes the ruler of the synagogue.

This was a vindication of Paul and his work, but it led him to believe that he must move on. The 'yet many days' of verse 18 may or may not be included in the eighteen months (ver. 11), but the Apostle's first visit to Corinth was about to end.

GALLIO

He came of a distinguished family. Seneca, his father, was a well-known rhetorician, and his brother was Seneca the Stoic, the tutor of Nero. He was a man of culture and refinement, and of amiable disposition. It was in the providence of God that he was in power in Corinth when the Jews rose against Paul.

THE INWARD JOURNEY
(xviii. 18-22)

QUESTIONS

It should be observed that the movements of the Apostle from the time he left Corinth to his arrival in Antioch in Syria are recorded by Luke in five verses! There is much we would like to know, but cannot. Presumably Timothy went with him eastward, but did Silas? And if not, what were *his* future movements?

Did Timothy at Ephesus leave Paul and go home to Lystra? If so, when and where did he next join up again with the Apostle? What was the nature of Paul's vow, and how can it be reconciled with his Christian principles and preaching? Why did not Paul sail from Ephesus to Seleucia, seeing that Antioch was his destination?

These and other questions are full of interest, and though Luke does not answer them we are not left wholly in the dark.

THE VOW AND HEAD SHAVING

It can be safely assumed that Paul took a temporary Nazarite vow, and this may well have been because of sickness. There is some reason to believe that Phoebe nursed him at Cenchreae (Rom. xvi. 1, 2), and being restored he shaved his head as the vow required, and made for Jerusalem to complete his undertaking.

TO EPHESUS

The sea journey from Cenchreae would, in ordinary weather, occupy about three days. Aquila, Priscilla and others accompanied the Apostle.

This was Paul's first visit to the Asian capital, but not his last (ch. xix), and on the Sabbath, or on one of the meeting-times of the Jews, he entered the synagogue and 'reasoned' with them. What this means we may gather from xiii. 15-41; xiv. 1-3, 17; xviii. 4. They were disposed to listen, and asked the Apostle to remain longer with them, but his movements were determined by his vow, and he had to hasten to Jerusalem.

'He left them there' in xviii. 19, means that when Paul left Ephesus Aquila and Priscilla remained.

To Jerusalem

Some have thought that by 'he went up and saluted the church' (xviii. 22) is meant the church at Caesarea but this does not make sense. To fulfil his vow Paul had to go to Jerusalem, which undoubtedly he did. He does not appear to have had much of a welcome there, and so he passed on.

At Jerusalem Paul met with 'courteous exchange of civilities, instead of brotherly talk and worship. Officialism, even apostolic, dislikes unconventional success, work done not according to its rules' (Lindsay).

This was his fourth visit to Jerusalem. The first time was shortly after his conversion; the second, when he took help from Antioch to the famine-stricken poor; the third, when he attended the Jerusalem Conference; and now.

It must have been a disappointing visit, and only illustrates the fact that too often the Church fails to recognise her great men.

To Antioch

This was the missionary base from which the Apostle had gone forth twice to evangelize, and from which he was to go once more. All that we are told of this visit is that 'he spent some time there' (xviii. 23). How much we would like to know what that statement embraces! The more carefully we read the Acts the more shall we wonder at the brevity of the record of momentous events.

THE SECOND JOURNEY

With this note of time Paul's second missionary journey ended.

The Apostle had been away from Syrian Antioch for about three years, and he had travelled some 2,800 miles; about 1,230 by sea, and about 1,570 by land, on foot so far as we know. These distances are nothing to us today, but in Paul's day they were very considerable. He had none of our present-day travel facilities or accommodation.

And, it should be remembered, he was not travelling as an official of the Empire, but on his own initiative, and to proclaim, what to those he addressed, both Jews and Gentiles, was a new religion. He had no Committee behind him, and no financial resources. The church at Antioch contributed nothing towards his support, so that while travelling and preaching he had to earn his own living, and, probably, had to support some of them that travelled with him. His health was precarious, and he was constantly subject, as Ramsay thinks, to malaria, and Luke must often have given him medical attention.

In addition to all this he had enemies who pursued and opposed him, especially Jews. He had no home-life, and was without the comfort and understanding of a loving wife.

The Second Journey took the Apostle much further afield than did the First, and though it cannot be claimed that he introduced Christianity into Europe, it is true that he first promulgated and established it there.

Much of the suffering catalogued in 2 Cor. xi. 23-28 was endured by the time Paul's Second Journey ended, and seeing that he had been preaching for about fifteen years, his store of vitality must have been considerably diminished.

Dr. Stalker says that the Second Journey 'was not only the greatest Paul achieved but perhaps the most momentous recorded in the annals of the human race. In its issues it far out-rivalled the expedition of Alexander the Great, when he carried the arms and civilisation of Greece into the heart of Asia, or that of Caesar, when he landed on the shores of Britain, or even the voyage of Columbus, when he discovered a new world. Yet, when he set out on it, he had no idea of the magnitude which it was to assume, or even the direction which it was to take'. Truly Paul was one of the greatest men God ever made!

PAUL'S TIRELESS ACTIVITIES

THE THIRD JOURNEY

Acts xviii. 23—xxi. 16

A.D. 54-58: 4 Years

PAUL'S THIRD MISSIONARY JOURNEY

(Acts xviii. 23-xxi. 16. A.D. 54-58)

Each journey the Apostle took grew in importance and wonder, as it did in matter of distance. It cannot be said that his ministry was untiring, but certainly it was unresting. The sense of urgency grew, as the record in xviii. 22, 23 shows: 'having landed', 'having gone up', 'having saluted', 'having stayed', 'passing through'. The Apostle must have been about fifty-two years of age when he left Antioch for his third missionary tour, and about eight years later he speaks of himself as 'the aged'. At sixty a man who had laboured and suffered as Paul had done may well have regarded himself as old, but his age had not abated his energy, nor had it weakened his determination to evangelize and teach while life lasted; and this ministry was both extensive and intensive. On his second journey Paul was a year and a half at Corinth, but on the third, he was from two to three years at Ephesus. These ministries, however, had widespread results, for of Paul's work in Ephesus it is said 'that all they that dwelt in Asia heard the word of the Lord, both Jews and Greeks' (xix. 10).

The following is an outline of the third period of Paul's missionary ministry, and though Luke's record is brief for a spell of about four years, yet from supplementary literature we can see how momentous a period it was.

III. THE THIRD MISSIONARY JOURNEY
(xviii. 23-xxi. 16. A.D. 54-58. 4 Years)

THE OUTWARD JOURNEY
(xviii. 23-xx. 3)

1. PAUL'S ACTIVITIES IN ASIA (xviii. 23-xix. 41)

(i) *The Itineration in Galatia and Phrygia* (23)

ANTIOCH (S)—TARSUS—DERBE—LYSTRA—ICONIUM—ANTIOCH (P).

412 miles

Antioch (S) to the Cilician Gates by Tarsus, about   200 miles

From the Cilician Gates by Derbe, Lystra, Iconium to
   Antioch (P) about   190 miles

The term 'Galatia and Phrygia' (23, cf. xvi. 6) may
   mean what is called the North Galatian theory, and
   would embrace the towns of

TAVIUM.   ANCYRA.   PESSINUS
This would add at least 600 miles to the journey.

(ii) *The Introduction of Apollos* (24-28)

Connecting EPHESUS and CORINTH with the story of Paul (xix. 1; xx. 2)

(*a*) Apollos at Ephesus (24-26)
(*b*) Apollos at Corinth (27-28; xix. 1)

(iii) *The Capital of Proconsular Asia* (xix)

(*a*) The Beginning of Paul's Ministry in Ephesus (1-7)

   (1) He meets ignorant disciples (1-4)
   (2) He further instructs them (5-7)

(*b*) The Progress of Paul's Ministry in Ephesus (8-20)

   (1) Ministry within the Synagogue (8, 9a)
       Duration of it (8)
       Theme of it (8)
       Manner of it (8)
       Rejection of it (9a)

   (2) Ministry outside the Synagogue (9b-20)
       Subjects of it (9)
       Frequency of it (9)
       Place of it (9)
       Duration of it (10)
       Extent of it (10)
       Endorsement of it (11, 12)
       Imitation of it (13-16)
       Success of it (17-20)

(*c*) The Conclusion of Paul's Ministry in Ephesus (21-41)

   (1) Paul's Plans for the Future (21, 22)

   (2) The Heathen Attack upon Paul (23-41)

       (*a*) The Mass Meeting (23-28)
           The Leader of the Disturbance (24a, 25a)
           The Ground of Complaint (23-27)
           The Effect on the Crowd (28)

(*b*) The Theatre Gathering (29-41)
    The arrest of Paul's companions (29)
    Paul's intervention prevented (30, 31)
    The confusion of the crowd (32)
    The refusal to hear Alexander (33, 34)
    The speech by the Town Clerk (35-41)

1 Corinthians. A.D. 57. From EPHESUS

PAUL'S THIRD MISSIONARY JOURNEY

O U T W A R D	FROM	I	ANTIOCH (S)	xviii. 22, 23	
	THROUGH		Galatia	xviii. 23, —xvi. 6	Cities of, visited
			Phrygia	xviii. 23, —	before.
			Upper Country	xix. 1	
	To	2	EPHESUS	xix. 1	
		3	TROAS	2 Cor. ii. 12, 13	
	THROUGH		Macedonia	xx. 1, 2.	Cities of, visited
				2 Cor. ii. 13	before.
	INTO	4	Greece, Corinth	xx. 2, 3	Corinth

PAUL'S THIRD MISSIONARY JOURNEY

Outward. In the record of this part of the Journey only *three* cities are named: (A. xviii. 22, 23; xix. 1. 2 Cor. ii. 12, 13), and four Provinces: Galatia, Phrygia, Macedonia, and Greece. But these Provinces represent many cities which the Apostle must have visited: Tarsus, Derbe, Lystra, Iconium, Antioch (P); and in Europe, Philippi, Thessalonica, Beroea and Corinth (A. xx. 2, 3. 2 Cor. xiii. 1). The record is very compressed, for Paul's programme must have been very full.

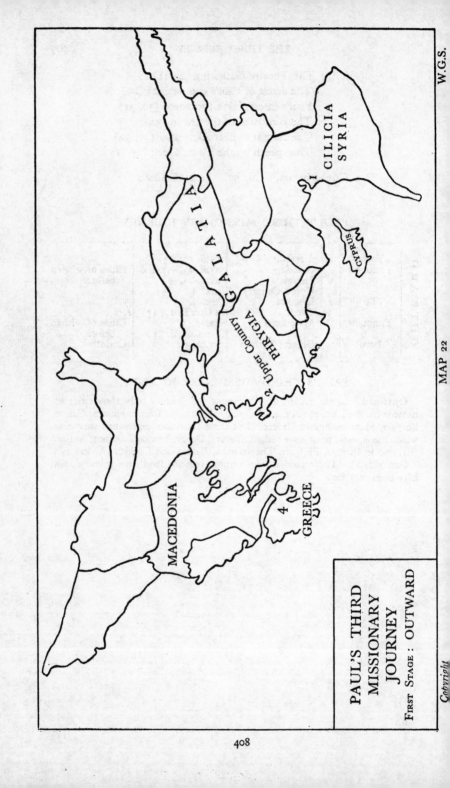

PAUL'S THIRD
MISSIONARY
JOURNEY

First Stage : OUTWARD

MAP 22

W.G.S.

Copyright

408

THE OUTWARD JOURNEY

1. PAUL'S ACTIVITIES IN ASIA

At Antioch in Syria

The Apostle must have arrived at his missionary base a tired and a sad man, yet he did not remain there for long (xviii. 23). He must have told the Church of his ministry in Europe, and of his intention to undertake a third journey 'if God will' (xviii. 20, 21). It may be also that at this time he heard from Timothy of the defection of the Galatians, though it is more probable that the news came later. This matter is immediately related to the disputed date of the Galatian letter (see p. 424).

A THIRD JOURNEY

'He departed, and went through the region of Galatia and Phrygia in order, stablishing all the disciples' (xviii. 23). This was Paul's third visit to eastern Asia Minor (chs. xiii. - xiv.; xv. 41), and it was his last. It appears that he entered upon the third journey *alone*, and went overland, passing once more through the Cilician Gates of Taurus, and visiting the churches he founded in Derbe, Lystra, Iconium, and Antioch in Pisidia. This may have occupied from two to three months. The brief summary 'stablishing all the disciples' would seem to suggest that the Galatian crisis had not yet arisen (Gal. i. 6-10; iii. 1-5).

TOWARDS EPHESUS

Paul went West 'through the upper country' (xix. 1) to Ephesus. He did not take the usual Roman road, but one further north, by-passing Colossae and Laodicea (Col. ii. 1). This visit was the fulfilment of a promise he had made (xviii. 20, 21). As a Christian strategist Paul concentrated on the great cities of his world, knowing that from these centres his message would spread to towns and villages. Of such centres were Philippi, Thessalonica, Corinth, and now Ephesus.

APOLLOS

At first sight it may seem that ch. xviii. 24-28 is interjected without reference to what precedes, but further consideration will show that it fills what otherwise would be a gap in the story which connects Paul with Ephesus and Corinth, and the references to Apollos in 1 Corinthians (i. 12; iii. 4, 5, 6, 22; iv. 6; xvi. 12. cf. Titus iii. 13).

What we are told of this man is most interesting and informing. He was a Jew; he hailed from Alexandria; he was cultured; he was learned in the Scriptures and powerful in his use of them; what he knew he taught with enthusiasm and accuracy; but his knowledge was limited; he was familiar with the Forerunner's baptism, but not with Christian baptism. He taught eloquently and boldly in the synagogue, and Priscilla and Aquila who heard him were much impressed, and in their home they helped him to fill up the gaps in his knowledge.

It may be that visitors from Corinth heard Apollos in the synagogue and invited him to come to their city. This he agreed to do, and Ephesian Christians wrote a letter to the Church at Corinth commending him.

At Corinth Apollos vigorously refuted the Jews, publicly proving from the Scriptures that Jesus is the Messiah. 1 Corinthians supplements this story as the references show.

There are those who think that Apollos wrote the Epistle to the Hebrews, but this is only a guess.

Much may be learnt from what is recorded of this man. Like a blazing comet in the ecclesiastical heavens we see him at Ephesus and Corinth striking down opposition and unbelief with the onslaught of his fervid and logical eloquence. Unlike most people of his ability he was teachable (xviii. 26b). The man who has finished his education never began it. Nobody knows all that the Bible has to teach, and we all may learn much from those who cannot wield our influence.

Ephesus

Two thousand years ago Ephesus was one of the great cities of the world. It has been spoken of as 'the Marseilles of the Aegaean', and 'the Vanity Fair of Asia'. Its position was unrivalled, its population was mixed and immense, and its wealth was vast. Farrar says, 'it was more Hellenic than Antioch, more oriental than Corinth, more populous than Athens, more wealthy and more refined than Thessalonica, more sceptical and more superstitious than Ancyra or Pessinus'.

Ephesus was one of the most immoral cities of its time, and the headquarters of numerous superstitions. Its famous temple was the city's chief ornament, and was numbered among the seven wonders of the world. It was of enormous proportions—about four times the size of the Parthenon. The construction of it occupied a hundred and twenty years. Its first great shrine was destroyed by fire on the night of the birth of Alexander the Great (B.C. 256), but it was rebuilt.

The goddess of this temple was not the Greek Artemis, the sister of Apollo, the Diana of the Romans, but an Ephesian Artemis (xix. 34), the mother-goddess of Asia Minor.

According to one authority this temple was 418 feet long by 239 feet broad, and it had, according to Pliny, 127 columns, each 60 feet high. Relics of it are in the British Museum.

The theatre was another of the features of Ephesus. It was an immense excavation in the hillside which could contain about 50,000 persons, and its ruins have recently been explored.

Many great names in early church history have been associated with Ephesus, for example, Polycarp, Irenaeus, Papias, and Polycrates, but its greatest associations are those which the New Testament records. Paul was there for a longer period than at any other place during his missionary travels, and to the church there he wrote an Epistle, which, however, was probably a circular letter. Later in the first century the Apostle John lived at Ephesus, and to the church there was sent one of the Seven Letters of the risen Lord (Rev. ii. 1-7). The warning in Rev. ii. 5 was fulfilled, and to-day the site of the city is marked by a few ruins, and its port is a marsh.

PAUL IN EPHESUS

The Apostle visited Ephesus at least three times (xviii. 19-21; xix; xx. 16, 17: 1 Tim. i. 3; iii. 14; iv. 13). When he said 'I know that ye all . . . shall see my face no more' (xx. 25), he was expressing 'a personal conviction based on human probabilities, which was over-ruled by subsequent events' (Knowling). His

MAP 23

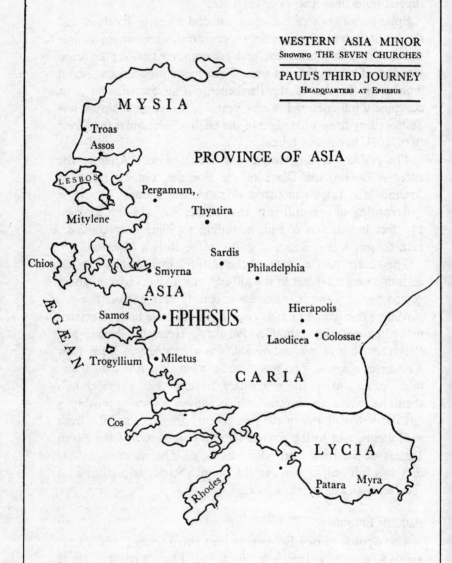

WESTERN ASIA MINOR
Showing THE SEVEN CHURCHES

PAUL'S THIRD JOURNEY
Headquarters at Ephesus

MYSIA

Troas
Assos

PROVINCE OF ASIA

LESBOS

Pergamum,

Mitylene

Thyatira

Chios

Sardis

Smyrna
Philadelphia

ASIA

ÆGEAN

Samos

EPHESUS

Hierapolis

Trogyllium
Miletus

Laodicea Colossae

CARIA

Cos

LYCIA

Rhodes

Patara Myra

MEDITERRANEAN

W.G.S.

association with this city put it on the map of the spread of Christianity in the first century. Farrar says: 'Ephesus was the third capital and starting-point of Christianity. At Jerusalem it was born in the cradle of Judaism; Antioch had been the starting-point of the Church of the Gentiles; Ephesus was to witness its full development, and the final amalgamation of its unconsolidated elements in the work of John the Apostle of Love.'

The record in Acts xix. is in two parts. Verses 1-22 tell of Paul's ministry in Ephesus from two to three years (xx. 31); and verses 23-41 tell of an incident which occurred at the end of this period, and at most cannot have occupied more than a day or two.

TWELVE DISCIPLES

This is a strange incident, and it leaves one wondering for what purpose it is recorded (xix. 1-7). Twelve men, called 'disciples' had been baptized 'into John's baptism', and yet they knew nothing of the Messiahship of Jesus, nor of the Holy Spirit. Not only had they no knowledge of Pentecost, but they were ignorant of the Baptist's teaching, for John had proclaimed the Messiah, and the Holy Spirit (Matt. iii. 3, 11).

How is it that these men had not made contact with Apollos, or with Priscilla and Aquila? They were teachable, at any rate, and received Christian baptism and the Holy Spirit with signs. With this incident their story begins and ends, and we may learn from it that there are lower and higher levels of Christian knowledge and experience, so that we should all 'press on unto perfection' (Heb. vi. 1).

MINISTRY IN THE SYNAGOGUE

Again and again one is astonished at the brevity of Luke's reports. Here he summarizes three months of Paul's work in seventeen words (xix. 8. Gr.).

> 'And he entered into the synagogue and spoke boldly for three months, arguing and persuading about the Kingdom of God.'

But carefully observe how much he says in these few words. Paul's subject was 'the Kingdom of God', by which he meant the grace of God in Jesus the Messiah; his method was to 'reason' and 'try to persuade'; and his manner was 'boldly'. So far as we know,

in no other place was he listened to for so long in a synagogue
(cf. xviii. 19, 20). The word 'to reason' occurs ten times in the
Acts, and in places it refers, almost certainly, to *conversation*.
The reference to *persuasion* tells of attempt, but not of success
(cf. xviii. 4, 6; xix. 8, 9). This must have distressed Paul not a
little. When the truth was met with *obstinacy*, *disobedience*, and
opposition the time had come to leave the unbelievers to their
choice (9a).

PUBLIC AND PRIVATE MINISTRY

This is distinguished from the synagogue witness, and it lasted
eight times as long (xix. 9b, 10; xx. 31). At Corinth Paul went
to the house of Titus Justus (xviii. 7), but in Ephesus he went to
a public hall (xix. 9).

The few words in xix. 9b are full of suggestion, and the
Western text adds to them 'from the fifth to the tenth hour'.
'School' refers to a place where one's *leisure* was spent. Probably
it was one of the five gymnasia which Ephesus had. Was
Tyrannus living? And if so, was he the lecturer in this hall, or
was he the landlord of it?

Paul hired the place and there proclaimed his message for 'two
years'. If the Bezan text is correct his time of witness was from
11.0 a.m. to 4.0 p.m. daily. 'That would be the time when the
serious work of the day was over and the citizens would frequent
the places of recreation' (Rackham). 'Daily' makes the present
day twice or thrice a week look foolish. In two years this would
mean over 700 addresses and over 3,500 hours of witness. We
do not know how much Paul paid for the hire of the 'school',
but we do know that he toiled at tent-making to defray the cost,
to keep himself, and, probably, others (xx. 33-35).

In addition to this public ministry Paul did much pastoral
work. He says that he taught 'from house to house'
(xx. 20; cf. 1 Cor. xvi. 19). A summary of his Ephesian ministry
is on record in his address to the Elders at Miletus (xx. 17-35);
and of it Luke says, 'all they that dwelt in Asia heard the word of
the LORD, both Jews and Greeks', and 'mightily grew the word
of the LORD and prevailed' (xix. 10, 20).

SPECIAL MIRACLES AND THE RESULTS

The record of chapter xix. 11-20 is of profound interest and importance, although in detail it does not allow of dogmatic interpretation. Four bits constitute the section: vv. 11, 12 say that miracles were performed by Paul; vv. 13-16 tell of the effect of this outside the church; vv. 17-19 tell of the effect within the church; and verse 20 summarizes the total effect of Paul's ministry in Ephesus so far.

NAPKINS AND APRONS

Every day Paul worked at tent-making to earn a living (xx. 34, 35; cf. xviii. 3; 2 Thess. iii. 7-9; Ephes. iv. 28). In the performance of this work he wore an 'apron', and as it was hard work he used 'cloths' or 'napkins' to wipe his *sweat*. Superstitious Ephesians, assuming that Paul had miraculous virtue in himself, concluded that this was communicated to things which touched his body, and so, apparently, they got his permission to take these 'napkins' and 'aprons' to people who were sick and could not come to the Apostle, and also to people who were demon-possessed (xix. 12). The effort was successful, and so these miracles are spoken of as 'not common', that is, 'extraordinary' (cf. xxviii. 1-6).

JEWISH EXORCISTS

Many Jews were professional exorcists and moved from place to place uttering incantations and claiming to cast out evil spirits. At Ephesus there were seven brothers who did this, and when they saw what Paul was doing they decided to use what they thought was his formula. Two of these brothers addressed a demon-possessed man, saying: 'I adjure you by Jesus whom Paul preaches'; whereupon the madman flew at them, and the demon in him cried: 'Jesus I acknowledge, and Paul I recognize; but who are you?' The two Jews stripped and wounded fled out of the house.

The Gospel necessarily must come into collision with every form of evil. Here it collides with magic and trickery, much to the humiliation of the latter.

Consider carefully the *presumption*, the *exposure*, the *judgment*, and the *result*. Christianity is always a challenge: it throws down the gauntlet to every would-be rival, and it always tests its strength in the open; and it is always victorious by preaching (8), persistence (10), power (11, 12), and progress (17-20).

Special attention should be given to verse 15, where two Greek words are translated 'know'. Paraphrased it reads, 'The Jesus whom you invoke is one whose authority I *acknowledge*; and the Paul whom you name I *recognize* to be the servant or messenger of God; but what sort of men are ye, who have been empowered to act as you do by neither?' (Lindsay). That's pretty good for a demon. The fact is, spiritual warfare cannot be waged with carnal weapons. God's work must be done by God's people, in God's way, for God's glory. Christ never asked for Caesar's acknowledgment or aid, and why should He? Wealthy, ungodly chairmen for religious meetings! Dance-floors to attract our youth to church! Raffles to prevent a deficit on church accounts! Away with this Laodiceanism.

CHRISTIANS AND A BONFIRE

The news of what had taken place spread rapidly in Ephesus and people were greatly impressed, heathen and Christian alike (xix. 17. cf. v. 1-11). Most of the Christians were converts from paganism, and many of them had continued to practise magic. By what had happened these were convicted and made open confession, and their genuine repentance was proved by their making a bonfire of their books of magical arts.

Mark here the conjunction of *faith, confession, sacrifice*, and *prosperity*. They cannot be separated. When one really *believes*, he will own up to wrong in his life, and then, at all costs, he will put that wrong away. These magical formulae were worth anything from £1,700 to £2,000. But the souls of these people were worth infinitely more. Observe, they did not *sell* these 'books', they *burnt* them. When you abandon what is wrong in your life, do not give it to someone else, for, or without, money; turn it into smoke, and it will come back to you in refreshing rain.

SUCCESS

The reports of Christian progress which are recorded in the
Acts are full of instruction and encouragement (vi. 7; ix. 31;
xii. 24; xvi. 5; xix. 20; xxviii. 31).

PAUL'S PLANS

Much is said in few words in xix. 21, 22. These verses are
wonderful, revealing as they do Paul's solicitude for his converts,
and his noble contempt of idleness. What dreams he dreamt!
MACEDONIA, ACHAIA, JERUSALEM, ROME! Truly neither Alexander,
nor Caesar, nor any hero of antiquity was a match for this little
Benjamite in the magnanimity of his designs.

Luke's record of Paul's designs and doings is brief and in-
complete. It is more than likely that the Apostle paid a visit to
Corinth from Ephesus during his two years in the Asian capital.
This seems to be implied in 2 Cor. ii. 1; xii. 14, 21; xiii. 1, 2.
But it is certain that, while at Ephesus, he wrote a letter to the
Corinthian Church (cf. Acts xix. 21, 22 with 1 Cor. xvi. 5-9). It
is our 1 Corinthians, but, in point of fact, it is his Second Epistle
to this Church (1 Cor. v. 9, 11), and our Second is the Third.

1 Corinthians

This Epistle was written from Ephesus in A.D. 57. The occasion
of it was news which had reached the Apostle (i. 11) concerning
the state of affairs in the Church at Corinth, and he wrote this
second letter (1 Cor. v. 9-11) to deal with these affairs. The
Epistle is in four parts, and deals with Divisions (i. 10-iv. 21);
Disorders (v-vi); Difficulties (vii. xiv); and Doctrine (xv).

The Apostle seems to have been somewhat unsettled at this
time as to what course he should pursue, and the Corinthians
charged him with inconstancy (2 Cor. i. 15-24).

His intention appears to have been to proceed from Ephesus
to Corinth, and then to go north to Macedonia; but he reversed
this plan and went through Macedonia to Corinth (Acts xix. 21, 22.
1 Cor. xvi. 5-9). Even when one is looking to God for guidance
a Christian often finds it difficult to be sure of what way he should

take. Our view is restricted, our knowledge is limited, and circumstances are kaleidoscopic; so that what at one time may seem to be clear, at another time is obscure.

A Riot

As Paul was anticipating a further period of ministry in Ephesus, that is, after the 'two years' (1 Cor. xvi. 8, 9), suddenly the situation became ugly, and degenerated so rapidly that the Apostle was compelled to leave the city (2 Cor. i. 8-11).

Neither the Government nor the Jews created this riot, but the leader of a trade. Religion and business intermingled to stir dangerous excitement, and, says Rackham, 'when devotion to religion coincides with self-interest, then the fury of fanaticism is resistless'. Mass emotion is a strange thing, and leads people to do together what they would never dream of doing separately (xix. 32). Paul and his associates had said nothing against the Ephesian temple and goddess (xix. 37), but their gospel was contrary to both, and this became evident in the reduced sales of models of the temple, or statuettes of Artemis; and Demetrius a silversmith gathered together his fellow-craftsmen in the agora and made an inflaming speech which filled the crowd with wrath, and they all started shouting 'Great is Artemis of the Ephesians'.

This illustrates the age-long conflict between truth and error, right and wrong, holiness and sin, Christ and the devil; for that's what it amounts to. Though what Demetrius says is exaggerated, he bears, unwittingly, a magnificent testimony to the power of the Gospel and the work of Paul (26).

Here is the first conference of a Trade Union (24, 25). A 'vested interest' was being attacked, and it squealed, as all such interests do, liquor, gambling, impurity. Christianity need not directly attack these to rouse them to hot hostility; it has only to proclaim itself, and that is the most powerful condemnation of all that is opposed to it. Of course, we should also attack directly. We see here how selfishness in private (25) can turn to piety in public (27). Here also, is an illustration of crowd psychology (32-34). There are no riots so dangerous as religious riots, nor so fanatical.

THEATRICALISM

Someone shouted 'Theatre' and this motley mob rushed to the immense excavation in the hillside which could accommodate 50,000 persons. On the way they laid hands on two of the evangelizing group, Gaius and Aristarchus, for they were in need of some quarry. When Paul heard of this he decided to go to the theatre and face the mob, but some disciples and friendly Asiarchs persuaded him not to do so, knowing that he would be murdered (2 Cor. i. 9-10).

The mad farce which had commenced in the agora was continued in the theatre. Alexander, a Jew, asked for a hearing, as he wanted it to be understood that not the Jews but the Christians had created this situation; but as the mob did not care who was responsible they would not listen to him.

THE TOWN CLERK

The Town Clerk appears to have been a very able man. He safeguarded Gaius, Aristarchus, and Alexander, defended Paul against the charge made (37), rebuked Demetrius (38), and warned the crowd (36-40), while upholding the City's paganism (35, 36). His speech is a model of diplomacy.

It should be noted that three things characterized the Christians at this time: *faithfulness* to Christ and the Gospel; *courage*, both physical and moral (30-33); and *prudence* (30, 31). We should relate and cultivate all virtues, and not develop one at the expense of another. Don't lose your head in a crowd. How impotent is godless wrath.

The Journey Home
(xx. 1-xxi. 16)

Assuming that Paul left Syrian Antioch for the third time in A.D. 54, his tour through Galatia and Phrygia (xviii. 23) and his stay in Ephesus would bring him to A.D. 57, and this would mean that it took the Apostle about a year to journey from Ephesus to Jerusalem, which he would reach in A.D. 58. Three months of this time were spent in Corinth (xx. 3).

The following is an outline of this year's ministry, which should be studied with Map 24 (p. 428).

THE INWARD JOURNEY
(xx. 3-xxi. 16)

I N W A R D	THROUGH		Macedonia	xx. 3
	TO	5	PHILIPPI	xx. 6
		6	Troas	xx. 6
		7	ASSOS	xx. 14
	OVER	a	MITYLENE	xx. 14
	AGAINST	b	Chios	xx. 15
	TOUCHED	c	Samos	xx. 15
	TO	8	MILETUS	xx. 15
	BY	d	Cos	xxi. 1
		e	Rhodes	xxi. 1
	TO	9	PATARA	xxi. 1
	BY	f	Cyprus	xxi. 3
	TO	10	TYRE	xxi. 3
		11	PTOLEMAIS	xxi. 7
		12	CAESAREA	xxi. 8
		13	JERUSALEM	xxi. 15

Inward. In the record of this part of the Journey only Philippi in Macedonia is named (A. xx. 6). A week was spent at Troas. Paul walked from Troas to Assos, and there boarded a ship (A. xx. 14). At Mitylene, Chios and Samos the company appear to have spent the night without landing. This applies also to Cos and Rhodes. But Paul landed at Miletus (A. xx. 15), and the whole company changed ships at Patara (A. xxi. 1). At each of the last four places named time was spent, and from Tyre to Jerusalem the journey was made on foot.

THE INWARD JOURNEY

2. PAUL'S EXPERIENCES IN EUROPE (xx. 1-6)

(i) The Circuit in MACEDONIA (xx. 1, 2a)

(via Troas and Neapolis)

2 Corinthians. A.D. 57. From MACEDONIA

(ii) The Conspiracy in ACHAIA (xx. 3)

No doubt at CORINTH

Three Months

Plot of the Jews to kill Paul

Galatians. A.D. 58. From CORINTH

Romans. A.D. 58. From CORINTH

(iii) The Convocation in PHILIPPI (3b-6a)

Attended the Feast of Unleavened Bread
(Luke rejoins Paul here: 'we')

Seven men sent forward to Troas

3. PAUL'S JOURNEY TO JERUSALEM (xx. 6-xxi. 16)

(i) His Experience during a week at TROAS (xx. 6-12)
  Meeting of the disciples on the first day of the week
    (7, 11; cf. ii. 42)
  Paul's discourse till late at night (7, 9)
  The accident to Eutychus, and his recovery (8-10, 12)
  The Breaking of Bread, and ministry till daybreak (7, 11)

(ii) His Farewell to his Friends at MILETUS (13-38)

(a) The Journey to MILETUS (13-16)

TROAS to ASSOS	20 miles
ASSOS to MITYLENE	40 miles
MITYLENE to CHIOS	70 miles
CHIOS to SAMOS	70 miles
SAMOS to MILETUS	50 miles
EPHESUS by-passed	

(b) The Discourse at MILETUS (17-35)

  (1) To the Audience in general (18-27)
    The Past is recalled (18-21)
    The Future is anticipated (22-24)
    The Present is estimated (25-27)
  (2) To the Elders in particular (28-35)
    The Charge (28-31)
    The Farewell (32-35)
  (c) The Departure from MILETUS (36-38)
    The Scene on the Shore
    Prayer. Emotion. Good-bye

(iii) The Voyage from MILETUS to JERUSALEM (xxi. 1-16)

MILETUS to COS (1)	about	40 miles
COS to RHODES (1)	about	85 miles
RHODES to PATARA (1)	about	70 miles
Changed ships		
PATARA to TYRE (2, 3)	about	400 miles
AT TYRE for a week (3-6)		

  The disciples sought out (4)
  The warning against going to Jerusalem (4)
  The pathetic farewell (5, 6)

TYRE to PTOLEMAIS (7)	about	25 miles

  Met the disciples, and remained with them
    for one day

PTOLEMAIS to CAESAREA (8-16)   about   30 miles

>   The guests of Philip and his daughters (8, 9)
>   The prophecy of Agabus (10, 11)
>   The effect of the prophecy on the company
>   and on Paul (12-14)

CAESAREA to JERUSALEM (15, 16)   about   64 miles

>   With certain Caesarean disciples, in addition
>   to Paul's companions, and with Mnason
>   who was to be the host in Jerusalem

Read again what has been said about Paul's Plans (p. 417).

2. PAUL'S EXPERIENCES IN EUROPE
(xx. 1-6)

DISCONSOLATE

The man who wrote, 'Rejoice in the LORD alway' was himself, on more than one occasion, thoroughly unhappy and miserable. He was this when he left Ephesus. Not finding Titus at Troas he was much agitated and 'had no relief for (his) spirit', and he says that, when he crossed over into Macedonia, his flesh had no relief, that he was afflicted on every side, that without were fightings and within were fears (2 Cor. i. 8; ii. 13; iv. 7; vii. 5)

It will be well for us to understand that Christians are subject, as are all others, to physical and mental laws. The believer is not exempt from the law of cause and effect. He is not exempt from the blast of a bomb which kills a neighbour; he is not immune from the sicknesses which befall mankind, nor from the sufferings which accompany them. The Christian is given no promise that he will be exempt from depression, dejection, despondency. This is not to say that such a state is excusable whenever it occurs, nor does it imply that the believer cannot find relief in Christ; but it does mean that difficult circumstances, if prolonged, may, and probably will affect our nerves, and will produce unhappy mental reactions. The experience of Paul proves this.

MACEDONIA

Paul went from Ephesus to Neapolis by sea, and all that Luke tells us of the Apostle's visit to Macedonia is that 'he went through those parts, and gave much exhortation' (xx. 1, 2).

It is safe to assume that by this statement is meant that Paul visited Philippi, Thessalonica, and Beroea where he had been five years before, in A.D. 52.

2 Corinthians

While at Philippi Titus reached Paul from Corinth and brought a cheering report of the effect upon the Church there of his First Epistle (2 Cor. vii. 5-16). This led him to write a Second Letter, which three of his companions took to the Church—Titus, perhaps Luke, and another, unnamed (2 Cor. viii. 17, 18, 22).

There are three notes in this intensely personal communication.

In chs. i-vii the note is one of *Consolation*, in which are explanation, exposition, and exhortation. In chs. viii-ix the note is one of *Solicitation*, in which he urges the Christians to be diligent in raising the promised collection for their fellow-believers in Jerusalem. In chs. x-xiii the note is one of *Vindication*, in which he defends his apostolic authority against Judaisers who were impugning it. These notes represent the mingled emotions of the Apostle at this time.

A matter which does not concern us at present may be mentioned here, namely the view which is influentially held that the Apostle wrote four letters to Corinth: (*a*) the lost letter of 1 Cor. v. 9; (*b*) our 1 Corinthians; (*c*) a stern letter (2 Cor. ii. 3; vii. 12), possibly 2 Cor. x. 1-xiii. 10; and (*d*) a glad letter, 2 Cor. i-ix; xiii. 11-14.

While 2 Corinthians was being communicated to Corinth it is not unlikely that Paul visited Illyricum (Rom. xv. 19), but passing over all the details which may be gathered from 1—2 Corinthians Luke simply says that Paul 'came into Greece' (the only time this name occurs in the Acts).

THREE MONTHS AT CORINTH

After an absence of four years Paul went back to Corinth, and stayed there for three months as the guest of Gaius (Rom. xvi. 23). Luke says nothing about this brief period which, it may be claimed, was the most fruitful period in the whole of Paul's ministry, because at this time he probably wrote GALATIANS, and certainly ROMANS, and no one else has ever done such great work in three months.

TWO EPISTLES

Galatians

There is considerable difference of opinion as to *when* this Epistle was written. One view relates it to the time immediately preceding the Apostle's third missionary journey and visit to the Galatian churches, about A.D. 54. Another view relates it to the time of Paul's last visit to Corinth, about A.D. 58. Discussion of the merits of these views lies outside the scope of this work, but we follow the later date.

Shortly before the Apostle's arrival in Corinth, or after his arrival, news reached him of the defection of the Galatian churches, due to the activities of Judaizing agents. In Galatia, as later in Corinth, these mischief-makers denied Paul's apostleship, and endeavoured to subject his converts to the Mosaic law. He was much hurt by the fickleness of the Galatian Christians, and wrote this Epistle to them in which he makes it crystal clear what Christianity is, and that the object of the Gospel was not to make Jews of the Gentiles, but to bring them into perfect spiritual liberty in Christ.

In chs. i. 1-ii. 21 Paul vindicates his apostolic authority; in chs. iii-iv he shows that justification is by faith in Christ alone; and in chs. v-vi he exhorts all Christians to enter into the full consequences of their emancipation.

Romans

It is practically certain that Paul wrote this Epistle during his three months stay in Corinth in A.D. 58. The similarity in essence of *Galatians* and *Romans* makes it most likely that *Galatians* was written at the same time, and that, in a sense, it served as a first draft of the longer Epistle.

The occasion of the Roman Letter was the fast approaching close of the Apostle's missionary ministry. He was well aware of this (Acts xx. 22-24; xxi. 10-14), and felt that the time had come for him to state in a more systematic form than hitherto the substance and scope of his Gospel. This he did, while at Corinth, in an Epistle which Luther described as 'the chief part of the New Testament, and the perfect gospel', and which Coleridge has called 'the most profound writing extant'. The Epistle is the classic of Christian Philosophy, and it is in three distinct parts: Philosophy of Salvation (i. 1-viii. 39); Philosophy of History (ix-xi); and Philosophy of Behaviour (xii-xvi); and that which gives unity to these parts is the fact and truth of the 'Righteousness of God' (i. 16, 17).

This wonderful Epistle was written by the hand of Tertius, and dispatched to Rome by the hands of Phoebe the deaconess of Cenchreae; and, of course, it prepared the way for the Apostle's visit to the capital of the Empire, which occurred three years later.

CONSUMMATION

One has the feeling when reading what may be known of Paul's three months in Corinth that events were moving toward a consummation; that Paul and his ministry were being directed towards a worthy completion, notwithstanding that this was to be on an executioner's block. Many a glorious life and work has had a violent end, an end which was its crown. A big stride toward this consummation was taken in Corinth in A.D. 58.

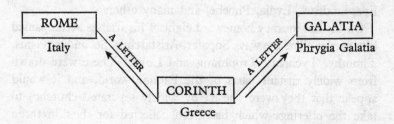

PLAN AND PLOT

The last time Paul was resident in Corinth, four to five years before the present date, the Jews who made an attack upon him were severely rebuffed (xviii. 12-17), and they had not forgotten it; so, when Paul returned to the city they resolved to have their revenge on him. They learned that he intended to sail, probably by a pilgrim ship, from Cenchreae to Jerusalem, to observe the

Passover, and they plotted to kill him at the port, or to throw him overboard if he sailed.

Paul heard of this, and decided to frustrate their evil design by going overland instead of by sea (xx. 3).

So while the Jews were waiting for him at Cenchreae, he went northward overland toward Philippi. The meaning of ch. xx. 5 is not certain, and the view may be correct that all the brethren named in verse 4 went with Paul from Corinth to Philippi, and only from Philippi went ahead of the Apostle to Troas, there to await his arrival (xx. 3-5).

In Paul's change of plan no mention is made of the Holy Spirit, but, of course, his movements were not determined merely by his sagacity, but by the guidance which certainly he would seek and receive. The plotters had only their wits to help them, but the planner had God to guide him.

PAUL'S COMPANIONS

Paul had a genius for friendship, and he drew to himself during his twenty years of missionary ministry a group of men, younger and older, and more and less distinguished, who as Staff Officers were devoted to their great General. Each of them has a right to remembrance on his and her own merits: Barnabas, Silas, Timothy, Luke, Titus, Aquila, Priscilla, Mark, Epaphroditus, Lydia, Phoebe, and many others.

On his last journey homeward eight of his friends accompanied him part or all of the way: Sopater, Aristarchus, Secundus, Gaius, Timothy, Tychicus, Trophimus and Luke. These were drawn from widely distant parts of the Pauline world, and it would appear that they were chosen by widely separated churches to take the offerings which had been collected for their brethren in Jerusalem (2 Cor. viii. 18-23). About three of them, or four, we know practically nothing, but all of them must have been to the tired Apostle a comfort and a joy.

'WE'

It is most important to observe that several parts of the Acts record are characterized by the use of 'we'—xvi. 10-17; xx. 5-16; xxi. 1-18; xxvii. 1-xxviii. 16. It is clear that in these sections the author of the record includes himself, and it is certain that the author is Luke. Where 'we' occurs Luke is with Paul, and this fact is illuminating. The first time they are seen together (in the record) is at Troas, and from there they go together to Philippi (xvi. 10-12); but when Paul left Philippi Luke did not go with him, and at that point '*they*' takes the place of '*we*' (xvii. 1), and it does not occur again until the point we have now reached (xx. 5, 6), about six years later. Presumably Luke spent these years in Philippi, to the great benefit of the church there. But from now, A.D. 58, he is Paul's companion to the end of his first Roman imprisonment in A.D. 63 (Col. iv. 14; Phile. 24), and when his second imprisonment ended in death (2 Tim. iv. 11). Why Luke ends the Acts record as he does, and does not write again, will be noticed later on.

3. PAUL'S JOURNEY TO JERUSALEM

(xx. 6-xxi. 16)

No part of Luke's record is so detailed as that which tells of Paul's voyage from Philippi to Jerusalem, which represents a period of from six to seven weeks. The following are the notes of time which Luke supplies.

Seven days, at least, at Philippi, to keep the Passover and the days of unleavened bread (xx. 6). *Five days* from Philippi to Troas (xx. 6). *Six days* at Troas (xx. 6). *Five days* (probably) from Troas to Miletus (xx. 13-15). *Two days* (probably) at Miletus (xx. 16-38). *Three days* from Miletus to Patara (xxi. 1). *Three or four days* from Patara to Tyre (xxi. 1-3). *Seven days* at Tyre (xxi. 4). *One day* from Tyre to Ptolemais (xxi. 6, 7). *One day* at Ptolemais (xxi. 7). *One day* from Ptolemais to Caesarea (xxi. 8). *Four* or *five days* at Caesarea (xxi. 8, 10, 15). *One day* from Caesarea to Jerusalem (xxi. 15).

This itinerary occupies the forty-nine days from Passover in Philippi to Pentecost in Jerusalem (xx. 6, 16). The period is brief, but within it much took place.

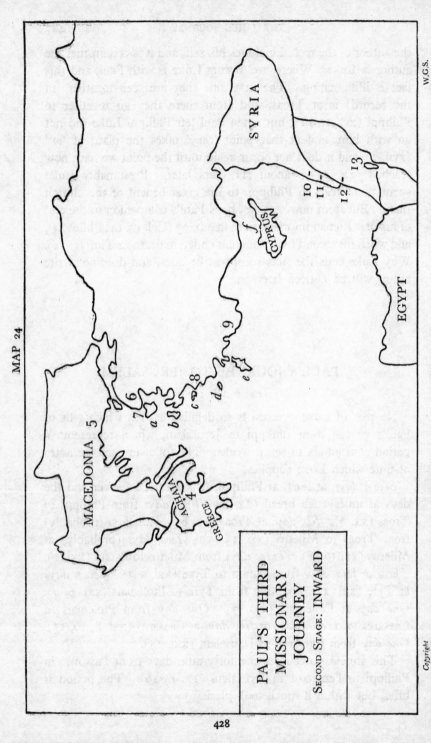

MAP 24

W.G.S.

SYRIA

13

10
11
12

CYPRUS

f

EGYPT

9

6
7
5
8
a
b
c
d
e

MACEDONIA

ACHAIA
4

GREECE

PAUL'S THIRD
MISSIONARY
JOURNEY

SECOND STAGE: INWARD

Troas

Paul was at Troas three times. (1) In A.D. 52, when it was revealed to him that he must extend his mission to Europe (xvi. 8-10). (2) In A.D. 57, on his way from Ephesus to Philippi. On this occasion Paul preached, but he was so distressed that Titus had not met him there with news of Corinth that he shortened his opportunity and went on to Philippi. (2 Cor. ii. 12, 13). (3) In A.D. 58, on his way for the last time to Jerusalem. On this occasion Paul remained a week in the city (xx. 7-12).

What he did throughout the week we are not told, but Luke gives a vivid account of the Apostle's last day there.

SUNDAY WORSHIP

'Upon the first day of the week—we were gathered together to break bread' (xx. 7). This is a statement of great importance for two reasons at least. (1) It supplies evidence of the Christian Sabbath, called the Lord's Day, and Sunday. The Jewish Sabbath is at the end of the week, but the Christian Sabbath is at its beginning, and the latter is accounted for by the resurrection of Jesus. It seems that this day was observed from the Church's beginning (1 Cor. xvi. 2). Jews work and then worship. Christians worship and then work. It is debatable whether or not the Christian Sunday can be insisted on from Exod. xx. 8. The Christian Sabbath is not imposed upon an ungodly world.

(2) The statement indicates also how 'the first day of the week' was spent. It appears that this day began at sundown on Saturday (when the Jewish Sabbath ended), and Christians 'gathered-together' for worship. This consisted of two meals— in what order cannot confidently be affirmed—the *Agape* or *Love-feast*, and the *Eucharist* or *Lord's Supper*; and to these were added the reading of Scripture, prayer, singing of psalms, and ministry of the Word (cf. ii. 46, 47; 1 Cor. xi. 20-34). These two facts explain the service at Troas having been held at night (xx. 7, 11).

FROM DEATH TO LIFE

During a long service, in the third floor of a house in Troas, a boy fell asleep, and, losing his balance, he fell to the ground and was killed. Paul immediately ceased preaching, and going down, with Luke no doubt, to where the lad lay, he 'fell on him, and embraced him', and life came back to him (cf. 1 Kings xvii. 17-24; 2 Kings iv. 32-37; Luke vii. 11-15; viii. 49-56). The medical doctor would know at once that the boy was dead, so that the only explanation of what happened is that Paul performed miracle.

It is astonishing that after this occurrence the service was continued 'till break of day', the Lord's Supper being observed.

What a service they had that Sunday, and what a preacher! (7). Paul might well have rested that night, for in the morning he was to start out on a long journey; but no—he talked *'till break of day'* (7, 11).

Very wrong inferences may be drawn from this incident. It is not a solemn warning to worshippers not to sleep in church, though, of course, they should not do so. Neither is it a rebuke to preachers who preach long sermons, though, of course, a sermon can be too long, as well as too short. The person who, falling asleep, fell and was killed, was a child, too young to appreciate Paul, and the room was very hot, but gladly did all the others sit up all night to listen to such a preacher. What preachers there were in bygone days! Yes, and what hearers! Eutychus was raised to life; and Paul caught his boat (10, 11) and Troas never forgot that week.

ALONE FOR TWENTY MILES

What seems a casual remark (xx. 13) deserves careful consideration. Why did Paul want to be alone from Troas to Assos? Think of all that had taken place in the past few months, and anticipate, as Paul must have done, what lay ahead for him, and one will understand how he craved to break away from his companions and be alone with his LORD.

Dr. Alexander Whyte has told how that, when on holiday one Christmas at Bonskied, he felt he just had to break away from the party and be alone for a while. He says: 'One afternoon I stole into my coat and hat, and took my staff, and slipped out of the house in secret. For two hours I walked alone and prayed. Two hours is a long time to steal away from one's books and companions to swing one's walking-stick, and to utter unavailing ejaculations to one's self in a wintry glen; but then, my two hours look to me now—as they tasted to me then—the best strength and the best sweetness of all my Christmas holiday'.

This is the kind of urge that Paul must have had, and so he decided to walk alone the twenty miles from Troas to Assos, that he might talk to God, and listen to Him, and receive from his LORD the comfort and courage he would need for the task confronting him. Do you ever feel that you *must* get away from nearest and dearest, on to the water, into the valley, up on the mountain, out in the country, anywhere, so long as you can be alone with God; do you?

FROM ASSOS TO MILETUS

How glad his friends must have been to see their leader again, and they were to be together now for the rest of the voyage. From Assos to Mitylene was about 40 miles; from Mitylene to Chios, about 70 miles; from Chios to Samos, about 70 miles; and from Samos to Miletus, about 50 miles. Allowing for anchoring a night at Mitylene, and one at Trogyllium, this 230 miles could be covered in from two to three days.

PAUL AND THE EPHESIAN ELDERS

About fifteen months after his sudden departure from Ephesus, Paul was again in the neighbourhood of that city. It is not easy to say what is meant by 'Paul had determined to sail past Ephesus' (xx. 16). Had he the control of the vessel? Or had he great influence over the captain? Or had he embarked on a fast ship which he knew would not call at the port of Ephesus? We do not know, but the boat passed Ephesus and called at Miletus, about 30 to 50 miles distant from the city. The ship was to be there long enough to allow of Paul sending to Ephesus to ask the Elders of the church to come to him, for he wanted to open his heart to them about the past and the future. Dearly did the Apostle love the church at Ephesus which he had nurtured for over two years, and so precipitate had been his departure from the city that he had had no opportunity to speak a farewell word, but such a word he must now speak to those who were the spiritual leaders in the church, the shepherds of the flock (xx. 28. cf. 1 Peter ii. 25).

In the first century 'elder' and 'bishop' described the same office, and must not be confused with meanings which later became attached to these terms (xx. 17, 28. Titus i. 5, 7).

THE FAREWELL ADDRESS

Time was short, and the word was weighty, and so, as at Troas, it was a night meeting—Saturday evening till Sunday morning—and the congregation consisted of the Ephesian Elders, Paul's companions, and other disciples (xx. 25). What Paul said to this company is recorded in xx. 18-35. Because of the unique circumstances this speech differs from all others which Paul delivered, and, having regard for the occasion and company, it may be variously analysed. Rackham says:

'It falls at once into two parts at verse 28 according to the audience in view—the church at large (18-27) and the presbyters (28-35). Again, there is a further division in the second part at verse 32; so that there are really three divisions of which the dominating ideas are: *vindication* (18-27); *charge* (28-31); *farewell* (32-35). But each of these ideas runs throughout the whole, and in relation to different spheres, viz.: (*a*) (18-27) the world at large; (*b*) (28-31) the church; (*c*) (32-35) the life of the individual' (*The Acts of the Apostles*, p. 385).

This is a pathetic and heroic farewell address. Our life is divided into two parts, past and future; the present is a mere point dividing the two. Paul looked *behind* with humble gratitude (18-21), and *before* with Christian courage (22-24). Pity the person that has no fruitful past, and no hopeful future. Paul's life was one of consecration (18, 19), fidelity (20, 27, 31), diligence and beneficence (33-35); and so he could anticipate suffering cheerfully (22, 23), for absorbed in his Master's service he was sublimely indifferent to his bodily estate (24).

The two dominating notes of his message at Ephesus were *repentance* and *faith* (21), and where these are wanting there is no Gospel. The personal element is very prominent in this farewell address as you will see from the occurrence of '*I*', '*me*', '*my*'. The occasion called for this, and the references are revealing. Note carefully the tenderness of Paul's farewell testimony (25-27), and the concern of the final exhortation (28-31). Let us all so live that we shall not be ashamed at last.

'March breast forward; never doubt that clouds will break.'

From a theological point of view we may say that verse 28 is the most important in the speech: 'The Church of God which He purchased with His own blood'. Here Jesus is called God, and spiritual life is by His atoning sacrifice. This verse reveals the Divine Trinity: '*The Holy Spirit* . . . the Church of *God* . . . *His own blood*'.

Much has been written on xx. 25, 38. Of Paul's statement, 'Ye all . . . shall see my face no more', Knowling says: 'No infallible presentiment or prophetic inspiration, but a personal conviction based on human probabilities, which was over-ruled by subsequent events. The word cannot fairly be taken to mean more than this, for in the same context the Apostle himself had distinctly disclaimed a full knowledge of the future (verses 22, 23).'

The Pastoral Epistles indicate that Paul did go to Ephesus again, and so was seen again by some to whom he had spoken at Miletus (1 Tim. i. 3; iii. 14; 2 Tim. i. 16-18). Divine Providence is under no necessity to follow our gloomy forecasts!

FROM MILETUS TO CAESAREA

The journey was uneventful from Miletus to Patara, but here Paul and his friends changed ships and got aboard one that was bound for Tyre, from 350 to 400 miles distant; and which took three or four days to cover the distance.

Here the ship was to unlade her cargo, and either necessarily or by arrangement (xxi. 4, 5) the Apostle had a week at his disposal in the city. He had probably been there before, on the way from Antioch to Jerusalem (ch. xi. 27-30), and knew that there were Christians there, but not knowing where they were, he had to 'search them out' (xxi. 4).

How the Apostle spent the week in Tyre we are not told, but may safely guess. He neither rested, nor went sight-seeing, but ministered to the church, and in such a way that at his departure the whole church and the children accompanied him to the ship, and knelt in prayer on the shore (xxi. 5, 6).

Another short day brought the ship to Ptolemais, and there also Paul found disciples and remained with them for one day. These groups of disciples everywhere (xxi. 4, 7, 8) must have been to these hungry hearts what food depots are to Arctic travellers. Wherever there is a Christian, God has a foothold.

This was the end of his journeys by ship until he sailed for Rome two years later. From Ptolemais the Apostle walked across the Plain of Sharon to Caesarea 44 miles distant.

Luke kept a diary. Mark the minute details of his record: a day here, seven there, an act, a warning, women and children— all in the mosaic of a Divine plan. As grains of sand make the shore, and drops of water the ocean, so do hours and days, words and deeds, tears and laughter, sorrow and rapture, make up what we call *life*. Everything counts. The outstanding lesson is that *each of us must do what God tells US to do*. God told Paul to go *to* Jerusalem.

In Caesarea

The few days that Paul spent in Caesarea—the political capital of Judaea—Luke records in seven verses (xxi. 8-14), but the record, though brief, is pregnant.

1. Paul stayed with 'Philip the evangelist'. He is described thus to distinguish him from Philip the Apostle. He was one of the first seven deacons appointed to attend to the 'business' of the Church (vi. 1-6); he evangelized the Samaritans after the death of Stephen (viii. 5 ff); he made the Ethiopian eunuch a convert and baptized him (viii. 26 ff); he made his home in Caesarea, and from there he engaged in itinerant evangelism, that is, as A. T. Robertson says, he 'gospelized communities'.

2. Luke mentions that Philip 'had four daughters, virgins, who did prophesy'. It is most probable that he obtained from them much of his knowledge of the beginnings of Christian history. Holy Scripture has not a little to say about the ministry of women

—Miriam, Deborah, Huldah, Hannah, Mary, Anna, Elisabeth, Philip's daughters, Lydia, Phoebe, Lois, Eunice, Priscilla, Euodia, Syntyche and others.

3. Agabus, a prophet, is twice mentioned in the 'Acts'. He predicted a famine, 'which took place in the days of Claudius' (xi. 27-30); and here he predicted symbolically what would happen to Paul at Jerusalem (xxi. 10, 11); but he did not advise the Apostle not to go to Jerusalem, as others did (xxi. 4, 12). For other symbolic actions see 1 Kings xxii. 11; Isa. xx. 1, 2 ff; Jer. xiii. 1 ff; Ezek. iv. 1 ff; *et al.*

4. Paul, who would not be persuaded to avoid Jerusalem used a striking word when he remonstrated with his friends (xxi. 13). '*"Breaking my heart"* is a rare word meaning to break up, to pound to bits, and, apparently from the use of washerwomen pounding clothes with stones, etc., in water, to bleach them, to whiten' (Jackson and Lake).

One of the most difficult problems of practical life is to know what are the fixed points on which we must not give way, to which all other considerations must yield, and what are the points which may be yielded under the pressure of conflicting circumstances. Never is the choice of a course made so difficult as when the pleading of our best friends is on the one side, and our convictions are on the other. Luther said: '*Were there as many devils in Worms as tiles on the roofs, yet thither will I go*'. And Paul said: '*I am ready to die for the name of the Lord Jesus*' (13). Weeping may break a heart (13), but it should not break a resolution formed in the sight of God and by His Spirit. IF HE BIDS THEE—RISE AND GO. Be unyieldingly true to God and your conscience.

There are distinct parallels between Paul's attitude and action at this time, and that of our Lord in Gethsemane—the resignation to God's will; the sorrowfulness; the reference to being 'delivered'; the kneeling in prayer; the kiss; the binding; the being parted from his friends; and the determination bravely to face danger and death. In the case of our LORD, of Paul, of Luther, and of many another this attitude is not one of obstinacy, but of obedience to a deeply rooted conviction.

JERUSALEM

The meaning of ch. xxi. 15, 16 seems to be that as the distance from Caesarea to Jerusalem was 64 miles horses were provided to carry the party and the baggage. This is what Chrysostom and Ramsay thought is meant by 'having packed up'. On the way they stayed a night with a venerable disciple, Mnason of Cyprus, and the next day they entered Jerusalem (xxi. 15, 16).

This is the end of Paul's third missionary journey, and the end of his personal freedom, for about five years. Having reference to his missionary journeys the Apostle's *Tireless Activities* are recorded in Acts xiii. 1-xxi. 16, and from this point to the end of the book are recorded his *Fruitful Captivities*.

CHART 137

	FIRST		SECOND		THIRD
	xiii. 1-xiv. 28		xv. 36-xviii. 22		xviii. 23-xxi. 16
	A.D. 47-50		A.D. 50-54		A.D. 54-58
O U T W A R D	ANTIOCH (S) Seleucia Salamis Paphos Perga Antioch (P) Iconium Lystra Derbe	**O U T W A R D**	ANTIOCH (S) Syria-Cilicia Derbe Lystra Phrygia-Galatia Troas Samothrace Neapolis PHILIPPI Amphipolis Apollonia Thessalonica Beroea Athens CORINTH	**O U T W A R D**	ANTIOCH (S) Galatia-Phrygia EPHESUS CORINTH EPHESUS Troas Neapolis PHILIPPI Illyricum Thessalonica Beroea CORINTH
I N W A R D	Lystra Iconium Antioch (P) Perga Attalia Seleucia ANTIOCH (S)	**I N W A R D**	Cenchreae Ephesus Caesarea JERUSALEM ANTIOCH (S)	**I N W A R D**	PHILIPPI Neapolis Troas Assos Mitylene Chios Samos Miletus Cos Rhodes Patara Tyre Ptolemais Caesarea JERUSALEM

PAUL'S FRUITFUL CAPTIVITIES

Acts xxi. 17-xxviii. A.D. 58-63. 5 Years

AT JERUSALEM

AT CAESAREA

AT ROME

Paul's Fruitful Captivities

(Acts xxi. 17-xxviii. 31. A.D. 58-63)

It was said of King George VI that latterly 'he walked with death'. This was pre-eminently true of the Apostle Paul for many years. Before he reached Jerusalem in A.D. 58, about nine years before his death, how greatly he had suffered, and how constantly he was in the shadow of death. Few of the Apostle's sufferings are recorded in the Acts, but the sufferer catalogues some of them in his second (third) letter to Corinth (A.D. 57).

> 'In stripes above measure, in prisons more frequent, in deaths, oft. Five times I received from Jews the forty stripes save one; thrice I was scourged with the Roman rods; once I was stoned; thrice I suffered shipwreck; a night and a day have I spent in the open sea. In journeyings often; in perils of rivers; in perils of robbers; in perils from my countrymen; in perils from the heathen; in perils in the city; in perils in the wilderness; in perils in the sea; in perils among false brethren. In toil and weariness; often in sleepless watchings; in hunger and thirst; often without bread to eat; in cold and nakedness' (2 Cor. xi. 23-28).

In addition to all this was the Apostle's ill health (2 Cor. iv. 7-12; xii. 7-12; Gal. iv. 13, 14), and the depressing knowledge that more suffering lay ahead for him (Acts xx. 22-25; xxi. 4, 10-14).

His actual captivity which began in Jerusalem in A.D. 58 and lasted, in Caesarea and Rome, until A.D. 63, brought the Apostle, not more suffering, but less, for he was under Roman protection, and in both Caesarea and Rome he was comfortably placed (xxiii. 35; xxviii. 16, 23, 30).

It should not be overlooked that the record of Paul's captivities, covering a period of five years, A.D. 58-63, is given $7\frac{1}{2}$ of the 28 chapters of the Acts, so that as the Book represents 33 years, A.D. 30-63, the record of the last five of them takes up a quarter of the whole. This will remind us of the fact that Luke, in his Gospel, devotes $9\frac{1}{2}$ of his 24 chapters to the last week of our LORD's life (xix. 28-xxiv), and these emphases reveal the author's sense of the importance of these two periods.

The following is an outline of the first captivity.

I. AT JERUSALEM (xxi. 17-xxiii. 30).   A.D. 58

1. THE APOSTLE'S DETENTION (xxi. 17-36)

(i) *Paul's Vow* (17-26)
(a) Paul meets and addresses the Elders (17-20a)
(b) The Elders advise Paul what to do (20b-25)
(c) Paul follows the advice of the Elders (26)

(ii) *Mob Violence* (27-36)
(a) The charge of the Asian Jews (27-29)
(b) The assault of the crowd upon Paul (30, 31a)
(c) The rescue of Paul by the Chief Captain (31b-36)

2. THE APOSTLE'S DEFENCE (xxi. 37-xxiii. 10)

(1) BEFORE THE CROWD (xxi. 37-xxii. 29)

(i) *The Request* (xxi. 37-40)
(ii) *The Speech* (xxii. 1-21)
(a) His upbringing and pre-Christian activities (1-5)
(b) His experience leading to conversion (6-16)
(c) His Divine commission to evangelize the Gentiles (17-21)

(iii) *The Effect* (xxii. 22-29)
(a) The frenzy of the mob (22, 23)
(b) The resolve of the Chief Captain to scourge Paul (24, 25a)
(c) The effective protest of Paul (25b-29)

(2) BEFORE THE SANHEDRIN (xxii. 30-xxiii. 10)
(i) Paul is brought before the Council (xxii. 30)
(ii) Paul's first word, and the High Priest's interruption (xxiii. 1, 2)
(iii) Paul's second word, and the Council's protest (xxiii. 3, 4)
(iv) Paul's third word, one of apology (xxiii. 5)
(v) Paul's fourth word and its effect on the Council (xxiii. 6-8)
(vi) The divided Council, and the Chief Captain's order
(xxiii. 9, 10)

3. THE APOSTLE'S DANGER (xxiii. 11-30)

(i) The Comforting Word of the Lord (11)
(ii) The Cunning Plot of the Jews (12-22)
(a) The oath of forty men, and their request of the Council
(12-15)
(b) Paul's nephew reveals the plot (16-22)
To Paul (16)
To the Captain (17-22)
(iii) The Counter Move of the Captain (23-30)
(a) His plan to send Paul to Caesarea (23, 24)
(b) His letter to Felix the Governor (25-30)

I. Paul's Captivity at Jerusalem
(Acts xxi. 17-xxiii. 30; A.D. 58)

Considered disproportion is in evidence in the first part of Paul's captivity, $2\frac{3}{4}$ chapters being given to the record of the events of twelve days (xxiv. 11). The following is a summary of these events.

PAUL AND THE ELDERS (xxi. 17-30)

This was Paul's fifth and last visit to Jerusalem, and his heart was heavy and apprehensive. For a long time he had been fulfilling his promise to collect funds for the poor Christians in Jerusalem (Gal. ii. 10), and now he presented these offerings, collected from many churches near and far (2 Cor. viii. ix); but, it appears, he got little thanks for his concern and contributions. Luke does not even mention the matter (cf. Rom. xv. 31).

Having delivered the offerings Paul reported to the Elders on the work he had been doing during the last three years (cf. Rom. xv. 18, 19), but all that Luke records of their reaction is that they 'glorified God' (xxi. 20), and from the following context it is evident that their minds were much more occupied with malicious gossip which was circulating in the city than with the evangelization of the world (xxi. 20-25).

THE REPORT

The many Christian Jews gathered at this time in Jerusalem had been told by non-Christian Judaisers that Paul was advocating *apostasy from Moses* (ver. 21 Gr.) James and the Elders did not believe this report, but, apparently, the many Christian Jews did, and there was likely to be trouble when they knew that Paul was in the city.

The truth was that the Apostle had never taught anything of the kind. Everywhere he had begun his ministry in the synagogue, if synagogue there was, and left it only when his message was rejected. He had had Timothy circumcised because he was half a Jew (xvi. 1-3); and when in Corinth he himself took a temporary Nazarite vow (xviii. 18); and he had written to the Corinthians that, where principle was not involved, to the Jews he became as a Jew, that he might gain Jews (1 Cor. ix. 19-22). 'His objection to Levitism was not an objection to external conformity, but only that substitution of externalism for faith to which conformity might lead' (Farrar).

How tragic it is that, without investigation, Christians are so ready to believe damaging reports of their fellows!

A Proposition Which Paul Adopted (xxi. 22-26)

The Elders proposed that, to disarm prejudice and prove the report to be a lie, Paul should take the vow of a temporary Nazarite, and also should pay the expenses of four others who had taken this vow.

This situation is of profound importance, and in speaking of it, caution rather than dogmatism is needed. *Mosaism was setting, and Christianity was rising*, and transition periods are always difficult. What is to be done? Are Gentile converts to be put under the Law? Or, are Jewish and Gentile Christians at once to enter into Christian liberty? Or are Jewish converts still to conform to the law, and Gentile converts to be absolved? The bigoted Jews were for the first; Paul's party were for the second; and James' party were for the third, which was a compromise of the other two. Now, compromises are delicate, and may easily be dangerous. If by a compromise, policy can be served without the sacrifice of principle, it is justifiable.

How often it happens that two parties, representing two different streams of thought or practice, are unavoidably thrown together. What is to be done? If both are unbending, something will break. But the question here is, Did Paul do right to take that vow? (23, 24, 26). We should not dogmatize on that point; but this may be said, that if his doing so was justifiable, it did not serve the purpose it was intended to; see what follows. This fact does not *prove* that he was wrong; it may prove that some people are irreconcilable, do what one will. On the other hand, the advice of many should never be allowed to stampede any of us into a false position.

Pay Their Expenses (Ver. 24)

A Nazarite vow was an expensive affair. The individual had to offer one he-lamb, one ewe-lamb, one ram, a basket of unleavened bread, cakes of fine flour mingled with oil, a meal offering and drink offerings. Also, the Nazarite had to shave his head and burn the hair (Num. vi. 13-20). If Paul did not offer these for himself, to pay for four men to do so was costly, and naturally we ask 'Where did Paul get the money?'

Sir Wm. Ramsay shows that at this time, and during the next four years, Paul had access to money, a fact which must have eased his hardship not a little; and he accounts for this on the supposition that Paul's father had died, and that the Apostle had inherited his share of the property. A number of details unite to make this supposition as likely as it is attractive. Rackham, however, favours the idea that Luke, or some other member of Paul's 'company', e.g., Aristarchus, may have met these expenses for the man to whom they were so devoted.

Paul made a compromise to avoid a conflict, but he did not succeed. If he had declined the advice of the Elders (18-25), the result could scarcely have been worse than it became, and it might have been better. Of course, it is easy to be wise after the event, but the whole affair calls our attention to *the desirability of compromise sometimes, and the peril of it at all times*.

DELIRIUM AND DELIVERANCE (xxi. 27-36)

The ignorant excitement which was stirred up at Ephesus (xix) is now seen at Jerusalem. A few voluble Jews threw the whole city into confusion by proclaiming the presence of Paul, and shouting certain charges against him—charges entirely untrue. The crowd severely manhandled him, and would have killed him, but news of the riot reached the Roman Commander who at once, with soldiers, appeared on the scene, rescued Paul, and took him to the castle of Antonia.

Here two things are thrown into sharp contrast by being related: *fanaticism* and *fortitude*; the Jews exhibiting the one, and Paul, the other. The things which marked the fanaticism of these Jews were *lying* and *violence*; and both are vices. Paul had raised no opposition to the Law (28, cf. 26); neither had he defiled the Temple, for he had *not* taken Trophimus into it (28, 29). '*They supposed*'. Yes, supposition has broken countless hearts, ruined families, and shaken the foundations of nations. A supposition is never strong enough to build upon. Is your attitude towards somebody just now, based on a supposition?

Why should Paul have been beaten before he was tried? (32). Truth and right are never dependent on, and never resort to, such methods. Over against all this we see Paul calm, courageous, energetic, resourceful, courteous, and sweetly reasonable. '*Away with him*' (36). That was said once before. Of whom? '*The servant is not greater than his LORD*'.

In this way began the captivity which was to last for five years; a captivity which, like Ezekiel's, and Daniel's, and John's, and Bunyan's, was to be richly fruitful.

PAUL'S SPEECHES

Ten of Paul's speeches are recorded in the Acts, and one in Galatians (ii. 14-21).

Of the ten in the Acts, four are briefly reported (xiv. 15-17; xxiii. 1-6; xxv. 10-12; xxviii. 17-20, 26-28), and six are given at greater length (xiii. 16-41; xvii. 22-31; xx. 18-35; xxii. 1-21; xxiv. 10-21; xxvi. 2-29). Of these six, three fall in the captivity period, and may be called the *Trial Speeches*. The first of these was delivered to the riotous crowd in Jerusalem (xxii. 1-21), the second was delivered before Felix (xxiv. 10-21), and the third was delivered before King Agrippa (xxvi. 2-29).

THE FIRST TRIAL SPEECH (xxii. 1-21)

What a pulpit (40), what a congregation (36), what a 'platform' (35), and what a preacher! (40). Ch. xxi.

Surely Paul was one of the most determined and courageous men who have ever lived. His physical condition at the time he was brought to the castle of Antonia must have been distressing, for he had been flogged by fanatical Jews, and painfully pushed about by an excited mob (xxi. 27-36). Yet, this notwithstanding, he asked the Roman Captain if he might address the crowd. Lysias thought he had captured an Egyptian revolutionary, but he was quickly disillusioned, and, no doubt, disappointed, when he heard his prisoner address him in Greek (xxi. 37, 38). Having been given permission to speak, Paul addressed the crowd in Aramaic, and up to a point they listened quietly.

Paul's speech is in three parts. In the first, he details his connections (3-5); in the second, he relates the story of his

conversion (6-16); and in the third, he tells of his Divine commission (17-21).

1. Paul's Connections (xxii. 3-5)

Probably most of the Jews in Jerusalem at this time did not
know Paul except by report, and so he began his speech by saying
who he was: a Jew, born in Tarsus, trained in Jerusalem, a pupil
of Gamaliel, a careful student of the Mosaic Law, characterized
by Judaic zeal, a relentless opponent of the Christians, and
commissioned by the leaders of Judaism in Jerusalem to round up
all such and bring them to headquarters for punishment
(cf. Phil. iii. 4-6; 2 Cor. xi. 22). This recital does not confirm
the charge brought against the Apostle (xxi. 28).

2. Paul's Conversion (xxii. 6-16)

The three accounts in the Acts of the event indicate what great
importance Paul attached to the fact and manner of it. The
Apostle's first account was given from the castle steps, and the
second, in his defence before Agrippa (xxvi. 12-18). Luke also
gives an account of this event which probably he received from
Paul himself (ix. 1-19a).

These narratives of this event show that Paul regarded it to be
an indisputable fact and the only possible explanation of his life
and work.

Ramsay has said:

'In the Divine reckoning Paul's life begins from his conversion and
his call to the Gentiles. The conversion is the epoch-making fact. On
our conception of that one event depends our whole view of his life,
and every action must be considered in its relation to the conversion.'

Consideration of the alleged discrepancies between the various
accounts of this event is not within the scope of our present purpose, but we endorse the opinion of Maurice Jones who has said:

'There is nothing in the variations themselves to destroy the evidence
of the three accounts as to the truth of the fact of the conversion. In
all three the spirit, the tone, and the essential features are the same.
As a matter of fact, the story of the conversion is not rejected because
of the discrepancies in the various editions of it, but on *a priori*
objections to the supernatural element connected with it.'

('St. Paul the Orator,' p. 263).

The late Lord Birkenhead has said that Paul's conversion is
one of the major events in all history.

3. Paul's Commission (xxii. 17-21)

Wherever the Apostle went he addressed himself first of all to the Jews, but there was never any doubt in his mind that he had been Divinely commissioned to take the Gospel to the Gentiles (ix. 15; xiii. 45-49; xviii. 5, 6; xix. 8-10; xxviii. 28; Gal. i. 16; Eph. ii. 11-22).

The word 'Gentiles' (ver. 21) was like a match to gunpowder, and the magazine exploded. No asylum ever built was big enough to hold that crowd. Ignorance and violence generally go together (xxii. 22, 23). No fanaticism is so senseless and vicious as religious fanaticism, and it has been responsible for rivers of blood. Where, in this dangerous hour, were the 'myriads' of Jews who had embraced the faith? (xxi. 20).

Justice Claimed (xxii. 24-29)

In circumstances which were similar Paul did not always act in the same way. In Philippi (xvi. 37) he did not speak of his Roman citizenship until after he was flogged, but on this occasion he claimed it to prevent his being tortured (xxii. 25). We must not suppose that his reason for making the claim was merely to avoid suffering, though this, after the flogging he had already endured (xxi. 31, 32), might well have proved fatal; but a crisis had arisen which precipitated a definite change of attitude to both the Jews and the Romans.

Claudius Lysias had broken the law in more than one respect, and this led him to action which eventuated in Paul putting himself under Roman protection for the future (xxv. 10-12). Henceforth he would be regarded, not as a Jew, but as a Roman.

It was now clear to the Apostle that he need hope for nothing from the Jews, Christian or non-Christian, so that, to continue his testimony, he resolved to employ the cover which the secular power afforded. This, of course, would greatly incense the Jews, who hated their Roman masters, but they had only themselves to thank for it.

Paul Before the Sanhedrin (xxii. 30-xxiii. 10)

Lysias gathered that Paul was charged with some infraction of Jewish law, and as he could not deal with that he resolved on assembling the Sanhedrin, which was the supreme Jewish Council, and consisted of seventy or seventy-two members, Pharisees and Sadducees. The emotions of the Apostle must have been mingled as he remembered that more than twenty years before, as a member of this Council, he gave his vote for the death of Stephen (vii. 58; viii. 1).

Paul was no more successful with the Sanhedrin than he had been with the crowd, and the record of the event raises some questions. There are few passages which present so many difficulties in so small a space as xxiii. 1-10. Was it right for Paul to speak as he did in verse 3? How was it that he did not know that the High Priest was presiding? If he was right in speaking as he did in verse 3, could he also be right in apologizing? (5). Did he do right in classifying himself with the Pharisaic party, seeing that he was so far removed from them in spirit? (6); and, in any case, was '*the hope and resurrection of the dead*' the count on which he had been arrested? Was he justified in adopting a policy which had for its design the breaking of the impact of opposition against himself? (7-9). These questions are as fair as they are difficult.

1. We need not say whether Paul spoke in *anger* or *indignation* in verse 3, but these should always be distinguished. We seldom do well to be angry; we often do well to be indignant. Anger suggests feeling mastering judgment; indignation suggests judgment giving character to feeling.

2. Several suppositions could clear up the second question (5a . Historically, this office at that time had fallen vacant, and Ananias, a deposed High Priest, was acting *pro tem*. But perhaps Paul was *short-sighted* (Gal. iv. 15).

3. Two replies may be given to the point of 5b: first, that it is possible greatly to respect an *office*, and yet have only contempt for the one who holds it; secondly, that if one is convinced he has made a mistake, it is the right, manly, and Christian thing to say so.

4. The last three questions, as indeed all of them, we must consider in the light of verse 11, '*Be of good cheer*'. The LORD

was pleased with Paul! This does not prove that Paul had acted wisely throughout, but it does show that his heart was right with God. But verse 6 remains a problem. What does ch. xxiv. 20, 21, mean?

UPLIFT AND ONLOOK (xxiii. 11)

'Take courage, for as you have testified about me at Jerusalem, so you must bear witness also at Rome' (R.S.V.).

After two days of incessant strain Paul was much depressed. Physical and mental reactions are inevitable. This great man had them, so we need not wonder if we have. *But light came in the night.* The LORD's words met Paul's need as key fits lock(11). '*Cheer up, Paul. Your Jerusalem witness has not been a failure; and your work is not done yet.*' If the Master praises, we need not trouble ourselves about men.

Jerusalem! Rome! You have; you must! Take courage!

Here are commendation, prediction, and exhortation, and the link between the past and the future is the present. Paul now knows that he will not be killed in his own country, and that his ambition to reach Rome with his message will be realized (xix. 21. Rom. i. 13). But what he does not yet know is what lies between Jerusalem and Rome.

It is well that we know not what awaits us, that God kindly veils our eyes; so let us believe that it is better to walk by faith with Him than to go alone by sight.

All the appearances of the Lord to Paul marked great crises in his life (ix. 4; xvi. 9; xviii. 9; xxii. 17; xxvii. 23f).

PLOT VERSUS PLAN (xxiii. 12-30)

God fulfils His purposes and promises in many ways; sometimes by *miracle*, but more often by *providence*. Here are more than forty men who are resolved to kill Paul (13). The LORD, on the other hand, says that he shall see Rome (11). The odds are all against the forty. What became of these men? (12).

Did they keep their vow?

Paul had a sister, and she had a son, and God used the lad to bring deliverance to his needy uncle. The nephew played his part well (16-22). We cannot all be engines, but we can be nuts and screws in the moral machinery of the world. Let no one imagine that his honest effort will not count. It will, and does.

The missionary prisoner travels like a king. Look at him, with a body-guard of four hundred and seventy soldiers, and riding, not walking! (23, 24). What a scene! Off to Caesarea, sixty-eight Roman miles from Jerusalem.

Here is the second *letter* in the 'Acts' (26-30; cf. xv. 23-29). Lysias did not speak the truth in verse 27.

Paul arrived at Caesarea, after about eighteen hours in the saddle. He has seen Jerusalem for the *last time*! It is now late A.D. 58. The shuttles fly to and fro; the dark and silver threads are interwoven; the tangled skein is working out on the upper side a perfect pattern. Why do we not leave the tapestry of our life in the hands of the Divine Weaver? He knows how to mend broken threads. In all our changes we have the changeless Christ.

CLAUDIUS LYSIAS

Study carefully CLAUDIUS LYSIAS, from xxi. 31 to xxiii. 30.

What we are told of this man, the commandant of the garrison at Jerusalem, is mostly to his credit. When he heard of the riot, caused by the recognition of Paul in the Temple, he immediately took soldiers and went down to the mob and rescued Paul (xxi. 32, 33). He allowed Paul to address the crowd from the castle steps (xxi. 37-39). He summoned the Sanhedrin that Paul might address them (xxii. 30). When he heard of the clamour in the Sanhedrin, he, a second time, rescued Paul (xxiii. 9, 10). Recognising the temper of the Jews in Jerusalem he, with expedition and under heavy escort, sent Paul to Caesarea to be examined by the Governor Felix (xxiii. 24). For this journey of about sixty-eight miles he provided a horse for the Apostle and his companions—probably Luke and Aristarchus—(xxiii. 24). He wrote a letter to Felix in which he presented Paul in a very favourable light (xxiii. 26-30).

It is true that Lysias ordered Paul to be tortured before he knew that he was a Roman (xxii. 24, 25); and true that in his letter to Felix he flattered himself, and misrepresented some of the facts, but, on the whole, he comes out of his ordeal well.

PAUL'S FRUITFUL CAPTIVITIES
(xxi. 17-xxviii)

Paul's second captivity was at Caesarea, and the following is an outline of the events.

II. AT CAESAREA (xxiii. 31-xxvi). A.D. 58-60: 2 Years

(A) PAUL BEFORE FELIX (xxiii. 31-xxiv. 27)

1. The Journey to Caesarea, and the Interview with Felix (xxiii. 31-35)
2. A Deputation from the Sanhedrin goes to Caesarea (xxiv. 1)
3. The Indictment of Tertullus, confirmed by the Jews (xxiv. 2-9)
    - (i) The opening word (2-4)
    - (ii) The Charge (5, 6 (7))
        - Sedition (5a).   Schism (5b).   Sacrilege (6)
    - (iii) The closing word (8 (9))
4. The Reply of the Apostle (xxiv. 10-21)
    - (i) His Compliment to Felix (10)
    - (ii) His Answer respecting Sedition (xxiv. 10-13)
    - (iii) His Answer respecting Schism (xxiv. 14-16)
    - (iv) His Answer respecting Sacrilege (xxiv. 17-19)
    - (v) His Challenge to the Sanhedrin (xxiv. 20, 21)
5. The Effect on Felix of Paul's Defence (xxiv. 22-27)
    - (i) His protection and indulgence of Paul (22, 23)
    - (ii) His interviews with Paul (24-26)
    - (iii) His recall to Rome, leaving Paul bound (27)

(B) PAUL BEFORE FESTUS (xxv. 1-12)

1. The Request of the Jews, and the Reply of Festus (1-5)
2. The Accusations of the Jews, and the Defence of Paul (6-8)
3. The Inquiry of Festus, and the Answer of Paul (6-12)

(C) PAUL BEFORE AGRIPPA (xxv. 13-xxvi. 32)

1. The Report of Festus to Agrippa (xxv. 13-22)
2. The Address of Festus to Agrippa in Paul's presence (xxv. 23-27)
3. The Speech of Paul before Agrippa (xxvi. 1-32)
    - (i) A courteous opening word to Agrippa (1-3)
    - (ii) A repudiation of the charge of apostasy from Judaism (4-11)
        - (a) His training as a Pharisee (4, 5)
        - (b) The charge against him involves all Israel (6-8)
        - (c) His pre-conversion attitude to the Christians (9-11)
    - (iii) The story of how he was converted (12-18)
    - (iv) His response to the Divine commission (19-21)
    - (v) A presentation of the Gospel to the assembly (22, 23)
    - (vi) The interruption of Festus, and Paul's reply (24-26)
    - (vii) Paul's appeal to the king, and the king's reply (27, 28)
    - (viii) The desire of Paul's heart (29)
4. The Effect of the Speech upon those addressed (30-32)

II. Paul's Captivity at Caesarea

(xxiii. 31-xxvi)   (A.D. 58-60)

CAESAREA

This city was built by Herod the Great in about twelve years, and was named Caesarea Sebaste in honour of Augustus Caesar. It was here that Agrippa I was smitten by God (xii. 19-23). Here Philip the evangelist and his family lived (viii. 40; xxi. 8). Here Cornelius the Roman centurion was stationed, and here Peter preached the Gospel and opened the door into grace for all Gentiles (ch. x), thus making it the mother-city of the Gentile churches. Paul was three times in Caesarea before the time of his imprisonment here (ix. 30; xviii. 22; xxi. 8). In late A.D. 58 the Apostle was sent by Claudius Lysias to Caesarea to be tried by Felix, and he was held in the city for two years.

It was a city of sumptuous palaces, and had a magnificent harbour. The Jews suffered great cruelties in this city, and in A.D. 548 a massacre of Christians took place. Eusebius was bishop of Caesarea in A.D. 313-340. To-day the place is a ruin, and its ancient glories are 'engulfed by the sand, or concealed by the encroaching sea'. Its rise was sudden, and its decay has been complete.

FELIX

Felix was Procurator or Governor in Palestine in A.D. 53-60. He began life as a slave, and as a slave, though of a different order, he ended it. Josephus and Tacitus are agreed as to his character. The latter says: 'He exercised all kinds of barbarity and extravagance as if he had royal authority, but with the disposition of a slave'. His wife, Drusilla, was the daughter of Herod Agrippa I, who slew James (xii); the sister of Agrippa II (xxvi); and the wife of Azizus, King of Emesa, from whom Felix enticed her.

This man was sensuous, cowardly, unjust, mercenary, tyrannical, and unscrupulous. Illegally, he held Paul a prisoner for two years, expecting him to pay for his release (xxiv. 26). He was quite willing to listen to Paul's message, but quite unwilling to act upon it (xxiv. 24-26).

His was Augustine's experience without Augustine's admissions.

'So was I assured that much better were it for me to give myself to Thy charity than to give myself over to my own cupidity; but though the former course satisfied me and gained the mastery, the latter pleased me and held me mastered.

'Nor had I anything to answer Thee calling to me, "Awake, thou that sleepest, and arise from the dead, and Christ shall give thee light."

'And when Thou didst on all sides show me that what Thou saidst was true, I, convicted by the truth, had nothing at all to answer, but only those dull and drowsy words, "Anon, anon," "presently," "leave me but a little." But "presently, presently," had no present, and my "little while" went on for a long while.'

So badly did this Governor govern that he was recalled to Rome to give an account of his actions, and thereafter he vanished into obscurity and disgrace.

PAUL AND FELIX (xxiii. 31-xxiv)

Relative to Paul, we have in chapter xxiv an *Indictment* (1-9), a *Defence* (10-21), and a *Result* (22-27). Construct the scene, and behold the characters. Felix, Paul, Ananias, Tertullus, Romans and Jews. What a conjunction of morality and immorality, of justice and injustice, of godliness and paganism.

Paul's contact with Felix lasted for two years, A.D. 58-60 (xxiv. 27). When the Apostle arrived at Caesarea, and the letter from Lysias had been read by Felix, the Governor ordered that Paul 'be kept in Herod's palace'. This was not a prison as in xvi. 23, 24, but the quarters of the Praetorian Guard (cf. Phil. i. 13). The Governor had to await the arrival from Jerusalem of Paul's accusers, and these came after five days—Ananias and certain Elders (xxiv. 1).

Paul was then brought up for trial, and there were two speeches —one by a Roman lawyer whose name was Tertullus, and the other by the Apostle, in reply.

After this Felix, instead of pronouncing sentence, dismissed the Court on the pretext that Claudius Lysias would have to come and bear witness. This was not necessary, nor did he come. It is evident that Felix considered Paul to be innocent, but he had not the courage to release him. Various motives lay behind this line of action (cf. xxiv. 26). Paul saw more of Felix than of any other Roman official, and addressed him more often and more plainly than he did any other (xxiv. 24-26).

THE SPEECH OF TERTULLUS (xxiv. 1-9)

This man was a professional lawyer, and, it would seem, he addressed the Court in Latin. He began his address in words of fulsome flattery of Felix, for the connection between the compliments and the facts is very slight.

Farrar speaks of this exordium as 'truly legal rotundity of verbiage', and of the speech as 'voluble plausibility'. When the deputation from Jerusalem assented to what Tertullus had said, Felix *nodded* to Paul to reply (xxiv. 10).

In his brief speech Tertullus brought three charges against Paul, the charge of *sedition* (5), of *schism* (5), and of *sacrilege* (6). The reference in the A.V. to Lysias (7) does not occur in the R.V. The word 'laid-hold' in verse 6 has been described as 'an excessively refined description of an attempt at lynching' (F. F. Bruce).

The address of Tertullus is characterized by two things—*flattery*, and *falsehood*. FLATTERY (2-4). This is a very dangerous thing, injuring both the flatterer and the flattered. Sir Walter Raleigh said that *'flatterers are the worst kind of traitors'*. Mark what this man said about Felix. But what are the facts? Tacitus, the Roman historian, says that Felix thought he could commit any crime with impunity, and speaks of him as a ruler of boundless cruelty and profligacy, using the power of a king with the temper of a slave. Within two years of this event he was recalled from his province, and accused by the Jews at Rome (27). Now read the speech of Tertullus again.

The second characteristic is FALSEHOOD (5-6). Listen to the rasp in these words—'*pestilence, sedition, ringleader, sect, the Nazarenes*'. Paul is charged with political rebellion, heresy, sacrilege, and disorder. A pack of lies! Poor indeed is that cause which must be propped up by untruth. All the Jews who *assented* were liars also (9). To nod to a lie is to tell one. There come times when silence is immoral, when not to protest is to connive at evil. These Jews were guilty of that.

Words are moral money—where are yours minted?

PAUL'S REPLY (xxiv. 10-21)

This follows the threefold charge which had been made against him. As to the charge of *sedition* (5) Paul points out that before his arrest he had been in Jerusalem about a week only, and that during that time he provoked no public discussion, collected no crowd, and caused no disturbance anywhere (11-13).

As to the charge of *schism* (5b), Paul admitted this, but affirmed that this was not an offence against either the Jews or the Empire, but that historically, doctrinally, and prophetically it was not contrary to Moses or the Hebrew Scriptures (14-16).

As to the charge of *sacrilege* (6), the Apostle declared, after referring to the offerings which he had brought to the Jewish Church, that so far from profaning the Temple he went into it to discharge certain obligations connected with a ceremonial vow which he had made, and he challenged those who had accused him to produce evidence (17-21).

What a contrast to the previous speech! Paul's reply is courteous, dignified, calm, frank, fearless, challenging, and conciliatory. It is both negative and positive: here we have a clear and bold denial, and a candid statement of facts. There is courtesy, but not flattery; truth, and not falsehood; fairness, and not malice; respect, and not contempt; argument, but not abuse, and let us remember, abuse is never argument.

Paul's defence is convincing because of its correctness, cogency, and calmness. The negative part of the defence is in 11-13; and the positive, in 14-21. Read verses 5 and 12 together. How could all that crime be committed in less than a fortnight, during the major part of which time Paul was under arrest? That lie gave itself away. Falsehood lacks the cement of consistency.

But after denial, is testimony (14-16). What these Jews called '*a sect*' (14, R.V.) was really '*The Way*' (14), with its beginning away back in the call of Abraham, and its end far on in resurrection and judgment (14, 15). Study verse 16, which describes *practical religion*. What is conscience? What its sphere? And what its limitation? The natural conscience is not infallible, but when enlightened and enlivened by the Spirit of God, it should be heard and heeded.

This speech, which was disconcerting to the Jews, made a favourable impression on Felix, and, postponing judgment, he ordered a centurion to look after Paul.

What pathetic reading verses 22-27 make! How terrible to know what is right, and yet, not to do it; to tremble at the truth, and yet, not to trust it (25). Felix was apparently free, but really bound. Paul was apparently bound, but really free. Think of the bound talking of giving liberty to the free! (23, 26, 27). It is better to be physically bound and morally free, than physically free and morally bound. What heroic courage Paul displayed on this occasion! (25). Are *you* waiting for a *'convenient season'*? It will never come. Now is God's time, and yours. There is a *'judgment to come'* (25).

Guard against moral and spiritual anaemia.

FREE CUSTODY (xxiv. 23)

Felix 'gave order to the centurion that (Paul) should be kept in charge, and should have indulgence; and not to forbid any of his friends to minister unto him'. Little imagination is needed to realize what this meant to Paul. Instead of being in a prison and cut off from all fellowship from without, he was comfortably housed, and all his friends had free access to him (cf. xxviii. 16, 17, 23, 30). We may be sure that Luke and Aristarchus would see him continually (xxvii. 2); and Philip the evangelist would be a frequent visitor, as well as other members of the Caesarean church. What times they would have together, and what valu-. able work was done, making possible much of the information which is found in the Acts. It was probably during this period that Luke gathered the material for his Gospel, and wrote part or all of it.

AN AUDIENCE OF TWO (xxiv. 24-26)

A heathen man and a Jewish woman frequently had Paul all to themselves, and he made the Governor to grovel (25). Some discourses are so diffusive that they reach no one. They aim at nothing and they hit it, but when Paul spoke to these two people he reached the target every time.

He spoke of *righteousness* to a man who was doing him a great injustice in not releasing him; he spoke of *self-control* to a couple who should not be husband and wife; and he spoke of *coming judgment* to people who did not wish to hear of such a thing. For speaking to Herod and Herodias as Paul was now doing to Felix and Drusilla, John the Baptist had his head taken off.

Paul's faithfulness made Felix tremble, but it seems to have left Drusilla unmoved. This girl of about eighteen years had a bad background. She was a daughter of Herod Agrippa I; her father murdered James; her great-uncle, Herod Antipas, slew John the Baptist; her great-grandfather, Herod the Great, killed the babes of Bethlehem. That did not give a girl much of a chance, and it is a wonder that she did not become a second Herodias (cf. Matt. xiv. 1-11); but Paul had received a promise (xxiii. 11).

A CONVENIENT SEASON (xxiv. 25)

There is no such time, and yet multitudes are banking on it. Procrastination when there is spiritual conviction is feeble, false, and fatal. No one should trifle with opportunity. Philip Henry says: 'The devil cozens us out of all our time by cozening us out of the present time'.

> To-morrow, and to-morrow, and to-morrow
> Creeps in this petty pace from day to day,
> To the last syllable of recorded time;
> And all our yesterdays have lighted fools
> The way to dusty death.
> (*Macbeth*, Act V, Sc. 5, l. 19-22).

To see the right way and not to take it is far worse than never to have seen it. Some will be beaten with few stripes, and some with many.

PAUL AND FESTUS (xxv. 1-12)

Not much is known about Festus, who succeeded Felix. He was made Procurator of Judaea by Nero in A.D. 60, and he died in A.D. 62. Josephus represents him as having been one of the best procurators ever sent to Judaea, and it has been said that 'he had a straightforward honesty about him. which forms a strong contrast to the mean rascality of his predecessor', and of his successor Albinus, of whom it is said that 'there was not any sort of wickedness that could be named but he had a hand in it'.

From Luke's record it is evident that Festus was active and energetic and just, although, because of the puzzling nature of the case of Paul, he attempted to shift the responsibility of a verdict from himself to the Sanhedrin (xxv. 9).

The story before us is one of persistent treachery and righteous tenacity. All Paul's Gentile examiners at home and abroad believed in his innocence, but Judaism was against him, and the 'myriads' of Christian Jews in Jerusalem did nothing to help him (xxi. 20).

Mark the persistent hatred of the Jews. Nothing could alter or mollify their venom. From the time of Paul's conversion to this hour they worried him from place to place. This is an Oriental, not an Occidental, trait. The Jews requested that Paul be brought to Jerusalem. Why? See verse 3, with xxiii. 12. No doubt these men were getting hungry.

Suppose Festus had done as they desired! We would never have had *Ephesians, Philippians, Colossians, Philemon,* and the *Pastoral Epistles*! Divine sovereignty controls human spite. God had said to Paul, *'thou must bear witness also at Rome'* (xxiii. 11). How unlikely that seemed at the time; but now the way to the Capital is cut clean through Jewish injustice and Roman indecision. There may happen in a moment what has not happened in a millennium. There is no such thing as a *cul-de-sac* in the Christian's path.

What these Jews lacked in integrity they made up for in imagination (7, cf. xxiv. 13); they were as fertile as they were false. In the main, so we judge from Paul's answer (8), their charges against him were of *heresy, sacrilege,* and *treason*. To each he gave a categorical denial. How great a thing it is to have a clear conscience and a clean heart.

Paul's appeal to Caesar must have come as a great surprise to his friends, to the Jews, and to Festus; nor could he himself have understood all that it would mean; yet, undoubtedly he was guided by God. Two words altered the whole complexion of the Paul-problem—*Kaisara epikaloumai*—'to Caesar I appeal'.

His strong desire to go to Rome, the LORD's promise that he would do so, the unsleeping hatred and pursuance of the Jews, the indecision of the Roman authorities, and his weariness of the Caesarean captivity, led the Apostle to utter these two words, words which foiled the Jews, relieved deputed Gentile authority, and secured for Paul a further spell of life and service.

There are times when we have to make up our minds quickly on some momentous issue, and then, much depends upon the state of our spiritual health. One who *lives* in the fellowship of God can sense much more quickly His will in a crisis than one who lives at a distance. The longest way round may be the safest way home.

FESTUS AND AGRIPPA II (xxv. 13-27)

This brief record is in two parts: first, Festus reports on Paul to Agrippa (13-22); and secondly, Festus introduces Paul to Agrippa (23-27), and both parts are very illuminating.

1. *Festus Reports on Paul to Agrippa* (13-22)

Four things here are worthy of notice: *justice, ignorance, contempt,* and *curiosity.* (*a*) A sense of fair-play is reflected in verses 13-17. Festus here enunciates an elemental principle of justice, namely, that one accused should have an opportunity to defend himself (16); yet in social and church life are we not constantly forming estimates of people, on report, without any attempt to learn the truth? Stop that! (*b*) Festus owns up to his ignorance of the matters under dispute (20 R.V.). He says he was perplexed, and that was due to his ignorance. Roman governors were not conversant with Jewish theology. (*c*) But with Festus' ignorance went contempt (19) '*of one Jesus*'! (19). Yet, that man was his Creator and Redeemer. Contempt of people is not a thing to cultivate. Contemptuous people are only exhibiting moral defect in themselves. (*d*) Curiosity may be good or bad (22). If it leads, as in the case of Zacchaeus, to concern and conversion, it is good; but if it is frivolous and fruitless, as in the case of Agrippa, it is bad.

The estimate which Festus formed of Paul is of considerable

importance. It is recorded in xxv. 14-21, 24, 25. He was not grateful for the 'left-over' of Felix (14). He cutely sensed that the Jews wanted to by-pass the law and to get him, newly arrived and inexperienced in this field, to hand over to them the prisoner, and he declined so to do (15, 16). He dealt with Paul's case immediately (17), and was surprised at the nature of the charge which the Jews brought against the prisoner (18, 19), and, he says, he was 'perplexed', because matters of the Jews' 'religion' lay outside his province as a judge. Going back, somewhat, on his principle of verse 16, he thought he might solve his problem if Paul were willing to be judged by the Sanhedrin (20), but Paul was not willing, and appealed to Caesar, by-passing, not the Jews only, but Festus also. This might have offended, and perhaps did somewhat offend the Governor, but this notwithstanding he told Agrippa that he found in the prisoner 'nothing worthy of death' (25).

2. *Paul and Agrippa II* (xxv. 23-xxvi.)

The AGRIPPA of this narrative is HEROD AGRIPPA II, the son of HEROD AGRIPPA I of chapter xii, and the brother of DRUSILLA, the wife of FELIX (xxiv. 24). BERNICE is AGRIPPA'S sister (13). This scene in the audience-chamber of the governor at Caesarea is indeed a strange one (xxv. 13-xxvi. 29). Gerok says it may be viewed in three ways: (1) It was a drawing-room of worldly glory, by reason of the splendour of the assembled nobility. (2) It was a lecture-room of holy doctrine, by reason of the testimony of the Apostle Paul. (3) It was a judgment-hall of Divine Majesty, by reason of the impression produced by the apostolic discourse.

BERNICE

Sister of Agrippa II, eldest daughter of Agrippa I, and sister of Drusilla, the wife of Felix, this woman was celebrated for her beauty and her profligacy, and she is frequently mentioned by Josephus and Roman writers. She was married to her uncle, Herod, the King of Chalcis, and on her husband's death, she resided incestuously, with her brother, Agrippa II, and we make acquaintance with her when the king came to pay his respects to the new governor, Festus, when they both met and heard Paul (xxv-xxvi).

'*Great pomp*' (23). This was soon only dust. What a ridiculous thing is proud dust! 'All flesh is as grass, and all the glory of man as the flower of grass' (cf. Isa. xl). The pomp of Agrippa and Drusilla did but serve to make their moral littleness the more conspicuous. Pomp can never be an ethical substitute for principle. Agrippa and Bernice were pomp-proud in the same city where their proud father was eaten of worms.

Festus was not asking Agrippa to judge of whether or not Paul was guilty, nor was he inviting him to say whether or not the prisoner's claim to be tried by Caesar was valid; he was simply entertaining and gratifying the curiosity of his two guests, and was wishful that he should get from Agrippa some guidance as to what report he should send, with the prisoner, to Nero.

THE PRISONER'S DEFENCE (xxvi. 1-29)

It has been said of this speech that 'of all the Apostle's utterances it is the most finished and elaborate in style, and it represents the high-water mark of his oratory'.

We may divide it into seven parts:—

1. Paul addresses Agrippa (2, 3).
2. Paul denies the charge of apostasy from Judaism (4-11).
3. Paul relates the story of his conversion (12-18).
4. Paul claims that he was Divinely commissioned to preach the Gospel to the world·(19-21).
5. Paul says that his Gospel is based on the Jewish Scriptures (22, 23).
6. Festus interrupts and Paul replies (24-26).
7. Paul appeals to Agrippa and the King answers him (27-29).

1. Gentile judges did not know enough about Jewish belief or custom to understand Paul's case, but he knew that Herod, a Jewish King, would understand, and in his courteous address to Agrippa he expresses this confidence (2, 3). Paul could speak with respect of Agrippa II, because, notwithstanding his sins, he was better than his forebears. Herod the Great had attempted to murder Jesus, Herod the Tetrach had murdered John the

Baptist, Herod Agrippa I had murdered James the Apostle, but Agrippa II, as Paul says, had knowledge of and interest in things spiritual. He was specially qualified to appreciate the prisoner's defence, because as a Jew he had a knowledge of Jewish affairs; as a King, he was invested with civil power; and as the guardian of the Temple, he possessed religious authority. This is why Paul felt himself 'happy' to address him.

2. In verses 4-11 Paul tells the story of his pre-Christian life, his upbringing, his Pharisaism, his zeal for Judaism, his hatred of the Christians, and his persecution of them. The implication of all this is 'that to arrest such a career of frenzied zeal required a very real and adequate cause'.

3. To this cause he now passes, and relates, for the second time, the story of his conversion (12-18; cf. ch. xxii). Luke's account of it is in ch. ix. How conclusive is his testimony, based as it always was, on facts. It is as though he said: 'Let the psychologists say what they please, the fact is that I was a wolf and am now a sheep, and the change came suddenly'. Facts should not be distorted to agree with our theories, but our theories should emerge from the facts.

4. Christ called the Apostle to be a missionary, and he instantly obeyed, calling both Jews and Gentiles to repentance; and for doing this, Jews in Jerusalem, and in other places, arrested him, and tried to murder him (19-21).

5. The Gospel which was so dear to him, and so obnoxious to the Jews, was based on the Jewish Scriptures. Jewish prophets had foreshadowed it, and the Mosaic Law was fulfilled in it (22, 23). Prof. Lindsay well says:

'Paul, speaking in the presence of Agrippa approaches the question of the Messiahship of Jesus from the Jewish side and not from the Christian. The great body of the Jews had fixed their thoughts on the glories of the Messiah's reign to such an extent, that they could not think of the possibility of a suffering Saviour.

'Hence a Christian addressing Jews had first of all to prove that the Christ could suffer, that a suffering Messiah was a possible thing, for a Christ crucified was a constant stumbling-block to the Jews.

'Paul, therefore, speaking to Jews, had to show two things—(1) that the Messiah was divinely destined to suffer, was *subject to suffering*; and (2) that the Messiah having suffered, and being the first-fruits of the resurrection from the dead, will proclaim light to the Jewish people and to the Gentiles.

'These two questions had to be proved from Scripture, from Moses and the prophets, ere Paul could proceed to the final proof, that Jesus of Nazareth has suffered, has risen, and has enlightened Jew and Gentile, and therefore fulfils the Old Testament description of the Messiah.'

This is what Paul affirmed, and evidently with great effect.

6. Festus, who could not have followed Paul's argument, was much impressed by his enthusiasm, and broke in on his speech with, 'Paul, you're mad, just dung donnart wi' learning'. It is strange that only *Christian* enthusiasm is put down to mental abnormality! (cf. Mark iii. 21). The Church urgently needs more madmen like Paul.

7. In closing his speech, Paul appealed point-blank to Agrippa, and caused the king much embarrassment (27-29). Agrippa, being in charge of the Temple, could not say that he did not believe the prophets, and if he said he did, he would be publicly agreeing with Paul, and as he did not wish to commit himself either way, he tactfully and playfully parried the appeal by saying: 'In a hurry you would fain make me a Christian'; 'in a short time'; 'with but little persuasion'; 'with small effort'. The word Agrippa used does not mean 'almost', and, in fact, Agrippa never was anywhere near becoming a Christian. So far as we know no Roman official Paul met became a Christian (cf. xiii. 12). This class of person is difficult to reach effectively with the Gospel, and, perhaps, we can appreciate some of their difficulties.

'CHRISTIAN' (xxvi. 28; xi. 26; 1 Pet. iv. 16)

This name was given to believers in Christ as a nickname by the Antiochenes. They derived it from the word *chrestos* which meant a good worthy fellow, and so Christ's followers were dubbed *the Chrestianoi*, the worthy folk. Agrippa's use of the word has in it a ring of contempt; and Peter's use of it shows that the designation was still used by outsiders of the disciples. Rackham says: 'the word is Greek, the idea Hebrew, and the form Latin' (cf. John xix. 19, 20). In the New Testament it is a name used of enemies, believers themselves preferring to be known as 'brethren', 'disciples', 'believers', 'saints', 'the faithful', 'the elect', and people of 'the Way'; but the appellation had come to stay, and when Christ's people were thrown to the beasts in Rome they were proud to confess, *Christianus sum*. The name, bestowed as a stigma, they accepted as a distinction.

Paul's reply to Agrippa was a noble conclusion to a noble speech: 'Whether short or long, I would to God that not only you but also all who hear me this day might become such as I am— except for these chains' (29).

Mark the great notes of Paul's message: '*repent, turn, do*'. No one can *do* until he *turns*, and no one will *turn* who does not *repent*. Don't try to begin at the end. He who will be faithful will be assailed (21). Is there anything more stupid than to suppose that truth is got rid of by killing the witness to it? He whom God helps will continue (22). In God's sight none is *small*, and none is *great*; or, in another view, all are small, and all are great. In earth's view, some are small, and some are great, though, in reality many of the small are great, and many of the great are small. Spiritual enlightenment can come only by way of Christ's death and resurrection (23).

THE END OF THE SCENE (xxvi. 30-32)

Agrippa spoke the last word: 'This man might have been set at liberty, if he had not appealed unto Caesar'. But suppose he had not appealed and had been set at liberty, what would have happened? Undoubtedly, he would have been murdered by the Jews, and there would have been no testimony at Rome, and the priceless Epistles, *Ephesians, Colossians, Philemon*, and *Philippians*; 1 *Timothy, Titus*, and 2 *Timothy* would never have been written. The universal Church should be deeply grateful, as already said, for the captivities of Daniel, Ezekiel, Paul, John, Bunyan, Rutherford, and others.

PAUL'S FRUITFUL CAPTIVITIES

Paul's first captivity was at Jerusalem; the second was at Caesarea; and the third was at Rome. The following is an outline of the last.

III. AT ROME (xxvii-xxviii). A.D. 60-63: 2 Years

1. ON THE SEA (xxvii)

(i) *The Start* (1-8)

Companions: LUKE, ARISTARCHUS, TITUS(?)

CAESAREA to SIDON	about 67 miles
At Sidon Paul went ashore to visit his friends (3)	
SIDON to MYRA	about 500 miles
At Myra the travellers changed ships (6)	
MYRA to 'over against' CNIDUS	about 130 miles
CNIDUS to 'over against' SALMONE	about 130 miles
SALMONE to FAIR HAVENS (8)	about 80 miles

(ii) *The Storm* (9-20)

    (a) Paul's advice and the Centurion's decision (9-12)

    (b) The Ship, leaving Fair Havens, runs into trouble (13-20)

        (PHOENIX, 40 miles W. of Fair Havens: 12)

        (CLAUDA, 50 miles from Phoenix: 16)

(iii) *The Shipwreck* (21-44)

    (a) Paul addresses the Ship's Company (21-26)

        A gentle rebuke (21)

        An assurance of safety (22)

        A ground of confidence (23, 24)

        An affirmation of faith (25)

        A word of warning (26)

    (b) Adrift in the Sea of Adria (27-29)

    (c) Paul prevents the flight of the sailors (30-32)

    (d) Paul persuades the company to eat (33-38)

FAIR HAVENS to MELITA (MALTA)	about 566 miles

    (e) The ship runs aground at Malta (39-41)

    (f) The whole ship's company get ashore (42-44)

2. AT THE ISLAND (xxviii. 1-10)

    (i) The welcome of the natives (1, 2)

    (ii) Paul and a viper (3-6)

    (iii) Paul heals many of the islanders (7-10)

3. IN THE CITY (xxviii. 11-31). A.D. 61-63: 2 Years

(i) Paul's Journey to Rome (11-16)

MELITA to SYRACUSE	about 80-90 miles
Tarried for three days	
SYRACUSE to RHEGIUM	about 80-90 miles
RHEGIUM to PUTEOLI	about 180-200 miles
Tarried a week with Christians	
PUTEOLI to APPIUS	about 80-100 miles
Met Christians	
APPIUS to THREE TAVERNS	about 10 miles
Met Christians	
THREE TAVERNS to ROME	about 33 miles

(ii) Paul's Interviews with Jews at Rome (16-28 (29))

(a) The First Interview (17-22)
   Paul explains his being in Rome (17-20)
   The Jews desire to hear more from him (21, 22)

(b) The Second Interview (23-28)
   The subjects of Paul's discourse (23)
   The effects of the discourse (24, 25a)
   Paul's indictment and resolve (25b-28(29))

(iii) Paul's Protracted Sojourn at Rome (30, 31)

(a) His Ministry by Word (30, 31)

(b) His Ministry by Letter

Ephesians. A.D. 62
Colossians. A.D. 62
Philemon. A.D. 62
Philippians. A.D. 63

III. Paul's Captivity at Rome
(xxvii, xxviii) A.D. 60-63

Paul's captivity at Rome did not extend beyond two years, but in this section of the record we include the journey to Rome, so that the period covered is from the autumn of A.D. 60 to the spring of A.D. 63, and it is in three distinct parts: ON THE SEA (xxvii), AT THE ISLAND (xxviii. 1-10), and IN THE CITY (xxviii. 11-31).

The Voyage to Rome
(xxvii. 1-xxviii. 10)

From the time of leaving Caesarea to the arrival at Rome was a period of about seven months, three of which were spent on the island of Malta. It cannot be an exaggeration to say that there is not in existence a record of a sea voyage and shipwreck so circumstantial and graphic as the one before us. Of nautical terms there are 37 words, 13 phrases, and 25 sentences (see Baumgarten's 'Acts', vol. III, pp. 237-8). The classic on Acts xxvii is *The Voyage and Shipwreck of St. Paul*, by James Smith of Jordanhill, and this should be consulted by any who would study the technical details, but into these we do not here enter.

There is not much in this chapter which requires expository treatment, but its outstanding value is in the revelation it gives of the personality of Paul, and its obvious application is to life as a voyage on a tempestuous sea.

THE START (xxvii. 1, 2)

Upon a ship sailing for the Asian coast were put a number of prisoners, probably convicted criminals, and with them *Paul*, *Luke*, and *Aristarchus*. In what capacity the last two travelled we are not told, but it could not have been as passengers. Ramsay says they must have gone as Paul's slaves, and this would give to the Apostle a degree of importance and attention which otherwise he could not have had.

These prisoners were under the authority of a centurion named JULIUS. Rackham says: 'The centurions of the New Testament strike us generally as a class of men of a high stamp of character, and Julius is no exception. He makes a worthy match to that other centurion of Caesarea—Cornelius'. Every reference to him is to his credit. He treated Paul kindly, and at Sidon gave him leave to go ashore to see his friends (3). It was natural that at Fair Havens he should act upon the advice of the master and owner of the ship instead of on Paul's (11), but later he acted on Paul's advice, and it saved the lives of all on board (30-32); and later still Julius gave orders which saved Paul's life, and that of all the prisoners (42, 43). We are not told that this centurion

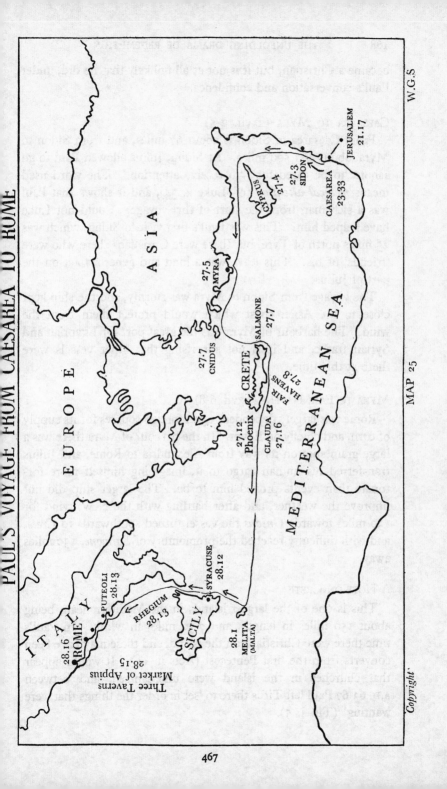

PAUL'S VOYAGE FROM CAESAREA TO ROME

MEDITERRANEAN SEA

EUROPE

ASIA

ITALY

ROME 28.16

PUTEOLI 28.13

RHEGIUM 28.13

SICILY

SYRACUSE 28.12

MELITA (MALTA) 28.1

Three Taverns
Market of Appius 28.15

CRETE

Phoenix 27.12

CLAUDA 27.16

FAIR HAVENS 27.8

SALMONE 27.7

CNIDUS 27.7

MYRA 27.5

CYPRUS 27.4

SIDON 27.3

CAESAREA 23.33

JERUSALEM 21.17

W.G.S

'Copyright'

MAP 25

became a Christian, but it is not at all unlikely that he did, under Paul's conversation and confidence.

CAESAREA TO MYRA (xxvii. 2-5)

From Caesarea to Sidon is about 67 miles, and from Sidon to Myra, about 460-500 miles. At Sidon, Julius allowed Paul to go ashore 'to be cared for', 'to receive attention.' The word used means *medical attention* (cf. Luke x. 34), and it shows that Paul was a sick man from the start of this voyage. Could not Luke have helped him? This was Paul's first visit to Sidon, which was 25 miles north of Tyre, but there were Christians there who were 'friends' of his. This leave was a kind and generous act on the part of Julius.

The voyage from Sidon to Myra was stormy, and the ship kept close to the Asian coast which would protect them from the wind. The harbour of Myra was the great port for Egyptian and Syrian traffic, and it is not surprising that other vessels were there at this time.

MYRA TO FAIR HAVENS (xxvii. 6-8)

Rome was largely dependent upon foreign sources for its supply of corn, and chiefly on Egypt. In the harbour of Myra there was a large grain ship on its way from Alexandria to Rome, and Julius transferred his human cargo to it, imagining himself more fortunate than events proved him to be. The larger ship did not improve the weather, and after battling with the N.W. wind for 130 miles towards *Cnidus* the vessel turned southwards to *Crete*, and with difficulty reached the promontory of *Salmone*, 130 miles away.

A NOTE ON CRETE

This is one of the largest islands in the Mediterranean, being about 150 miles in length, and 7-30 miles in width. In Paul's time there were Christians on the island, and these may have been converts from the first Pentecost (Acts ii. 11). It would appear that churches in the island were unorganized, and between A.D. 63-67 Paul left Titus there to 'set in order the things that were wanting' (Tit. i. 5).

The Cretans were a brave and turbulent race, and had a reputation for avarice, mendacity and drunkenness (Tit. i. 10-16). A word was coined to describe these people which meant that 'to out-Cretan a Cretan was to outwit a knave'.

MAP 26

W.G.S.

The Alexandrian vessel coasting along the southern side of the island reached *Fair Havens* 80 miles west of Salmone. This harbour was not protected from bad weather, and a council was held on board to decide whether the vessel should remain there for the winter—all hope having been abandoned of reaching Italy in that season—or to endeavour to reach *Phoenix*, a seaport 40 miles west of Fair Havens.

THE COUNCIL (xxvii. 9-12)

This Council is of interest for several reasons. It consisted of Julius the centurion, who, militarily, was in charge of the vessel; the captain and the owner of the ship, who were responsible for its navigation; the crew; and Paul.

No other prisoner was present, but Paul was on special terms with Julius, and the centurion knew that he had had much ocean experience.

All were agreed that the navigating season was practically at an end, for from September to November the sea was dangerous, and after that it was impossible till the spring, and already it was the end of September, for the Day of Atonement—which the Jews on board had observed—was past (xxvii. 9). The only matter, therefore, to be determined was where the ship would spend the winter. On this two views were expressed. Paul's view was that they should remain where they were, at Fair Havens; but the captain and the owner of the ship regarded this harbour as incommodious, and proposed that they should move on to Phoenix (Phenice), about 40 miles to the west, where the harbour was good. When the matter was put to the vote, Paul's advice was rejected.

THE STORM (xxvii. 13-20)

A most terrifying experience is summarized in these few verses, and, remember, it is the record of one who was on board. The blowing of a gentle south wind seemed to justify the majority vote, but when the vessel reached Cape Matala, a hurricane tore down upon them from the north, wind and sea combining to make a dangerous whirlwind. The wind is called *Euroclydon* or *Euraquilo*. No further progress could be made towards Phoenix, and the ship was 'driven' south-westward. An island was reached, called *Clauda*, or *Cauda*, where certain adjustments and preparations were made, in the hope that the vessel should not be cast upon the *Syrtis*, 'sand-banks off the coast of Tunis and Tripoli'. The situation swiftly deteriorated, and as they had no guidance from sun or stars, they did not know where they were.

They kept throwing overboard all that could be spared so as to lighten the ship, but to little effect. By the third day all on board were 'famishing wretches in a fast-sinking ship, drifting, with hopes that diminished day by day, to what they regarded as an awful and a certain death' (Farrar).

'CHEER UP' (xxvii. 21-26)

Paul interposed four times during this voyage (xxvii. 10, 21-26; 31; and 33-35). If these passages were eliminated from the story it would lose all value as a Christian record. It is Paul who dominates the events of the journey from Caesarea to Rome, and it is because of this that the story has survived. It seems worse than ironical to tell 276 sea-sick men to 'cheer up'. Such advice is not a known cure for this malady! Yet this is what Paul said to this haggard crowd, and his justification was not wishful thinking but Divine revelation. Doubtless Paul was feeling as seedy as any of them, but he had what most of them had not, a God whom he could trust (23, 25). But for him, everyone on that vessel would have been drowned (24).

Paul told them that though their ship would never reach its distination, they would. One wonders what Julius and the ship's captain thought of this!

The Apostle's 'You should have listened to me', was not 'I told you so', a hit back at the captain and crew, but was intended to induce them to follow his present counsel. If they had heeded him at Fair Havens they would not have 'gained this loss'. We can both gain a loss and lose a gain (2 John 8).

TREACHERY BAULKED (xxvii. 27-32)

Fourteen days after leaving Clauda the vessel was still adrift, but to the trained ears of the sailors it was evident that they were nearing land. There are times when latent baseness in human nature is given expression, and here is an illustration of it. The sailors attempted to quit the ship and leave all on board to their fate (30). But Paul was not sleeping, and discerning their intention, he told Julius and his soldiers what the sailors were about, and declared that if they succeeded all would be lost, for the sailors only could handle the ship in the present dilemma.

At once the soldiers frustrated the design by sending the boat adrift, and so, thanks to Paul once again, the situation was saved. Most of the Divine promises can be fulfilled only if and when human conditions are co-operative. Means and end must harmonize (24, 31). Paul said: 'Unless . . . *you* cannot be saved'. He knew that he himself would reach Rome.

FOOD AND HOPE (xxvii. 33-38)

The pitiable condition of this shipload of human beings can scarcely be imagined. For a fortnight they had been battered about on a raging sea; much of the ship's equipment was already lost, including, probably, their cooking utensils; much of their food would have been sodden by sea-water; all of them must have been violently sick; and they had been living in hourly peril of foundering. Because of these circumstances they had not eaten anything since they left Clauda, and must have been near the end of human endurance (33). If ever there was reason for despair it was now, but once more Paul dominates the situation.

Evidently some of the food on board was still eatable, and Paul exhorted them all—commander, captain, owner, soldiers, sailors, and prisoners, 276 souls—to eat what they could; and to encourage them he took a loaf, thanked God for it, broke it, began to eat, and no doubt gave of it to Luke and Aristarchus, if the latter had not left the company at Myra.

Though the word for 'giving-thanks' is that from which eucharist is derived, we must not suppose that this was a celebration of the Supper.

Food brought cheer and hope to this pitiful crowd, and as they would not need any more of the wheat they threw it overboard to lighten the ship (38, cf. ver. 18).

A Note on Malta

Melitene, Melita, Malta. From Clauda to Malta the ship travelled about 480 miles; and the journey of the ship's company from Malta to Rome, by sea and land, would be a distance of about 470 miles.

This island is about 17 miles long, and 8 miles broad. Its old capital was Citta Vecchia, and its present capital is Valetta. The island is without rivers, lakes, and trees. In Paul's day it was sparsely populated, but to-day it has over half a million inhabitants. St. Paul's Bay is the traditional scene of the wreck. At the ancient capital a grotto is shown, where, it is supposed, the Apostle lived during his three months' stay on the island.

During the second world war, in the battle of Malta, 15,000 buildings were destroyed, including 70 churches, 18 convents or monasteries, 22 schools, 8 hospitals, and 10 theatres; and over 14,000 tenements were damaged by blast.

Because of Malta's noble service in the Second World War it was presented in 1942 with the George Cross.

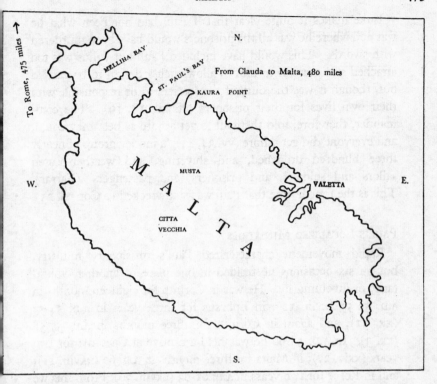

N.

MELLIHA BAY

ST. PAUL'S BAY

From Clauda to Malta, 480 miles

KAURA POINT

W.

M A L T A

MUSTA

VALETTA

E.

CITTA
VECCHIA

S.

Copyright   MAP 27.   W.G.S.

THE SHIPWRECK (xxvii. 39-44)

Luke records briefly the wreck of the ship on which Paul and he were travelling. The captain and sailors did not recognize the land which they saw, not because they had not been to Malta before, but because the harbour into which ships went—Valetta—was seven miles away, E.S.E. They saw a beach on which they planned to run the ship, but, instead, they struck a sandbank where two seas met, and the ship began to break up.

> And now, lashed on by destiny severe,
> With horror fraught the dreadful scene drew near.
> The ship hangs hovering on the verge of death;
> Hell yawns, rocks rise, and breakers roar beneath,
> Uplifted on the surge to heaven she flies,
> Her shattered top half-buried in the skies,
> Then, headlong, plunging, thunders on the ground,
> Earth groans, air trembles, and the deeps resound.
>
>   (Falconer)

Luke makes it quite clear that if Paul had not been what he was and where he was all the prisoners would have been murdered with swords. This would have included Paul, but Julius was too attached and grateful to him to allow such a design to be carried out, though it was the duty of the soldiers to be responsible with their own lives for their prisoners (cf. xii. 18, 19). The commander, therefore, told them all to get ashore as best they could, and everyone did get ashore (vv. 34, 44), 'a motley group of nearly three hundred drenched, and shivering, and weather-beaten sailors and soldiers, and prisoners, and passengers' (Farrar). This is the fourth time that Paul was shipwrecked (2 Cor. xi. 25).

PAUL'S LOCALIZED MINISTRIES

Rapid movement characterized Paul's missionary ministry, but on six occasions he resided in one place or another, voluntarily or involuntarily. He was in Corinth for eighteen months in A.D. 52-53 (xviii. 11); in Ephesus for three years in A.D. 54-57 (xx. 31); and again in Corinth for three months in A.D. 57-58 (xx. 3). In A.D. 58-60 he was held a captive at Caesarea for two years (xxiv. 27); in Malta for three months in A.D. 60 (xxviii. 11); and in Rome for two years in A.D. 61-63 (xxviii. 30). From this we see that nine years of his ministry were localised, $4\frac{3}{4}$ years voluntarily, and $4\frac{1}{4}$ involuntarily. During his first residence at Corinth the Apostle wrote 1-2 Thessalonians, and during his second visit he wrote Galatians and Romans. While at Ephesus he wrote 1 Corinthians. During his residence at Caesarea and at Malta he wrote nothing that has survived, but while in Rome the first time, he wrote Ephesians, Colossians, Philemon, and Philippians.

THREE MONTHS AT MALTA (xxviii. 1-10, 11a)

One would think and wish that Luke would have told us more about these three months at Malta, for much of great importance must have happened. What were the wrecked people doing—Julius, Luke, the captain, and the owner of the ship, the sailors, the soldiers, and the prisoners? And where were they located? Where was Paul resident, and what was he doing all this time? From November to the end of January!

Luke selects two incidents only—the event of a viper fastening on Paul's hand (1-6), and the healing ministry of the Apostle and its results (7-10).

THE MALTESE (xxviii. 1, 2)

By calling the inhabitants of Malta 'barbarians' Luke does not mean they were uncivilized—for they were not—but only that they were not Greeks.

When these drenched and shivering men landed on the island it was November and very cold, and it was pouring rain. They had lost everything in the wreck, and were in a pitiable condition, but the Maltese treated them handsomely. The word 'no common kindness' is *philanthrōpia*, which occurs here and in Titus iii. 4 only, and the adverb *philanthrōpōs* occurs in Acts xxvii. 3 only. These references are worth studying together. Luke says that the inhabitants 'kindled a fire', and 'took us all to themselves' (cf. xviii. 26).

THE VIPER INCIDENT (xxviii. 3-6)

Paul is altogether astonishing. He had dominated the situation on the ship from Clauda to Malta, and now he dominates the situation on the island. By gathering brushwood he helped to keep going the fire which others had started; and while doing so a viper, awakened by the heat darted out and fastened itself on his hand.

Some writers say that this was quite a natural and common experience; and others say the story is not true because there were no vipers on the island; and one is left wondering why Luke, so careful an historian, should have bothered to record what was of no importance, or to invent what was not true! The story clearly implies that the viper either bit or poisoned Paul, and that he was supernaturally saved from the consequences. The natives, who saw what had happened, expected Paul to drop down dead, and as he did not, they concluded that he was a god (cf. xiv. 8-18). This event, happening soon after Paul got ashore, had much to do with the great influence he exercised throughout his three months stay on the island.

PAUL AND PUBLIUS (xxviii. 7-10)

Publius appears to have been the Governor of the island, and his headquarters were, probably, Citta Vecchia (see Map 27, p. 473). Luke presents him as a man humane and generous. The 'us' of verse 7 certainly means Paul and his companions, and, perhaps, Julius also. His entertainment was all the more estimable seeing that his father was a very sick man. His ailment is described with medical accuracy by Luke as 'fever and dysentery'. Paul, hearing of this, got permission to visit him, and, having prayed and having laid (his) hands on him, he healed him. This news rapidly circulated and caused a great sensation, with the result that many miracles of healing were performed. Perhaps the 'us' of verse 10 implies that Luke's medical skill was employed in this good work.

Though nothing is said about Paul evangelizing the natives we may be quite sure that he did so, and that there were conversions to Christianity, and that the nucleus of a church was formed before the Apostle left the island.

Further Thoughts on the Journey

FROM CAESAREA TO MALTA

This record may well be regarded as a picture of LIFE'S JOURNEY.

Bunyan wrote an immortal allegory of the Christian course as a journey *by land*. Here, we see it as a journey *by sea*. What a variety of companionship there is! What a strange admixture of fellow-travellers, from whose company we cannot altogether dissociate ourselves! Like the *captain* there are those who have a right to command us; like the *soldiers*, those in whose power we stand; like the *sailors*, those whose duty it is to care for our safety; like *Paul*, those who can enlighten us; like *Luke*, those who can heal us; like *Aristarchus*, those who can refresh us; and like the *prisoners*, those who are our fellow-sufferers.

The presence here of Romans, Macedonians, Alexandrians, Hebrews, and others, reminds us that this is a world of nations, and that we cannot stand clear of one another. On life's journey there can be no absolute seclusion, or refined retirement. And if there could be, how would experience be gained, and where would be found the means of discipline and self-sacrifice? '*No man liveth to himself.*'

We are all on the ship and on the sea.

We cannot always choose our company.

Looking at this record as a picture of our journey over life's ocean, we have seen how varied is our company. But there are other points of analogy. On such a journey, difficulties, hardships, and peril are certainties; the winds are sure to be contrary, and the sea may be tempestuous. Sometime or other sunshine will give place to storm. The changing drama of nature mirrors the story of the human soul. Life is not all radiant calm: we must expect also cyclonic disturbance. If, sometimes, our nights are turned into day by happy providences, sometimes our days are turned into night by that same Wisdom (xxvii. 20). What is it that avails at such times? Only faith in God (xxvii. 23-25).

Paul was the only hope of this ship, and though a prisoner, he was really the ruler. The centurion and master of the ship may typify that blind obstinacy which will persevere with its designs in the teeth of nature's laws. But only the Christian religion can bring comfort and hope (xxvii. 24) in such circumstances as these.

It is worthy of notice that, though no doubt Paul and his companions prayed, they also worked (xxvii. 19). God is in charge of the storm, but He will not handle '*the tackling of the ship*'; we have to do that. With piety should go prudence, and with entreaty, effort. There is no use our telling men what they should not have done, unless we also can tell them what they now should do.

No matter what our circumstances may be, we should witness for Christ (xxvii. 23); '*whose I am, and whom I serve*', said Paul. You cannot serve Him unless you are His. Paul kept his head in this storm, and God kept his heart! The world, like this ship, is greatly blessed because Christians are in it. Only Christian faith can be triumphant in the face of black despair.

Life is not a picnic, but a probation.

What an amazing story this is (xxvii.) Think of these two hundred and seventy-six souls not having eaten for a fortnight, during which time they were blown about and lashed by the reckless sea!

Then, see Paul among them, cheering them, and getting them to eat, serving them with food, and in the presence of them all asking God's blessing on the bread (33-37). He must have been a good sailor. There's nothing like a storm at sea to show what's in a man, or what is not.

The *shipmen*, whose duty it was to abide by the ship to the last, tried to escape (30). The *soldiers* thought the best thing to do was to kill the prisoners (42). The *Apostle* saved both situations; the one by his presence of mind (31), and the other, by his presence of body (43). The whole narrative is exceedingly graphic, and could have been given only by an eye-witness, and one with nautical knowledge. The world may not like Christians, but it cannot get on without them.

Verse 41 tells of a wreck, and may well lead us to think of the *intellectual*, *moral*, and *spiritual* shipwrecks which so many are making every day. Have you *run aground*? Is your will stuck, and is your conscience broken? (41). It is said even of Peter that he began to sink, but happily for himself, he knew it, and cried to Christ for help. Alas for people who do not know it!

The closing verses (43, 44) tell of a landing. There are different ways of getting ashore—applying this to Christians, some with bold stroke swim in, and others miserably drift in on debris. How are you going Home?

Life's providences mysteriously and marvellously interlock, but the mind and hand behind them all are God's. If you cannot be a good leader, be a good follower.

Observe how carefully Luke kept his diary, notwithstanding the trying circumstances. The record is that of an eye-witness, and the notes of *time* are given with exactness: in ch. xxvii: '*the next day*' (3); '*many days*' (7); '*much time*' (9); '*after no long time*' (14); '*the next day*' (18); '*the third day*' (19); '*many days*' (20); '*long*' (21); '*the fourteenth night*' (27); '*about midnight*' (27); '*a little space*' (28); '*while the day was coming on*' (33); '*the fourteenth day*' (33); '*when it was day*' (39); in ch. xxviii: '*three days*' (7); '*after three months*' (11); '*three days*' (12); '*after one day*' '*the second day*' (13); '*seven days*' (14).

Mark also these particulars: MALTA, PUBLIUS, THE TWIN BROTHERS, SYRACUSE, RHEGIUM, PUTEOLI, MARKET OF APPIUS,

THE THREE TAVERNS, ROME. Note also the references to *bar-barians, rain, cold, sticks, viper, murdered, god, entertained, fever, dysentery, cured, honours.*

Paul and his company spent *three months* at Malta, as we have seen; 276 of them, Christians and criminals, soldiers and sailors, Romans and Jews! It is PAUL who dominates the scene. The Church's greatest theologian gathers sticks for the fire. The heathen are hospitable and show that *kindness* is universally a human quality. They also are superstitious (4), and unstable (6). It's a long stride from 'murderer' to 'god', but these people easily took it. There is peril in the noblest service, and out of the fires of devotion vipers may fasten on us; but let us *shake them off*, and get on with the work.

Luke records the healing at CITTA VECCHIA, the old capital of the island, but Paul wrought it; it was the preacher and not the physician who effected the cures, or some of them at any rate. Medical missions are an essential part of the redeeming enter-prise. I doubt not Paul left some Christians on this island whom he did not find there when he landed.

Christ would have us fit into our circumstances.

FROM MALTA TO ROME (xxviii. 11-16)

The journey from the island to the city, from Malta to Rome, about 475 miles, is briefly related. In late February or early March the sea was open again for navigation, and another Alexandrian ship which had harboured at Malta set sail for Rome, and it had on board the 276 men who had been wrecked off Malta the previous November.

The Maltese showed their gratitude to Paul and his com-panions by supplying them with things they would need on their journey to Rome. This may have been clothing and food (xxviii. 10).

The places of call were *Syracuse*, about 80 miles from Malta; *Rhegium*, 80-90 miles from Syracuse; *Puteoli*, about 180 miles from Rhegium; the *Appii Forum*, about 80 miles from Puteoli; *Three Taverns*, about 10 miles from Appii Forum; and *Rome*, about 33 miles from Three Taverns. These distances are only approximate, but they indicate relatively what ground was covered by the Apostle on his way to the Capital. From Caesarea to Malta is about 1,395 miles, and adding the distance—about 475 miles—from Malta to Rome, the Apostle travelled not less than 1,870 miles, mostly by sea.

SYRACUSE was the chief city of Sicily, and on the way to it from Malta Paul would see the giant cone of volcanic Etna. The ship remained at Syracuse for three days, but it is not said why; nor do we know how Paul used the time. The next stop was at *Rhegium*, in the straits of Messina, where they tarried for a day, and then proceeded to *Puteoli*, in the Bay of Naples, which Howson has called 'the Liverpool of Italy'. On the way to this city they would see the smoke of the Stromboli volcano, and on reaching it they would get a view of Vesuvius. Not far from Puteoli was Pompeii, which in A.D. 79 was destroyed by an eruption of Vesuvius.

Puteoli was the port at which travellers to Rome were landed, and from here Paul and his companions proceeded to Rome—120 miles away—overland.

The outstanding fact at this point is that there was a Christian Church at Puteoli, and contact was made between Paul and the brethren. They invited him to stay with them for a week, which Julius allowed him to do. What a week that must have been, and how great is our loss in not having any account of it. Evidently news was sent from Puteoli to the Christians at Rome that Paul was on the way thither, and one group met him at *Appii Forum*, 43 miles from Rome, and another group met him at *Three Taverns*, ten miles nearer the Capital.

This kindly welcome led Paul to thank God, and to take courage. As he neared Rome his emotions must have been very mingled, but these fellow-believers brought him much cheer.

'And so we came to Rome' (14)

It has been rightly said that this is the climax of the book of Acts (xix. 21; xxiii. 11), but not the close of Paul's career.

Before looking at the few details which are given of the Apostle's two years' captivity in the imperial capital, something must be said about the City and the Emperor of Rome.

ROME

SOCIAL CONDITIONS IN ROME

Details of the lay-out of this ancient city would not serve our present purpose, but a few particulars of another kind may help us to realize what sort of a place Rome was in Paul's day. The population was about 2,000,000, of which half were slaves. Accommodation for all these had to be found in the city's 1,790 palaces and 46,602 jerry-built tenement houses. Magnificence and squalor, architecturally and socially, lived side by side; ostentatious luxury and chronic pauperism were characteristics of this vast city; gorgeous gluttonies and gilded rottenness were everywhere to be seen.

Paul's indictment of the inhabitants of Rome in Romans i. 18-32 is one of the most terrible passages in literature. Seneca spoke of Rome as a cesspool of iniquity, and Juvenal pictured her as a filthy sewer, and in like vein wrote Tacitus and Suetonius. The miserable multitude sought solace in superstition, sensuality, or stoicism.

Of course there were finer elements in the vast community, represented by Epictetus and Aurelius, by Seneca also, and his brother Gallio, but Nero murdered both of them.

THE JEWS IN ROME

The Jewish population in Rome was very large. They resided chiefly in a quarter of the city called Trans-Tiberine, or Over Tiber. They had many synagogues there, and were allowed much freedom in all questions touching their own law, though in all civil matters they were subject to their Roman masters.

CHRISTIANS IN ROME

When and how the Christian Church appeared in Rome it is not possible to say, but in all likelihood it may have stemmed from the first Pentecost at Jerusalem (Acts ii. 9). That Christians were numerous is witnessed to by writers of the period, and Paul tells us that they were to be found even in 'Caesar's household' (Phil. iv. 21).

It was some time before Rome distinguished between Judaism and Christianity, and they were treated alike by Roman tolerance and justice.

It is impressive that Paul's greatest Epistle was sent to the Church at Rome, and its chapter xvi throws much light on the Assembly there.

NERO

The Roman Emperors before Nero were:

Augustus, B.C. 30-A.D. 14 (Luke ii. 1); *Tiberius*, A.D. 14-37 (John xix. 12); *Caligula*, A.D. 37-41; *Claudius*, A.D. 41-54 (Acts xviii. 2); and then followed *Nero*, A.D. 54-68 (Acts xxv. 12), the fifth Emperor, and so far the worst.

Of him it is said in *Chambers' Encyclopaedia* (1950);

> 'Nero was vain and timid, an unbridled voluptuary and a dilettante aesthete who, living in an atmosphere of intrigue and conspiracy, abused his unlimited power and became a suspicious and cruel tyrant.
>
> 'Irresponsible and indifferent to the problems of Government, he satisfied his vanity by displaying himself as a musician, versifier, and charioteer before adulatory audiences in South Italy and in Greece where he staged a triumphal tour.'
>
> (Vol. ix. 763*a*).

His father and mother were persons of ungovernable temper and immoral character, so that Nero had a start in life loaded on the side of evil. He was responsible for the death of his brother, Britannicus, and his mother, who had committed every sin for his advancement, was put to death by his order.

In A.D. 54-62 the State was under the joint administration of two worthy men—*Burrus*, who held the post of Praetorian Prefect, and *Seneca*, the brother of Gallio (Acts xviii. 12), Nero's tutor, and the most elegant scholar of his day. During this period the devil in Nero was kept somewhat in check, but in A.D. 62-68 there was a rapid and terrible decline. In A.D. 62 Burrus was removed by poison, and after this event Seneca lost his power, and himself was murdered in A.D. 65. Released from the influence and advice of these great men, Nero came completely under the power of two wicked people—*Poppaea*, who became his wife, who was a proselyte to Judaism, and of whom Tacitus said that she had every recommendation except a virtuous mind.

The other evil influence in Nero's life was *Tigellinus*, the instigator of his crimes, the associate of his debaucheries, and the murderer of Christians, of whom Juvenal wrote:

> 'Paint Tigellinus and your fate will be
> To burn with brimstone at the martyr's tree,
> While, as the flames consume the living brand,
> A crimson rill runs trickling o'er the sand.'
>
> (Sat. I. v. 155).

In A.D. 64 Rome was largely destroyed by fire, and Nero was suspected of the event. While the city was blazing he stood on Maecenas' Tower and sang 'The Fall of Troy' to his everlasting guitar. To evade the suspicion which fell on him he propagated the calumny that the Christians were the criminals, and this led to a horrible massacre of them. Of this Tacitus says:

> 'Their sufferings at their execution were aggravated by insult and mockery, for some were disguised in the skins of wild beasts, and worried to death by dogs; some were crucified, and others were wrapped in pitched shirts, and set on fire when the day closed, that they might serve as lights to illuminate the night. Nero lent his own gardens for these exhibitions, and exhibited at the same time a mock Circensian entertainment, being a spectator of the whole in the dress of a charioteer, sometimes mingling with the crowd on foot, and sometimes viewing the spectacle from his car.'
>
> (Annales, xv. 44).

Nero was the first Emperor to persecute the Christians, and he did so, not because it was illegal to be a Christian, but because he needed scapegoats.

Of his brief life Farrar says that he 'was stained through and through with every possible crime, and steeped to the very lips in every nameless degradation. A wholesale robber, a pitiless despot, an intriguer, a poisoner, a murderer, a matricide, a liar, a coward, a drunkard, a glutton, incestuous, unutterably depraved, of whom pagans said that he was 'a mixture of blood and mud'.

This was the man that Paul appealed to (Acts xxv. 11; xxvi. 32), before whom he stood, and who finally relegated him to the executioner's block. He came to the throne when he was seventeen years of age, and fourteen years later, in A.D. 68, he committed suicide.

Paul at Rome

(xxviii. 16-31)

WHERE HE DWELT (xxviii. 16. 23, 30)

On reaching Rome, Julius, the centurion, would in all probability hand over his prisoners to the Prefect of the Praetorium who, at this time, was *Burrus* (see p. 482). The correspondence, handed over at the same time, would call the attention of the Prefect to the case of Paul who was commended by Festus, Agrippa, and by Julius, no doubt. Seeing how different he was from the other prisoners, Burrus separated him from them and 'suffered (him) to abide by himself, with the soldier that guarded him' (xxviii. 16). In verse 23 there is a reference to 'his lodging', and in verse 30 to 'his own hired dwelling'.

Verse 23 may read, the Jews came to him '*to receive his hospitality*' (cf. Phile. 22); and verse 30, 'he abode two whole years *on his own earnings*,' or '*at his own expense*'.

These renderings have led to the view that Paul's accommodation in verse 23 was not the same as in verse 30; that in verse 23 he was the guest of friends—maybe Aquila and Priscilla—and that in verse 30 he had rooms for the use of which he paid, either out of the gifts of friends (Phil. iv. 10-19), or from his toil at tent-making, if he had permission, and if his chain did not hinder. In verse 23 is exhibited the grace of Christian hospitality, where it was almost incriminating to show it, and in verse 30 is seen Paul's noble independence; how perfect a gentleman he was.

In the house he occupied for two years there must have been several rooms at his disposal, and one of them must have been large (xxviii. 23). We are not told if Luke and Aristarchus, and later, Timothy and Mark, lodged with him, but they may have, and, perhaps, messengers who came to him from afar would find shelter under his roof. In all likelihood, it was in this house that Epaphroditus fell ill (Phil. ii. 25-30), and Luke would attend to him. There must have been constant coming and going, so that, as one has said, Paul's abode was 'The Church Offices', and the General Secretary was chained to his seat (Mackinnon).

CHAINED

It has been pointed out that there were several kinds of custody recognized by the Roman law: (*a*) confinement in the public gaol—a horrible experience (cf. xvi. 22-24); (*b*) free custody— the mildest kind; and (*c*) military custody, in which the prisoner was the charge of a soldier to whom he was chained. The last was Paul's form of bondage (cf. xxiv. 23; Eph. vi. 19, 20; Col. iv. 3; Phile. 9; Phil. i. 13). The guard was changed frequently so that Paul had much opportunity to witness for Christ, and he would not be slow to take it (Phil. i. 13).

Two years of this must have been very wearying, but his captivity was infinitely better than many had to endure, and for longer periods, in German concentration camps in the last Great War (1939-45). It is probably true that in appearance he was not distinguished, and his much suffering must have left its mark on his body and face; but from what he endured and achieved— especially on the voyage to Rome—it is evident that he was physically tough. Yet he refers to the physical as 'a fragile vessel of clay', 'a common earthenware jar', 'a clay pot' (2 Cor. iv. 7: Rotherham; Phillips; Williams). What always matters, of course, is not the shell but the nut.

PAUL'S PERSONAL APPEARANCE

In this regard nothing, of course, can be authentic, yet descriptions of the Apostle of different dates which have features in common may be said to have a degree of probability as to his appearance.

The 'Acts of Paul and Thekla' describe him as of moderate height, scanty hair, bow-legged, with large eyes, meeting eyebrows, and a rather long nose.

Another description, of the 6th century, says that 'Paul was in person round-shouldered, with a sprinkling of grey on his head and beard, with an aquiline nose, greyish eyes, meeting eyebrows, with a mixture of pale and red in his complexion, and an ample beard'.

In the 15th century, Nicephorus wrote: 'Paul was short and dwarfish in stature, and, as it were, crooked in person and slightly bent. His face was pale, his aspect winning. He was bald-headed, and his eyes were bright. His nose was prominent and aquiline, his beard thick and tolerably long, and both this and his head were sprinkled with white hairs'.

Paul says it was reported that 'his bodily presence is weak'; and 'ye would have plucked out your eyes and given them to me'; and from his summary of his sufferings we may draw certain conclusions, as also from the description of his voyage to Rome (Gal. iv. 15; 2 Cor. x. 10; xi. 23-30; Acts xxvii).

PAUL AND THE JEWS IN ROME
(xxviii. 17-28)

FIRST INTERVIEW (xxviii. 17-22)

By the groups of Christians who met Paul as he approached Rome he was assured of his welcome by the Church there, but, as yet, he did not know how he would be received by the Jews. Desirous to find out their attitude, as soon as he had settled down in his 'lodging' he invited the 'chief' among them, the rulers and leaders of the synagogues, to visit him (as he could not visit them) so that he might explain his position (verses 17-20). He denied that he was guilty of any act of disloyalty to his own people and customs; that his Roman examiners had affirmed his innocence and would have liberated him; and that, because of the attitude of the Jews in Jerusalem and Caesarea, he had been compelled to appeal to Caesar, not in order to accuse the Jews, but that he might receive justice.

The reply of the rulers was courteous and non-committal. They were unprejudiced so far as Paul was concerned, and were willing that he should tell them what exactly his teaching was, but they were aware that the sect of the Nazarenes, of whom Paul was a leader (xxiv. 5), was in ill repute among the Jews (xxiv. 21, 22).

SECOND INTERVIEW (xxviii. 23)

A day was appointed for a further meeting at which Paul could expound his teaching. This time the rulers brought with them many others (23), so that all available room was occupied, and he addressed them 'from morning till evening' (cf. xix. 9; xx. 7, 11).

Paul's subject was the *Kingdom of God*, and, no doubt, it followed the lines which characterized his presentation of Christianity to the Jews (cf. xiii. 14-41). The Messiah was the King, and Jesus was the Messiah, the fulfilment of the law and the prophets (cf. Luke xxiv. 46, 47; Acts xvii. 3; xxvi. 23).

PAUL'S FINAL BREACH WITH JUDAISM (xxviii. 24-28)

As so often before, 'some believed, and some disbelieved'. Paul's experience at Antioch, and Corinth, and Ephesus was repeated at Rome, but now it was for the last time. The revelation which the Jews now finally refused, sealed their fate, for in less than ten years the nation, as such, was destroyed (A.D. 70).

The passage from the Jewish Scriptures which Paul quoted—Isaiah vi. 9, 10—is quoted also by Jesus (Matt. xiii. 14, 15; Mark iv. 12; Luke viii. 10; and in John xii. 40). In Rom. ix-xi the Apostle had outlined comprehensively the history of Israel—past, present, and future—but the Jews were both blind and deaf, and their last chance to acknowledge the Messiah had come and gone. Refusing to see the salvation of God they dismissed themselves (ver. 25); literally, 'they loosened themselves from'.

TWO YEARS OF CAPTIVITY MINISTRY (xxviii. 30, 31)

Here is a wonderful end to a wonderful record:

> '*He* (Paul) *lived there* (at Rome) *two whole years at his own expense* (or, in his own hired dwelling), *and welcomed all who came to him, preaching the Kingdom of God, and teaching about the Lord Jesus Christ quite openly and unhindered.*'

This brings into view a number of matters of much importance.

DELAY OF PAUL'S TRIAL

The Apostle who had been held for two years in Caesarea, and had had a terrible voyage from Caesarea to Rome, had to wait in the Imperial City for two years before he was called up for trial. There were three charges against him: (1) causing disturbances among the Jews throughout the Empire; (2) being a ringleader of the sect called the Nazarenes; and (3) profaning the Temple at Jerusalem. Before he could be convicted his accusers would have to reach Rome and in person charge him, and they could delay doing this indefinitely, and did delay, as we see, for two years. But for Paul the edge was taken off this waiting time by two circumstances—his relatively comfortable quarters, and his great opportunities to bear his witness.

ORAL MINISTRY

The text says '*preaching* and *teaching*', and it says also what he preached and taught—the Kingdom and the Messiah. This summarizes Paul's message of the gospel and gives to the Acts record a certain completeness, for as it began so it ends, on the notes of Christ and the Kingdom. What Paul *preached* would be for all, but what he *taught* was, probably, for those only who were ready for it.

The total of '*all who came to him*' must have been very great in the course of two years, and, Luke says, they were all made '*welcome*'.

The Apostle was allowed perfect liberty of speech and he made great use of it. His utterances were '*with all freedom . . . and without hindrance*'. What a note to end upon—'UNHINDERED'. Nothing really can hinder the Christian Church but itself, and nothing can prevent the triumph of the gospel but a hesitant or faulty presentation of it.

The word *akōlutōs*, *a* and *kōlutōs*, which occurs nowhere else in the New Testament, is a positive negatived. To *hinder, withstand, forbid*, occurs six times in the Acts (viii. 36; x. 47; xi. 17; xvi. 6; 23; xxvii. 43), but in xxviii. 31 it has the negative prefix, and so, *not hindered, not withstood*, and *not forbidden*. In God's good providence the Christian Church has the Roman Prefect to thank for that.

WRITING MINISTRY

Paul did more than speak, he also wrote, and never wrote to greater purpose. We here assume that what are called the Prison Epistles were written at Rome in A.D. 61-63, and not at Caesarea, or anywhere else. Three of the four were sent to Asia—*Ephesians*, *Colossians*, and *Philemon*, and one—*Philippians*—to Macedonia. We shall look at these Epistles in detail later on, but it can be said now with confidence that, excepting *Romans* perhaps, they are Paul's greatest epistolary work in their richness and profoundness.

In the Apostle's time there was no such postal system as now exists, and Paul's letters could be transmitted only by carefully chosen persons. We do not know in every case who these were, but it is clear that *Philippians* was carried by Epaphroditus (ii. 28); *Colossians* and *Philemon* by Tychicus and Onesimus (Col. iv. 7-9); and *Ephesians*, so-called, which appears to have been a circular letter, sent in the first instance to the Church at Laodicea, was also conveyed by Tychicus (Col. iv. 7, 8, 16). Paul, therefore, had his own postmen, and from his rooms in Rome immortal messages were radiated to far-distant places and so were made available to the Christian Church for 1,900 years so far.

ONESIMUS

It is most impressive that the sin of a slave should have been so used by Providence that 'out of the eater has come forth meat, and out of the strong, sweetness'. We are not told how this man and Paul made contact. He may have been seen in Rome by a friend of Philemon, and taken to Paul; or he might have heard that Paul—whom he may have seen before—was in the city, and felt an urge to meet him; or, in the performance of some casual job, he may have visited the house where Paul was. The thing that matters, however, is that he met Paul and by him was led to Christ, and out of this event came the priceless letter to Philemon. How great is that unwritten story! What did the slave tell the prisoner, and what did the prisoner say to him, and what did the soldier think who heard it all?

COMPANIONS IN ROME

Paul had a genius for friendship, and the two years of his first captivity in Rome were enriched by many friends. Not fewer than ten are mentioned: Timothy, Epaphras, Luke, Aristarchus, Tychicus, Mark, Epaphroditus, Demas, Justus, Onesimus, and almost certainly must be added Aquila and Priscilla, and other Christians in Rome; nor should we exclude

Julius, Paul's centurion friend of the tragic voyage, and, maybe, other Romans who were reached and impressed by the Apostle (Phil. iv. 22).

The comfort and encouragement which these friends brought to the captive Paul cannot be exaggerated, and the spiritual influence he had on them cannot be assessed. Demas defaulted, but Mark made good, and to Timothy two of his thirteen letters were written.

'Two Whole Years'

This note of time implies either that at the conclusion of it some change took place affecting either Paul, or Luke, or both, or that Luke wrote up to the limit of his knowledge at that time, and intended to write more when he had more to write.

After the 'Two Whole Years'

Some think that Luke, having traced the progress of the Gospel from Jerusalem to Rome, had no need to carry the narrative further, and had no intention of doing so, and that chapter xxviii. 30, 31 makes a natural and a satisfactory conclusion. But others, perhaps in the majority, regard the last two verses as abrupt and unfinished, and look for traces, biblical or extrabiblical, of what happened to Paul at or after the end of the 'two years' referred to.

When was Paul tried, and what was the verdict? Was there but one Roman imprisonment? Do *Philippians* and *Philemon* warrant the view that the verdict was likely to go in Paul's favour? If it be assumed that the Pastoral Epistles—1-2 *Timothy* and *Titus*—were written by Paul, can they be placed in the story of the Acts, or must they be accounted for beyond the Acts record? Has tradition anything to say on this subject?

These and other questions, naturally arise, and though much is left in obscurity there are data which present a fairly consistent picture of the five years which immediately followed the conclusion of the Acts.

1. When Paul wrote *Philippians*, probably in A.D. 63, he was anticipating release from his Roman imprisonment. He speaks

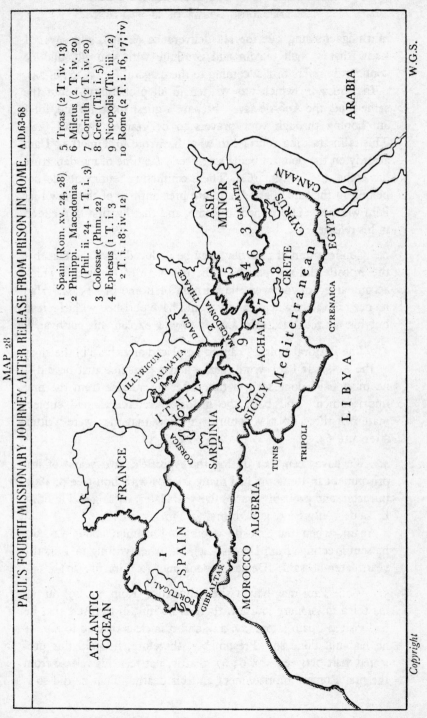

MAP 28

PAUL'S FOURTH MISSIONARY JOURNEY AFTER RELEASE FROM PRISON IN ROME. A.D. 63-68

1 Spain (Rom. xv. 24, 28)
2 Philippi. Macedonia
   (Phil. ii. 24. 1 T. i. 3)
3 Colossae (Phm. 22)
4 Ephesus (1 T. i. 3
   2 T. i. 18; iv. 12)

5 Troas (2 T. iv. 13)
6 Miletus (2 T. iv. 20)
7 Corinth (2 T. iv. 20)
8 Crete (Tit. i. 5)
9 Nicopolis (Tit. iii. 12)
10 Rome (2 T. i. 16, 17; iv.

W.G.S.

Copyright

of things turning out for his deliverance (i. 19), and says: 'I know that I shall remain and continue with you all', and he confidently refers to his 'coming to them again' (i. 25, 26; ii. 24).

In *Philemon*, which was written in all probability, about the same time, the Apostle says: 'Prepare a guest room for me, for I am hoping through your prayers to be granted to you' (22). This is in startling contrast to what he wrote to Timothy, 'I am already on the point of being sacrificed; the time of my departure has come' (2 Tim. iv. 16). These conflicting sentiments do not belong to the same period, and are presumptive of the view that Paul was twice imprisoned in Rome, and that his first trial ended in his release.

2.   Confirmation of this view may be deduced from the fact that the Apostle did not perish in the massacre of Christians which accompanied or followed the burning of Rome in A.D. 64.   Had he been in the city he certainly would have perished with the rest, but his alleged release in A.D. 63 would explain his survival.

3.   The Pastoral Epistles cannot be placed anywhere in the story of the Acts.   If Paul wrote them—and we assume that he did— he must have done so at a time after his release from the first imprisonment, and both the historical references and subject matter of these Epistles confirm the view that they were written after A.D. 63.

4.   We have seen that during the Apostle's 'two years' of imprisonment in Rome he had many friends with him (see p. 489), but later, and probably four to five years later, writing to Timothy, he said: 'Only Luke is with me' (2 Tim. iv. 11).

Again, when the Apostle wrote to Philemon about A.D. 63, he sent greetings from Demas (24), but when writing to Timothy years later he said: 'Demas forsook me' (2 Tim. iv. 10)

5.   While Paul may have visited Illyricum (Rom. xv. 19) during his third missionary journey, there is no hint in the Acts that he had visited Spain (Rom. xv. 24), and it is clear that up to A.D. 58 he had not done so.   Presumably, therefore, he paid this projected visit between A.D. 63-67, that is, between his release from the first Roman imprisonment and his death.   That he did so is

not without the confirmation of tradition—Clement of Rome, Chrysostom, Jerome, Theodoret, and others, but we are completely without the details of such a visit.

6.   In the Pastoral Epistles there are references to Crete, Ephesus, Macedonia, Troas, Corinth, Nicopolis, Miletus, Thessalonica, Galatia, and Dalmatia, which cannot be fitted into the Acts, and so, presumably, refer to a period after the close of it, i.e. between A.D. 63-67.   See: Rom. xv. 24, 28.   1 Tim. i. 3; 2 Tim. i. 18; iv. 12. Phil. ii. 24.   Phile. 22.   2 Tim. i. 16, 17; iv. 13, 20; iv.   Tit. i. 5; iii. 12.

In these Epistles occur also the names of people, some of whom at least Luke would have mentioned if they had belonged to the period of his Acts record—Phygelus, Hermogenes, Onesiphorus, Crescens, Carpus, Alexander, Eubulus, Pudens, Linus, Claudia, Artemas, Hymenaeus, and Zenas.

All these details look in one direction, and point to a period of freedom which Paul had between two Roman imprisonments, the second of which was fatal.

This, then, was the end, an end which was an endless beginning.

> Faithfulness can feed on suffering,
> And knows no disappointment.
>
> (Spanish Gipsy)

2 Timothy ch. iv tells of the final trials before Nero of this greatest of all missionaries, the second of which ended in his martyrdom.   There is something wrong with the person who can read this chapter without deep emotion.   This great soul had fought the fight, run the race, and kept the trust, and now he was looking forward to meeting his Lord whom he had served so devotedly.

> No more to tread the desert's burning sand,
> Or climb the pass where mountain snows congeal!
> No more to brave the robber's ruffian hand,
> Or plough the stormy seas with treacherous reel!
> No more the ignominious lash to feel,
> Or drag the galling chain!   Now dawns the day
> That sets to long-tried faith the welcome seal,
> And lightened of its weary load of clay,
> The spirit rests with Him who 'wipes all tears away'.

CHART 138
PAUL'S LAST FIVE YEARS

A.D.	PAUL	CONTEMPORARY EVENTS
63	Roman trial and acquittal In Macedonia—Philippi (Phil. ii. 24) At Colossae (Phile. 22)	
64	To Spain (Rom. xv. 24, 28)	Great fire at Rome, and the persecution of Roman Christians under Nero
65	- - - - - - -	Death of Seneca
66	At Ephesus (1 Tim. i. 3) In Macedonia (1 Tim. i. 3) At Ephesus	The Jewish War begins
67	Writes 1 *Timothy* At Miletus—Corinth (2 Tim. iv. 20) Writes to Titus At Nicopolis (Tit. iii. 12) Re-arrested and taken to Rome Writes 2 *Timothy* Trial and execution at	
68	Rome	Death of Nero